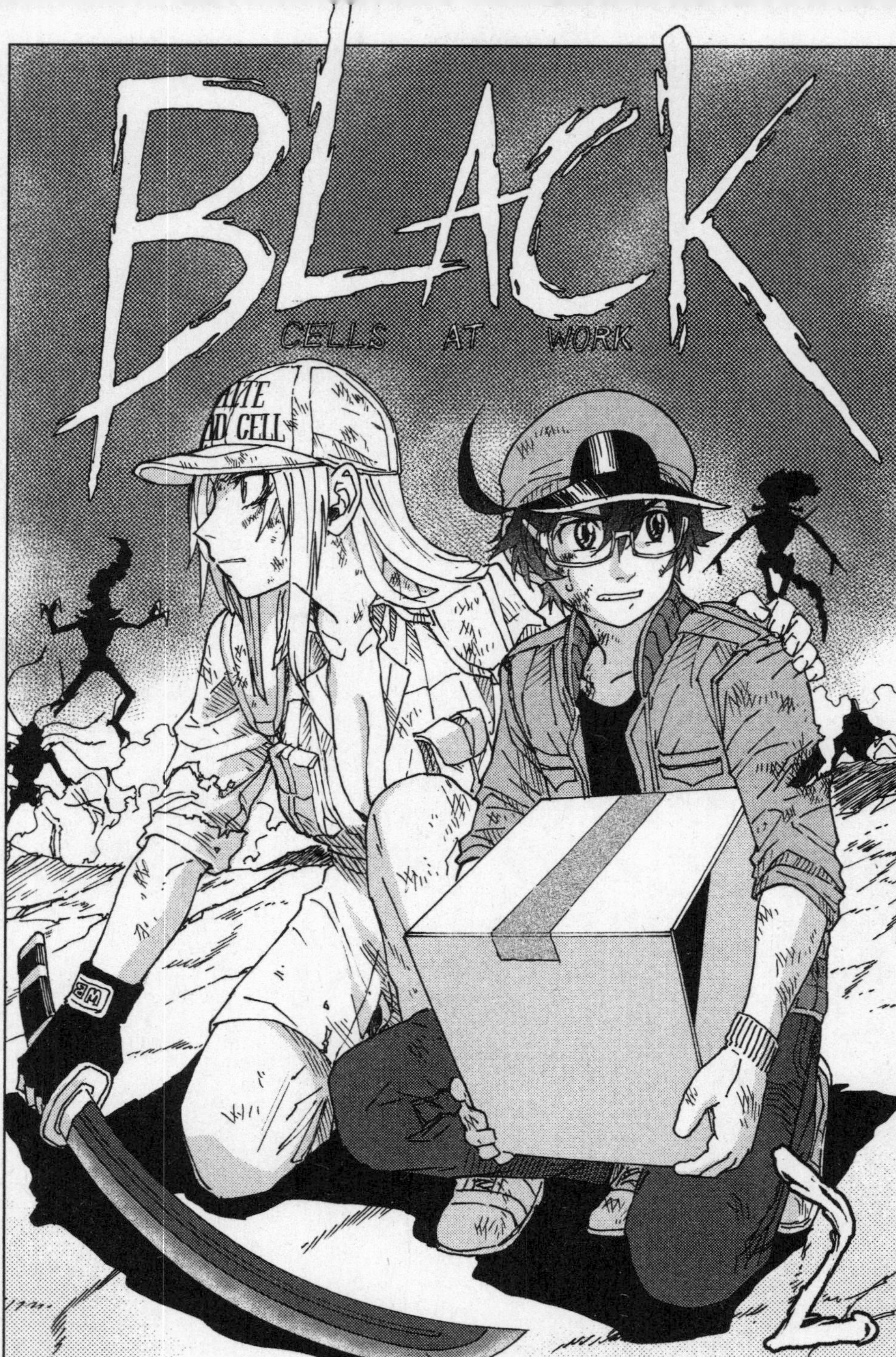
BLACK
CELLS AT WORK

CHAPTER 6: CALAMITY, ATHLETE'S FOOT, AND THE MEANING OF WORK

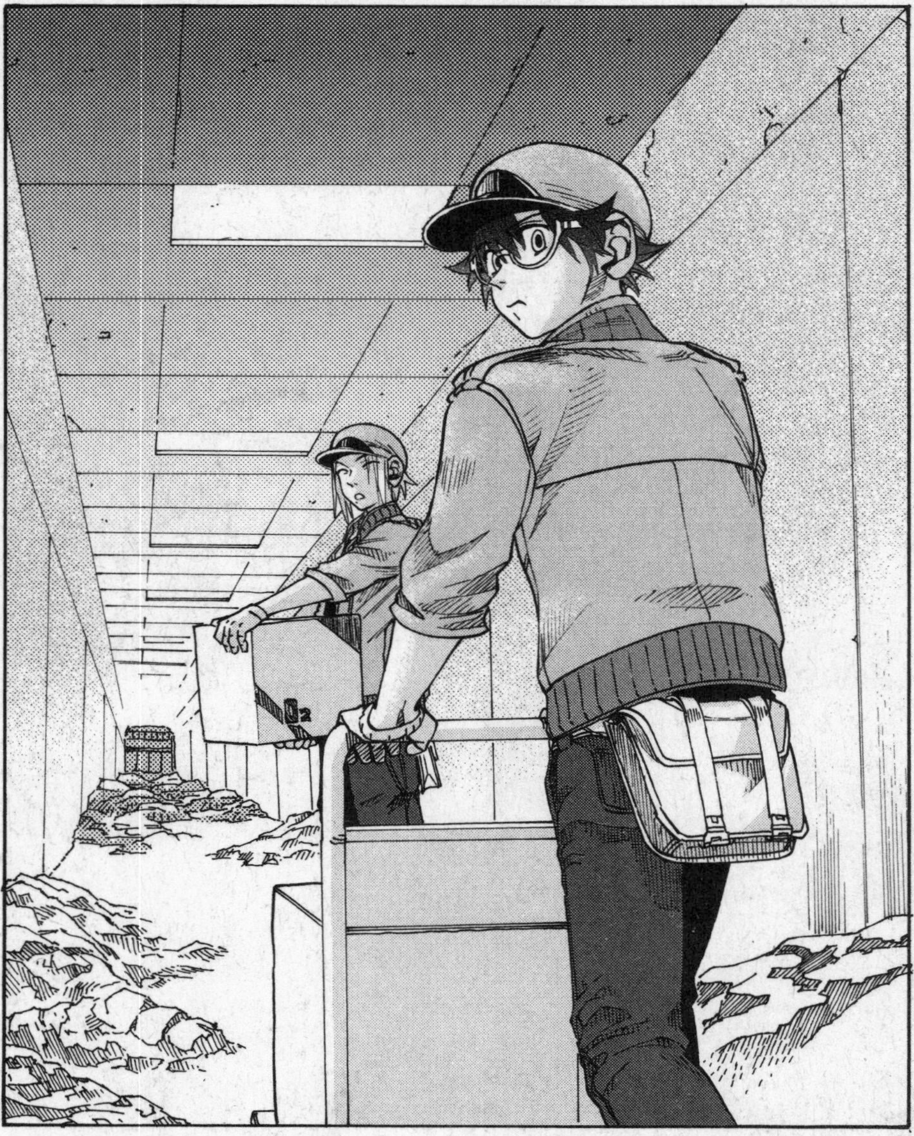

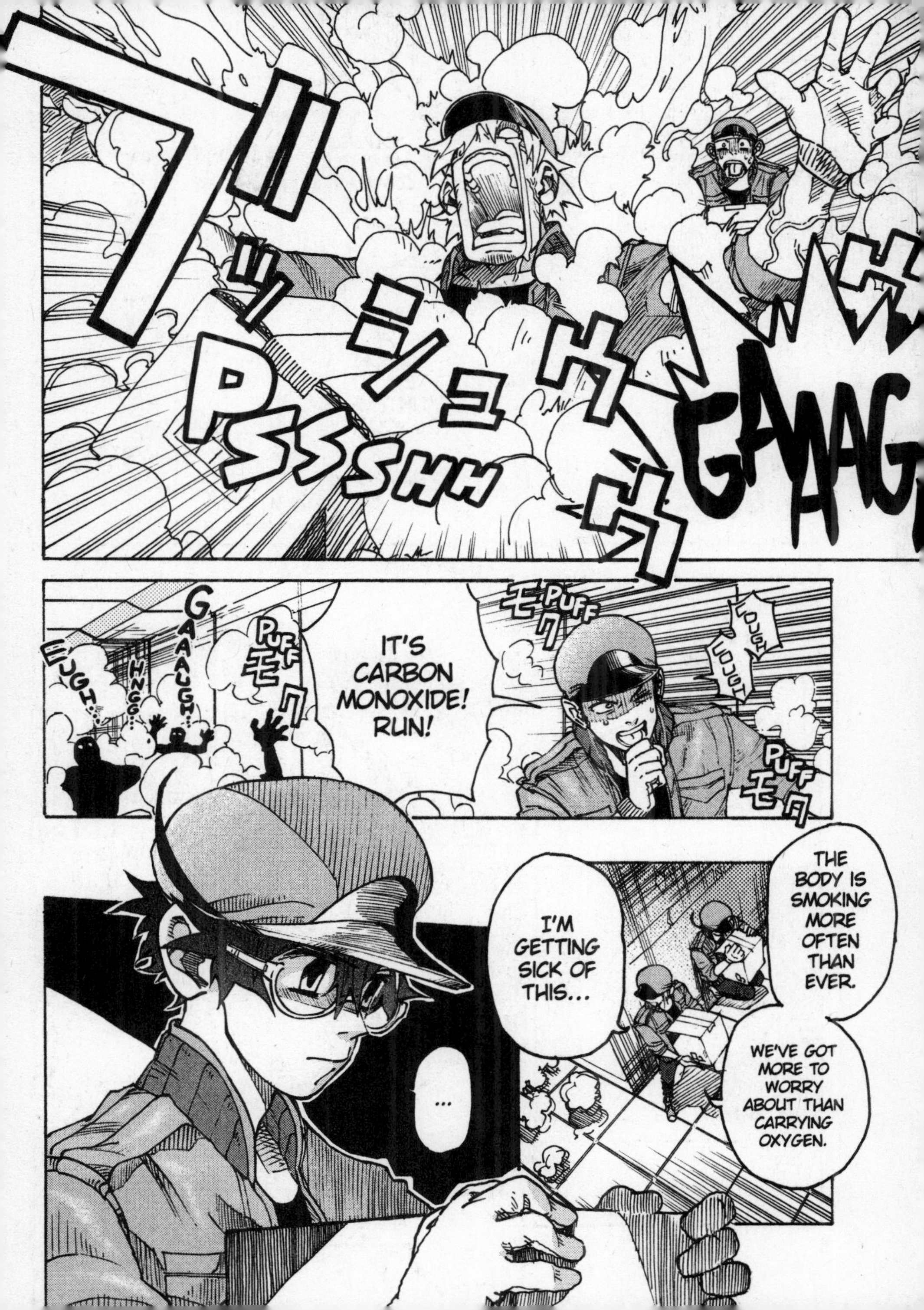
GAAAG
PSSSHH
PUFF
COUGH
COUGH
PUFF
IT'S CARBON MONOXIDE! RUN!
PUFF
GAAAUGH...
HNGG...
EUGH...
THE BODY IS SMOKING MORE OFTEN THAN EVER.
WE'VE GOT MORE TO WORRY ABOUT THAN CARRYING OXYGEN.
I'M GETTING SICK OF THIS...
...

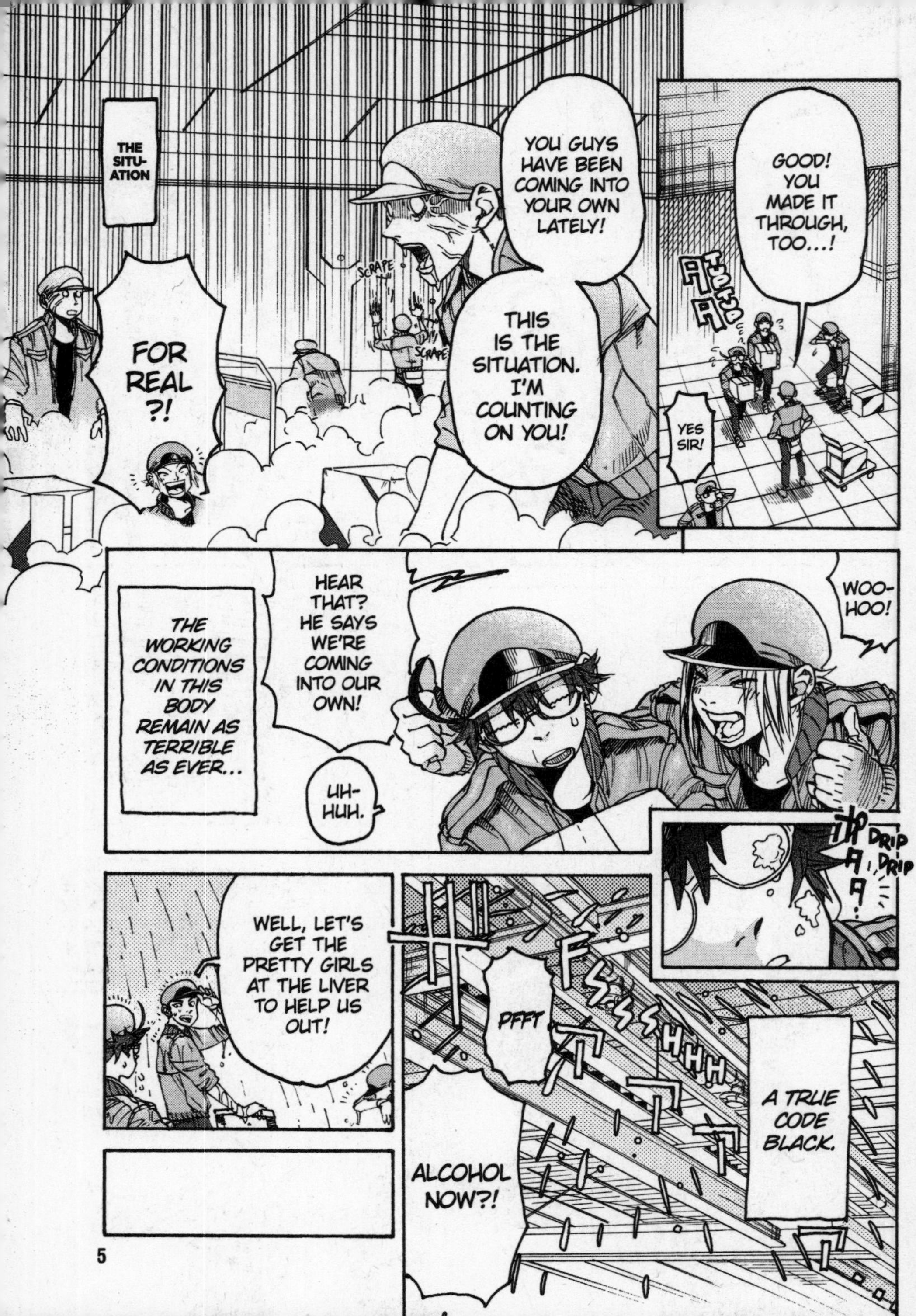
GOOD! YOU MADE IT THROUGH, TOO...!
YES SIR!
YOU GUYS HAVE BEEN COMING INTO YOUR OWN LATELY!
THIS IS THE SITUATION. I'M COUNTING ON YOU!
SCRAPE
SCRAPE
FOR REAL ?!
THE SITUATION
WOO-HOO!
HEAR THAT? HE SAYS WE'RE COMING INTO OUR OWN!
UH-HUH.
THE WORKING CONDITIONS IN THIS BODY REMAIN AS TERRIBLE AS EVER...
DRIP DRIP
FSSSHHHH
PFFT
A TRUE CODE BLACK.
ALCOHOL NOW?!
WELL, LET'S GET THE PRETTY GIRLS AT THE LIVER TO HELP US OUT!

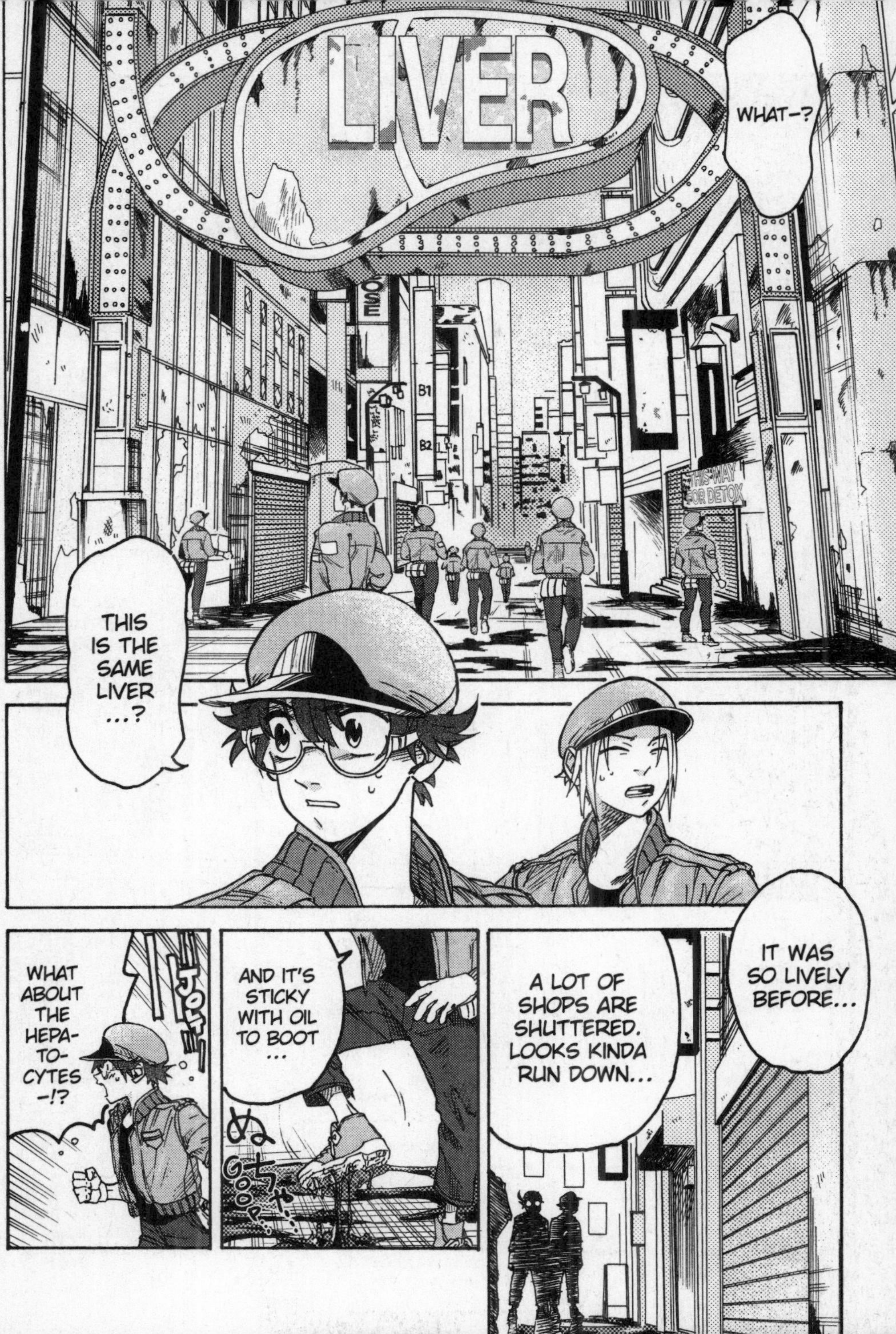

WHAT–?
LIVER
THIS WAY FOR DETOX
THIS IS THE SAME LIVER ...?
IT WAS SO LIVELY BEFORE...
A LOT OF SHOPS ARE SHUTTERED. LOOKS KINDA RUN DOWN...
AND IT'S STICKY WITH OIL TO BOOT ...
ぬちゃ...
GOOOP...
WHAT ABOUT THE HEPA-TO-CYTES –!?
JOLT

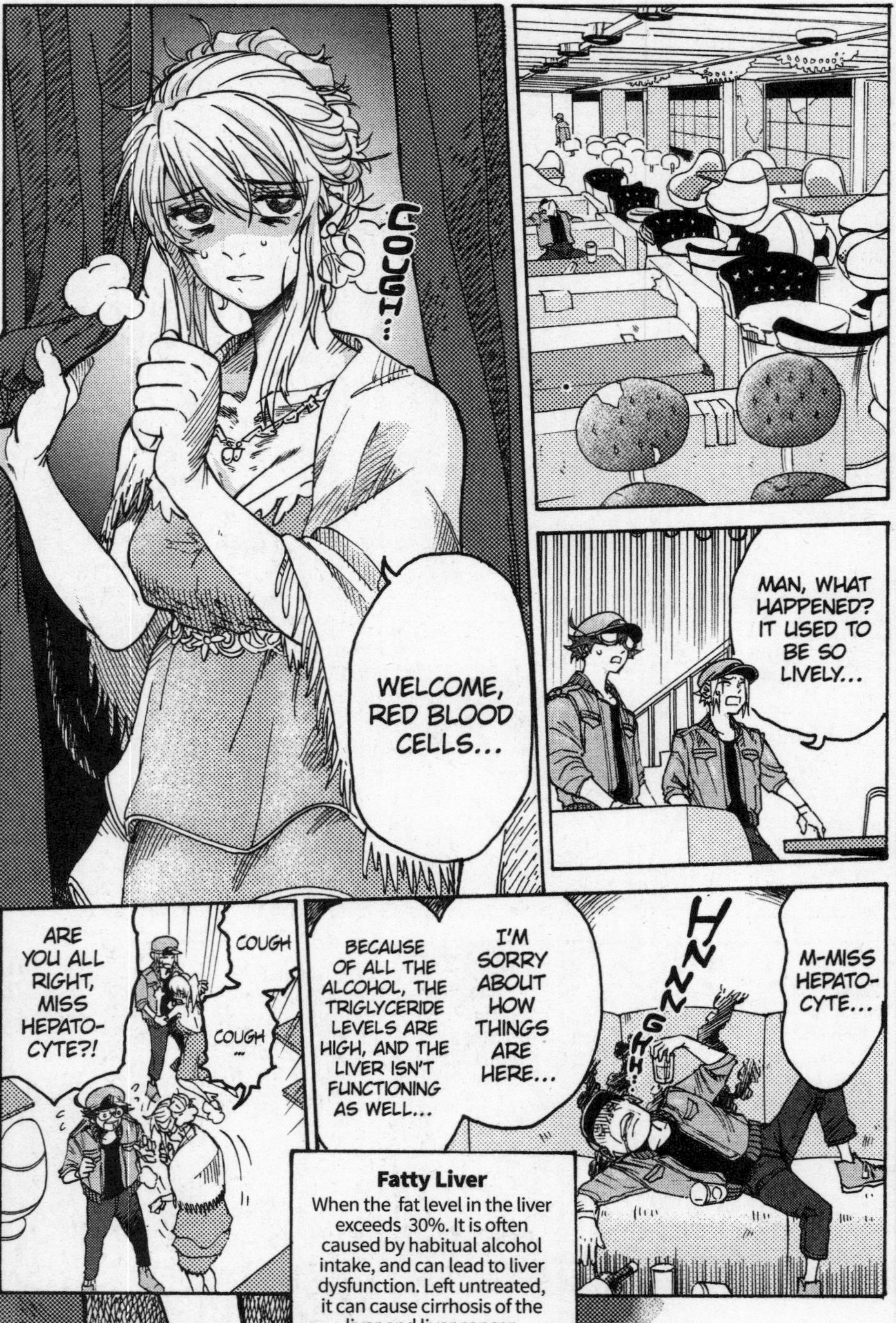
MAN, WHAT HAPPENED? IT USED TO BE SO LIVELY...
COUGH...
WELCOME, RED BLOOD CELLS...
M-MISS HEPATOCYTE...
HNNNGHH...
I'M SORRY ABOUT HOW THINGS ARE HERE...
BECAUSE OF ALL THE ALCOHOL, THE TRIGLYCERIDE LEVELS ARE HIGH, AND THE LIVER ISN'T FUNCTIONING AS WELL...
Fatty Liver
When the fat level in the liver exceeds 30%. It is often caused by habitual alcohol intake, and can lead to liver dysfunction. Left untreated, it can cause cirrhosis of the liver and liver cancer.
COUGH
COUGH...
ARE YOU ALL RIGHT, MISS HEPATOCYTE?!

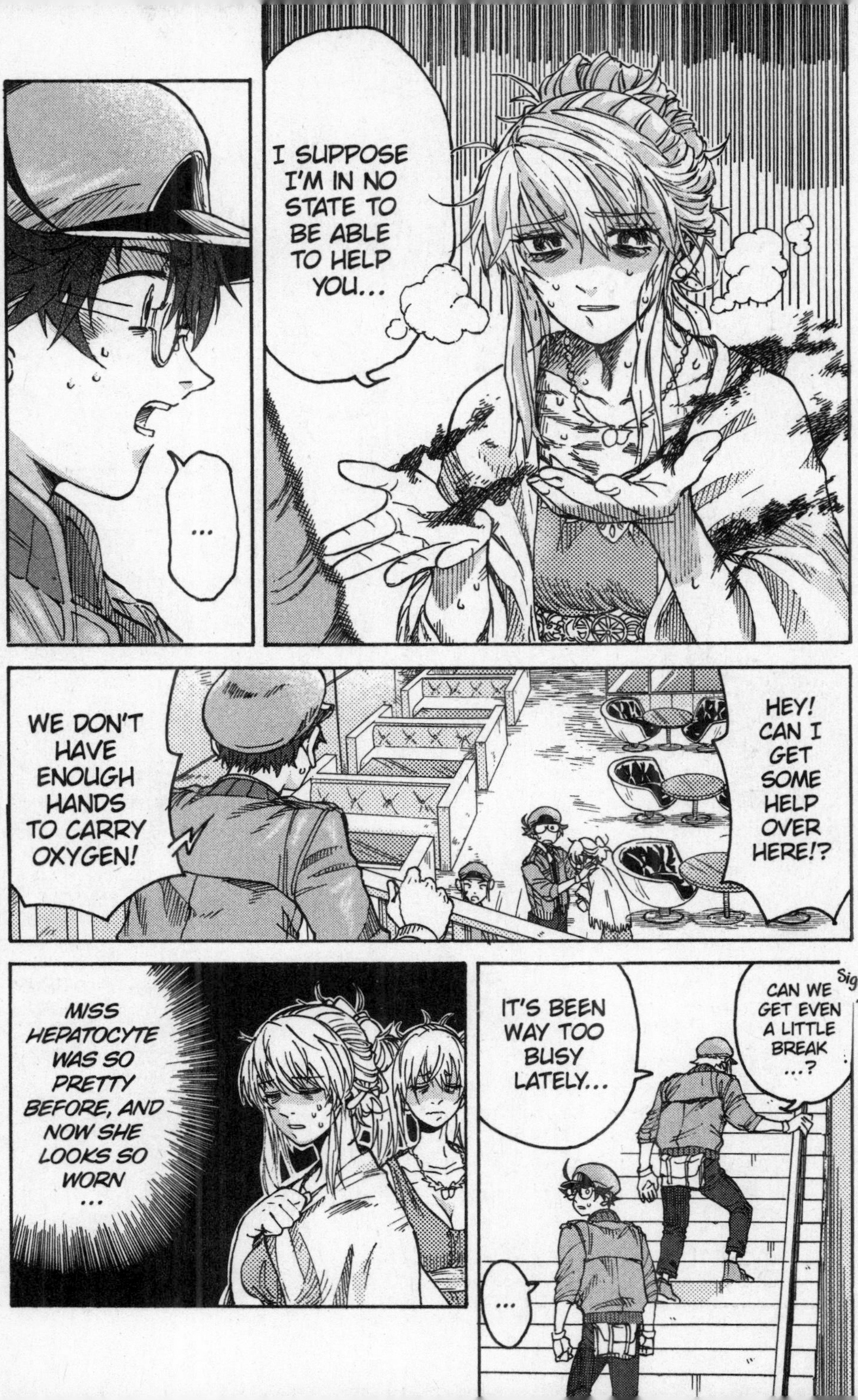
I SUPPOSE I'M IN NO STATE TO BE ABLE TO HELP YOU...
...
HEY! CAN I GET SOME HELP OVER HERE!?
WE DON'T HAVE ENOUGH HANDS TO CARRY OXYGEN!
Sigh...
CAN WE GET EVEN A LITTLE BREAK ...?
IT'S BEEN WAY TOO BUSY LATELY...
...
MISS HEPATOCYTE WAS SO PRETTY BEFORE, AND NOW SHE LOOKS SO WORN ...

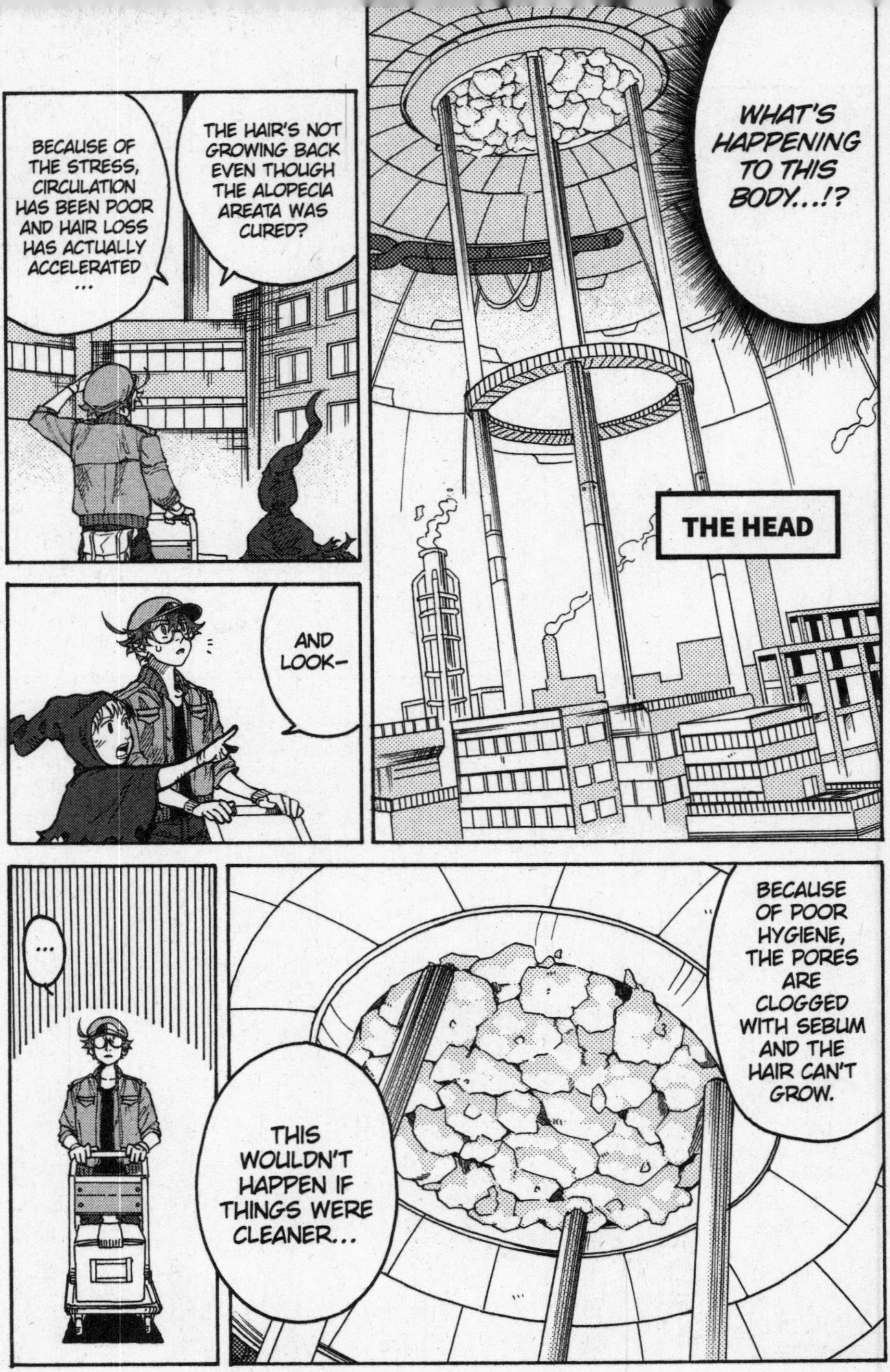
WHAT'S HAPPENING TO THIS BODY...!?
THE HEAD
THE HAIR'S NOT GROWING BACK EVEN THOUGH THE ALOPECIA AREATA WAS CURED?
BECAUSE OF THE STRESS, CIRCULATION HAS BEEN POOR AND HAIR LOSS HAS ACTUALLY ACCELERATED ...
AND LOOK-
BECAUSE OF POOR HYGIENE, THE PORES ARE CLOGGED WITH SEBUM AND THE HAIR CAN'T GROW.
THIS WOULDN'T HAPPEN IF THINGS WERE CLEANER...
...

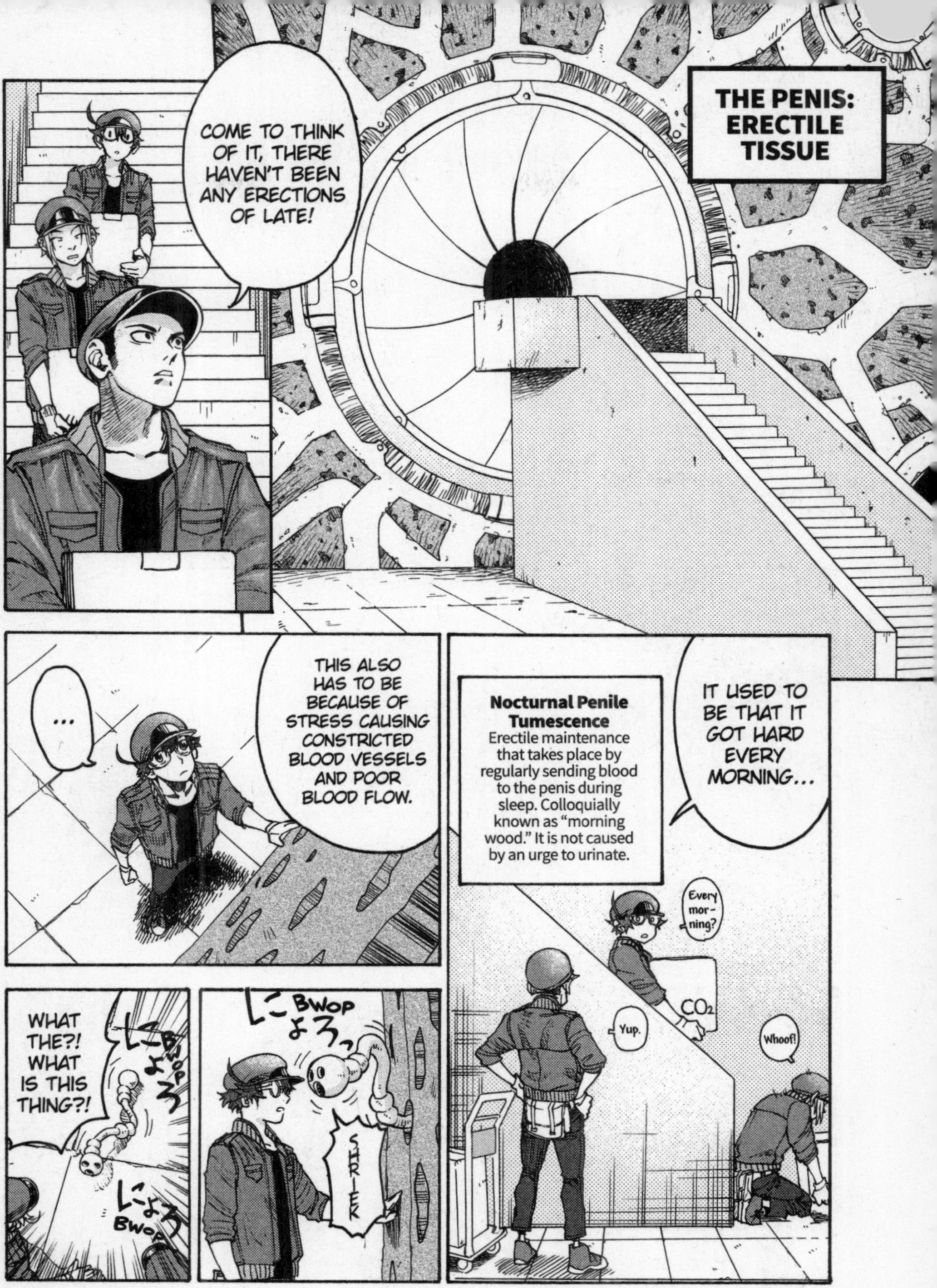
THE PENIS: ERECTILE TISSUE
COME TO THINK OF IT, THERE HAVEN'T BEEN ANY ERECTIONS OF LATE!
IT USED TO BE THAT IT GOT HARD EVERY MORNING...
Nocturnal Penile Tumescence
Erectile maintenance that takes place by regularly sending blood to the penis during sleep. Colloquially known as "morning wood." It is not caused by an urge to urinate.
Every mor-ning?
Yup.
Whoof!
CO2
THIS ALSO HAS TO BE BECAUSE OF STRESS CAUSING CONSTRICTED BLOOD VESSELS AND POOR BLOOD FLOW.
...
BWOP
SHRIEK
WHAT THE?! WHAT IS THIS THING?!
BWOP
BWOP

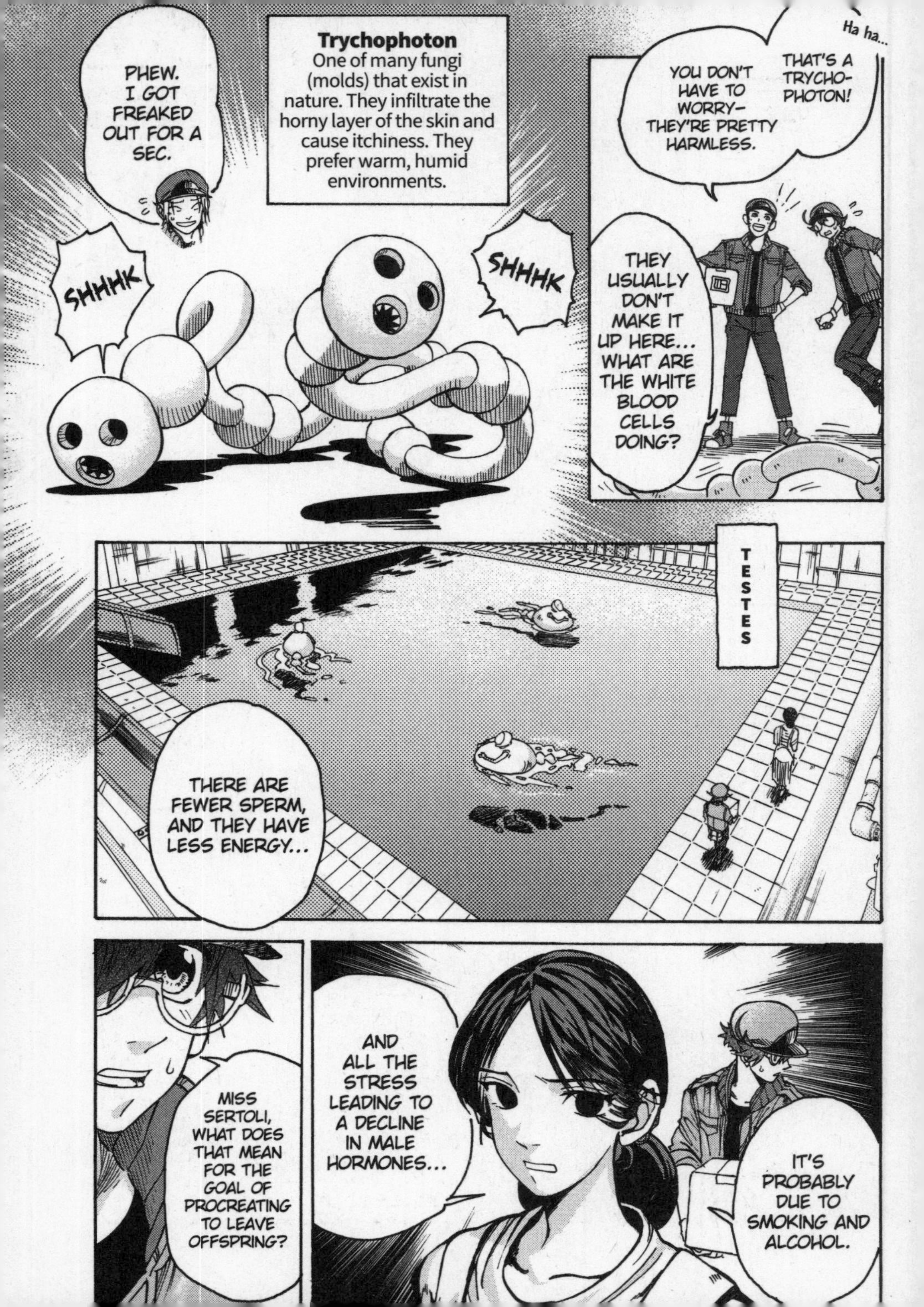
Ha ha...
THAT'S A TRYCHO-PHOTON!
YOU DON'T HAVE TO WORRY— THEY'RE PRETTY HARMLESS.
THEY USUALLY DON'T MAKE IT UP HERE... WHAT ARE THE WHITE BLOOD CELLS DOING?
Trychophoton
One of many fungi (molds) that exist in nature. They infiltrate the horny layer of the skin and cause itchiness. They prefer warm, humid environments.
PHEW. I GOT FREAKED OUT FOR A SEC.
SHHHK
SHHHK
TESTES
THERE ARE FEWER SPERM, AND THEY HAVE LESS ENERGY...
IT'S PROBABLY DUE TO SMOKING AND ALCOHOL.
AND ALL THE STRESS LEADING TO A DECLINE IN MALE HORMONES...
MISS SERTOLI, WHAT DOES THAT MEAN FOR THE GOAL OF PROCREATING TO LEAVE OFFSPRING?

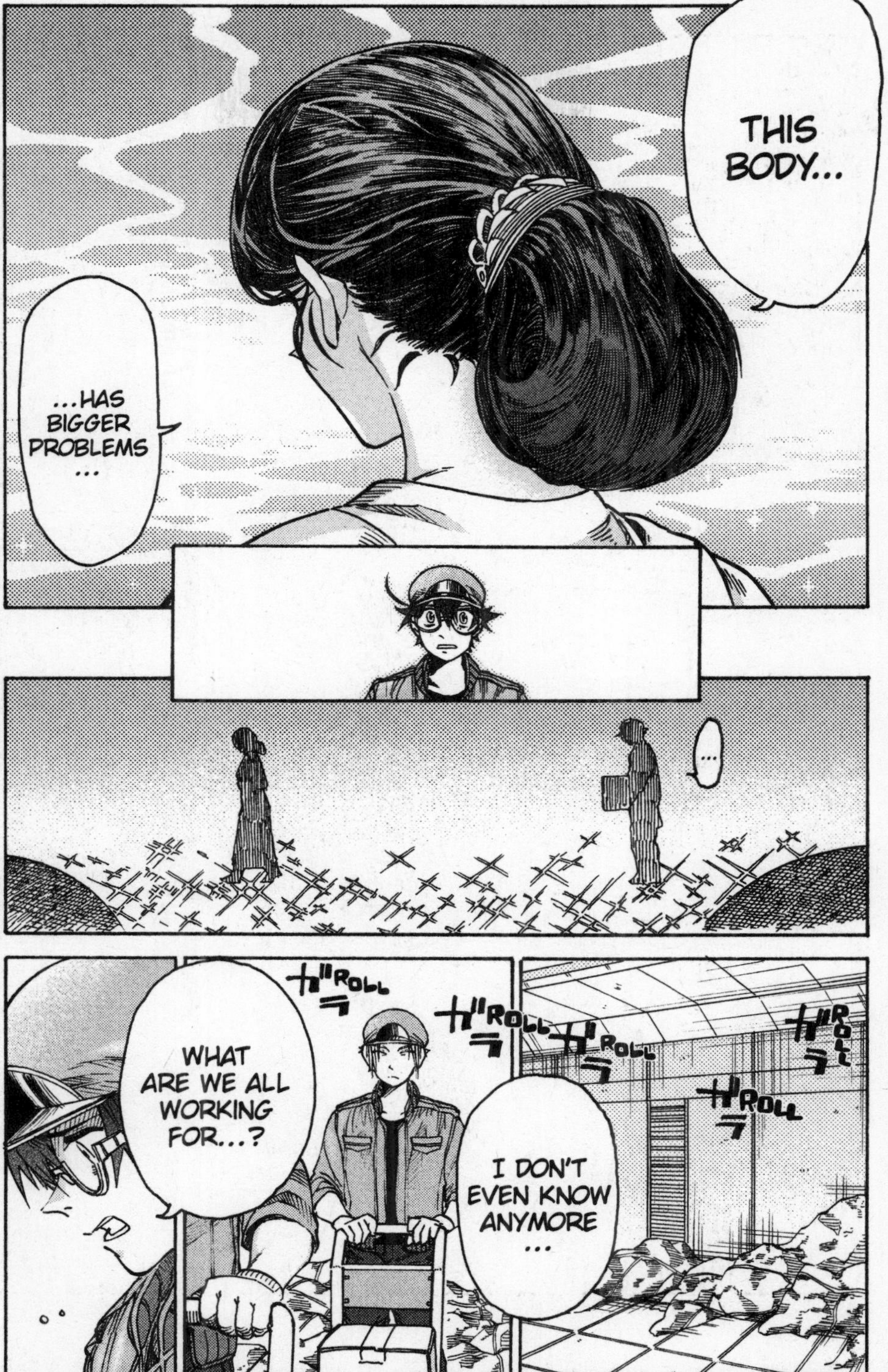
THIS BODY...
...HAS BIGGER PROBLEMS...
...
ガ"ROLLラ
ガ"ROLLラ
ガ"ROLLラ
ガ"ROLLラ
ガ"ROLLラ
WHAT ARE WE ALL WORKING FOR...?
I DON'T EVEN KNOW ANYMORE...

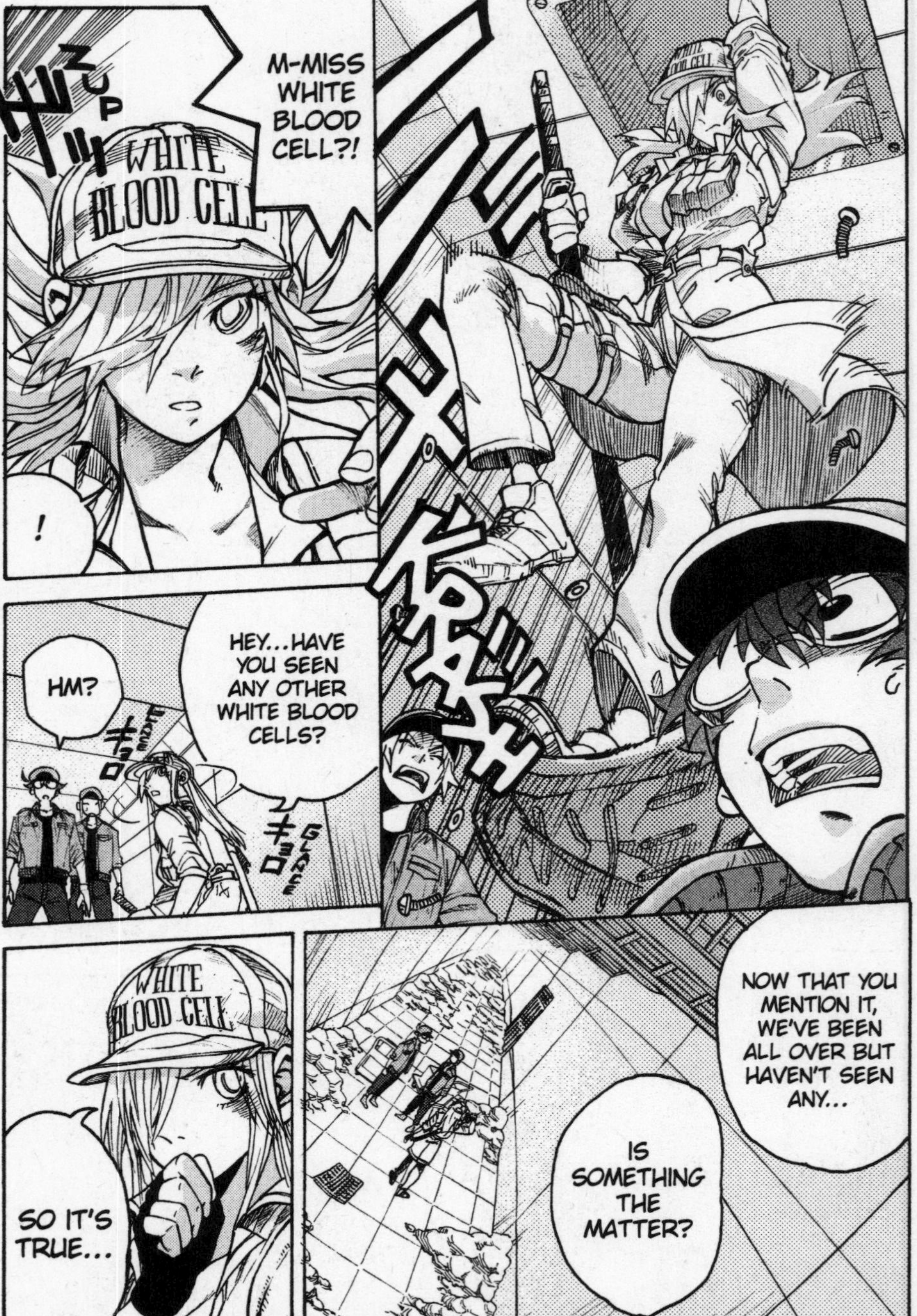
KRASH
ZUP
M-MISS WHITE BLOOD CELL?!
!
HEY...HAVE YOU SEEN ANY OTHER WHITE BLOOD CELLS?
HM?
GLANCE
GLANCE
NOW THAT YOU MENTION IT, WE'VE BEEN ALL OVER BUT HAVEN'T SEEN ANY...
IS SOMETHING THE MATTER?
SO IT'S TRUE...

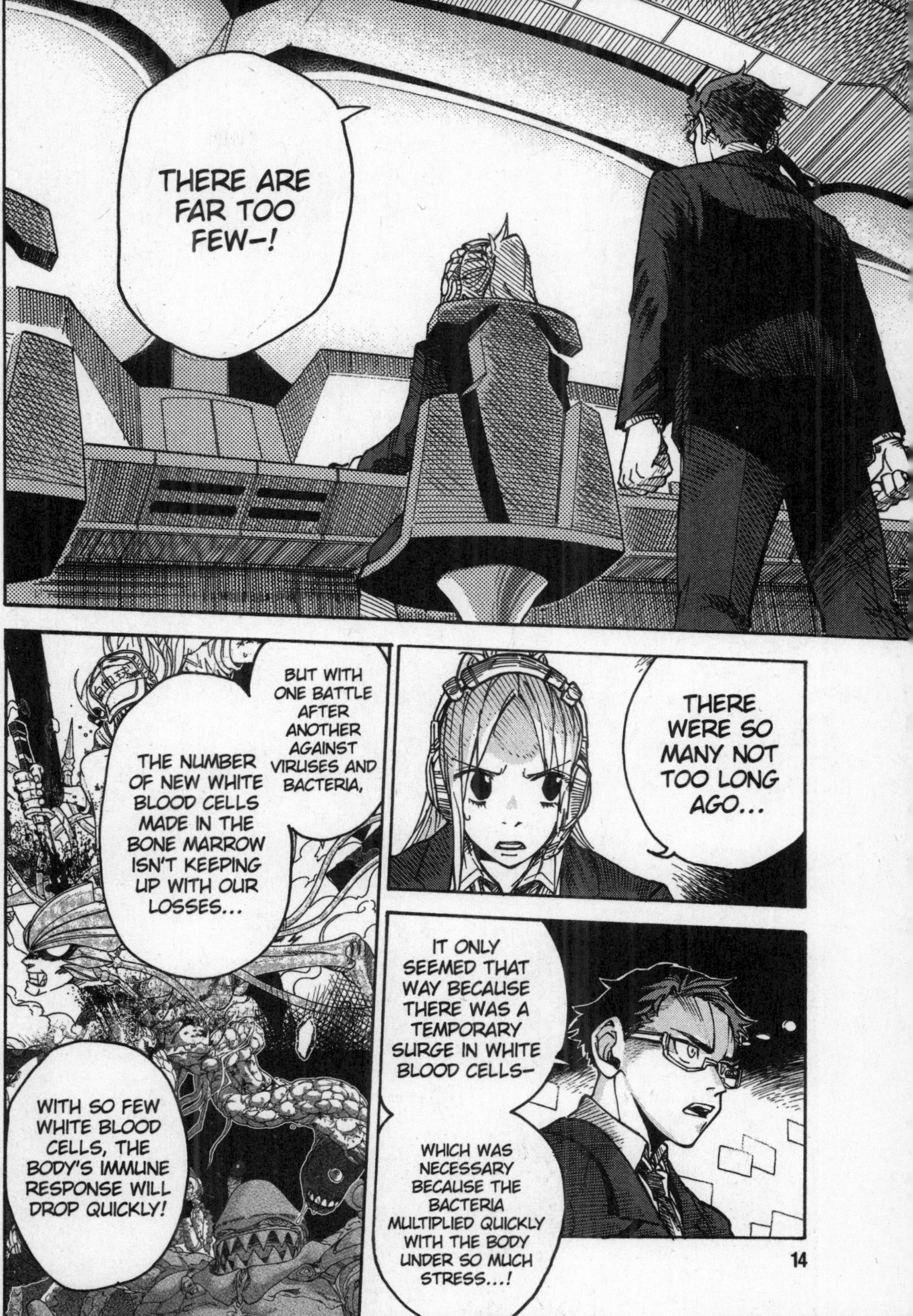
THERE ARE FAR TOO FEW–!
THERE WERE SO MANY NOT TOO LONG AGO...
IT ONLY SEEMED THAT WAY BECAUSE THERE WAS A TEMPORARY SURGE IN WHITE BLOOD CELLS–
WHICH WAS NECESSARY BECAUSE THE BACTERIA MULTIPLIED QUICKLY WITH THE BODY UNDER SO MUCH STRESS...!
BUT WITH ONE BATTLE AFTER ANOTHER AGAINST VIRUSES AND BACTERIA,
THE NUMBER OF NEW WHITE BLOOD CELLS MADE IN THE BONE MARROW ISN'T KEEPING UP WITH OUR LOSSES...
WITH SO FEW WHITE BLOOD CELLS, THE BODY'S IMMUNE RESPONSE WILL DROP QUICKLY!

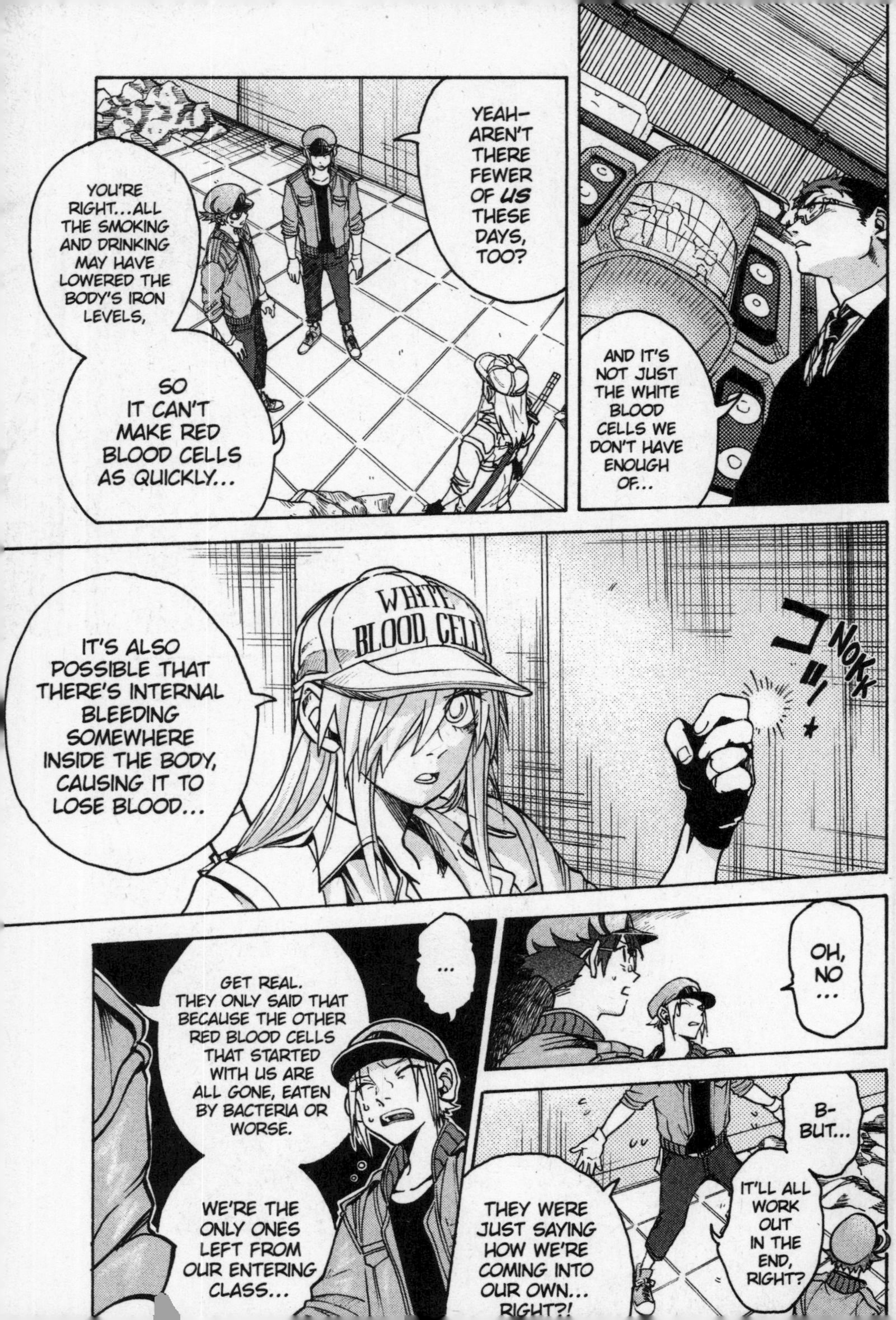
AND IT'S NOT JUST THE WHITE BLOOD CELLS WE DON'T HAVE ENOUGH OF...
YEAH- AREN'T THERE FEWER OF *US* THESE DAYS, TOO?
YOU'RE RIGHT...ALL THE SMOKING AND DRINKING MAY HAVE LOWERED THE BODY'S IRON LEVELS,
SO IT CAN'T MAKE RED BLOOD CELLS AS QUICKLY...
WHITE BLOOD CELL
NOKK
IT'S ALSO POSSIBLE THAT THERE'S INTERNAL BLEEDING SOMEWHERE INSIDE THE BODY, CAUSING IT TO LOSE BLOOD...
OH, NO ...
B- BUT...
IT'LL ALL WORK OUT IN THE END, RIGHT?
THEY WERE JUST SAYING HOW WE'RE COMING INTO OUR OWN... RIGHT?!
...
GET REAL. THEY ONLY SAID THAT BECAUSE THE OTHER RED BLOOD CELLS THAT STARTED WITH US ARE ALL GONE, EATEN BY BACTERIA OR WORSE.
WE'RE THE ONLY ONES LEFT FROM OUR ENTERING CLASS...

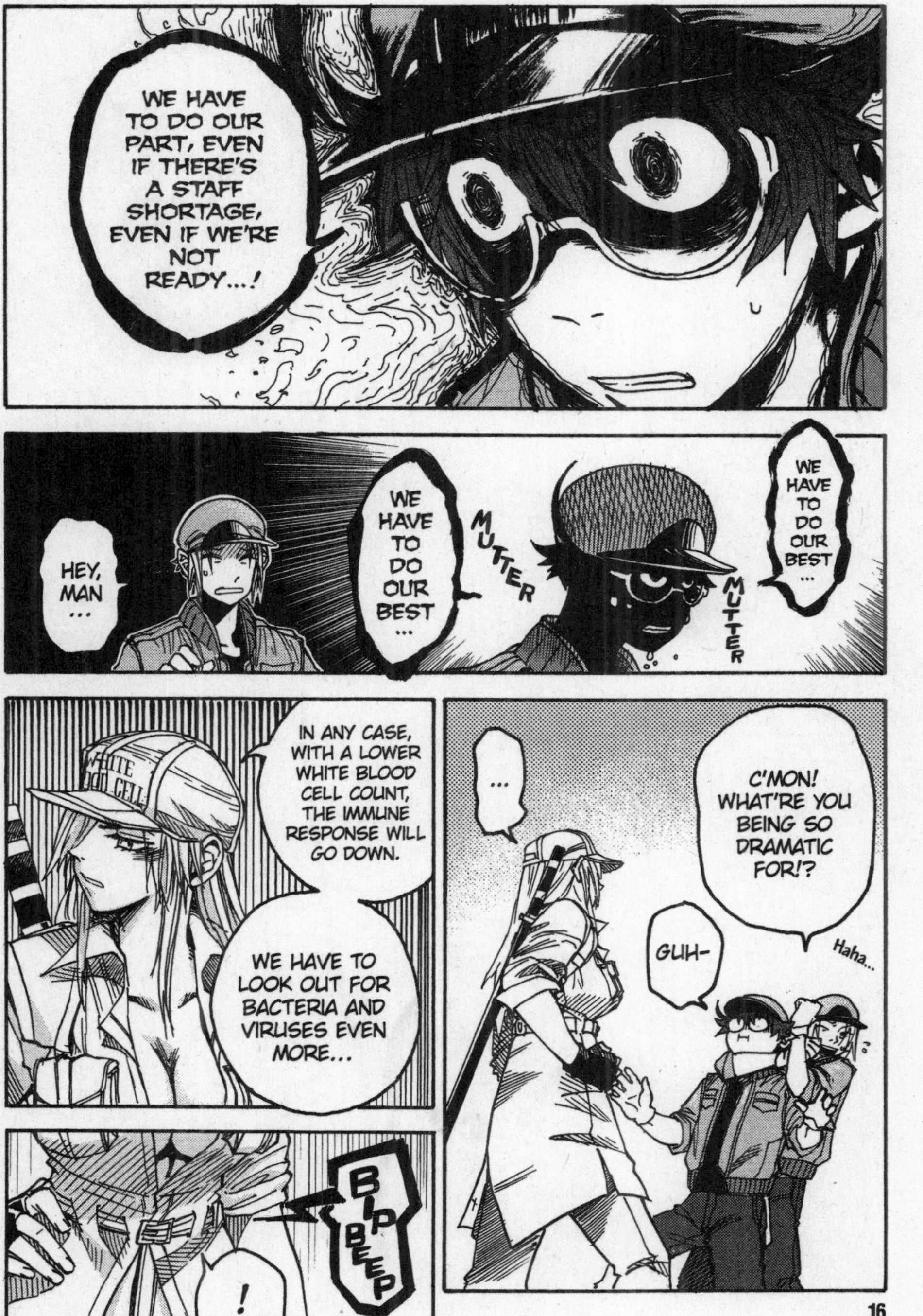
WE HAVE TO DO OUR PART, EVEN IF THERE'S A STAFF SHORTAGE, EVEN IF WE'RE NOT READY...!
WE HAVE TO DO OUR BEST...
MUTTER
WE HAVE TO DO OUR BEST...
MUTTER
HEY, MAN...
C'MON! WHAT'RE YOU BEING SO DRAMATIC FOR!?
...
Haha...
GUH-
IN ANY CASE, WITH A LOWER WHITE BLOOD CELL COUNT, THE IMMUNE RESPONSE WILL GO DOWN.
WE HAVE TO LOOK OUT FOR BACTERIA AND VIRUSES EVEN MORE...
BIP BEEP
!

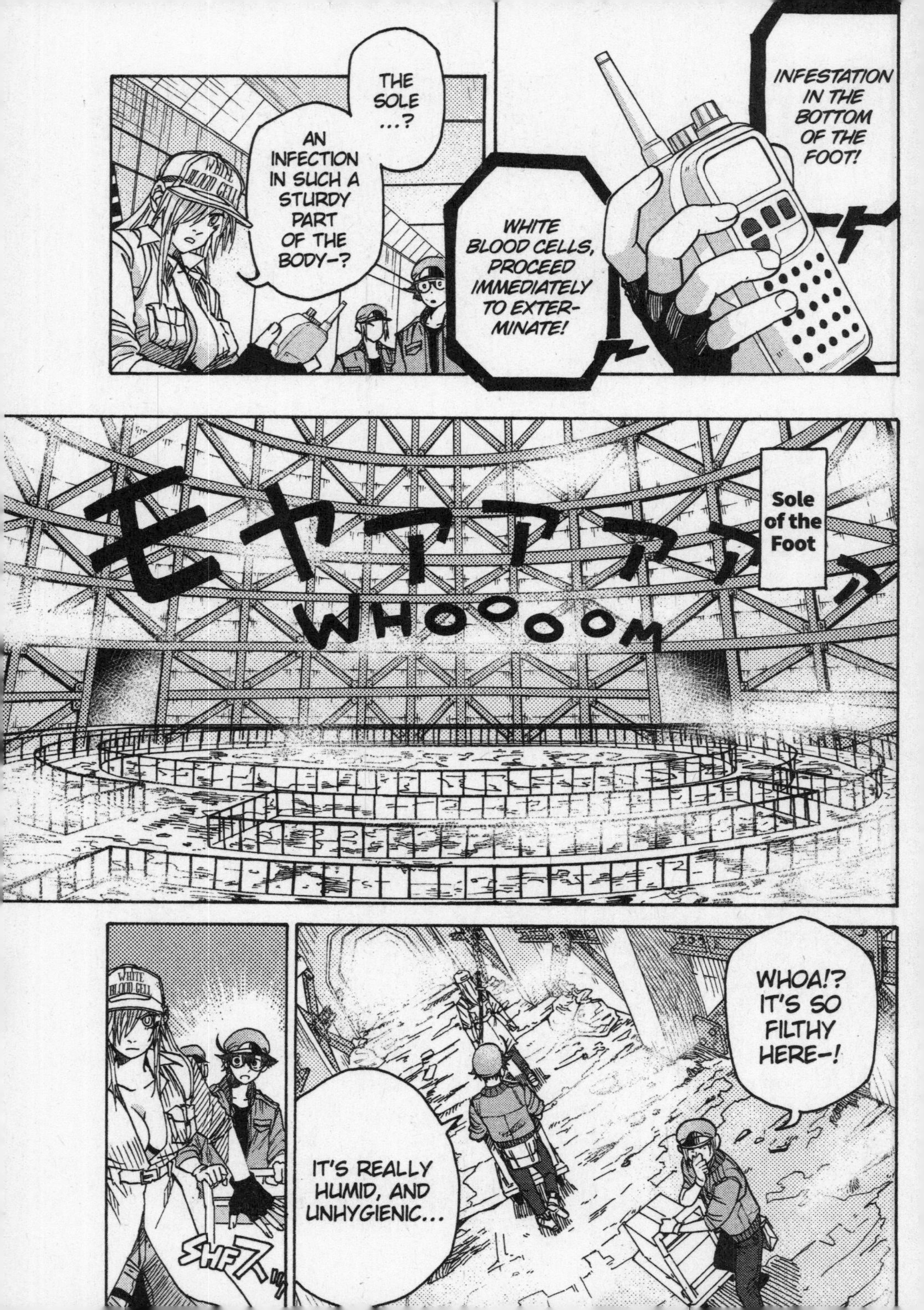
INFESTATION IN THE BOTTOM OF THE FOOT!
WHITE BLOOD CELLS, PROCEED IMMEDIATELY TO EXTER-MINATE!
THE SOLE ...?
AN INFECTION IN SUCH A STURDY PART OF THE BODY-?
Sole of the Foot
モヤアアア
WHOOOOOM
WHOA!? IT'S SO FILTHY HERE-!
IT'S REALLY HUMID, AND UNHYGIENIC...
SHF

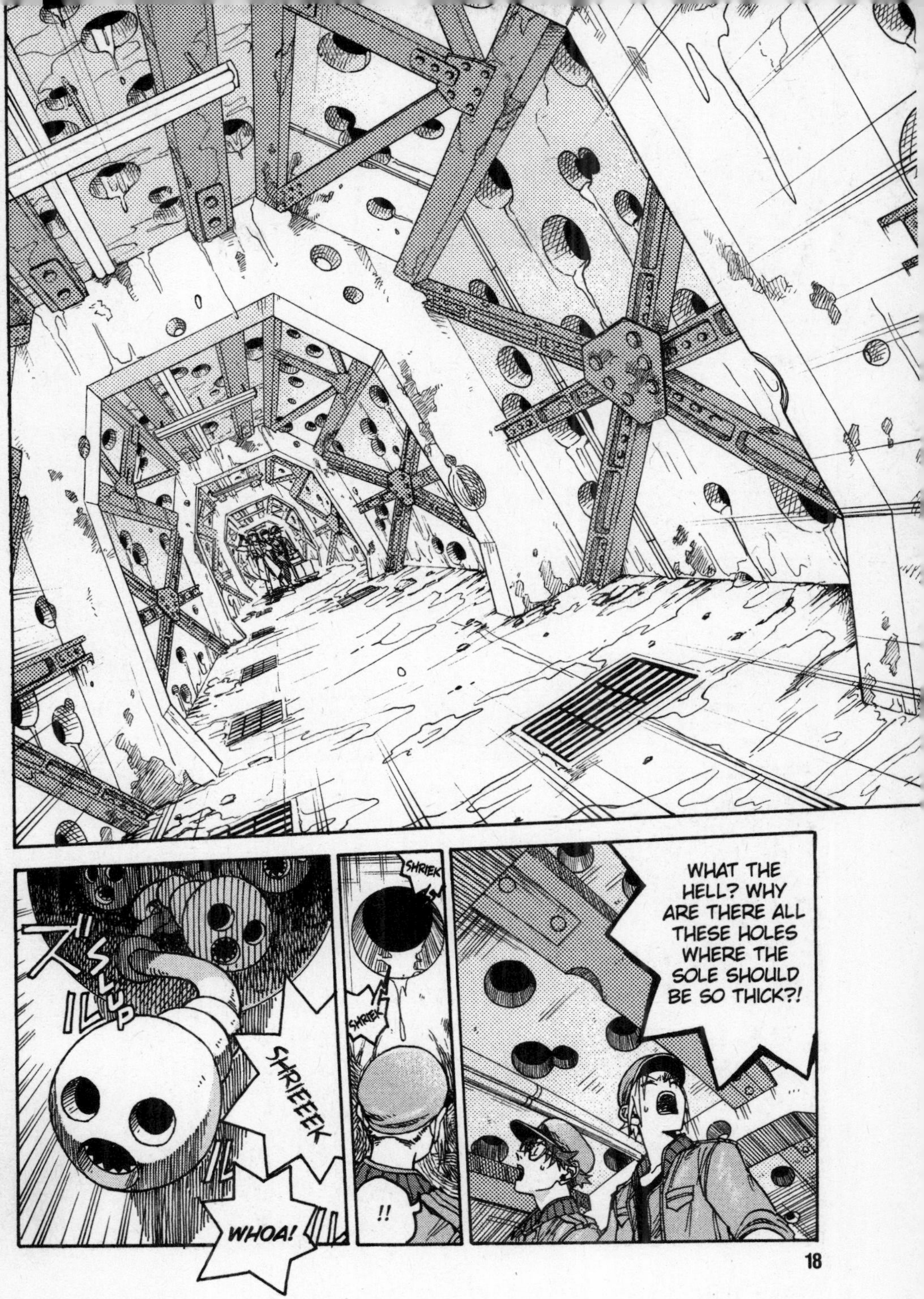
WHAT THE HELL? WHY ARE THERE ALL THESE HOLES WHERE THE SOLE SHOULD BE SO THICK?!
SHRIEK
SHRIEK
!!
SLUP
SHRIEEEK
WHOA!

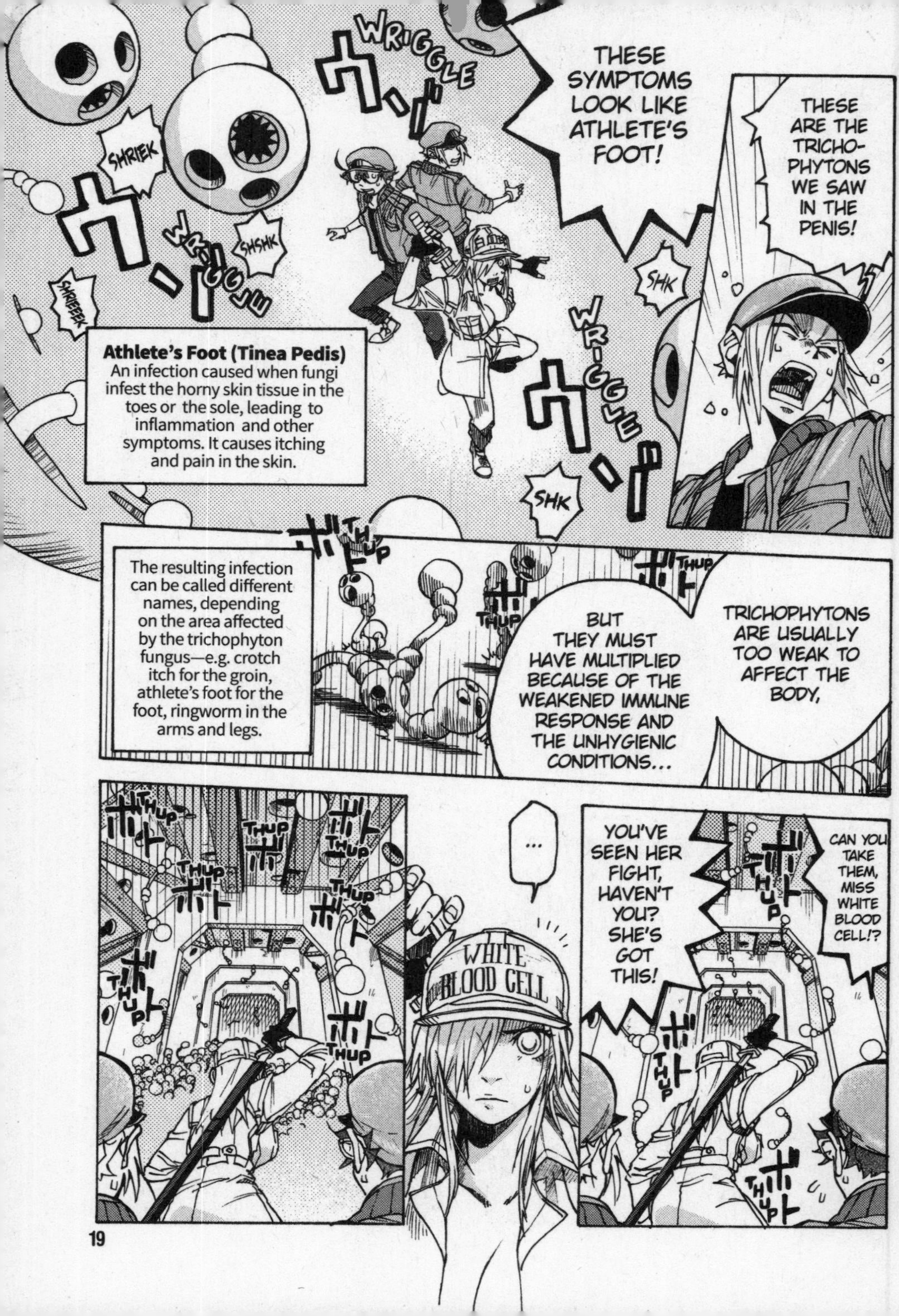
THESE ARE THE TRICHO-PHYTONS WE SAW IN THE PENIS!
SHK
WRIGGLE
SHK
THESE SYMPTOMS LOOK LIKE ATHLETE'S FOOT!
WRIGGLE
SHRIEK
SHSHK
WRIGGLE
SHRIEEEK
Athlete's Foot (Tinea Pedis)
An infection caused when fungi infest the horny skin tissue in the toes or the sole, leading to inflammation and other symptoms. It causes itching and pain in the skin.
THUP
TRICHOPHYTONS ARE USUALLY TOO WEAK TO AFFECT THE BODY,
BUT THEY MUST HAVE MULTIPLIED BECAUSE OF THE WEAKENED IMMUNE RESPONSE AND THE UNHYGIENIC CONDITIONS...
THUP
THUP
The resulting infection can be called different names, depending on the area affected by the trichophyton fungus—e.g. crotch itch for the groin, athlete's foot for the foot, ringworm in the arms and legs.
CAN YOU TAKE THEM, MISS WHITE BLOOD CELL!?
YOU'VE SEEN HER FIGHT, HAVEN'T YOU? SHE'S GOT THIS!
THUP
THUP
THUP
...
WHITE BLOOD CELL
THUP
THUP
THUP
THUP
THUP
THUP
THUP

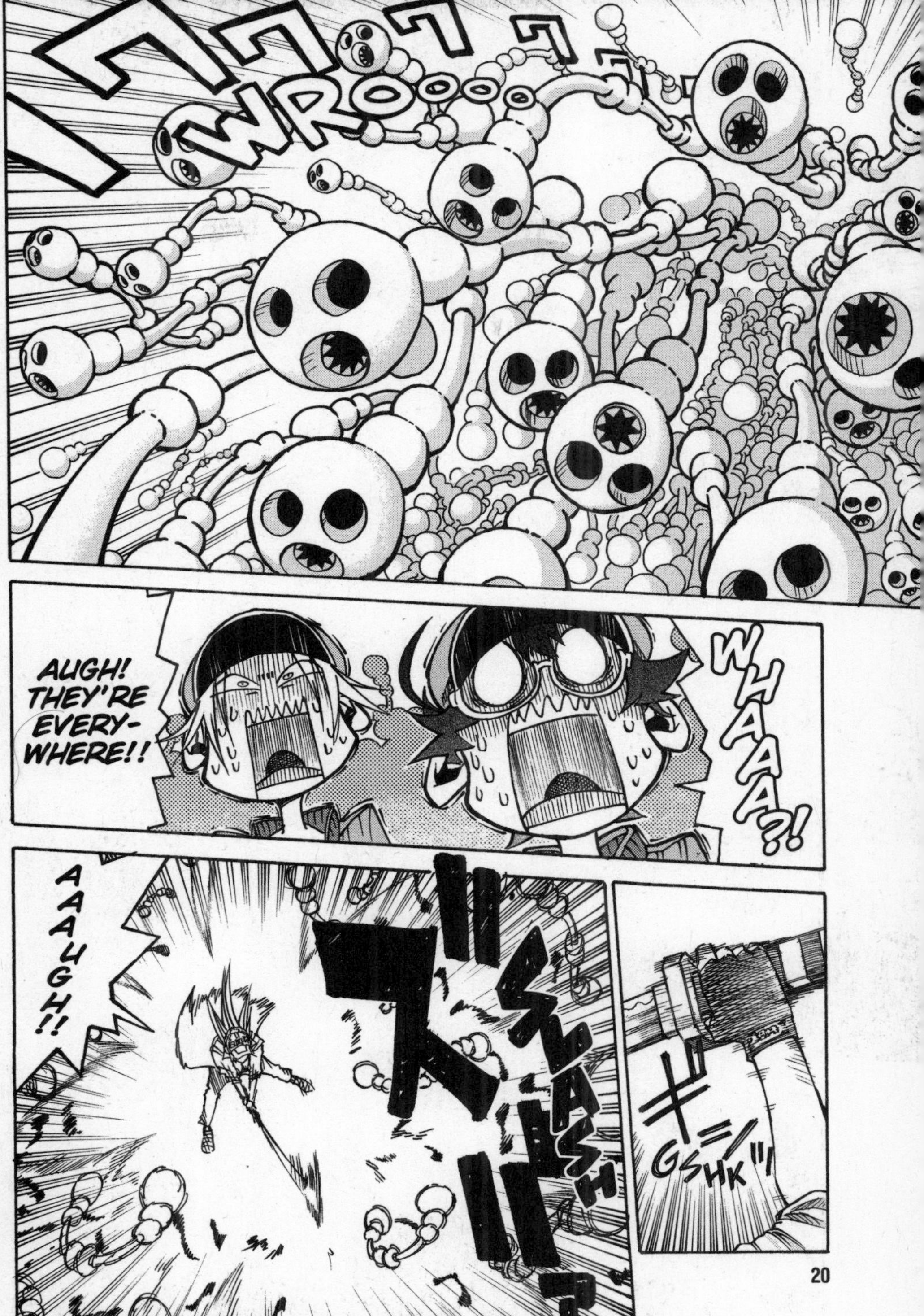
WROOOO
WHAAAA?!
AUGH! THEY'RE EVERY-WHERE!!
GSHK
SLASH
AAAAUGH!!

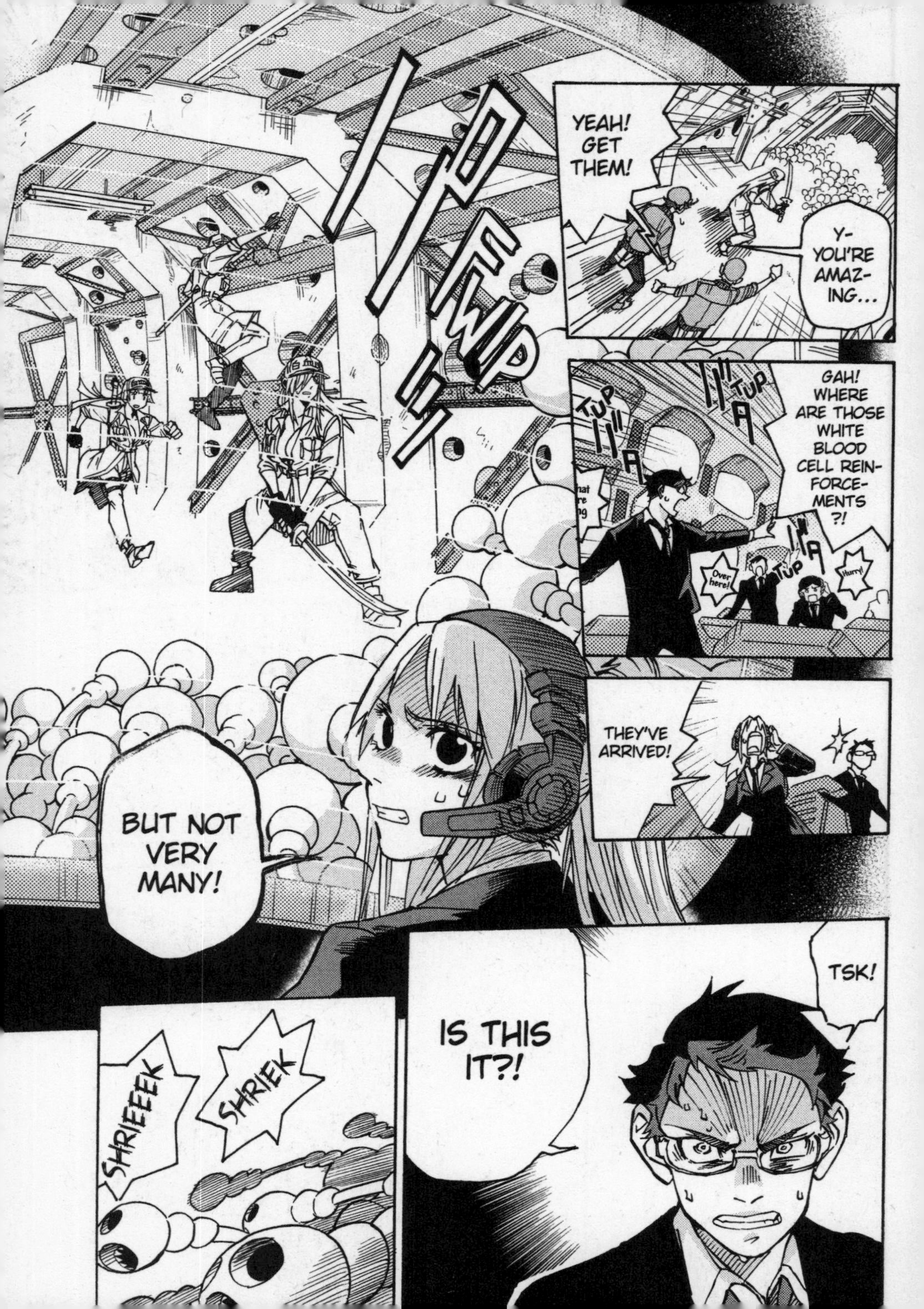
YEAH! GET THEM!
Y-YOU'RE AMAZING...
GAH! WHERE ARE THOSE WHITE BLOOD CELL REINFORCEMENTS?!
TUP TUP TUP
Over here!
Hurry!
THEY'VE ARRIVED!
PEWIP
BUT NOT VERY MANY!
TSK!
IS THIS IT?!
SHRIEK
SHRIEEEK

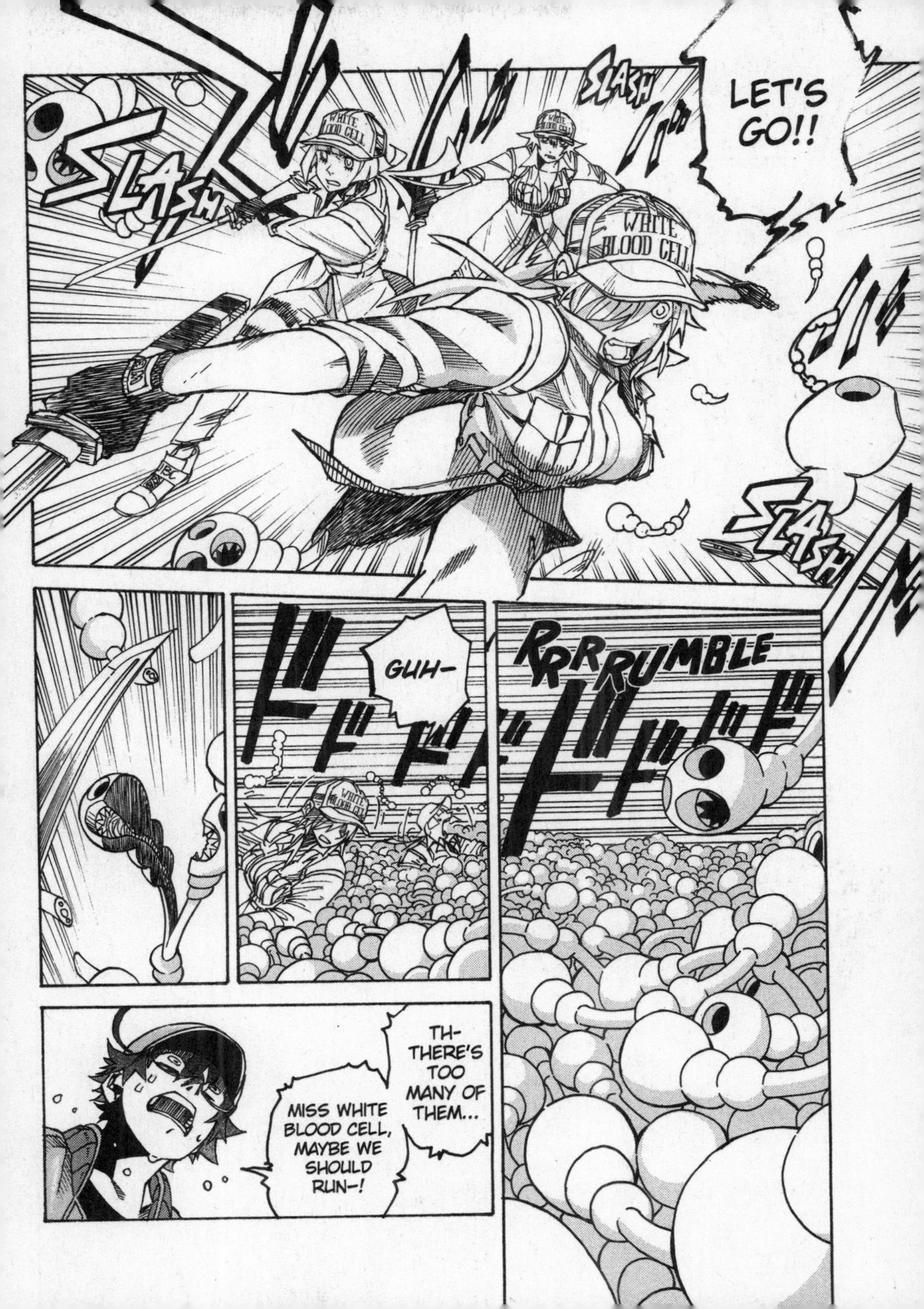
LET'S GO!!
SLASH
WHITE BLOOD CELL
SLASH
SLASH
RRRRUMBLE
GUH-
TH-THERE'S TOO MANY OF THEM...
MISS WHITE BLOOD CELL, MAYBE WE SHOULD RUN-!

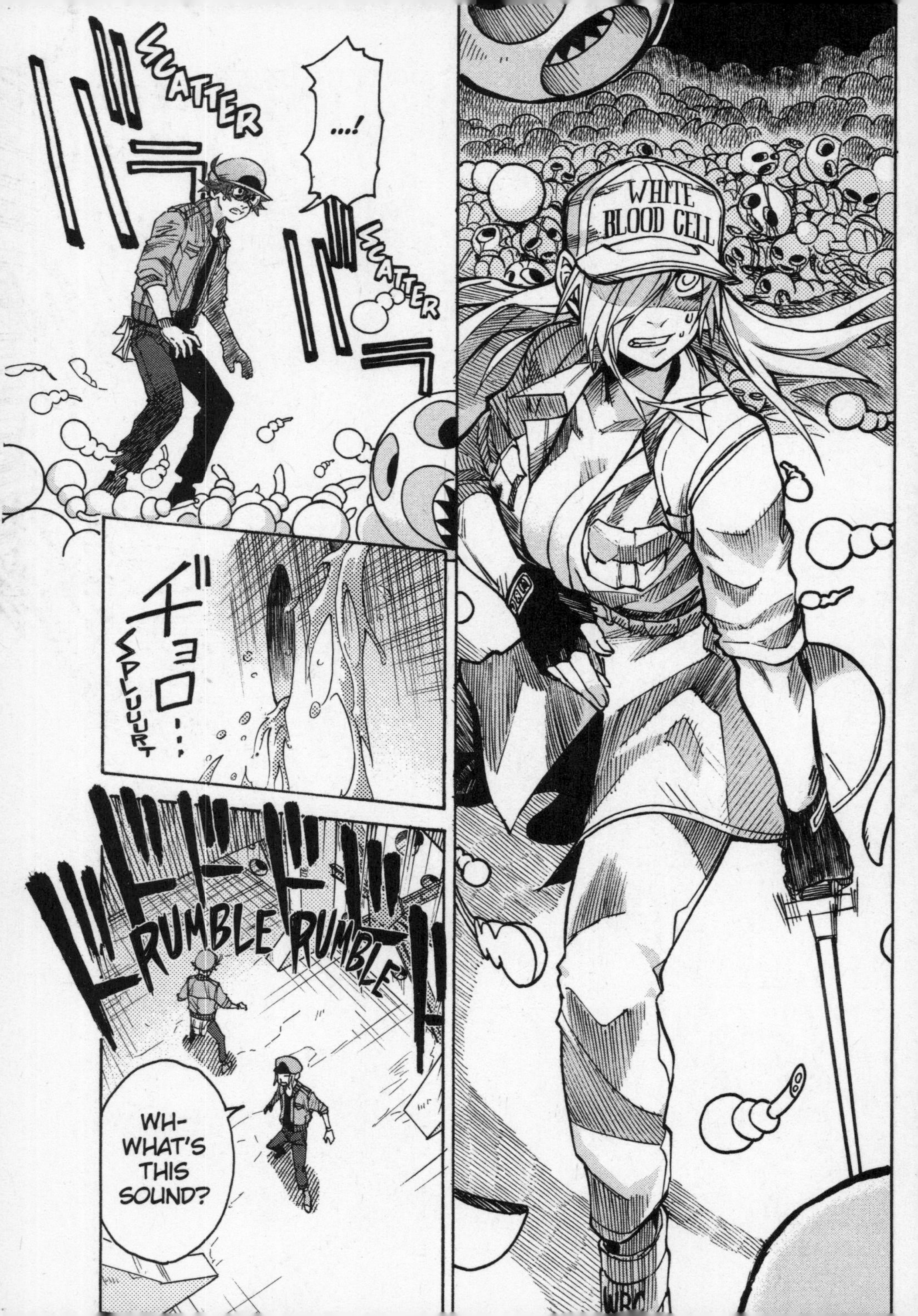

WHITE BLOOD CELL
...!
バラ
SCATTER
バラ
SCATTER
ギョロ…
SPLUUURT
ドドドドド
RUMBLE RUMBLE
WH- WHAT'S THIS SOUND?

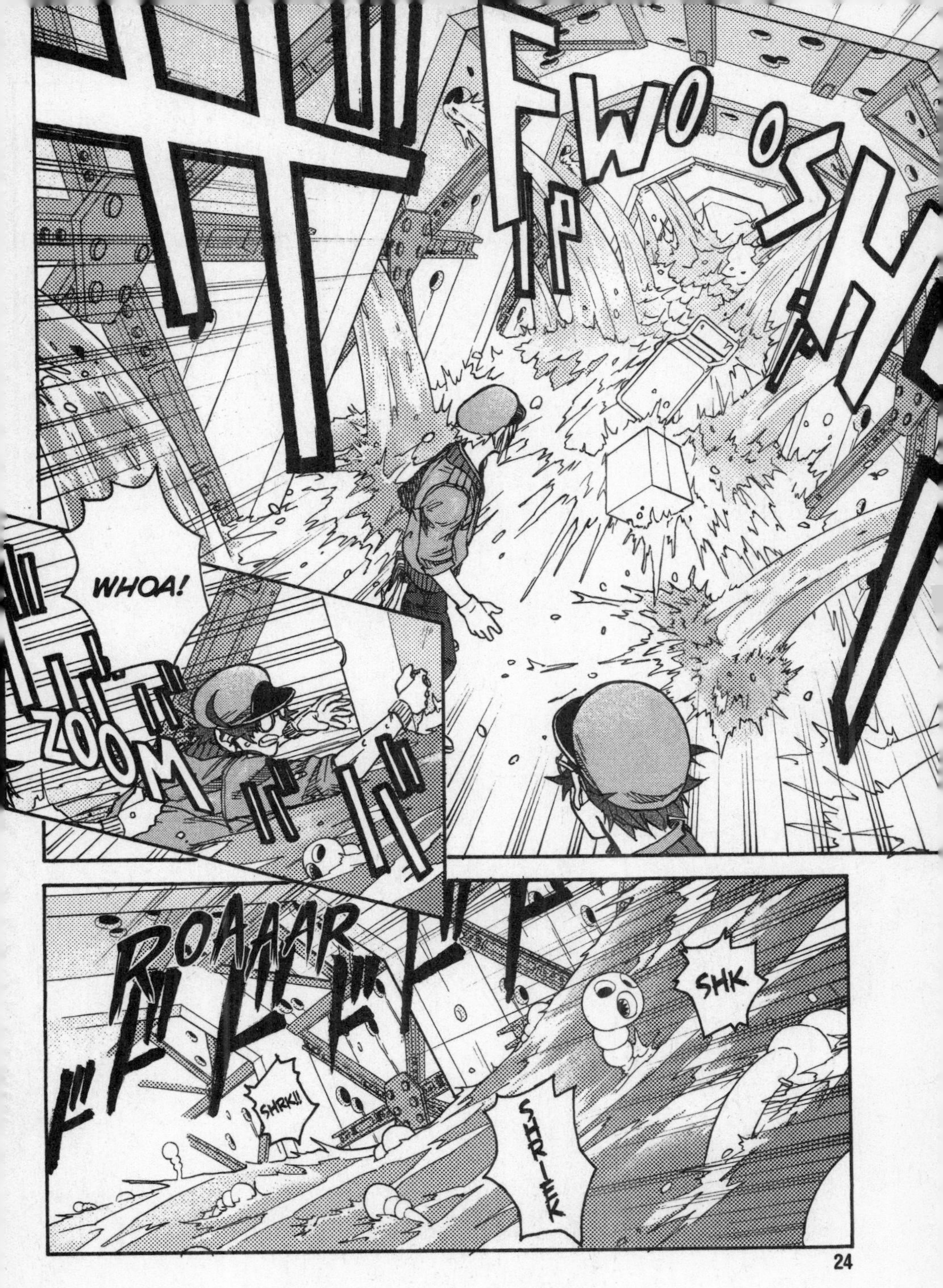
FWOOSH
WHOA!
ZOOM
ROAAAR
SHK
SHRK!!
SHRIEK

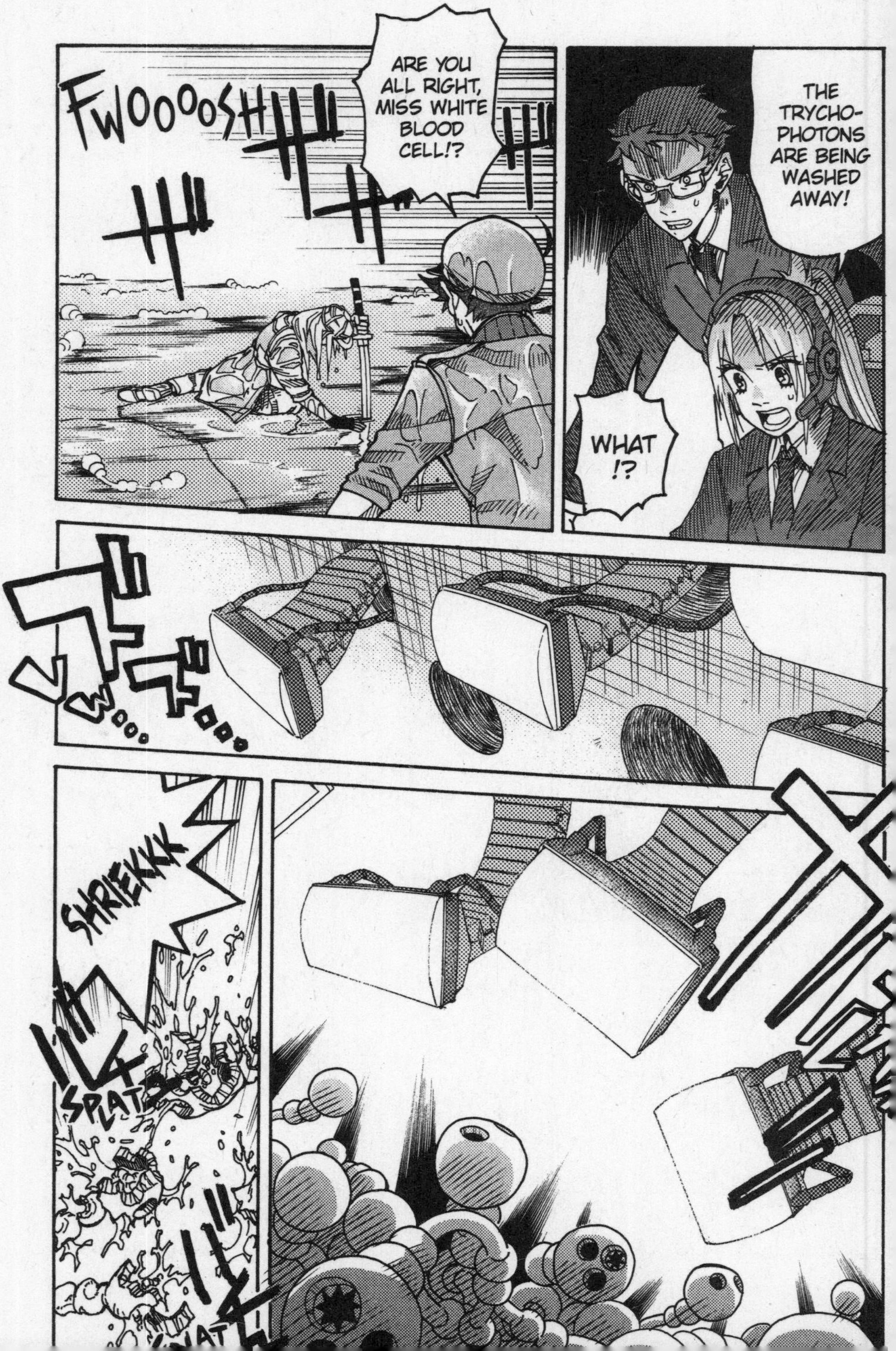
THE TRYCHO-PHOTONS ARE BEING WASHED AWAY!
WHAT!?
ARE YOU ALL RIGHT, MISS WHITE BLOOD CELL!?
FWOOOOSH
SHRIEKKK
SPLAT

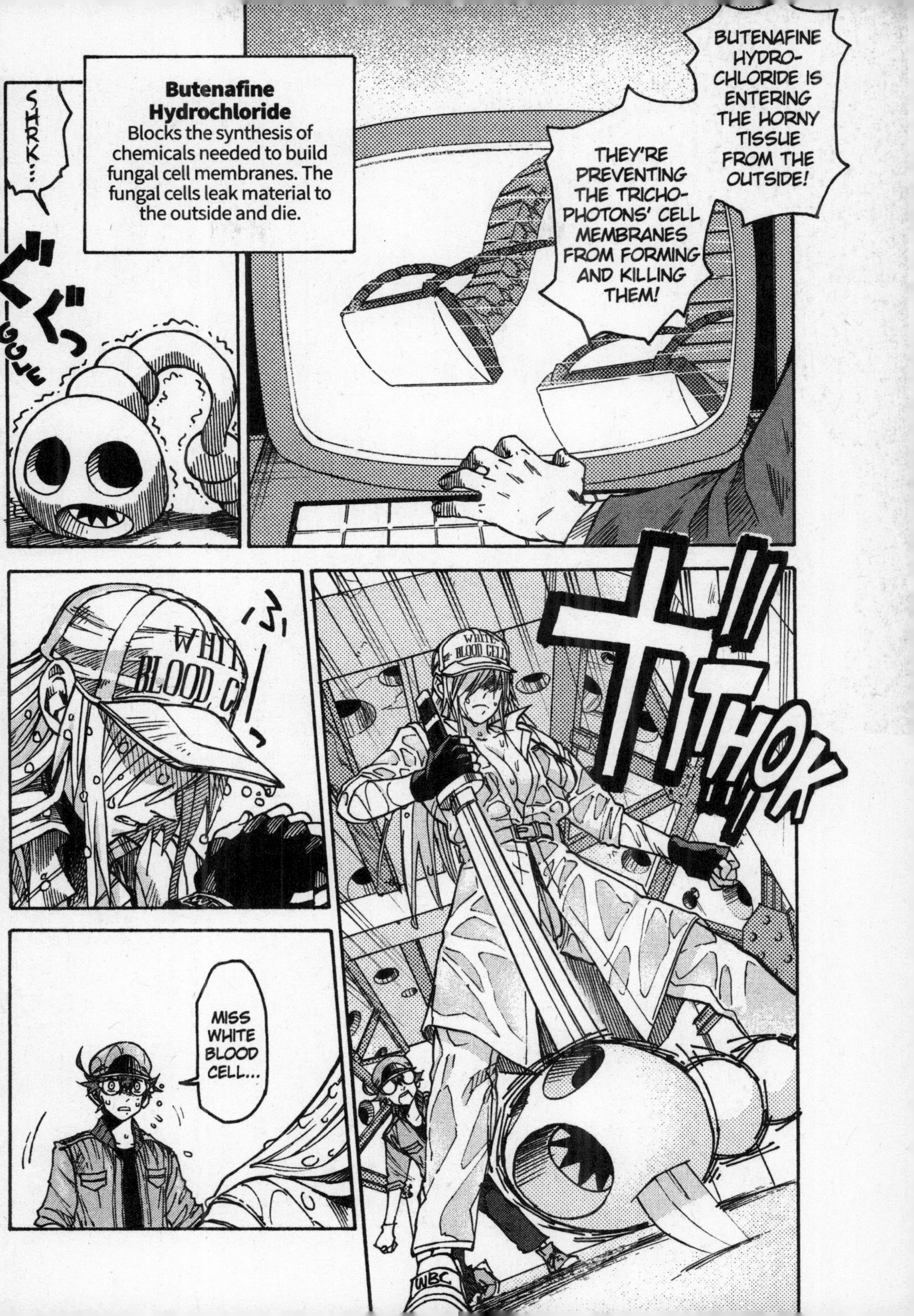
BUTENAFINE HYDROCHLORIDE IS ENTERING THE HORNY TISSUE FROM THE OUTSIDE!
THEY'RE PREVENTING THE TRICHOPHOTONS' CELL MEMBRANES FROM FORMING AND KILLING THEM!
Butenafine Hydrochloride
Blocks the synthesis of chemicals needed to build fungal cell membranes. The fungal cells leak material to the outside and die.
SHRK...
GGLE
THOK
WHITE BLOOD CELL
MISS WHITE BLOOD CELL...

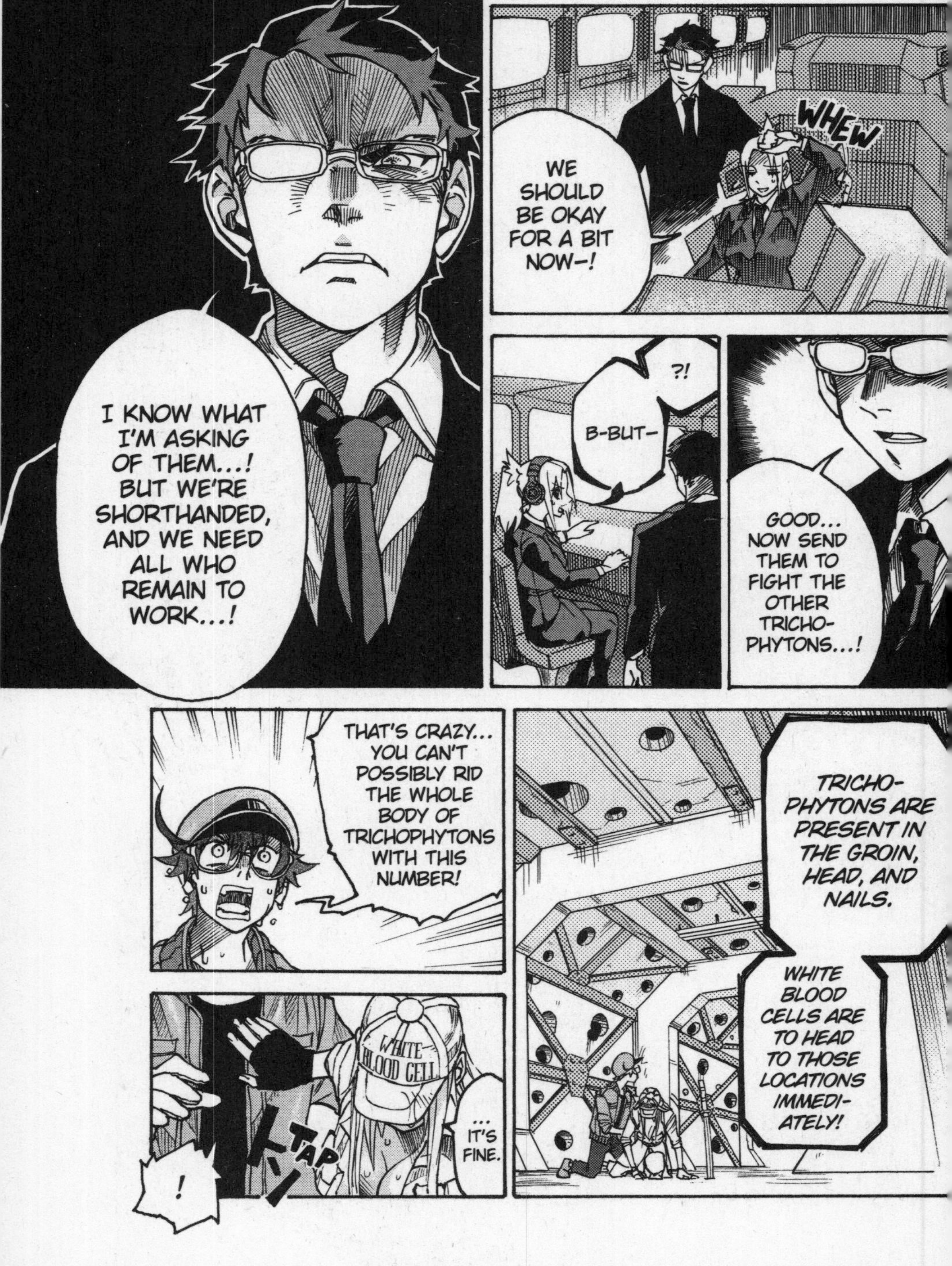
WHEW
WE SHOULD BE OKAY FOR A BIT NOW-!
GOOD... NOW SEND THEM TO FIGHT THE OTHER TRICHO-PHYTONS...!
?!
B-BUT-
I KNOW WHAT I'M ASKING OF THEM...! BUT WE'RE SHORTHANDED, AND WE NEED ALL WHO REMAIN TO WORK...!
TRICHO-PHYTONS ARE PRESENT IN THE GROIN, HEAD, AND NAILS.
WHITE BLOOD CELLS ARE TO HEAD TO THOSE LOCATIONS IMMEDI-ATELY!
THAT'S CRAZY... YOU CAN'T POSSIBLY RID THE WHOLE BODY OF TRICHOPHYTONS WITH THIS NUMBER!
WHITE BLOOD CELL
... IT'S FINE.
TAP
!

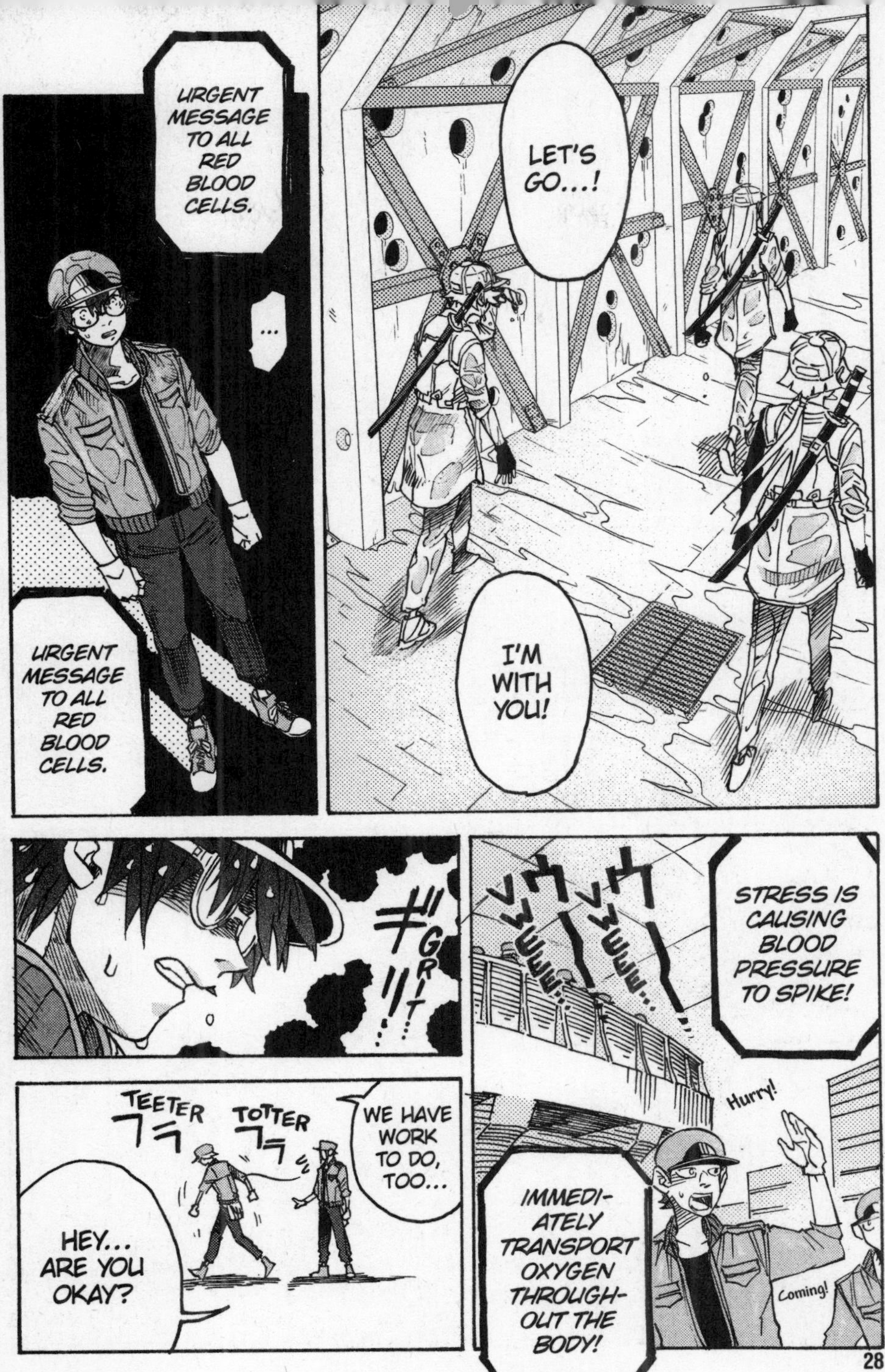
LET'S GO...!
I'M WITH YOU!
URGENT MESSAGE TO ALL RED BLOOD CELLS.
...
URGENT MESSAGE TO ALL RED BLOOD CELLS.
STRESS IS CAUSING BLOOD PRESSURE TO SPIKE!
VWEEEE...
VWEEEE...
Hurry!
IMMEDI-ATELY TRANSPORT OXYGEN THROUGH-OUT THE BODY!
Coming!
GRIT...!!
WE HAVE WORK TO DO, TOO...
TEETER
TOTTER
HEY... ARE YOU OKAY?

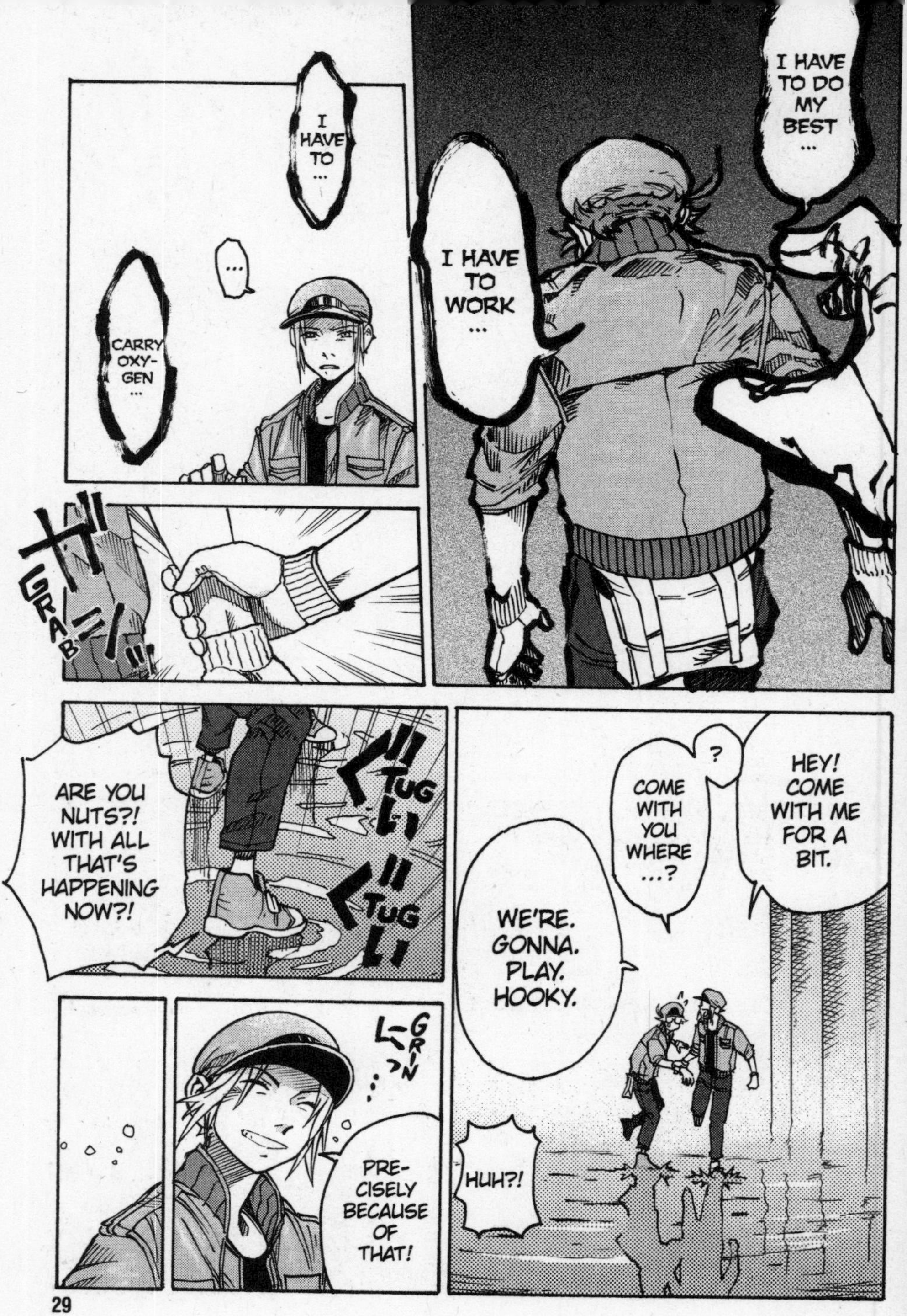
I HAVE TO DO MY BEST ...
I HAVE TO WORK ...
I HAVE TO ...
...
CARRY OXY-GEN ...
GRAB
HEY! COME WITH ME FOR A BIT.
?
COME WITH YOU WHERE ...?
WE'RE. GONNA. PLAY. HOOKY.
HUH?!
TUG
TUG
ARE YOU NUTS?! WITH ALL THAT'S HAPPENING NOW?!
GRIN
PRE-CISELY BECAUSE OF THAT!

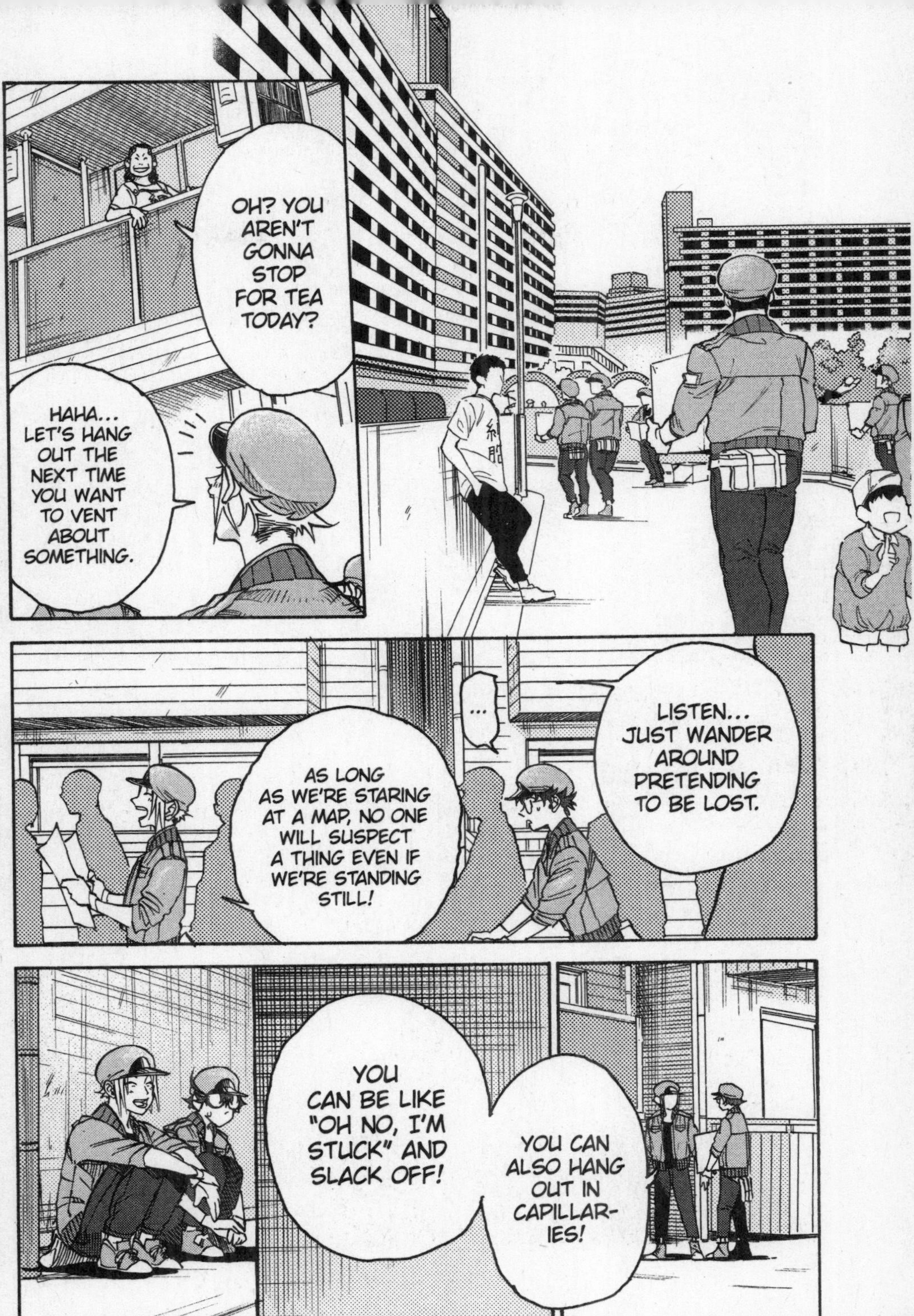
OH? YOU AREN'T GONNA STOP FOR TEA TODAY?
HAHA... LET'S HANG OUT THE NEXT TIME YOU WANT TO VENT ABOUT SOMETHING.
LISTEN... JUST WANDER AROUND PRETENDING TO BE LOST.
...
AS LONG AS WE'RE STARING AT A MAP, NO ONE WILL SUSPECT A THING EVEN IF WE'RE STANDING STILL!
YOU CAN BE LIKE "OH NO, I'M STUCK" AND SLACK OFF!
YOU CAN ALSO HANG OUT IN CAPILLARIES!

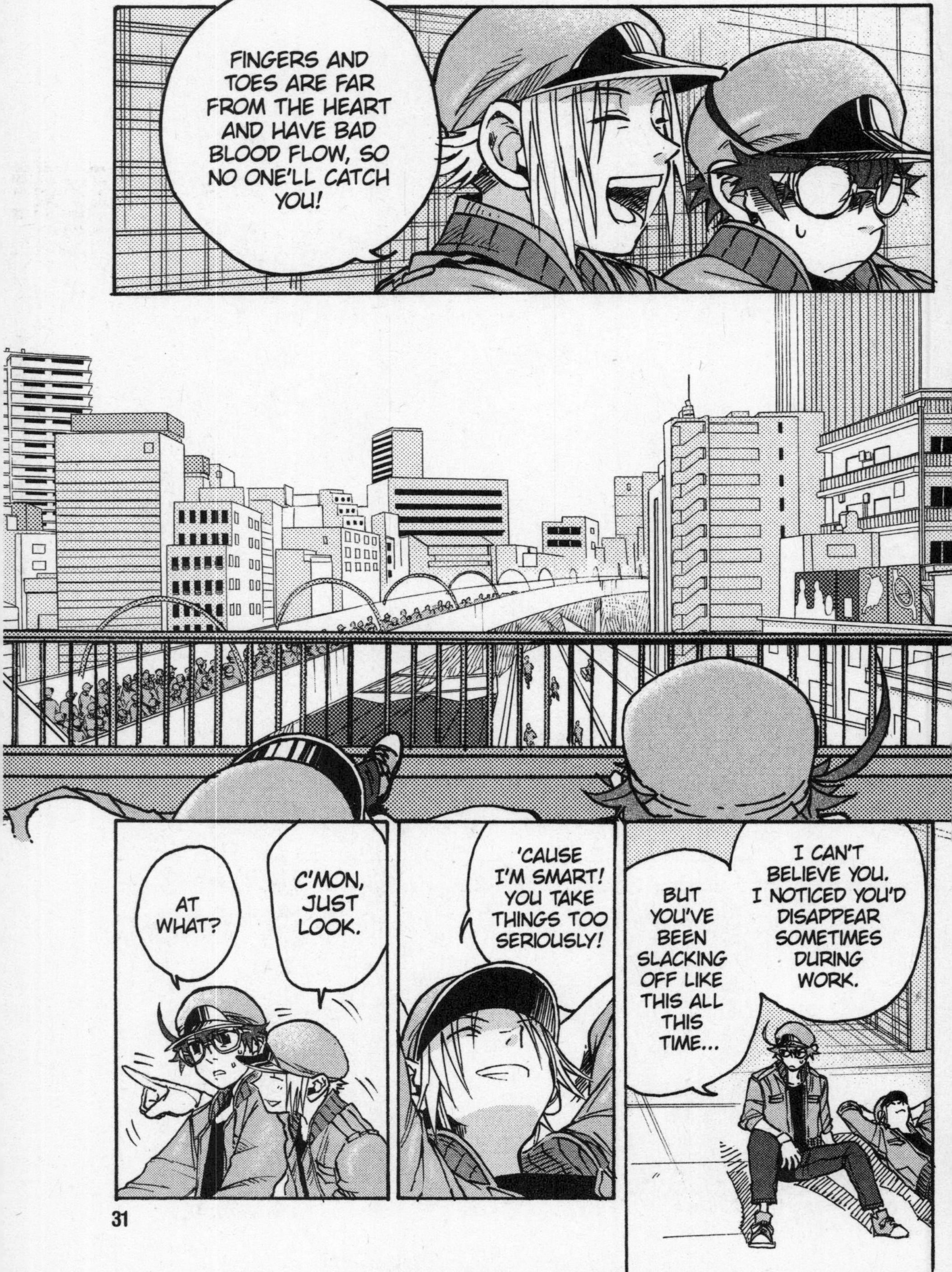
FINGERS AND TOES ARE FAR FROM THE HEART AND HAVE BAD BLOOD FLOW, SO NO ONE'LL CATCH YOU!
I CAN'T BELIEVE YOU. I NOTICED YOU'D DISAPPEAR SOMETIMES DURING WORK.
BUT YOU'VE BEEN SLACKING OFF LIKE THIS ALL THIS TIME...
'CAUSE I'M SMART! YOU TAKE THINGS TOO SERIOUSLY!
C'MON, JUST LOOK.
AT WHAT?

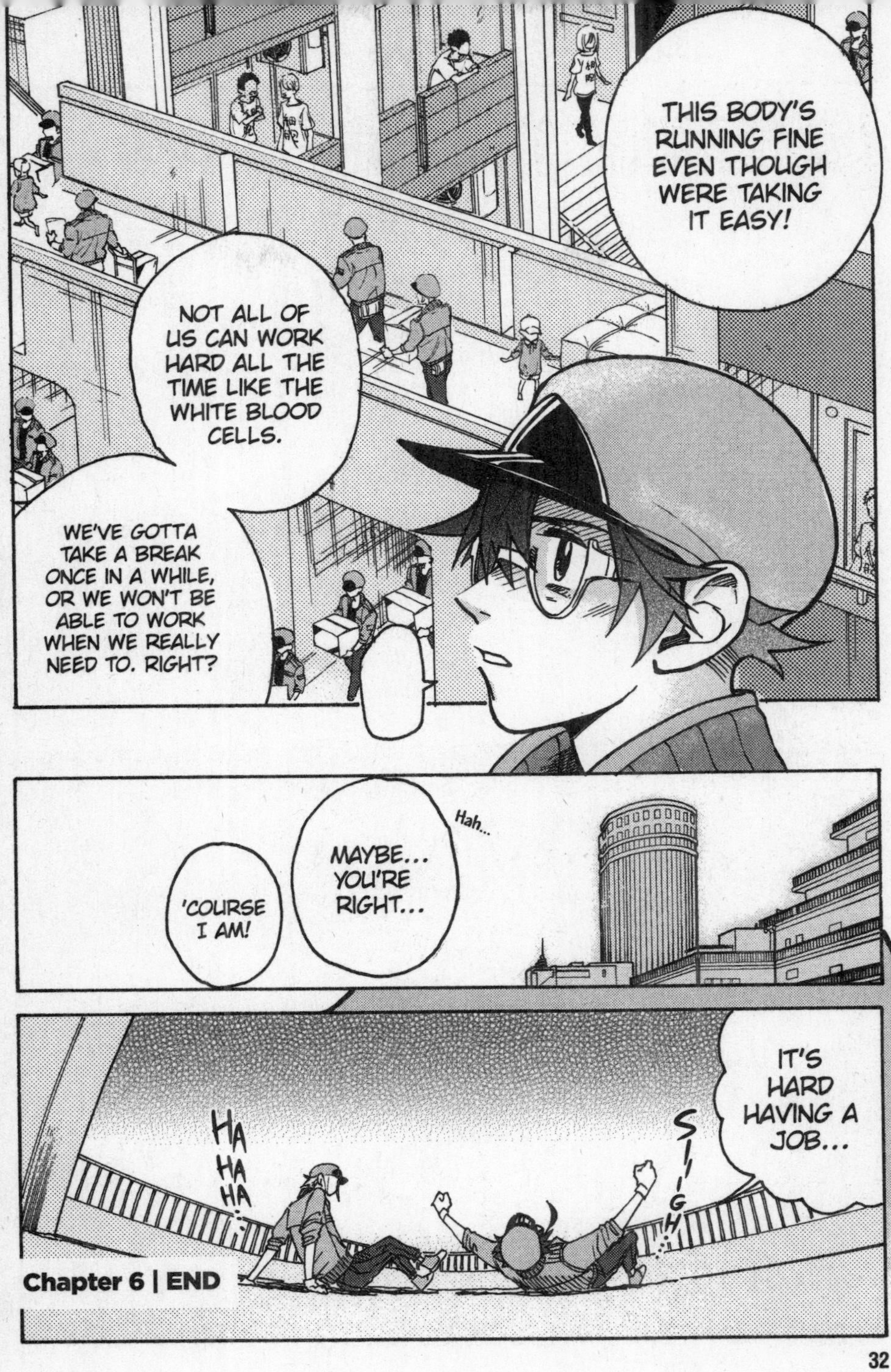
THIS BODY'S RUNNING FINE EVEN THOUGH WERE TAKING IT EASY!
NOT ALL OF US CAN WORK HARD ALL THE TIME LIKE THE WHITE BLOOD CELLS.
WE'VE GOTTA TAKE A BREAK ONCE IN A WHILE, OR WE WON'T BE ABLE TO WORK WHEN WE REALLY NEED TO. RIGHT?
Hah...
MAYBE... YOU'RE RIGHT...
'COURSE I AM!
IT'S HARD HAVING A JOB...
SIIIGH...
HA HA HA...
Chapter 6 | END

CHAPTER 7: STOMACH ULCER, FRIENDSHIP, AND LOSS

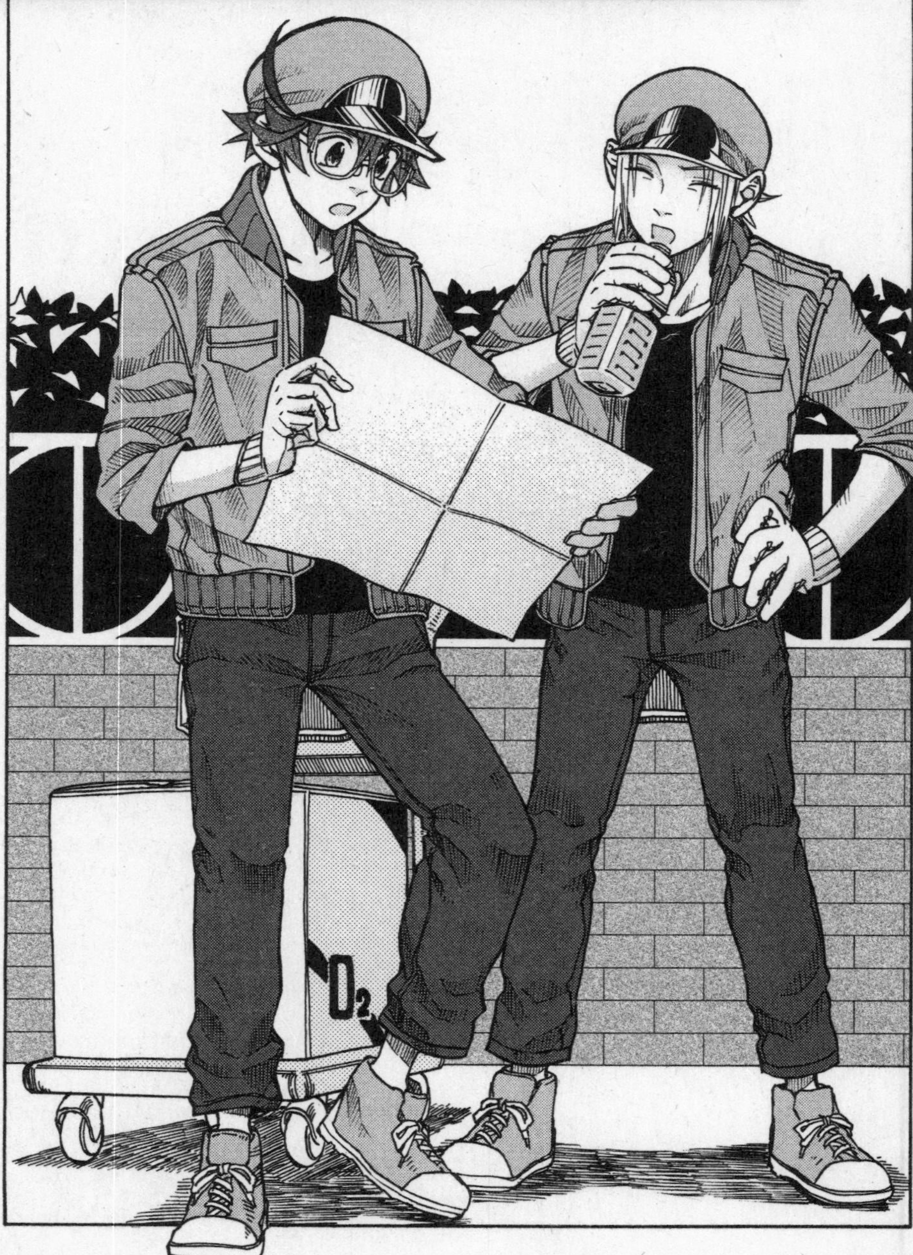

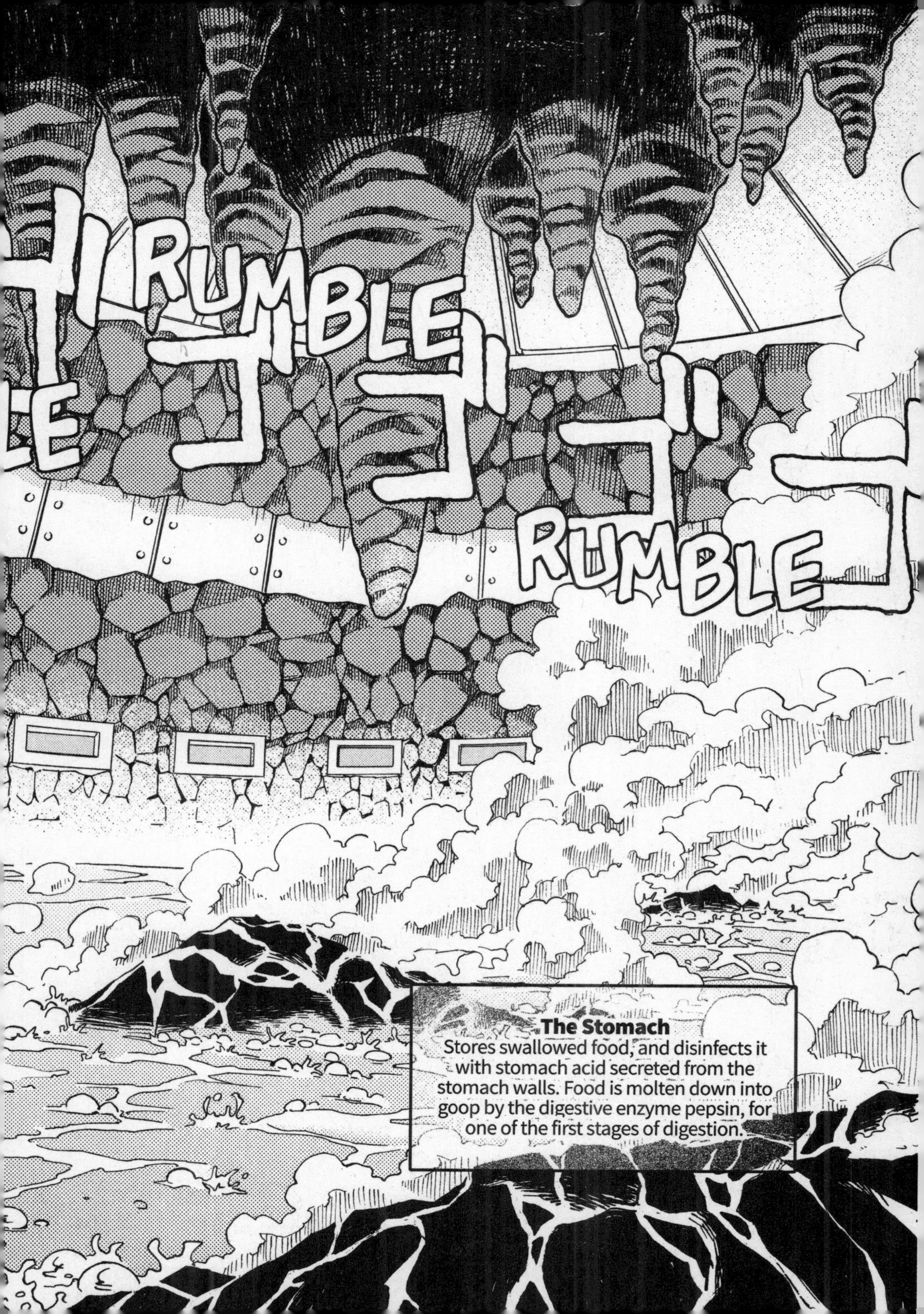
RUMBLE
RUMBLE
The Stomach
Stores swallowed food, and disinfects it with stomach acid secreted from the stomach walls. Food is molten down into goop by the digestive enzyme pepsin, for one of the first stages of digestion.

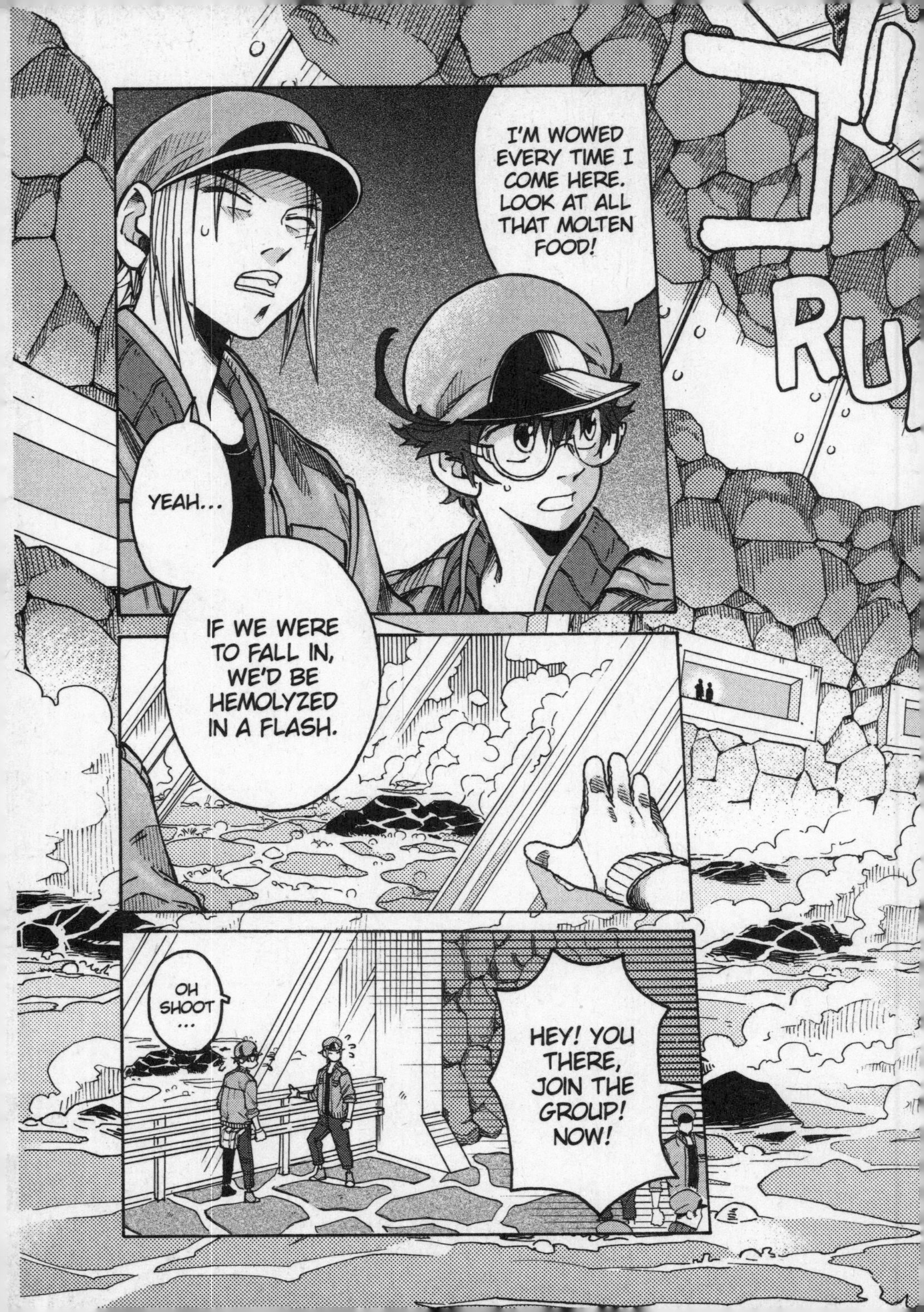
RU
I'M WOWED EVERY TIME I COME HERE. LOOK AT ALL THAT MOLTEN FOOD!
YEAH...
IF WE WERE TO FALL IN, WE'D BE HEMOLYZED IN A FLASH.
HEY! YOU THERE, JOIN THE GROUP! NOW!
OH SHOOT ...

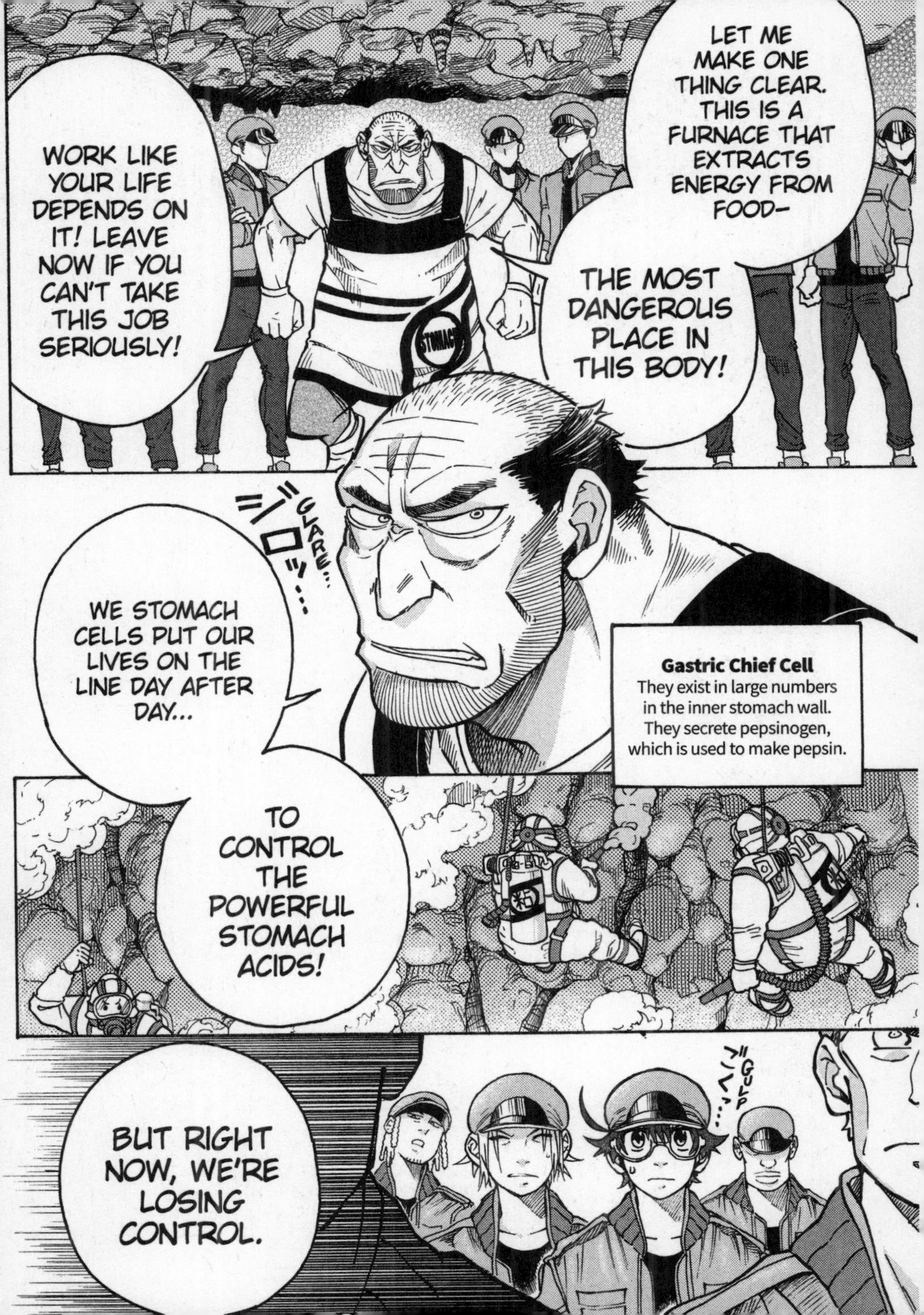
LET ME MAKE ONE THING CLEAR. THIS IS A FURNACE THAT EXTRACTS ENERGY FROM FOOD–
THE MOST DANGEROUS PLACE IN THIS BODY!
WORK LIKE YOUR LIFE DEPENDS ON IT! LEAVE NOW IF YOU CAN'T TAKE THIS JOB SERIOUSLY!
STOMACH
ジロッ…
GLARE...
Gastric Chief Cell
They exist in large numbers in the inner stomach wall. They secrete pepsinogen, which is used to make pepsin.
WE STOMACH CELLS PUT OUR LIVES ON THE LINE DAY AFTER DAY...
TO CONTROL THE POWERFUL STOMACH ACIDS!
ゴクッ…
GULP...
BUT RIGHT NOW, WE'RE LOSING CONTROL.

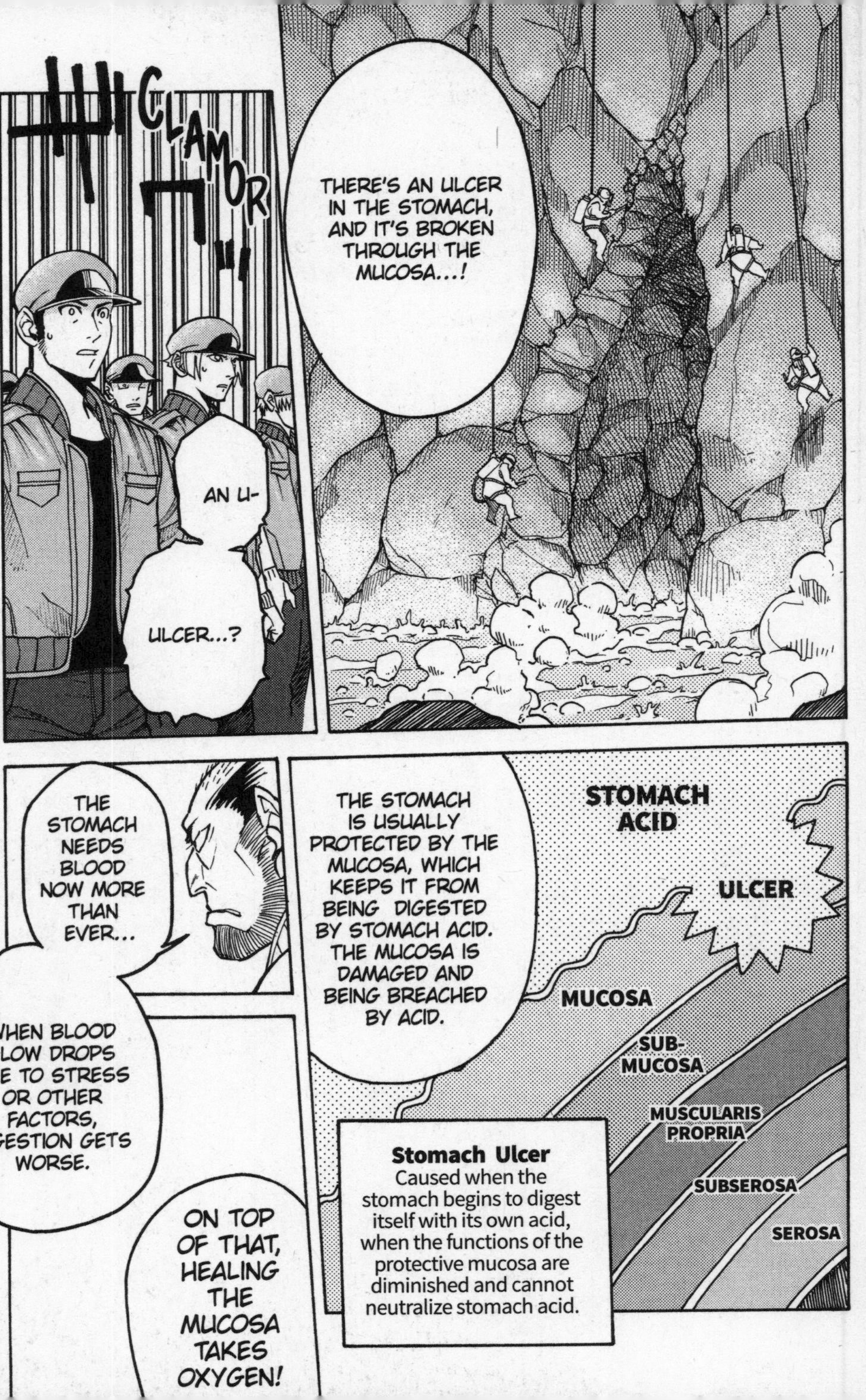
THERE'S AN ULCER IN THE STOMACH, AND IT'S BROKEN THROUGH THE MUCOSA...!
CLAMOR
AN U-
ULCER...?
THE STOMACH IS USUALLY PROTECTED BY THE MUCOSA, WHICH KEEPS IT FROM BEING DIGESTED BY STOMACH ACID. THE MUCOSA IS DAMAGED AND BEING BREACHED BY ACID.
STOMACH ACID
ULCER
MUCOSA
SUB-MUCOSA
MUSCULARIS PROPRIA
SUBSEROSA
SEROSA
Stomach Ulcer
Caused when the stomach begins to digest itself with its own acid, when the functions of the protective mucosa are diminished and cannot neutralize stomach acid.
THE STOMACH NEEDS BLOOD NOW MORE THAN EVER...
WHEN BLOOD FLOW DROPS DUE TO STRESS OR OTHER FACTORS, DIGESTION GETS WORSE.
ON TOP OF THAT, HEALING THE MUCOSA TAKES OXYGEN!

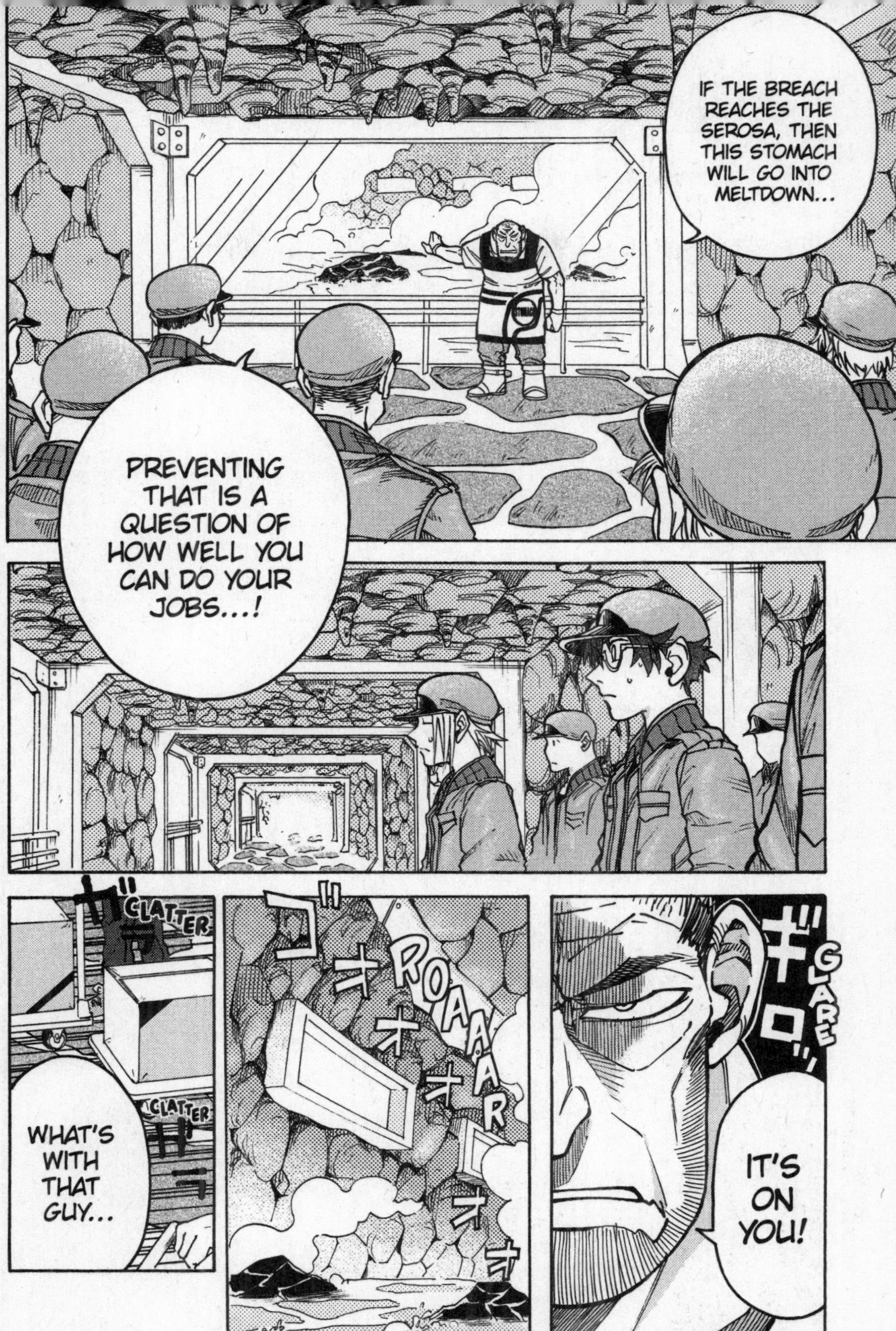
IF THE BREACH REACHES THE SEROSA, THEN THIS STOMACH WILL GO INTO MELTDOWN...
PREVENTING THAT IS A QUESTION OF HOW WELL YOU CAN DO YOUR JOBS...!
GLARE
IT'S ON YOU!
ROAAAAR
CLATTER
CLATTER
WHAT'S WITH THAT GUY...

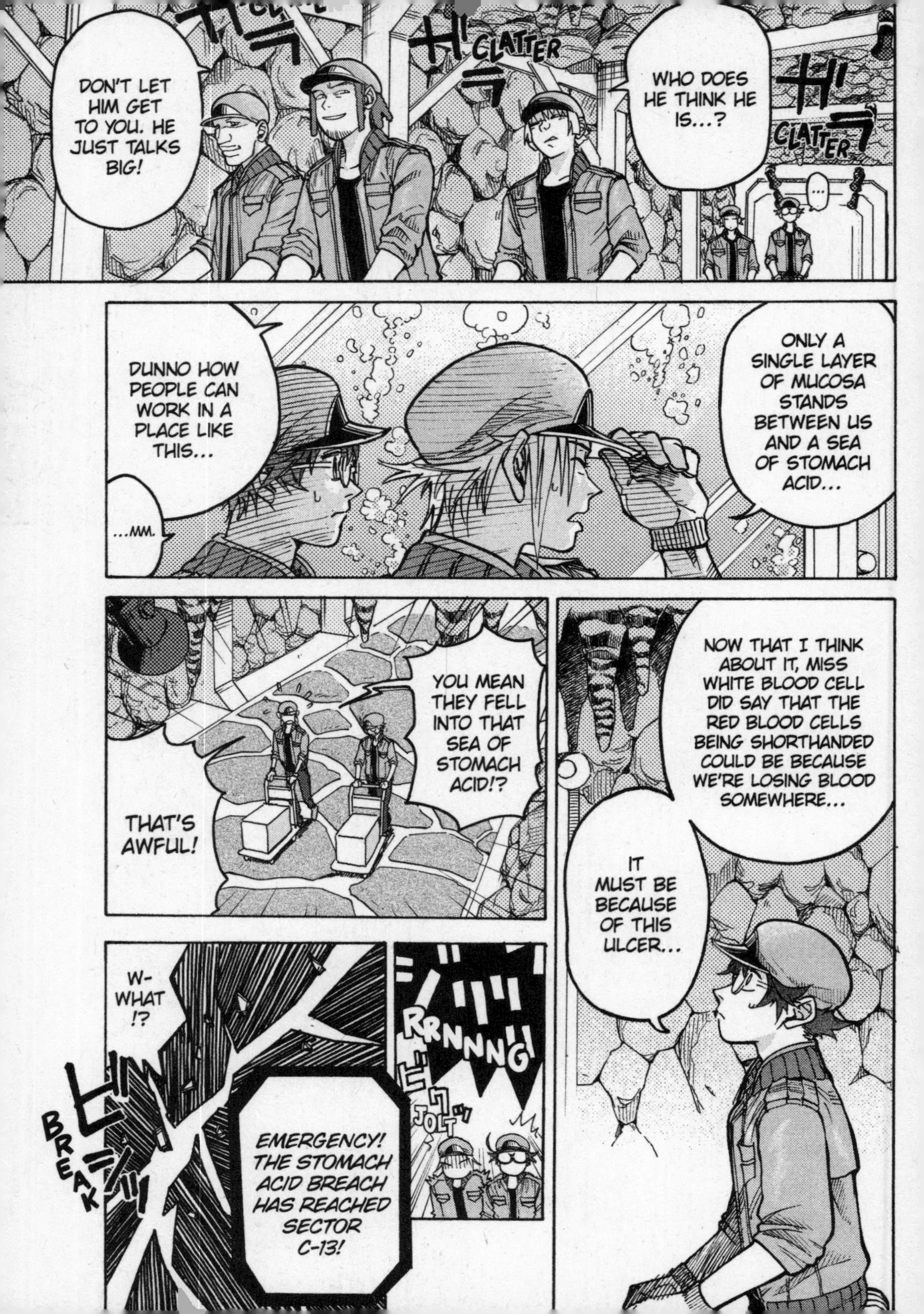
CLATTER
...
WHO DOES HE THINK HE IS...?
CLATTER
DON'T LET HIM GET TO YOU. HE JUST TALKS BIG!
ONLY A SINGLE LAYER OF MUCOSA STANDS BETWEEN US AND A SEA OF STOMACH ACID...
DUNNO HOW PEOPLE CAN WORK IN A PLACE LIKE THIS...
...MM.
NOW THAT I THINK ABOUT IT, MISS WHITE BLOOD CELL DID SAY THAT THE RED BLOOD CELLS BEING SHORTHANDED COULD BE BECAUSE WE'RE LOSING BLOOD SOMEWHERE...
IT MUST BE BECAUSE OF THIS ULCER...
YOU MEAN THEY FELL INTO THAT SEA OF STOMACH ACID!?
THAT'S AWFUL!
RRNNNG
JOLT
W-WHAT!?
BREAK
EMERGENCY! THE STOMACH ACID BREACH HAS REACHED SECTOR C-13!

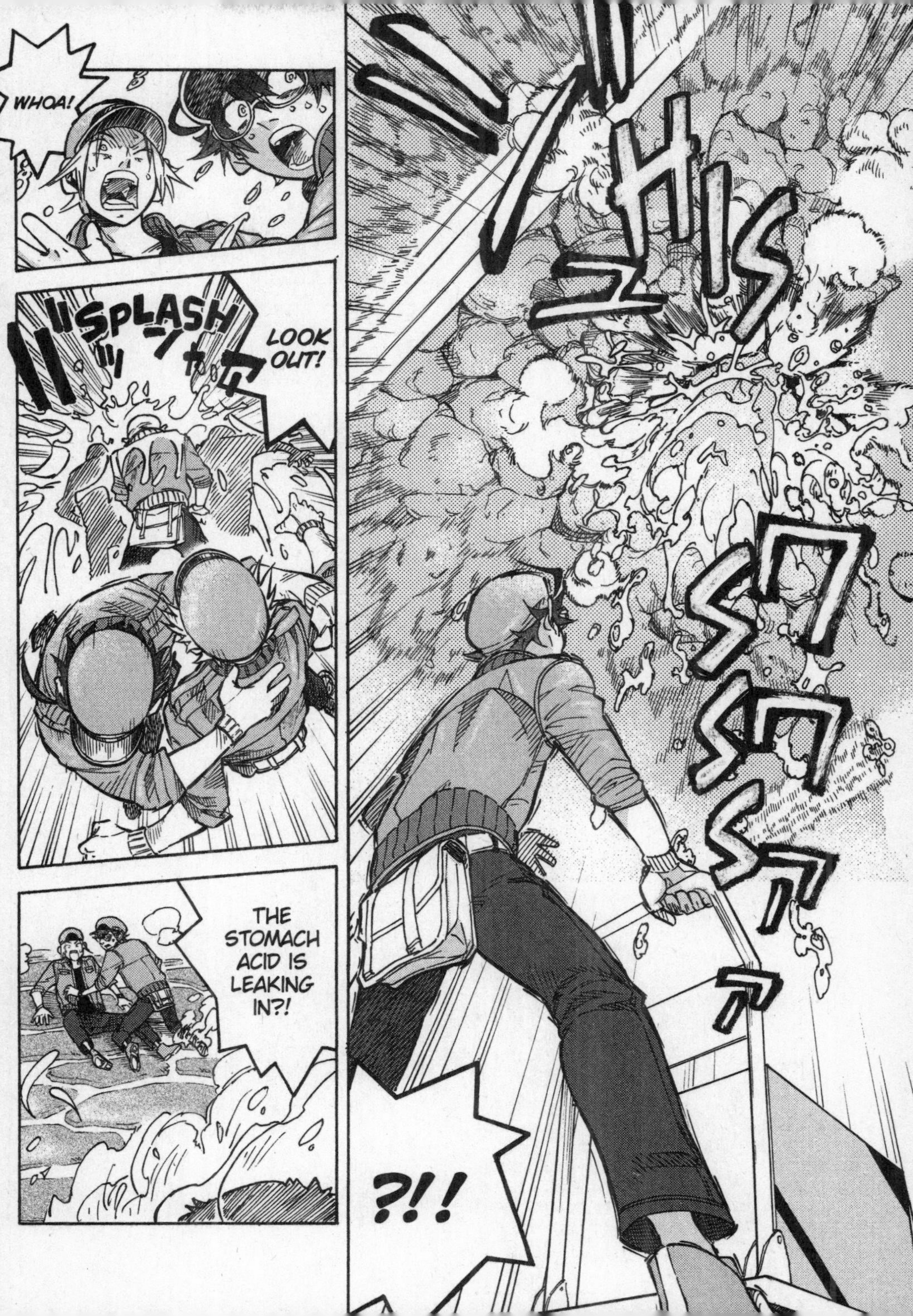
HISS
?!!
WHOA!
SPLASH
LOOK OUT!
THE STOMACH ACID IS LEAKING IN?!

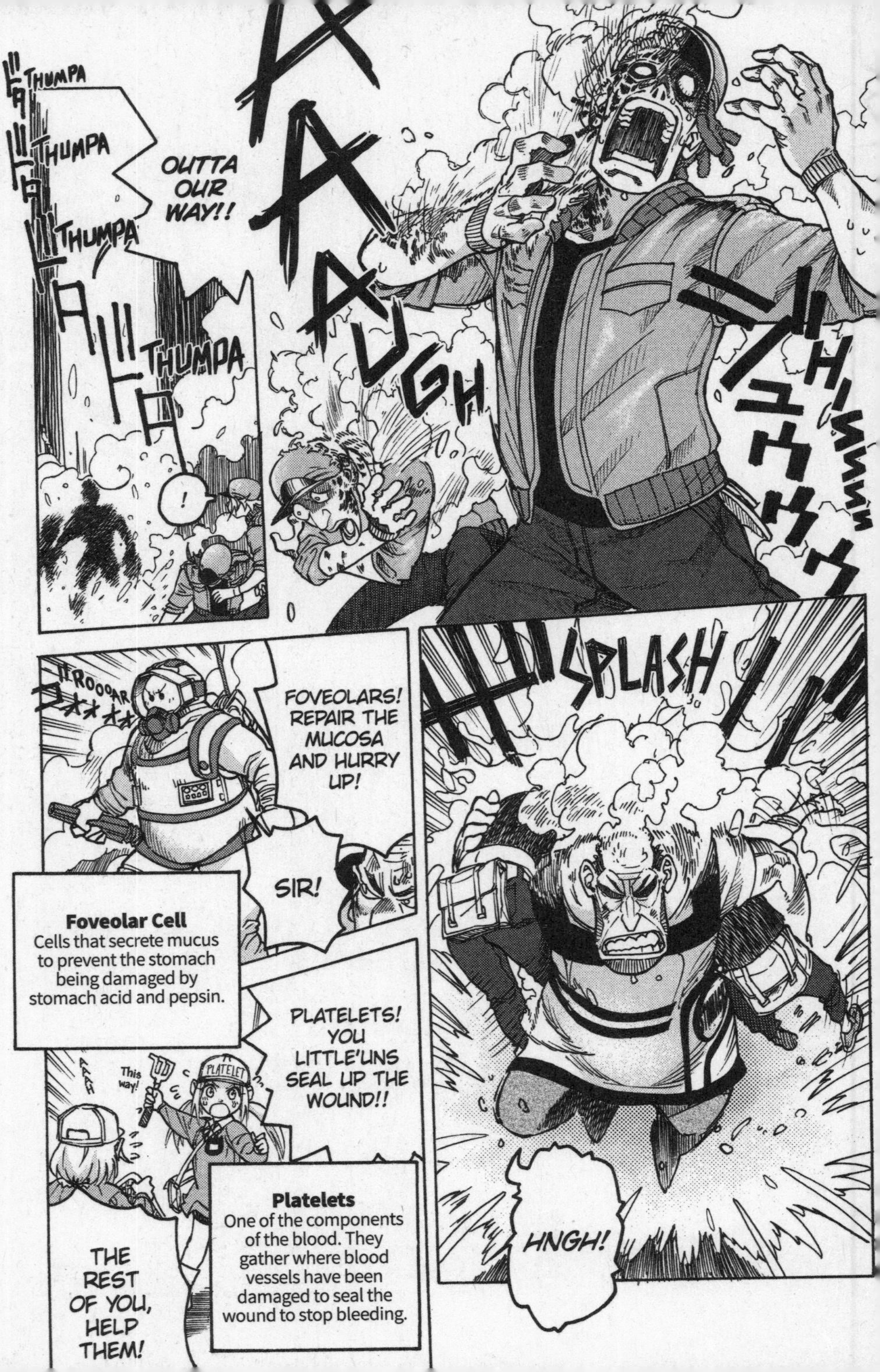
AAUGH
HISSSS
THUMPA
THUMPA
THUMPA
THUMPA
OUTTA OUR WAY!!
!
SPLASH
HNGH!
ROOOAR
FOVEOLARS! REPAIR THE MUCOSA AND HURRY UP!
SIR!
Foveolar Cell
Cells that secrete mucus to prevent the stomach being damaged by stomach acid and pepsin.
PLATELETS! YOU LITTLE'UNS SEAL UP THE WOUND!!
PLATELET
This way!
Platelets
One of the components of the blood. They gather where blood vessels have been damaged to seal the wound to stop bleeding.
THE REST OF YOU, HELP THEM!

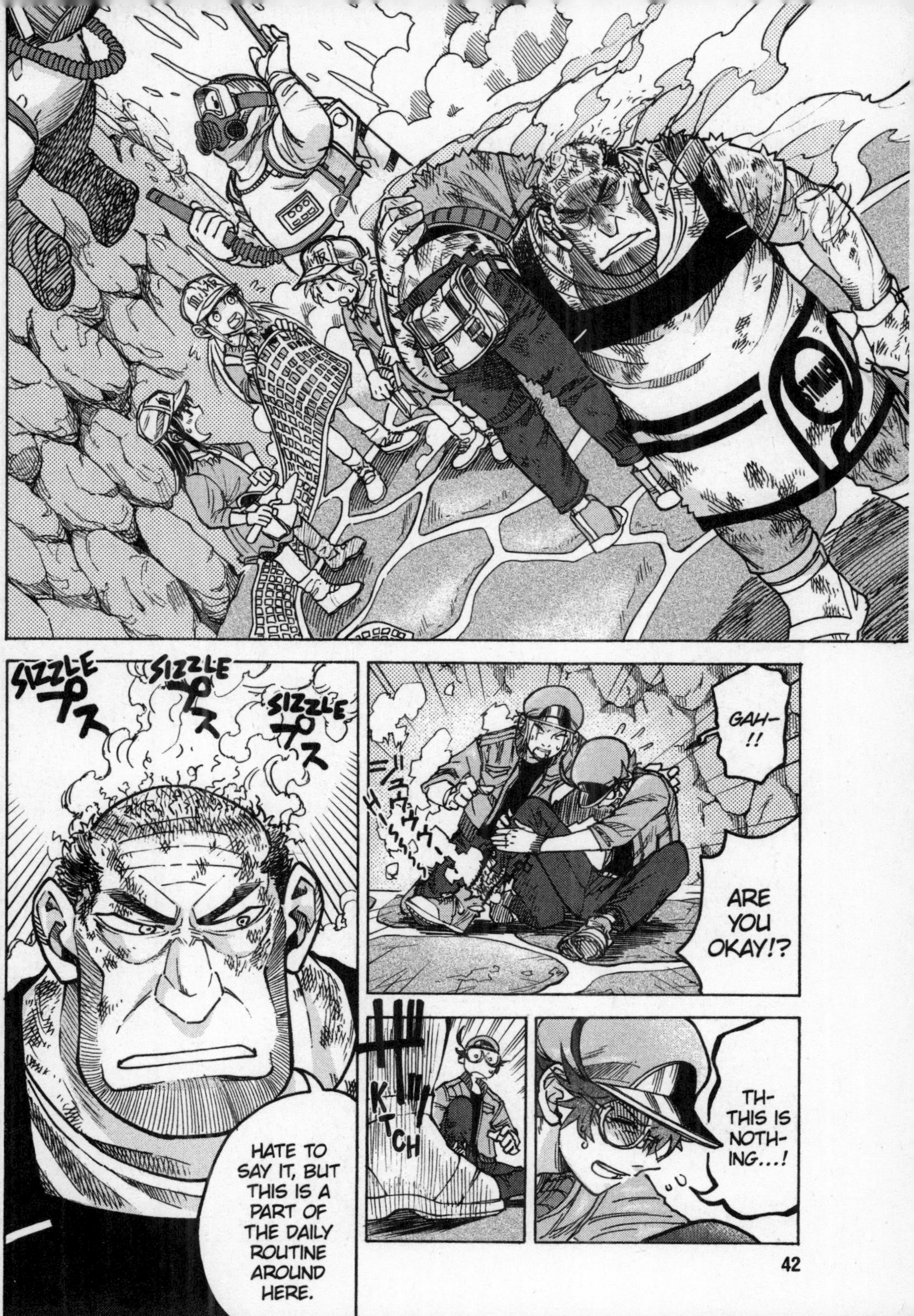
GAH-!!
ARE YOU OKAY!?
TH-THIS IS NOTHING...!
KTCH
SIZZLE プス
SIZZLE プス
SIZZLE プス
HATE TO SAY IT, BUT THIS IS A PART OF THE DAILY ROUTINE AROUND HERE.

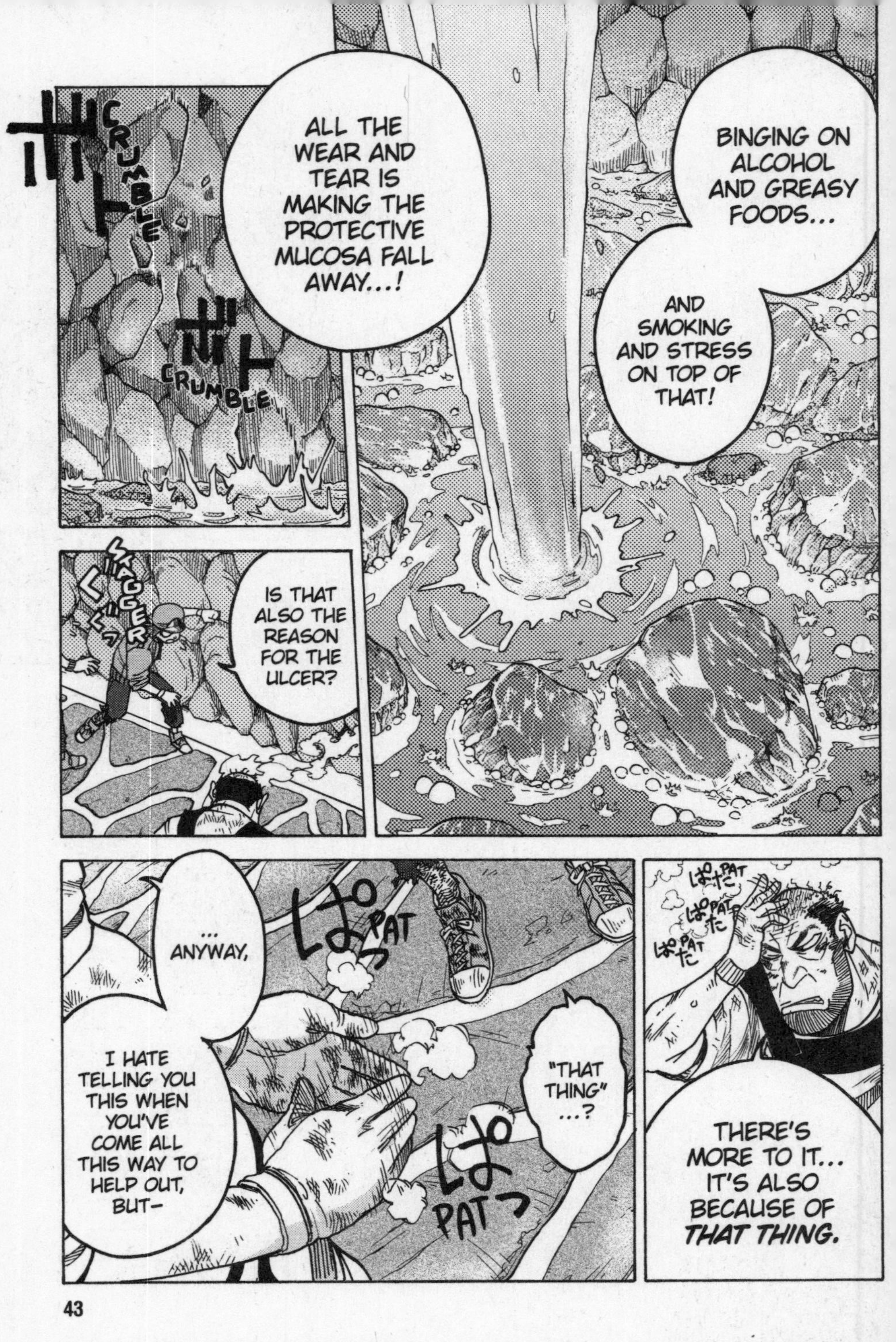
BINGING ON ALCOHOL AND GREASY FOODS...
AND SMOKING AND STRESS ON TOP OF THAT!
ALL THE WEAR AND TEAR IS MAKING THE PROTECTIVE MUCOSA FALL AWAY...!
CRUMBLE
CRUMBLE
STAGGER
IS THAT ALSO THE REASON FOR THE ULCER?
PAT
PAT
PAT
THERE'S MORE TO IT... IT'S ALSO BECAUSE OF *THAT THING.*
... ANYWAY,
PAT
"THAT THING" ...?
I HATE TELLING YOU THIS WHEN YOU'VE COME ALL THIS WAY TO HELP OUT, BUT—
PAT

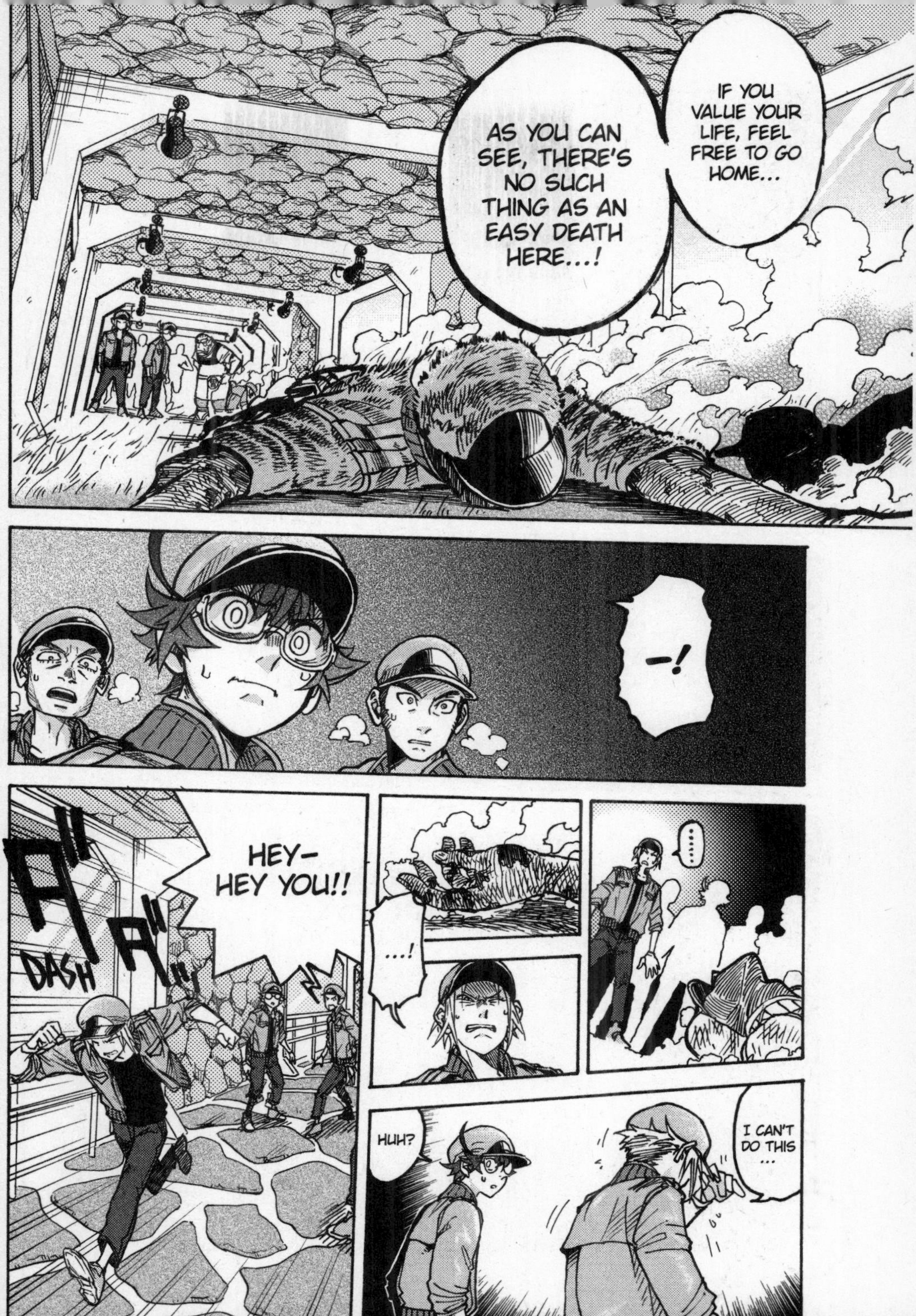
IF YOU VALUE YOUR LIFE, FEEL FREE TO GO HOME...
AS YOU CAN SEE, THERE'S NO SUCH THING AS AN EASY DEATH HERE...!
—!
......
...!
HEY— HEY YOU!!
DASH
I CAN'T DO THIS ...
HUH?

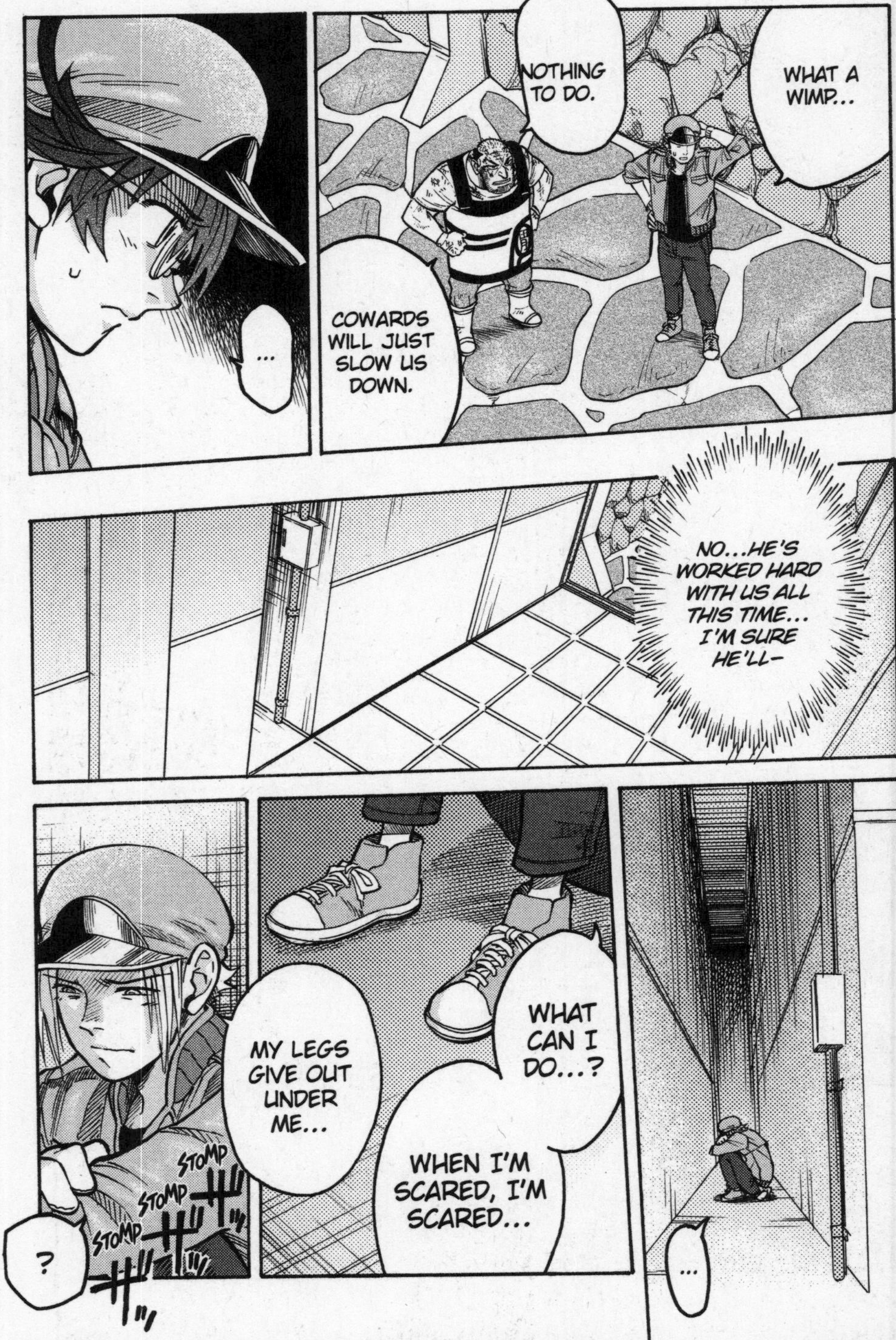
WHAT A WIMP...
NOTHING TO DO.
COWARDS WILL JUST SLOW US DOWN.
...
NO...HE'S WORKED HARD WITH US ALL THIS TIME... I'M SURE HE'LL-
...
WHAT CAN I DO...?
WHEN I'M SCARED, I'M SCARED...
MY LEGS GIVE OUT UNDER ME...
STOMP
STOMP
STOMP
?

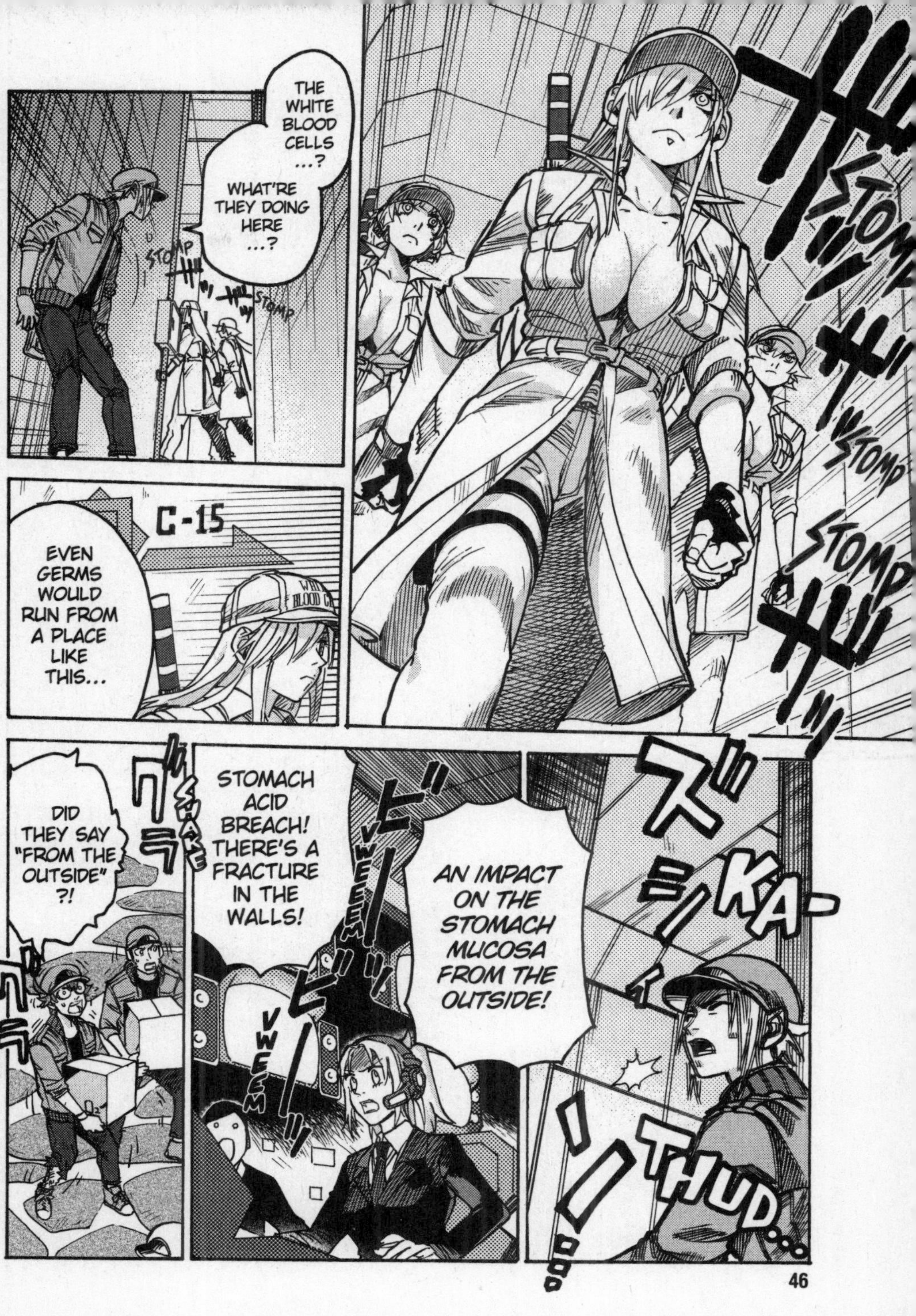
STOMP
STOMP
STOMP
THE WHITE BLOOD CELLS ...?
WHAT'RE THEY DOING HERE ...?
STOMP
STOMP
C-15
EVEN GERMS WOULD RUN FROM A PLACE LIKE THIS...
KA-
AN IMPACT ON THE STOMACH MUCOSA FROM THE OUTSIDE!
THUD...
STOMACH ACID BREACH! THERE'S A FRACTURE IN THE WALLS!
VWEEM
VWEEM
SHAKE
DID THEY SAY "FROM THE OUTSIDE"?!
SHAKE

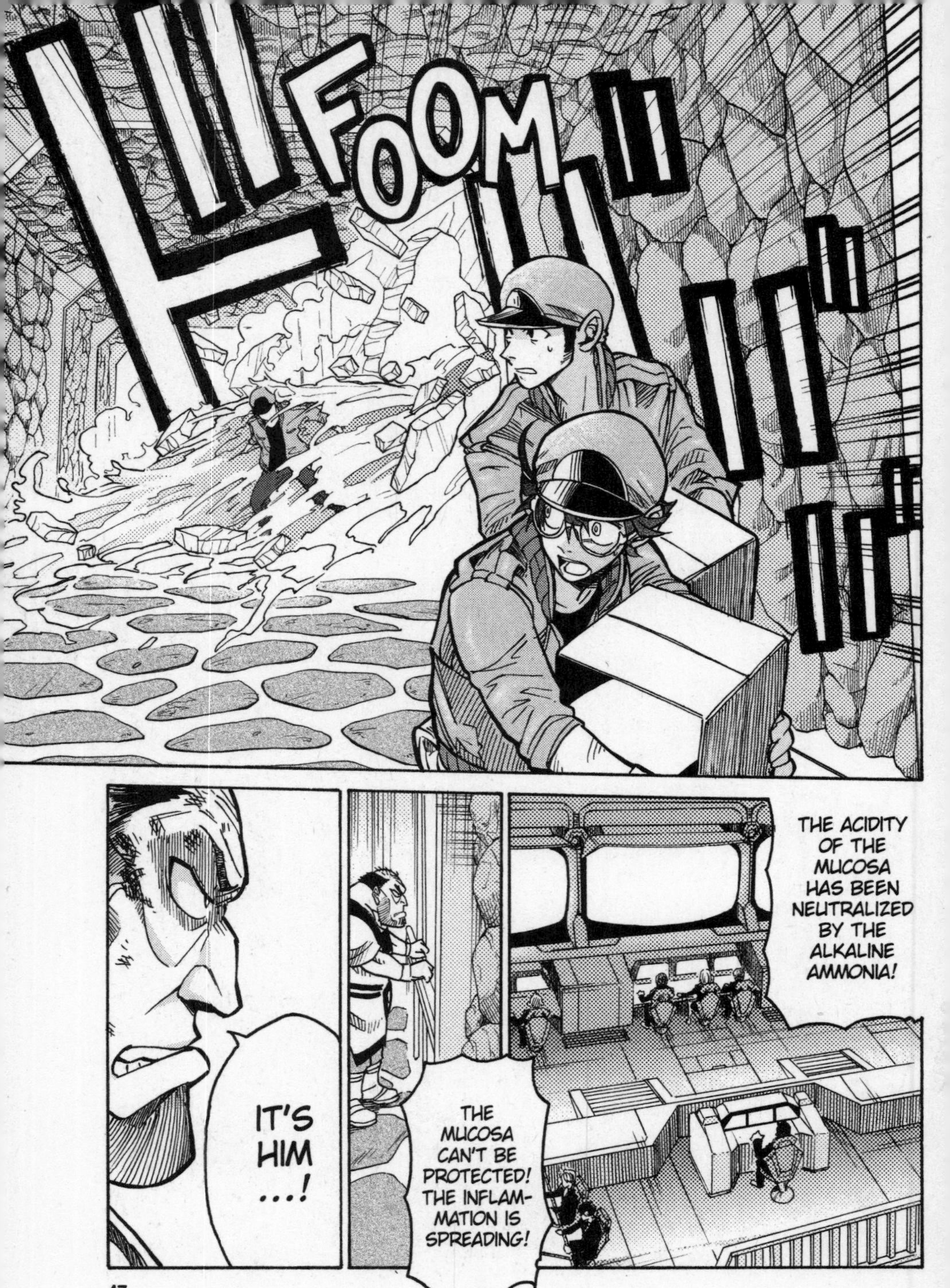
FOOM
THE ACIDITY OF THE MUCOSA HAS BEEN NEUTRALIZED BY THE ALKALINE AMMONIA!
THE MUCOSA CAN'T BE PROTECTED! THE INFLAMMATION IS SPREADING!
IT'S HIM ...!

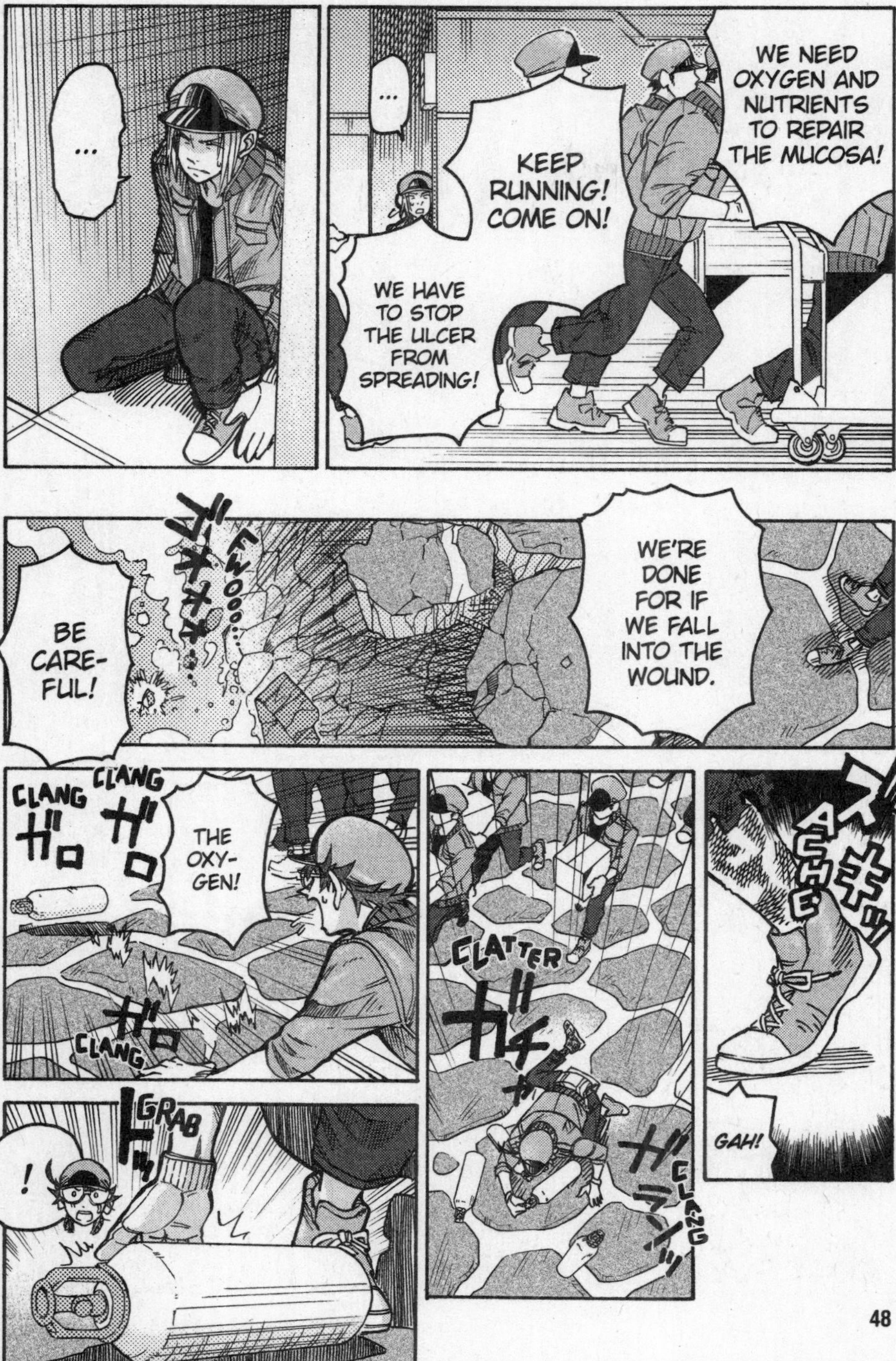
WE NEED OXYGEN AND NUTRIENTS TO REPAIR THE MUCOSA!
KEEP RUNNING! COME ON!
WE HAVE TO STOP THE ULCER FROM SPREADING!
...
...
WE'RE DONE FOR IF WE FALL INTO THE WOUND.
FWOOO...
BE CAREFUL!
ACHE
GAH!
CLATTER
CLANG
CLANG
CLANG
THE OXYGEN!
CLANG
GRAB
!

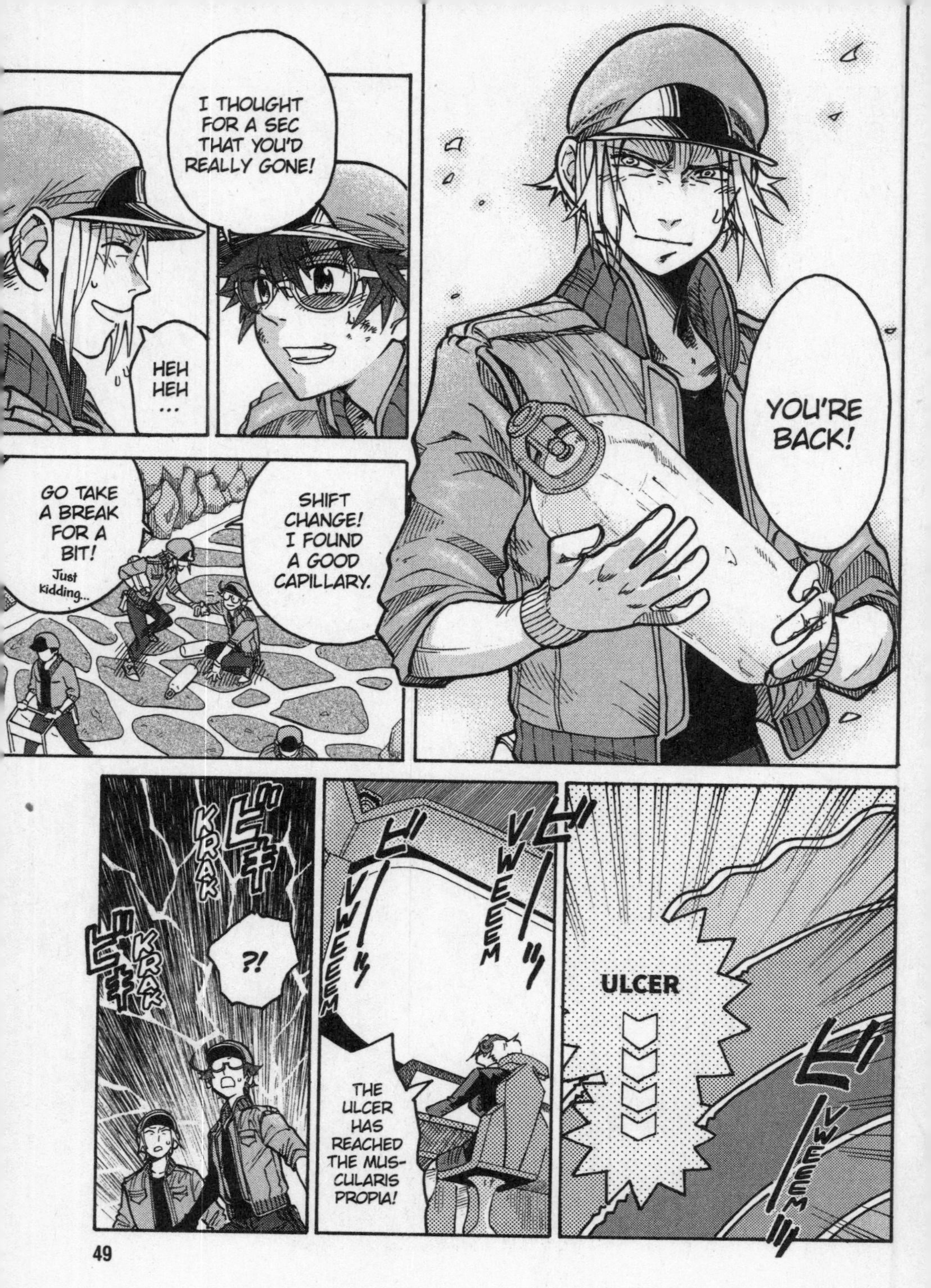
YOU'RE BACK!
I THOUGHT FOR A SEC THAT YOU'D REALLY GONE!
HEH HEH ...
SHIFT CHANGE! I FOUND A GOOD CAPILLARY.
GO TAKE A BREAK FOR A BIT!
Just kidding...
ULCER
ビー
VWEEEM
ビー
VWEEEM
VWEEEM
THE ULCER HAS REACHED THE MUSCULARIS PROPIA!
ビキ
KRAK
ビキ
KRAK
?!

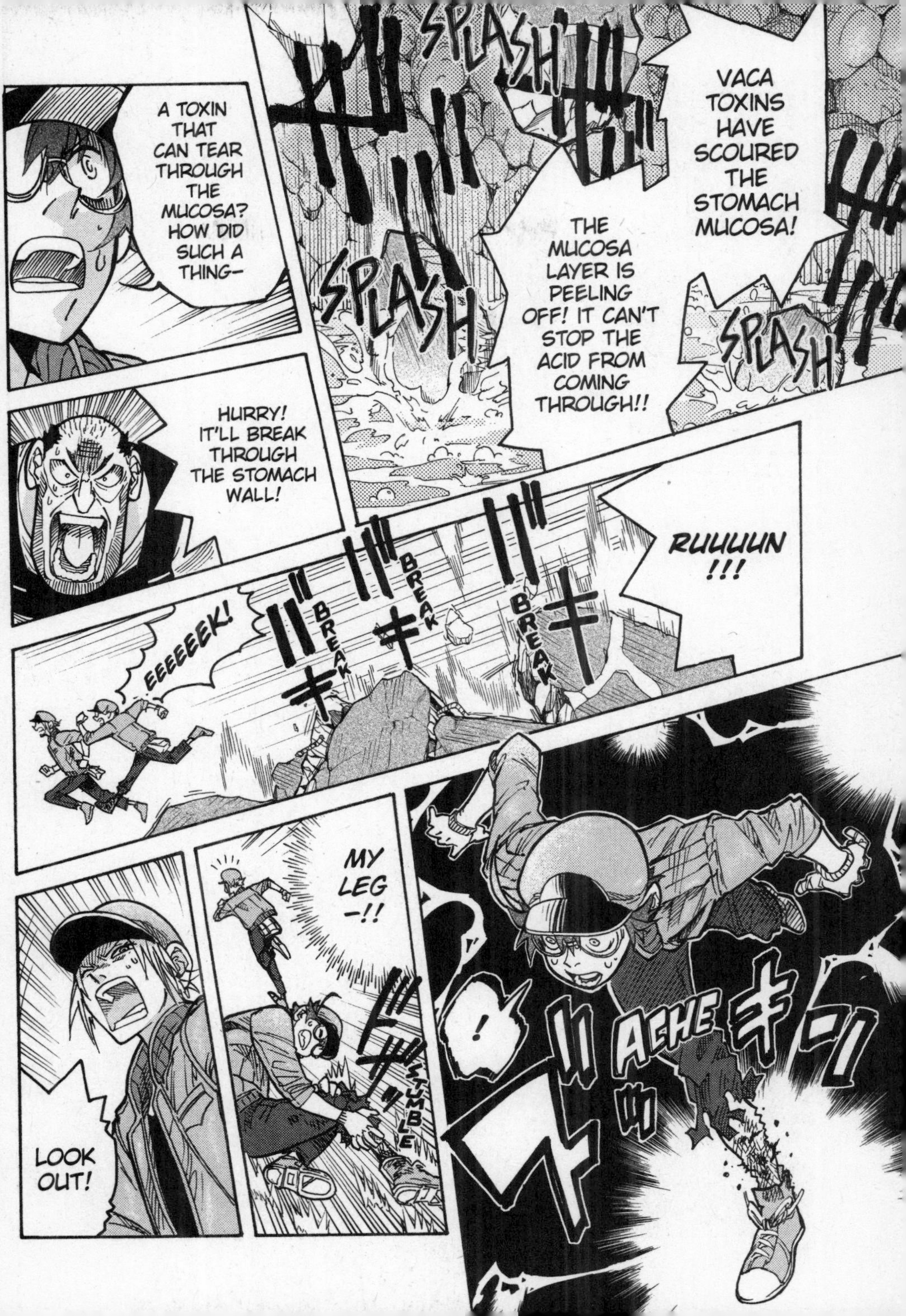
SPLASH
VACA TOXINS HAVE SCOURED THE STOMACH MUCOSA!
THE MUCOSA LAYER IS PEELING OFF! IT CAN'T STOP THE ACID FROM COMING THROUGH!!
SPLASH
SPLASH
A TOXIN THAT CAN TEAR THROUGH THE MUCOSA? HOW DID SUCH A THING-
HURRY! IT'LL BREAK THROUGH THE STOMACH WALL!
RUUUUN !!!
BREAK
BREAK
BREAK
EEEEEEK!
!
ACHE
MY LEG -!!
STUMBLE
LOOK OUT!

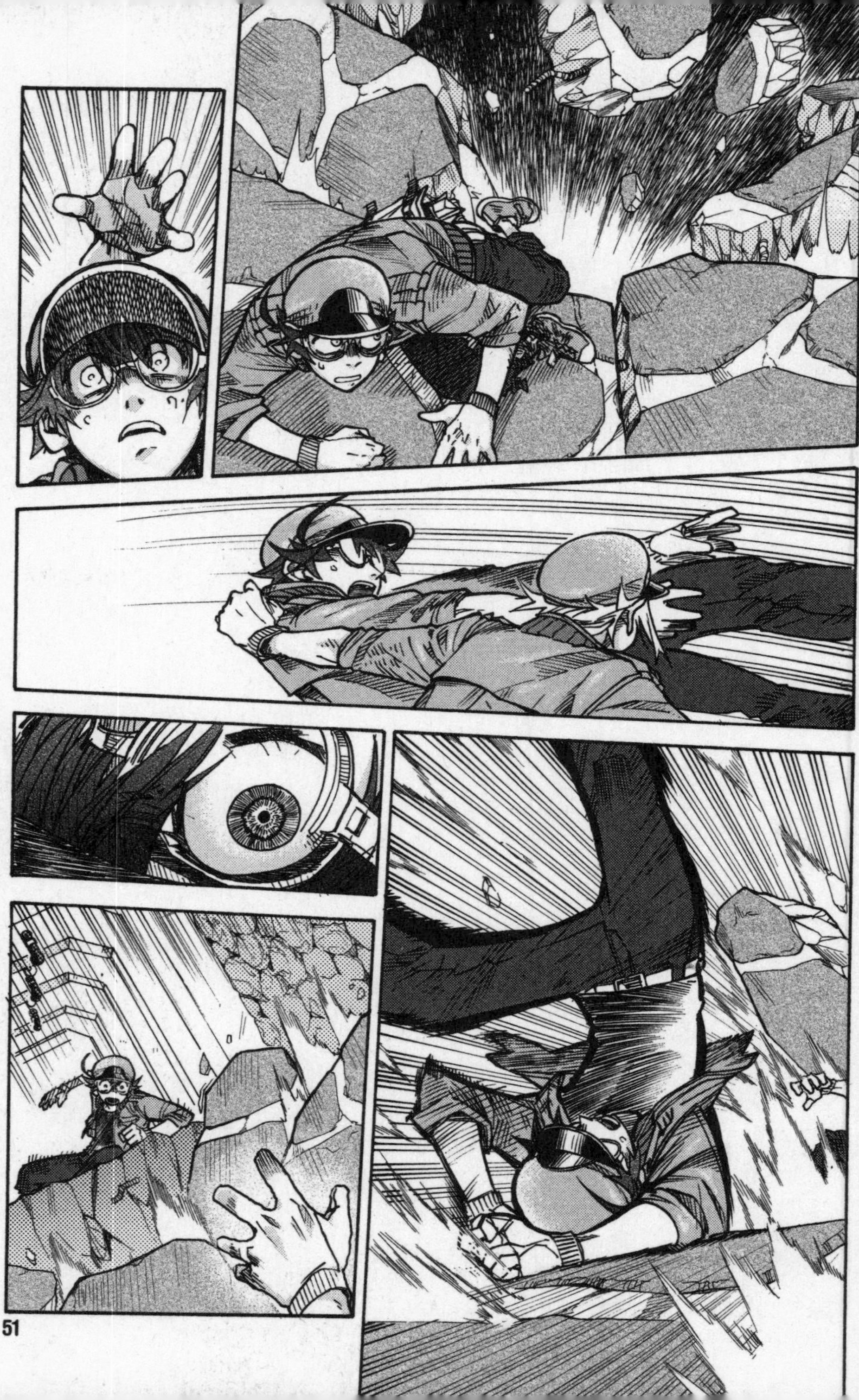

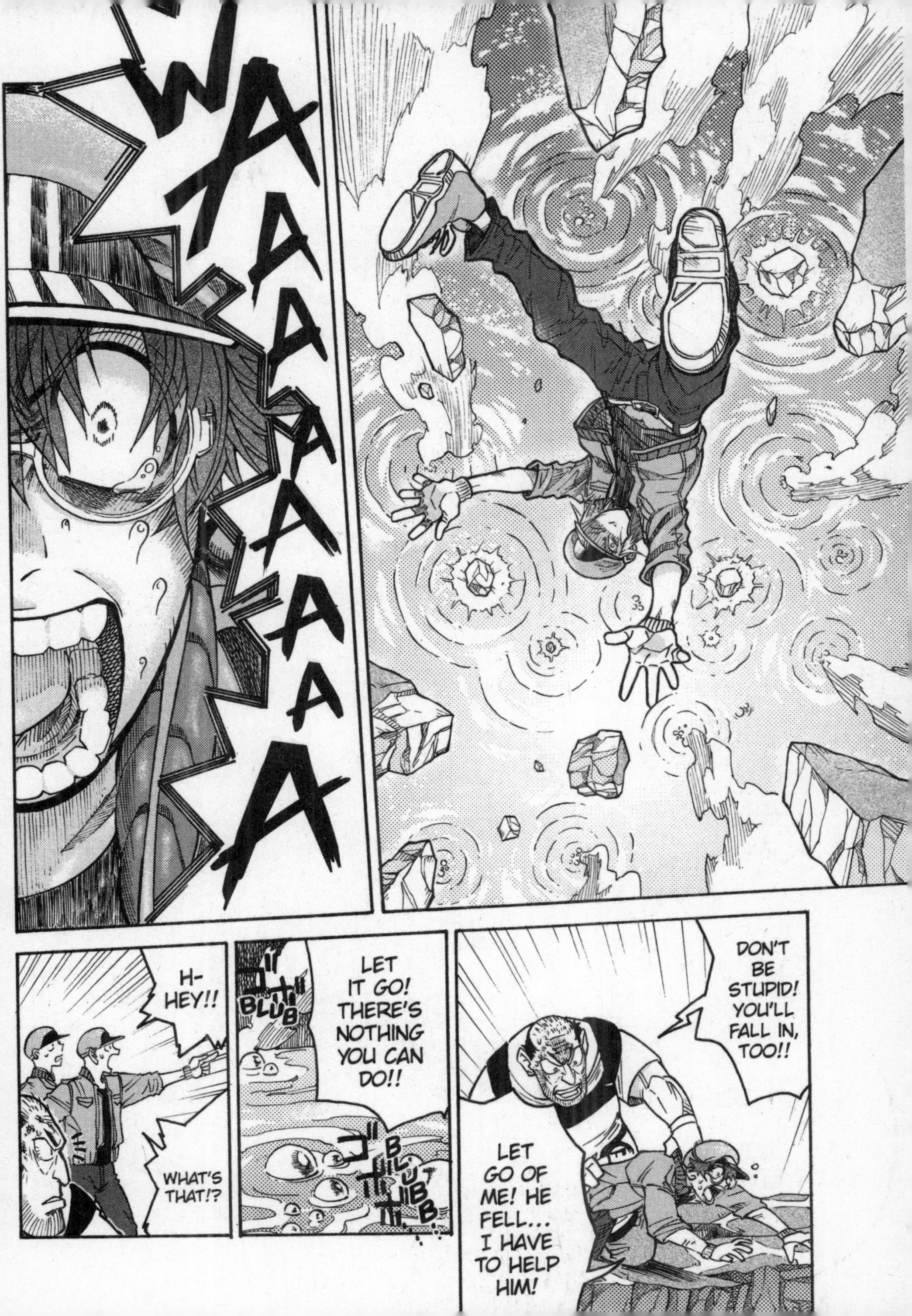

WAAAAAAAA
DON'T BE STUPID! YOU'LL FALL IN, TOO!!
LET GO OF ME! HE FELL... I HAVE TO HELP HIM!
BLUB
LET IT GO! THERE'S NOTHING YOU CAN DO!!
BLUBB
H-HEY!!
WHAT'S THAT!?

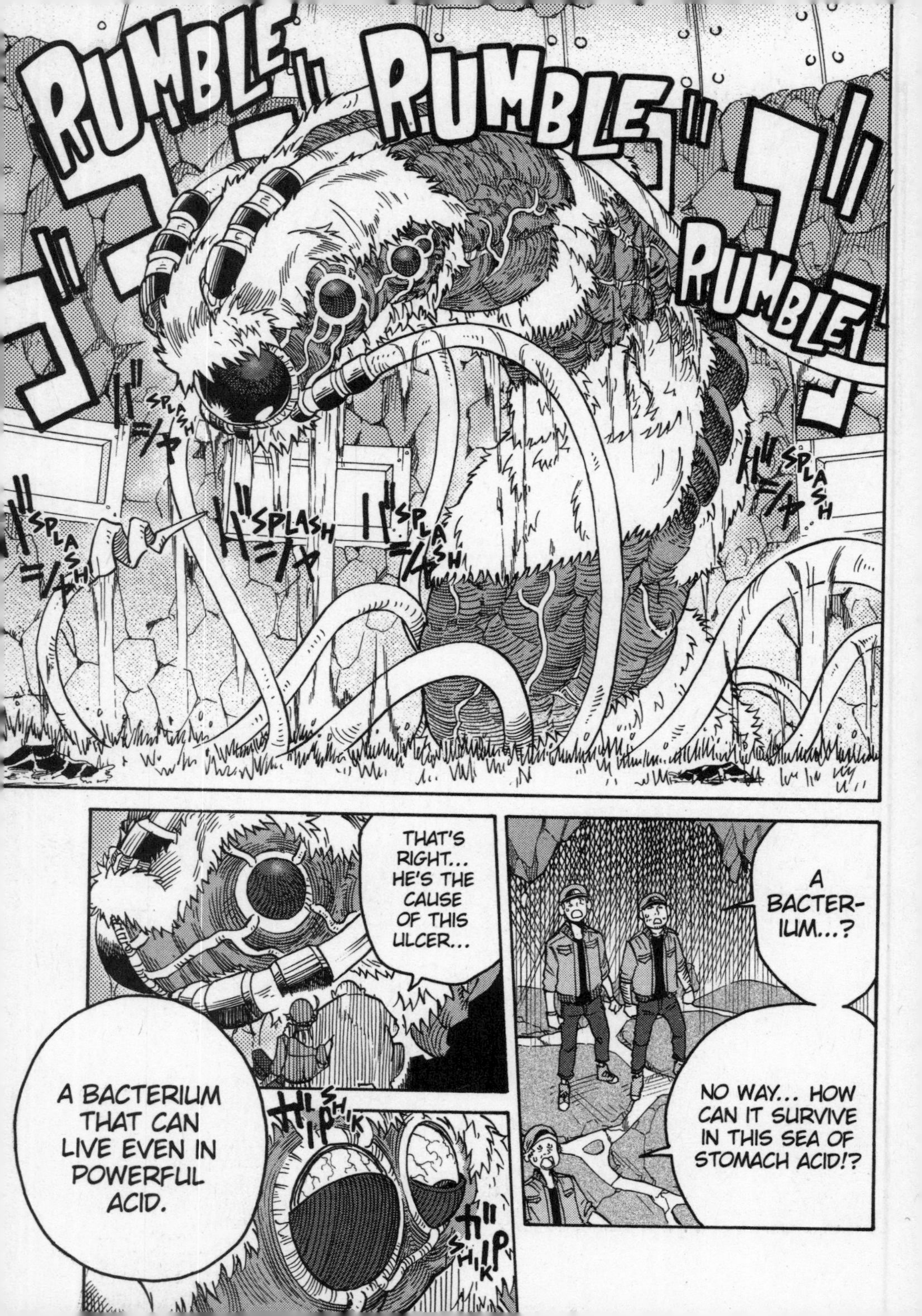
RUMBLE
RUMBLE
RUMBLE
SPLASH
SPLASH
SPLASH
SPLASH
SPLASH
A BACTERIUM...?
NO WAY... HOW CAN IT SURVIVE IN THIS SEA OF STOMACH ACID!?
THAT'S RIGHT... HE'S THE CAUSE OF THIS ULCER...
A BACTERIUM THAT CAN LIVE EVEN IN POWERFUL ACID.
SHIK
SHIK

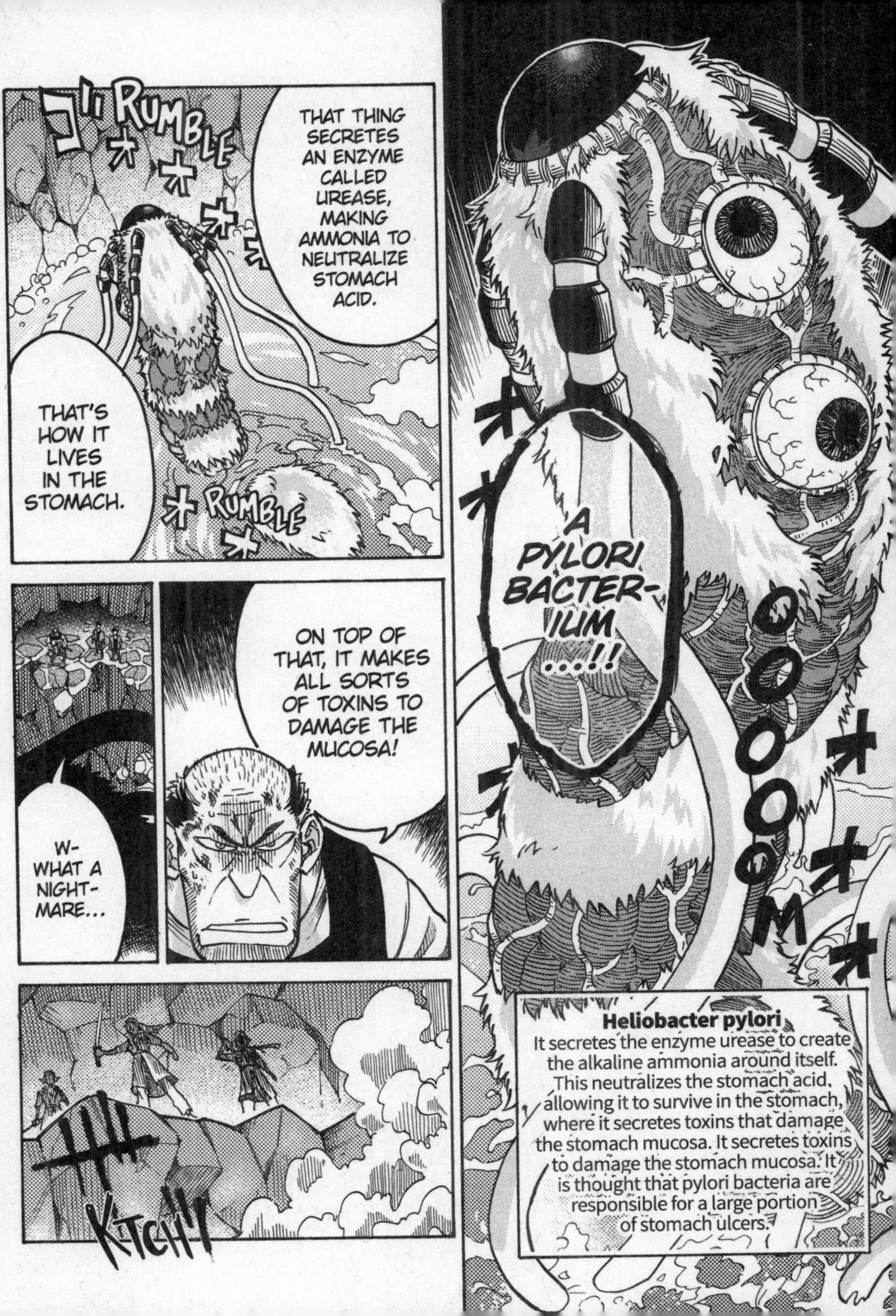
A PYLORI BACTER-IUM ...!!
OOOOOOM
Heliobacter pylori
It secretes the enzyme urease to create the alkaline ammonia around itself. This neutralizes the stomach acid, allowing it to survive in the stomach, where it secretes toxins that damage the stomach mucosa. It secretes toxins to damage the stomach mucosa. It is thought that pylori bacteria are responsible for a large portion of stomach ulcers.
RUMBLE
THAT THING SECRETES AN ENZYME CALLED UREASE, MAKING AMMONIA TO NEUTRALIZE STOMACH ACID.
THAT'S HOW IT LIVES IN THE STOMACH.
RUMBLE
ON TOP OF THAT, IT MAKES ALL SORTS OF TOXINS TO DAMAGE THE MUCOSA!
W-WHAT A NIGHT-MARE...
KTCH!!

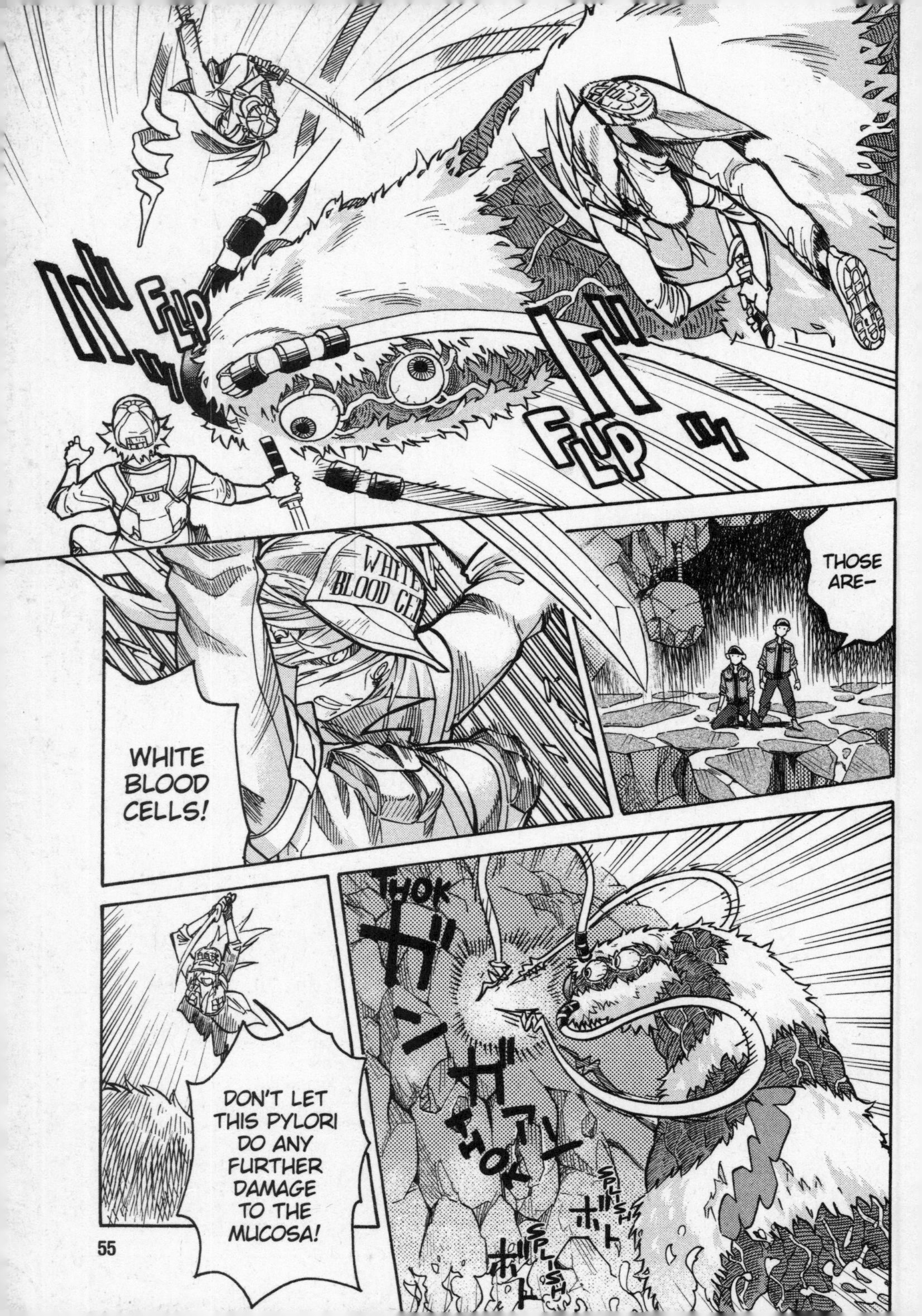

FLLP
FLLP
WHITE BLOOD CELL
THOSE ARE-
WHITE BLOOD CELLS!
THOK
THOK
SPLISH
SPLISH
DON'T LET THIS PYLORI DO ANY FURTHER DAMAGE TO THE MUCOSA!

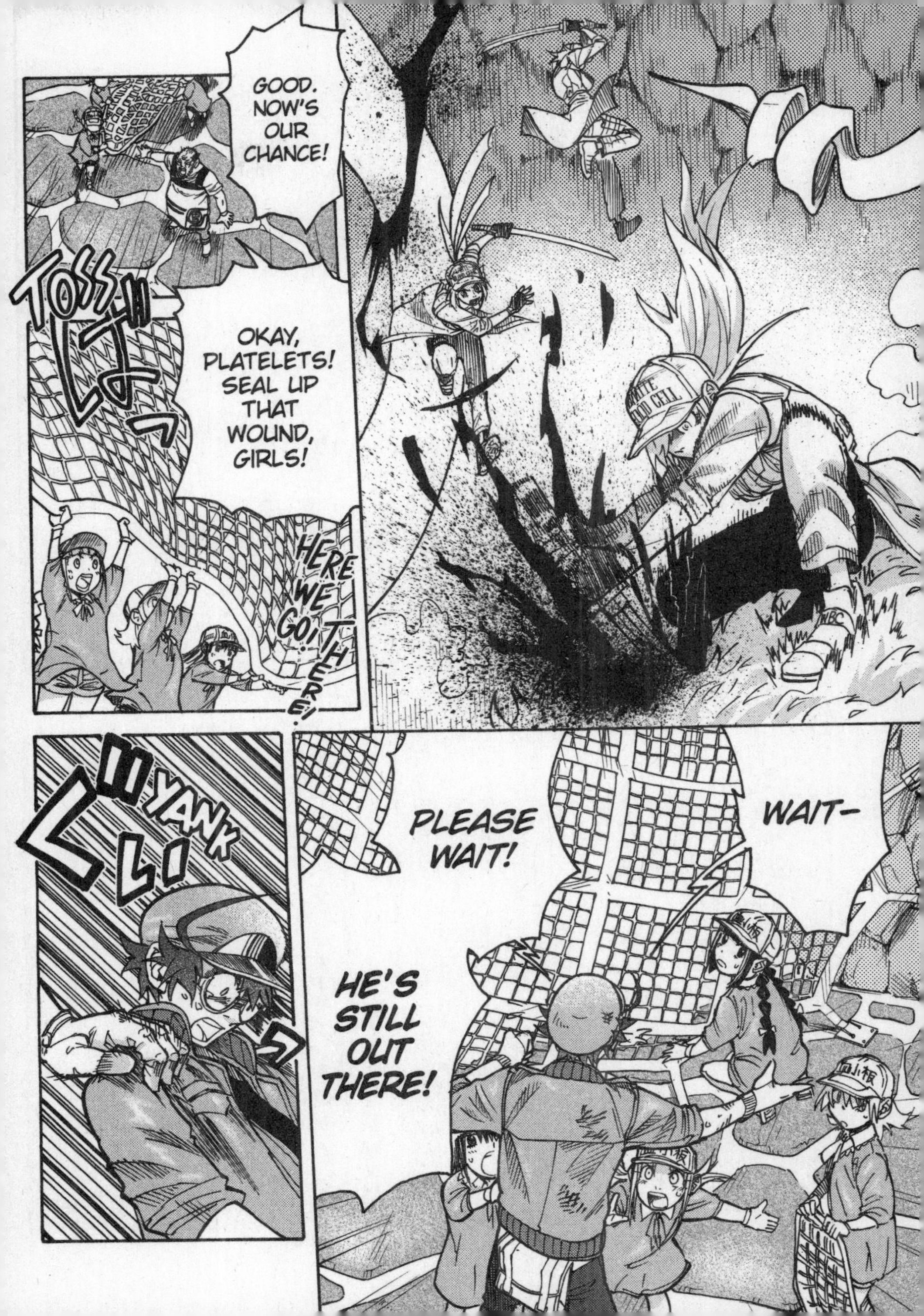
GOOD. NOW'S OUR CHANCE!
TOSS
OKAY, PLATELETS! SEAL UP THAT WOUND, GIRLS!
HERE WE GO! THERE!
WAIT-
PLEASE WAIT!
HE'S STILL OUT THERE!
YANK

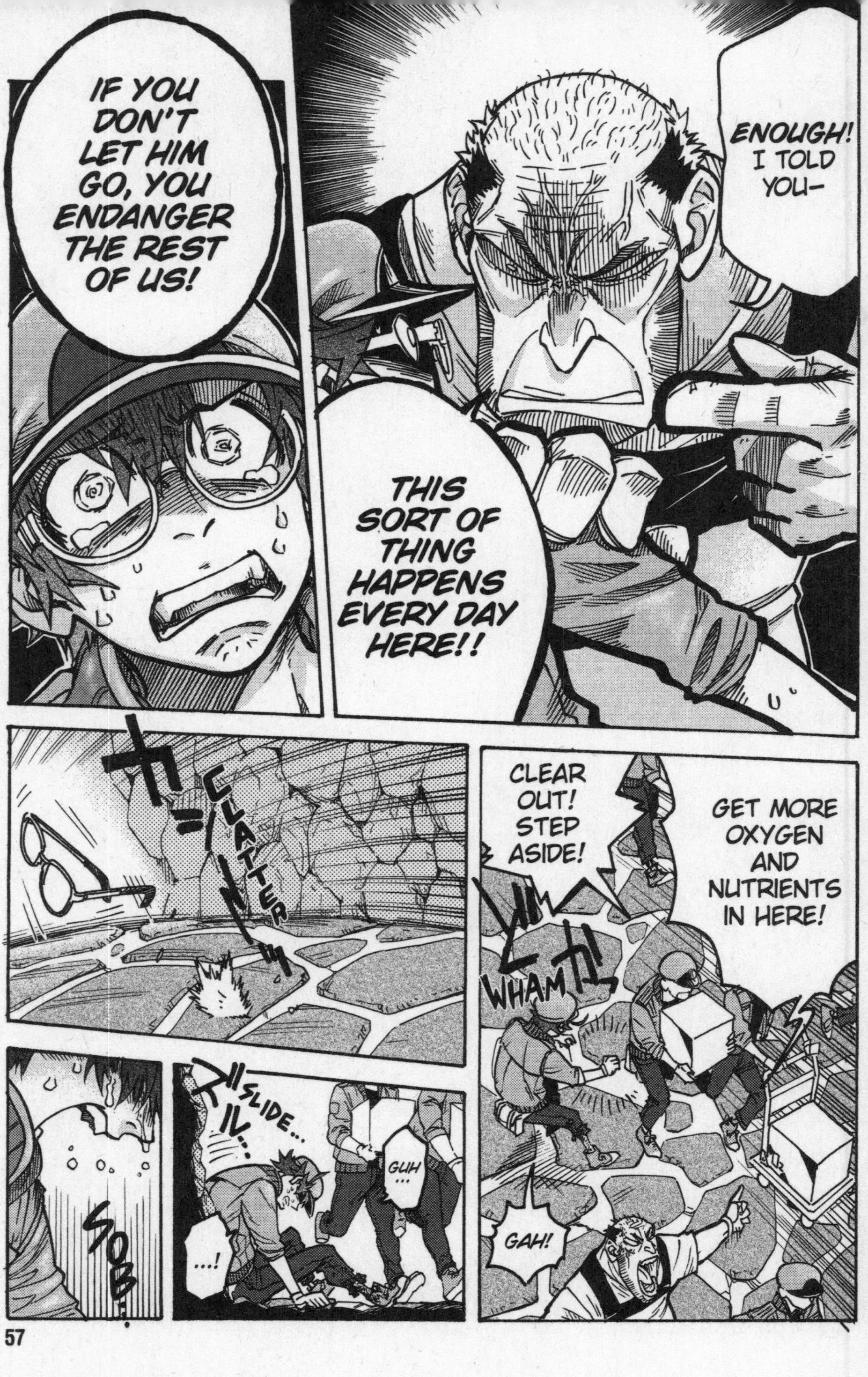
ENOUGH! I TOLD YOU-
THIS SORT OF THING HAPPENS EVERY DAY HERE!!
IF YOU DON'T LET HIM GO, YOU ENDANGER THE REST OF US!
GET MORE OXYGEN AND NUTRIENTS IN HERE!
CLEAR OUT! STEP ASIDE!
WHAM
GAH!
CLATTER
SLIDE...
GUH ...
...!
SOB...

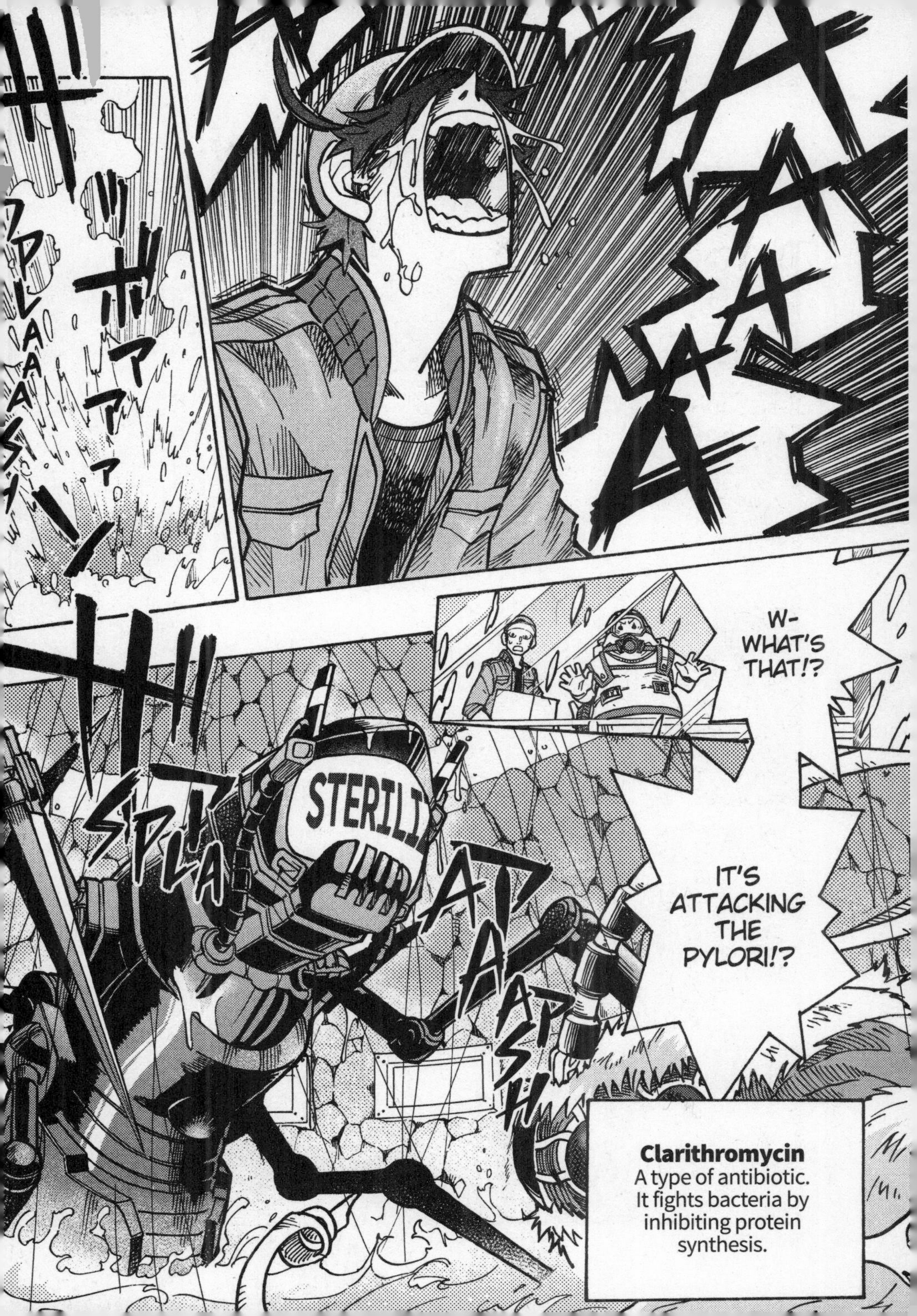
SPLAAASH
W-WHAT'S THAT!?
IT'S ATTACKING THE PYLORI!?
STERILI
Clarithromycin
A type of antibiotic. It fights bacteria by inhibiting protein synthesis.

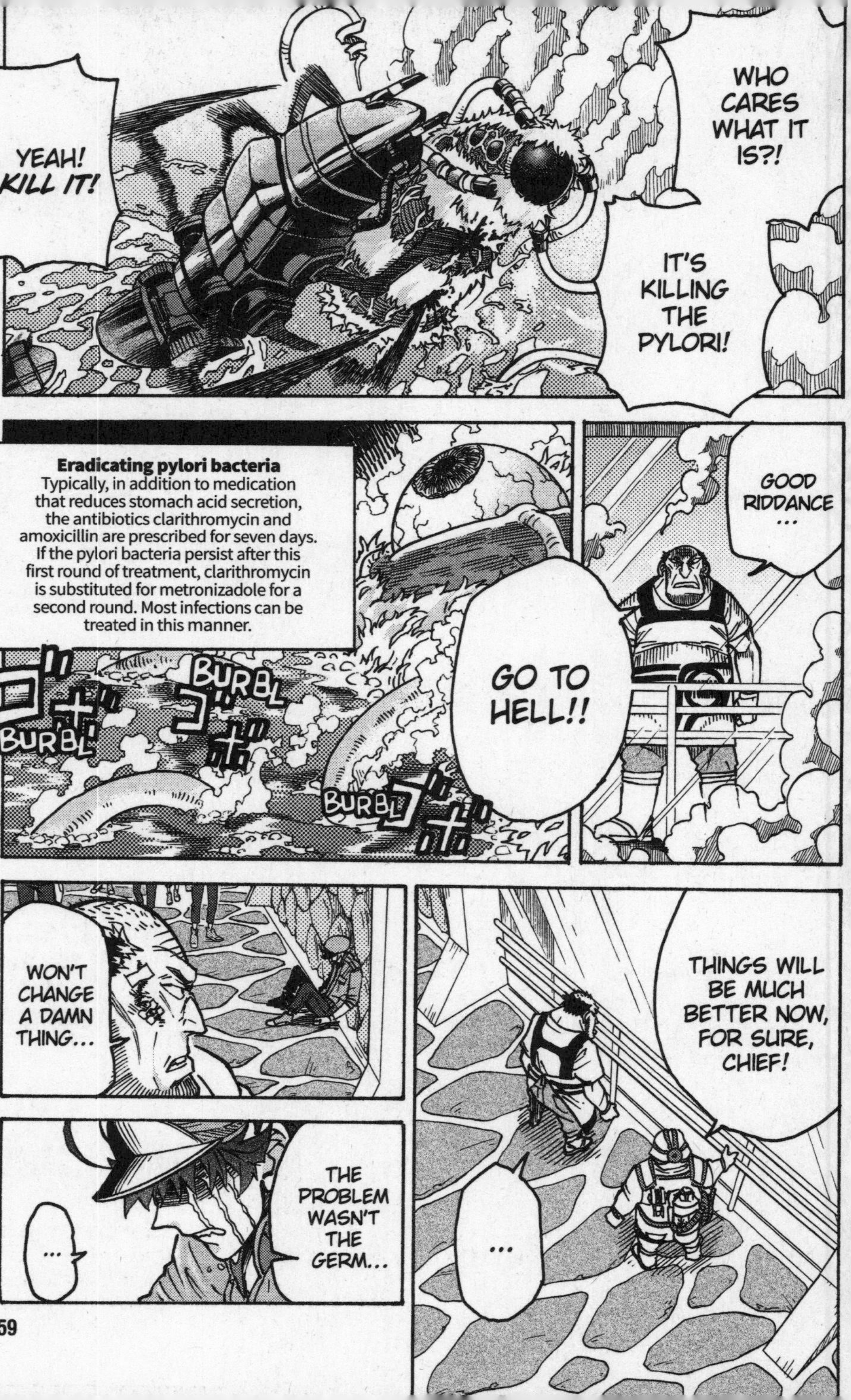
WHO CARES WHAT IT IS?!
IT'S KILLING THE PYLORI!
YEAH! KILL IT!
GOOD RIDDANCE...
GO TO HELL!!
Eradicating pylori bacteria
Typically, in addition to medication that reduces stomach acid secretion, the antibiotics clarithromycin and amoxicillin are prescribed for seven days. If the pylori bacteria persist after this first round of treatment, clarithromycin is substituted for metronizadole for a second round. Most infections can be treated in this manner.
BURBL
BURBL
BURBL
THINGS WILL BE MUCH BETTER NOW, FOR SURE, CHIEF!
...
WON'T CHANGE A DAMN THING...
THE PROBLEM WASN'T THE GERM...
...

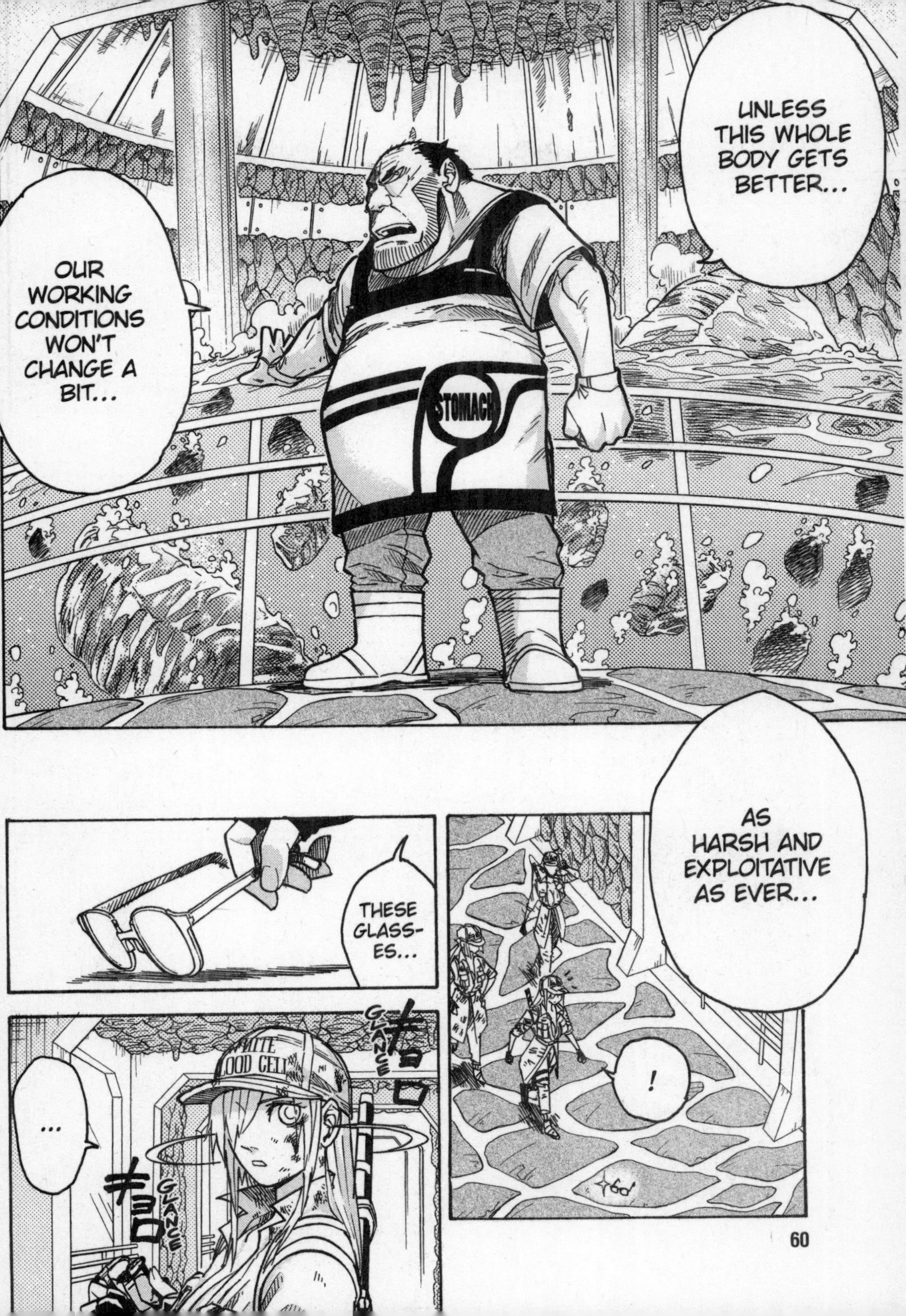
UNLESS THIS WHOLE BODY GETS BETTER...
OUR WORKING CONDITIONS WON'T CHANGE A BIT...
STOMACH
AS HARSH AND EXPLOITATIVE AS EVER...
!
THESE GLASS-ES...
GLANCE
...
GLANCE

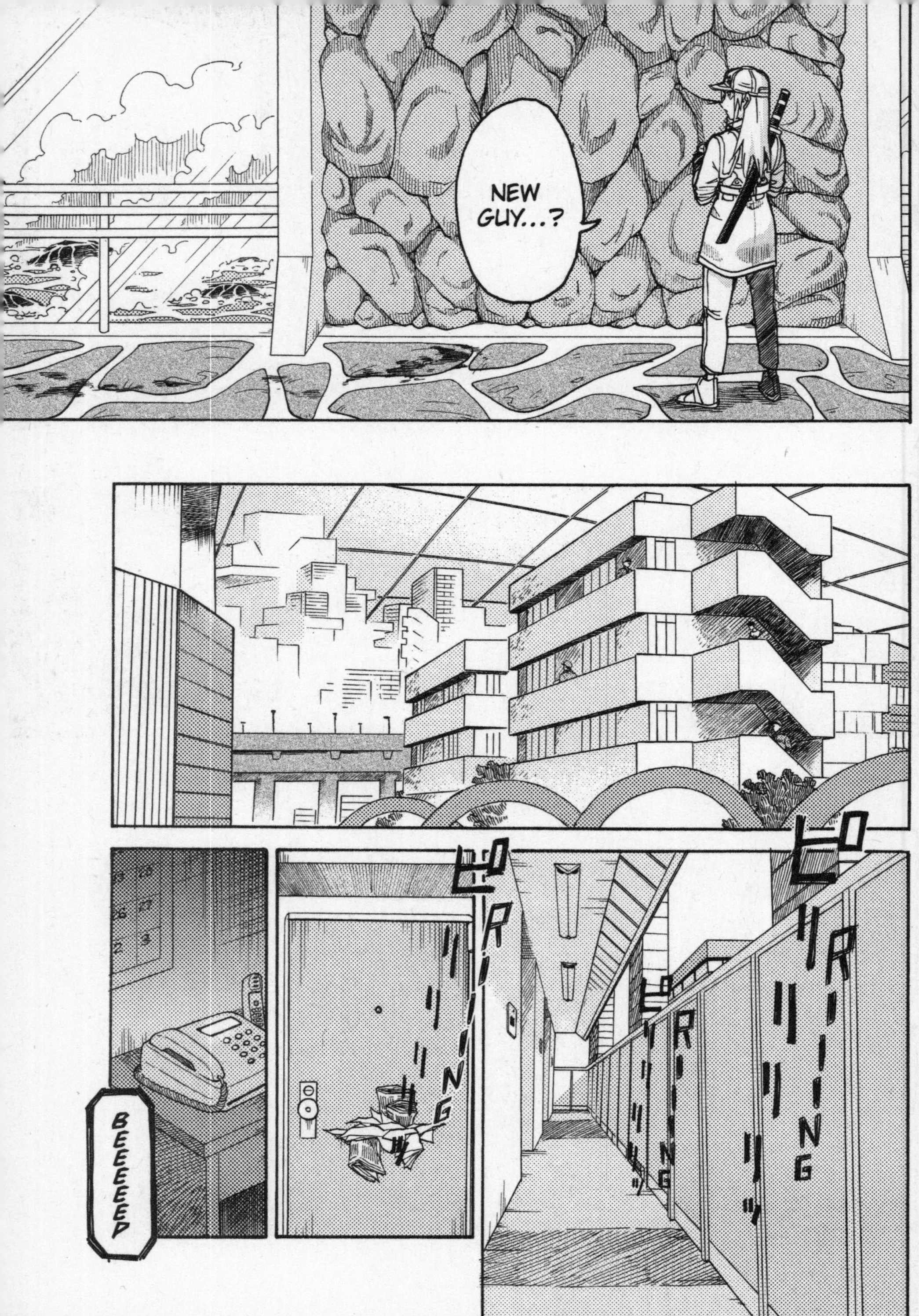
NEW GUY...?
ピロ
RIIIING
ピロ
RIIIING
ピロ
RIIIING
BEEEEEP

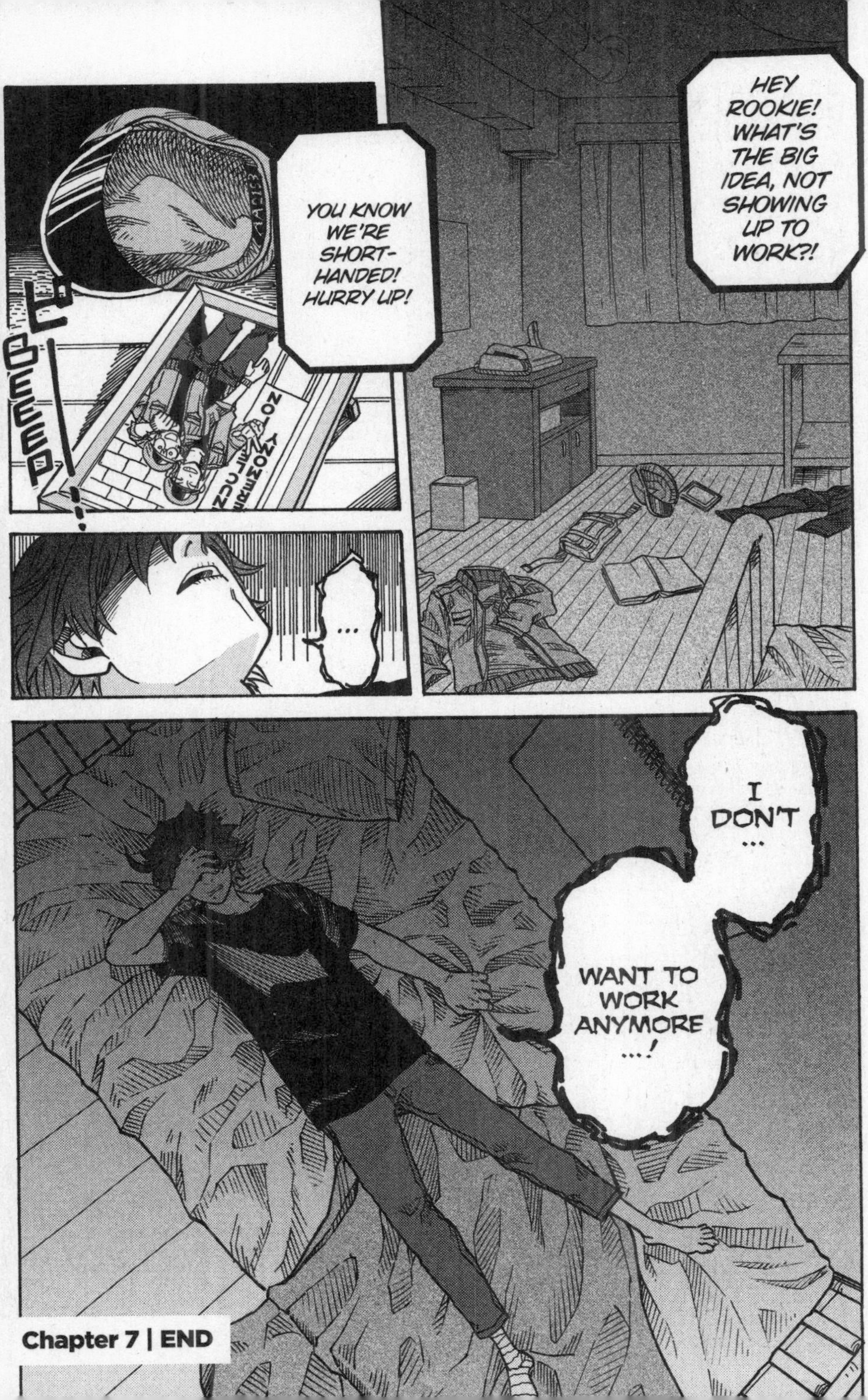
HEY ROOKIE! WHAT'S THE BIG IDEA, NOT SHOWING UP TO WORK?!
YOU KNOW WE'RE SHORT-HANDED! HURRY UP!
ピ
BEEEP—!
...
I DON'T...
WANT TO WORK ANYMORE...!
Chapter 7 | END

CHAPTER 8: DESPERATION, GOUT, AND REBELLION

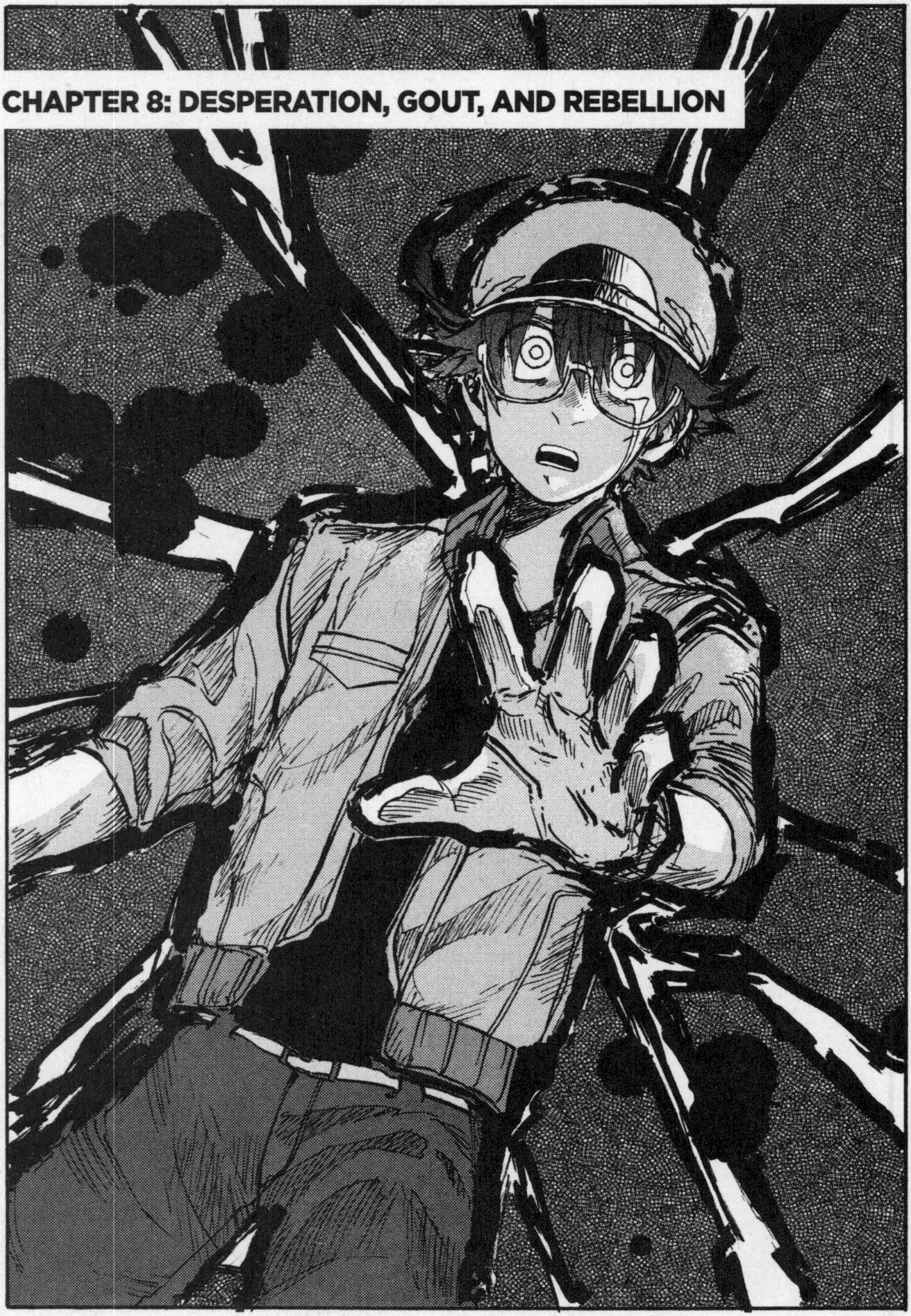

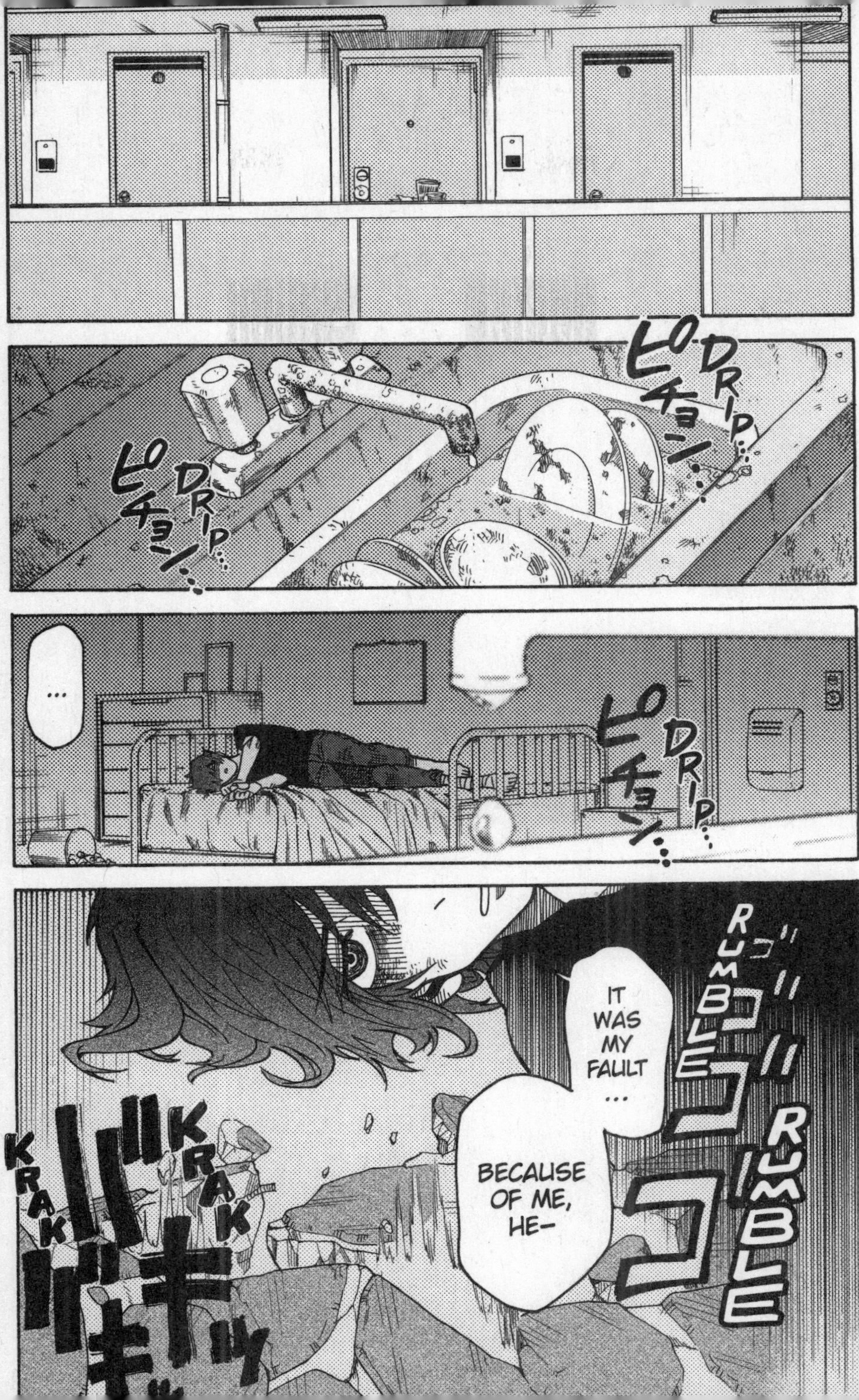
ピチョン…
DRIP…
ピチョン…
DRIP…
ピチョン…
DRIP…
…
ゴゴゴ
RUMBLE
RUMBLE
IT WAS MY FAULT…
BECAUSE OF ME, HE–
バキッ
KRAK
KRAK

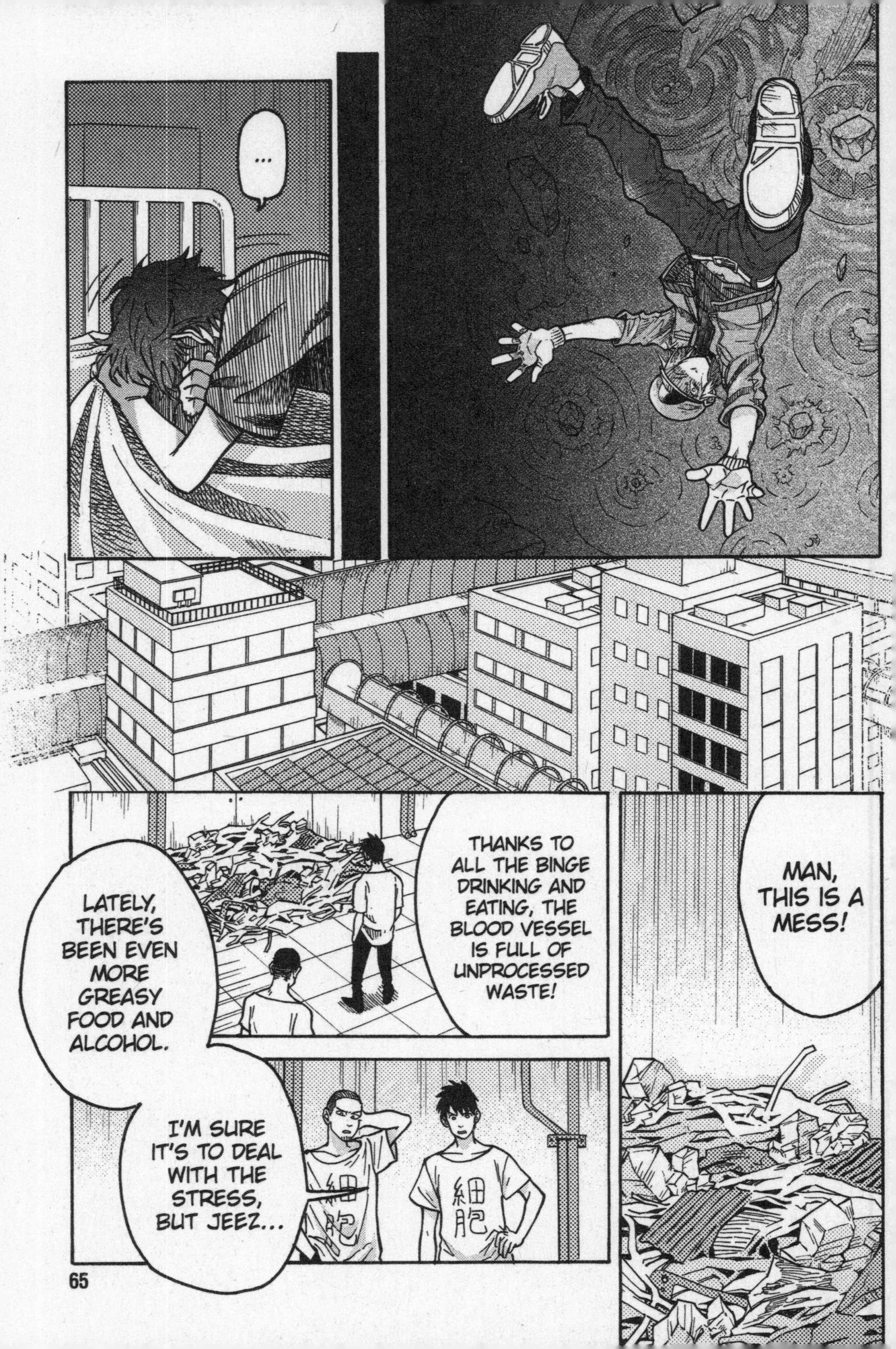
...
MAN, THIS IS A MESS!
THANKS TO ALL THE BINGE DRINKING AND EATING, THE BLOOD VESSEL IS FULL OF UNPROCESSED WASTE!
LATELY, THERE'S BEEN EVEN MORE GREASY FOOD AND ALCOHOL.
I'M SURE IT'S TO DEAL WITH THE STRESS, BUT JEEZ...

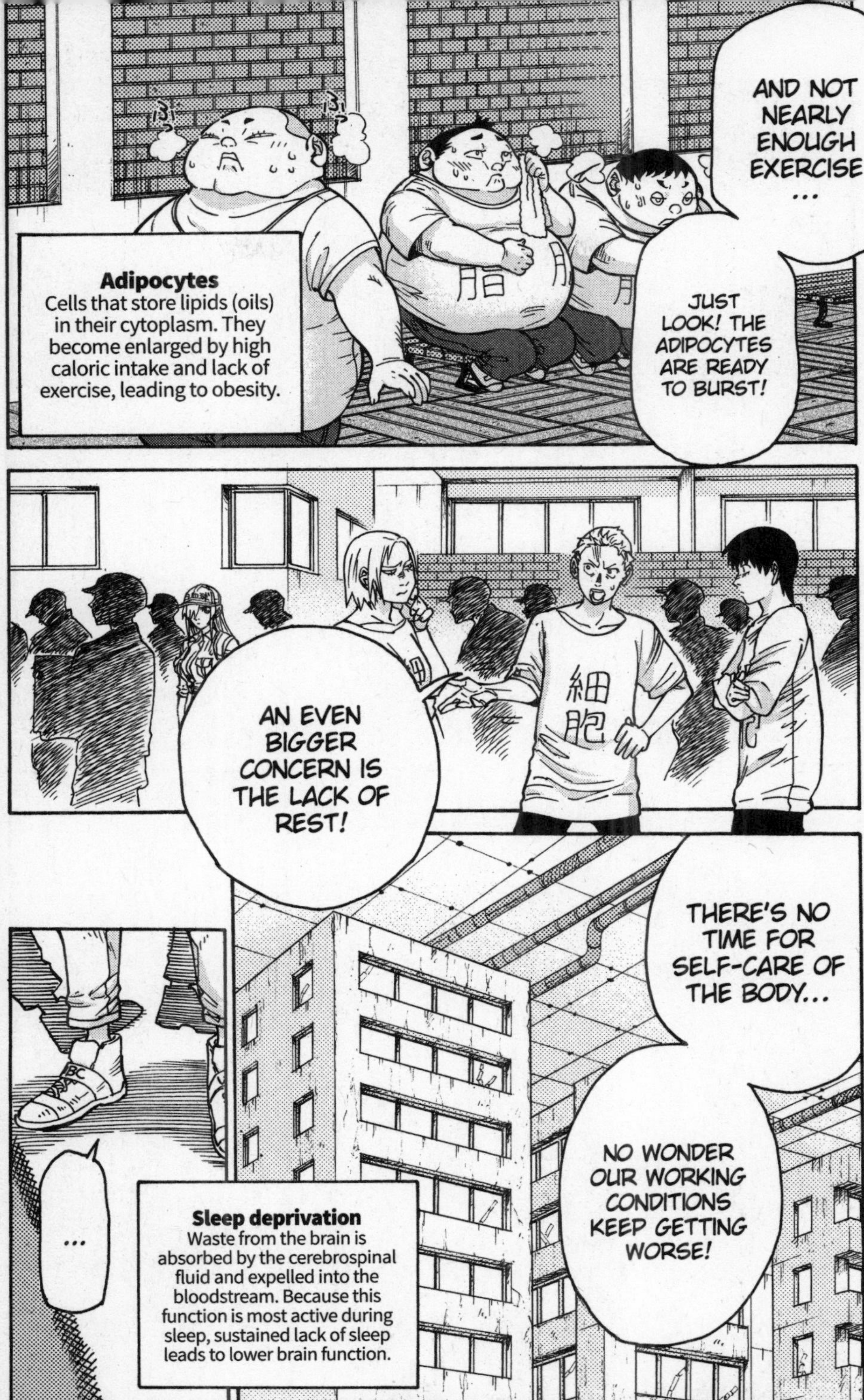
AND NOT NEARLY ENOUGH EXERCISE...
JUST LOOK! THE ADIPOCYTES ARE READY TO BURST!
Adipocytes
Cells that store lipids (oils) in their cytoplasm. They become enlarged by high caloric intake and lack of exercise, leading to obesity.
AN EVEN BIGGER CONCERN IS THE LACK OF REST!
THERE'S NO TIME FOR SELF-CARE OF THE BODY...
NO WONDER OUR WORKING CONDITIONS KEEP GETTING WORSE!
Sleep deprivation
Waste from the brain is absorbed by the cerebrospinal fluid and expelled into the bloodstream. Because this function is most active during sleep, sustained lack of sleep leads to lower brain function.
...

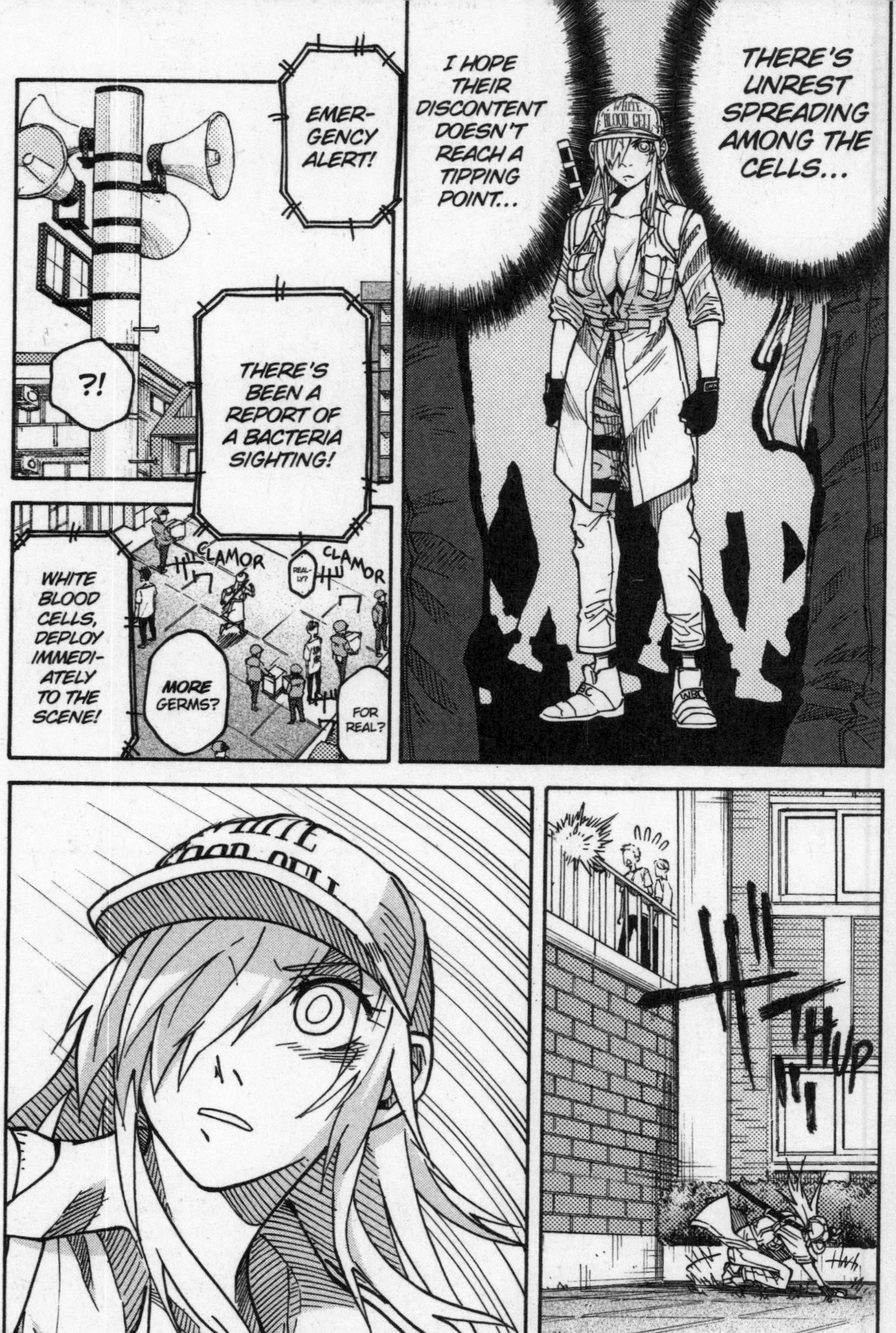
THERE'S UNREST SPREADING AMONG THE CELLS...
I HOPE THEIR DISCONTENT DOESN'T REACH A TIPPING POINT...
EMERGENCY ALERT!
?!
THERE'S BEEN A REPORT OF A BACTERIA SIGHTING!
CLAMOR
REALLY?
CLAMOR
WHITE BLOOD CELLS, DEPLOY IMMEDIATELY TO THE SCENE!
MORE GERMS?
FOR REAL?
THUP

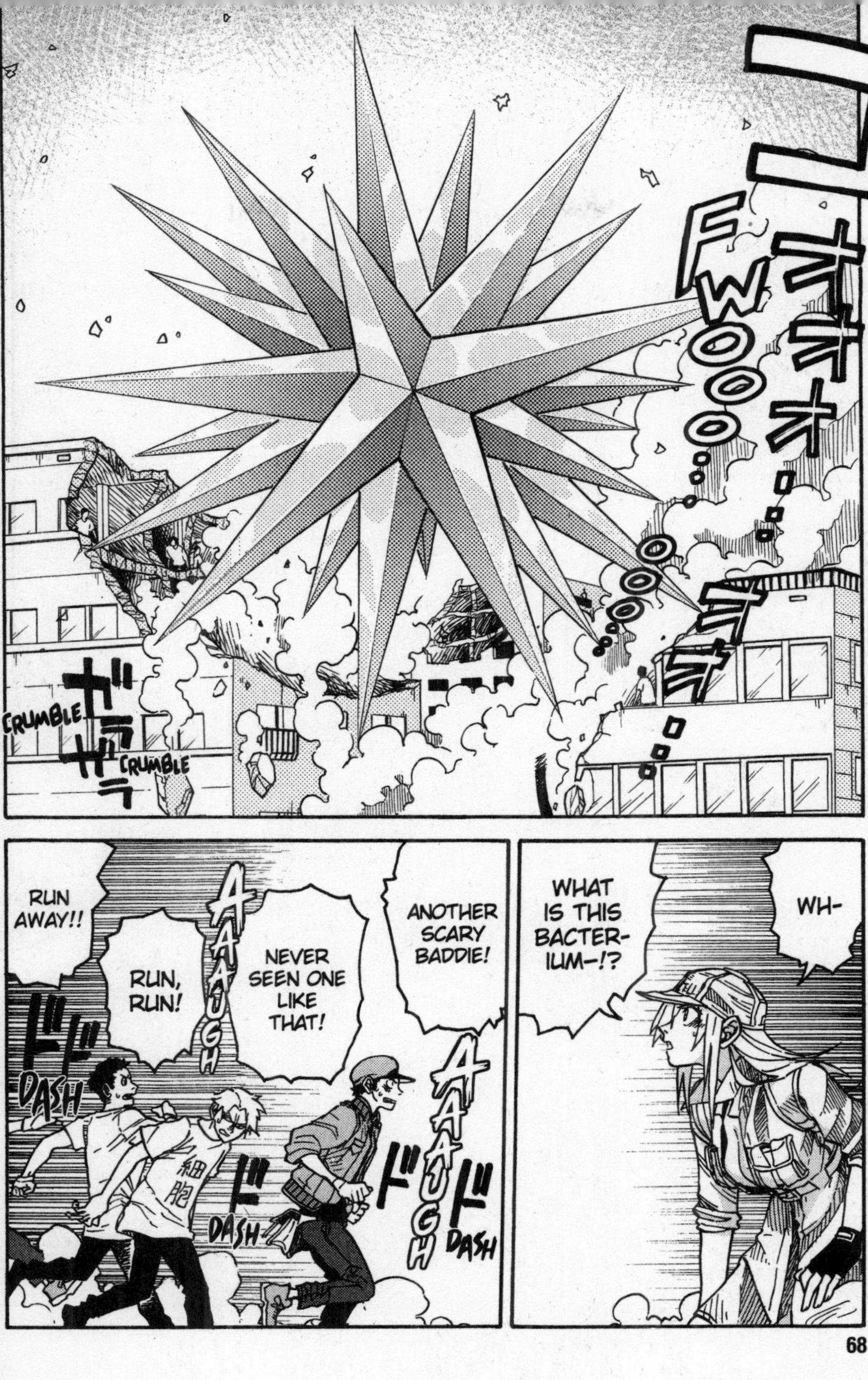
FWOOOO...OOOO...
CRUMBLE
CRUMBLE
WH-
WHAT IS THIS BACTER-IUM-!?
ANOTHER SCARY BADDIE!
NEVER SEEN ONE LIKE THAT!
AAAUGH
RUN, RUN!
RUN AWAY!!
AAAUGH
DASH
DASH
DASH

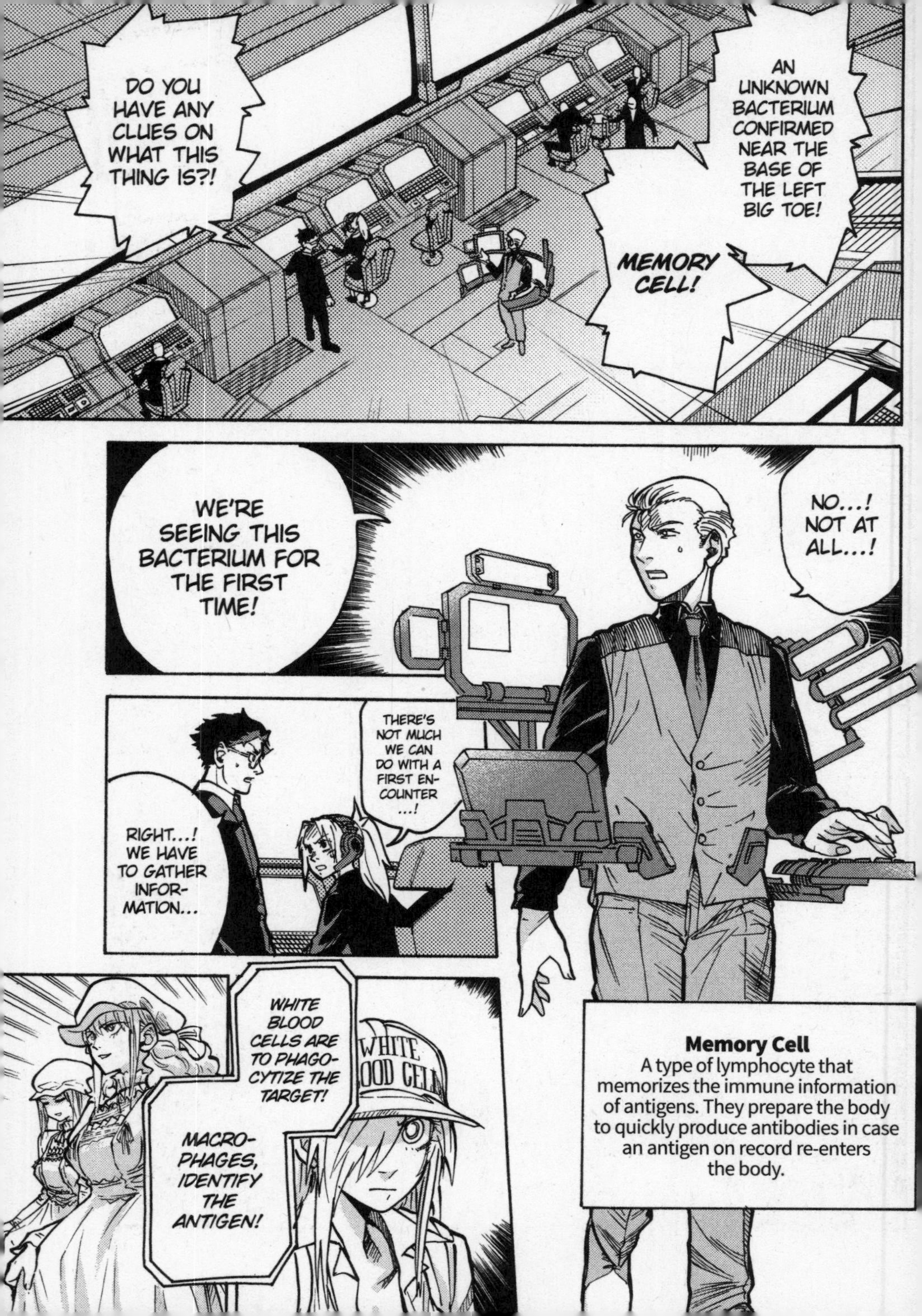
AN UNKNOWN BACTERIUM CONFIRMED NEAR THE BASE OF THE LEFT BIG TOE!
MEMORY CELL!
DO YOU HAVE ANY CLUES ON WHAT THIS THING IS?!
NO...! NOT AT ALL...!
Memory Cell
A type of lymphocyte that memorizes the immune information of antigens. They prepare the body to quickly produce antibodies in case an antigen on record re-enters the body.
WE'RE SEEING THIS BACTERIUM FOR THE FIRST TIME!
THERE'S NOT MUCH WE CAN DO WITH A FIRST EN-COUNTER ...!
RIGHT...! WE HAVE TO GATHER INFOR-MATION...
WHITE BLOOD CELLS ARE TO PHAGO-CYTIZE THE TARGET!
MACRO-PHAGES, IDENTIFY THE ANTIGEN!

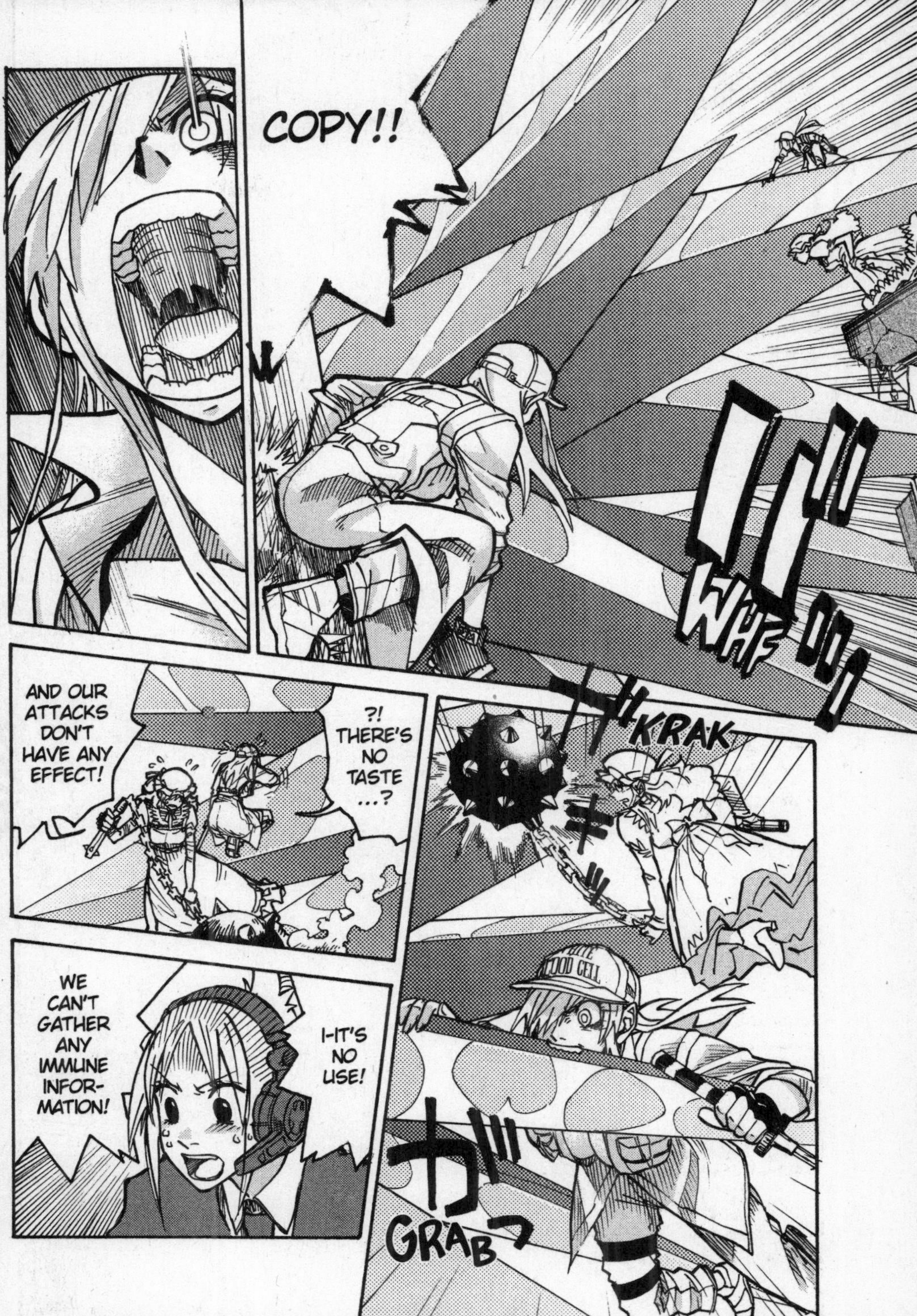
WHFOOM
COPY!!
KRAK
?! THERE'S NO TASTE ...?
AND OUR ATTACKS DON'T HAVE ANY EFFECT!
GRAB
I-IT'S NO USE!
WE CAN'T GATHER ANY IMMUNE INFORMATION!

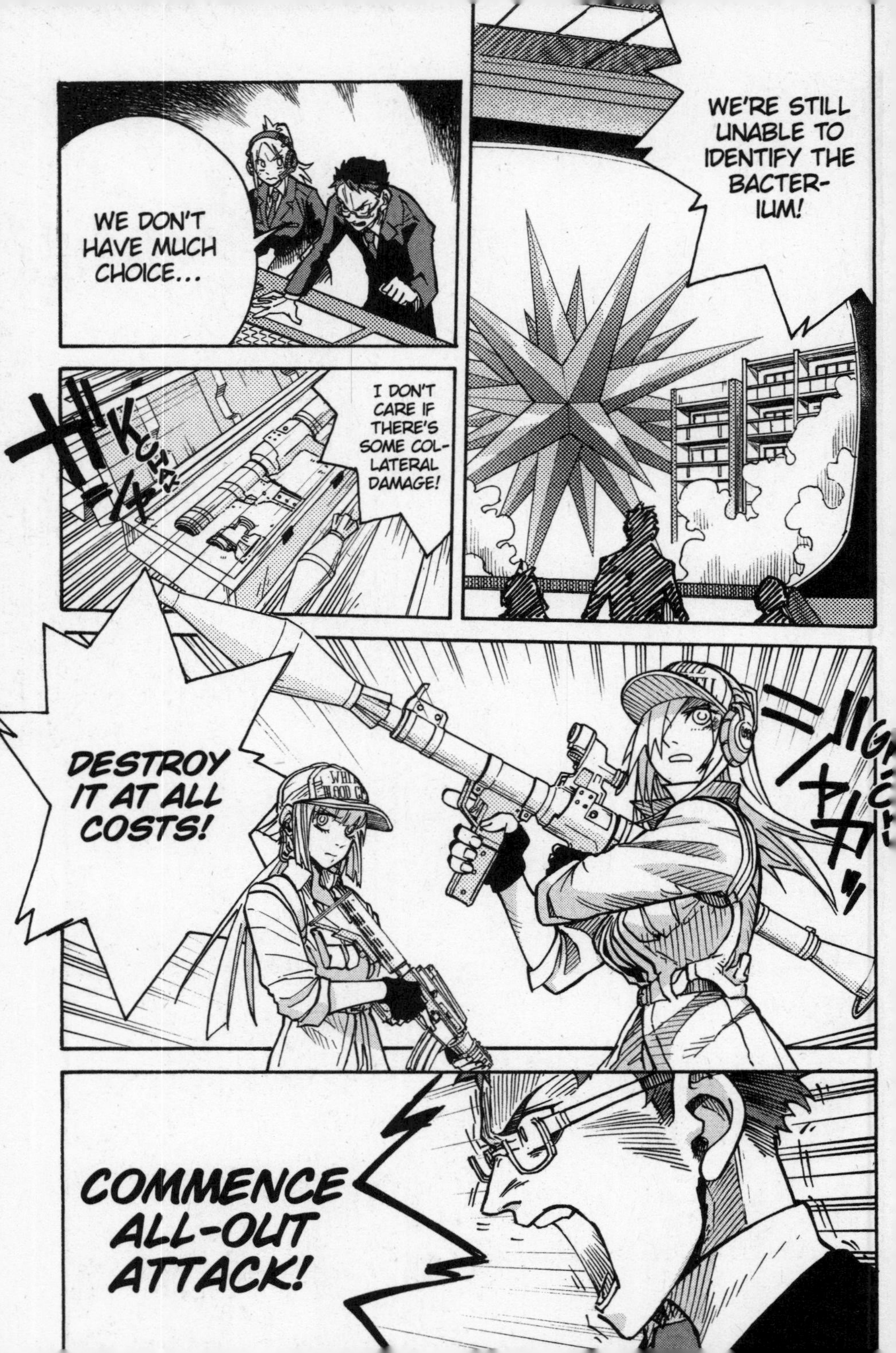
WE'RE STILL UNABLE TO IDENTIFY THE BACTER-IUM!
WE DON'T HAVE MUCH CHOICE...
I DON'T CARE IF THERE'S SOME COL-LATERAL DAMAGE!
KCHAK
DESTROY IT AT ALL COSTS!
COMMENCE ALL-OUT ATTACK!

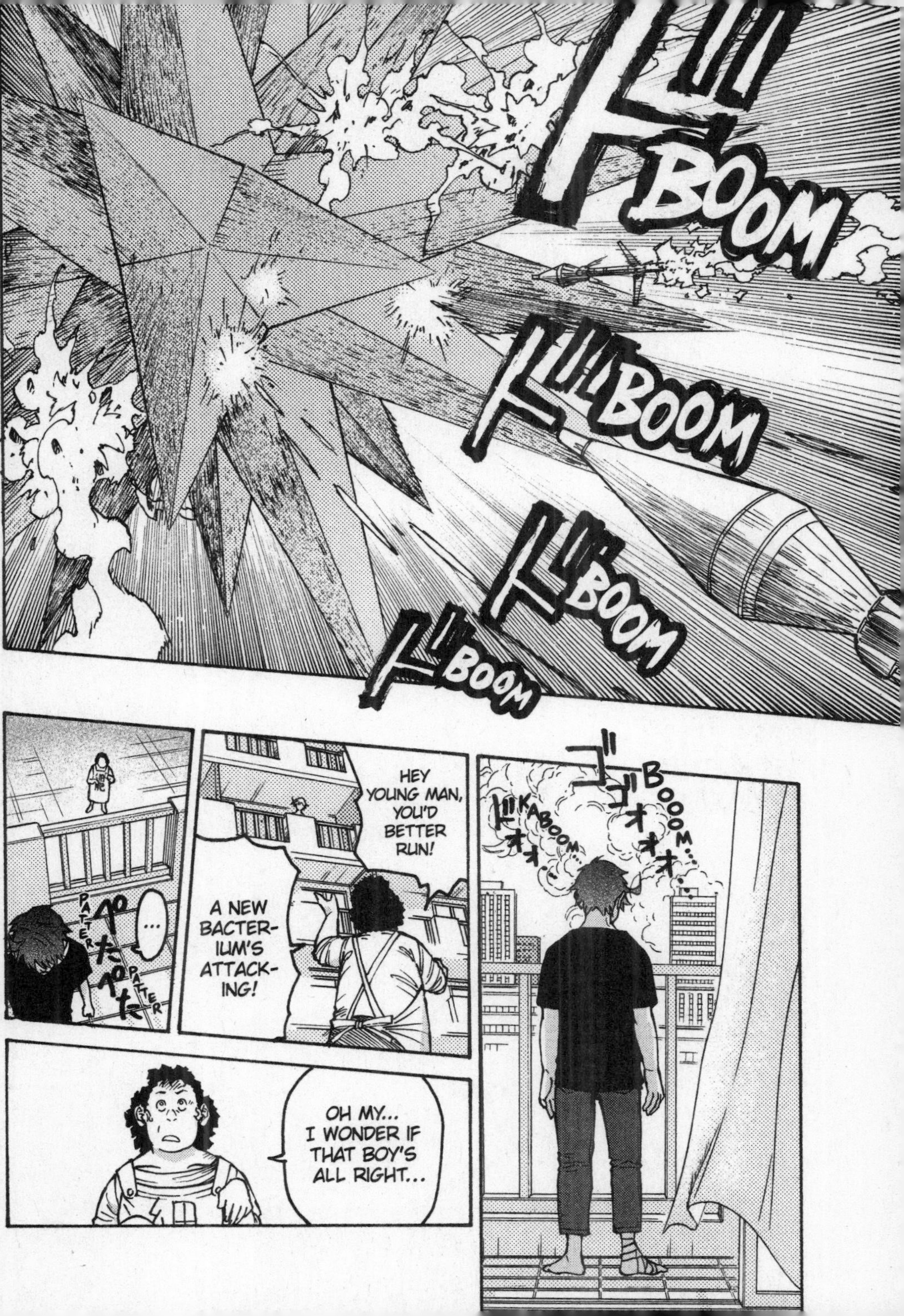
BOOM
BOOM
BOOM
BOOM
BOOOM...
KABOOM...
HEY YOUNG MAN, YOU'D BETTER RUN!
A NEW BACTERIUM'S ATTACKING!
...
PATTER
PATTER
OH MY... I WONDER IF THAT BOY'S ALL RIGHT...

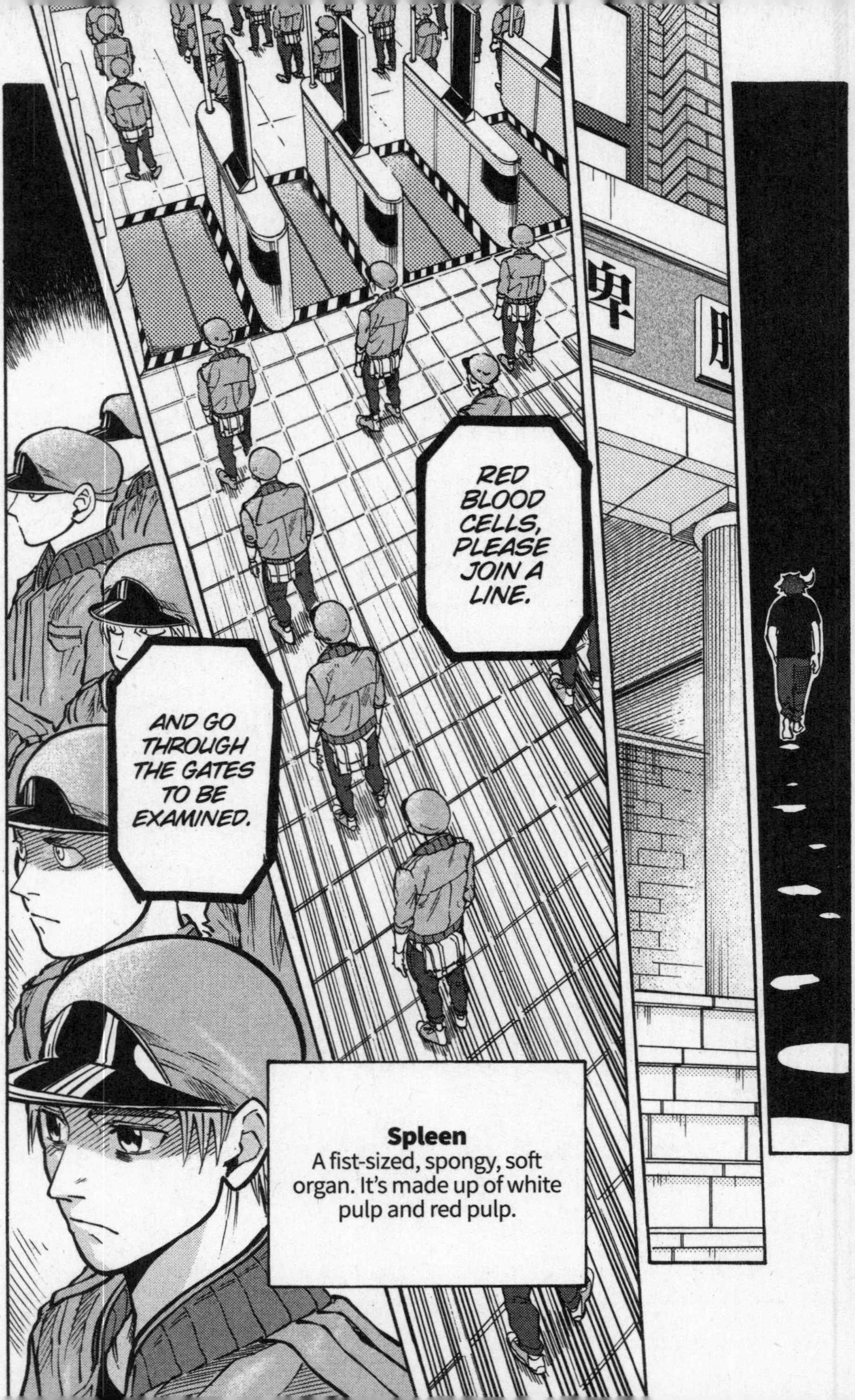
RED BLOOD CELLS, PLEASE JOIN A LINE.
AND GO THROUGH THE GATES TO BE EXAMINED.
Spleen
A fist-sized, spongy, soft organ. It's made up of white pulp and red pulp.

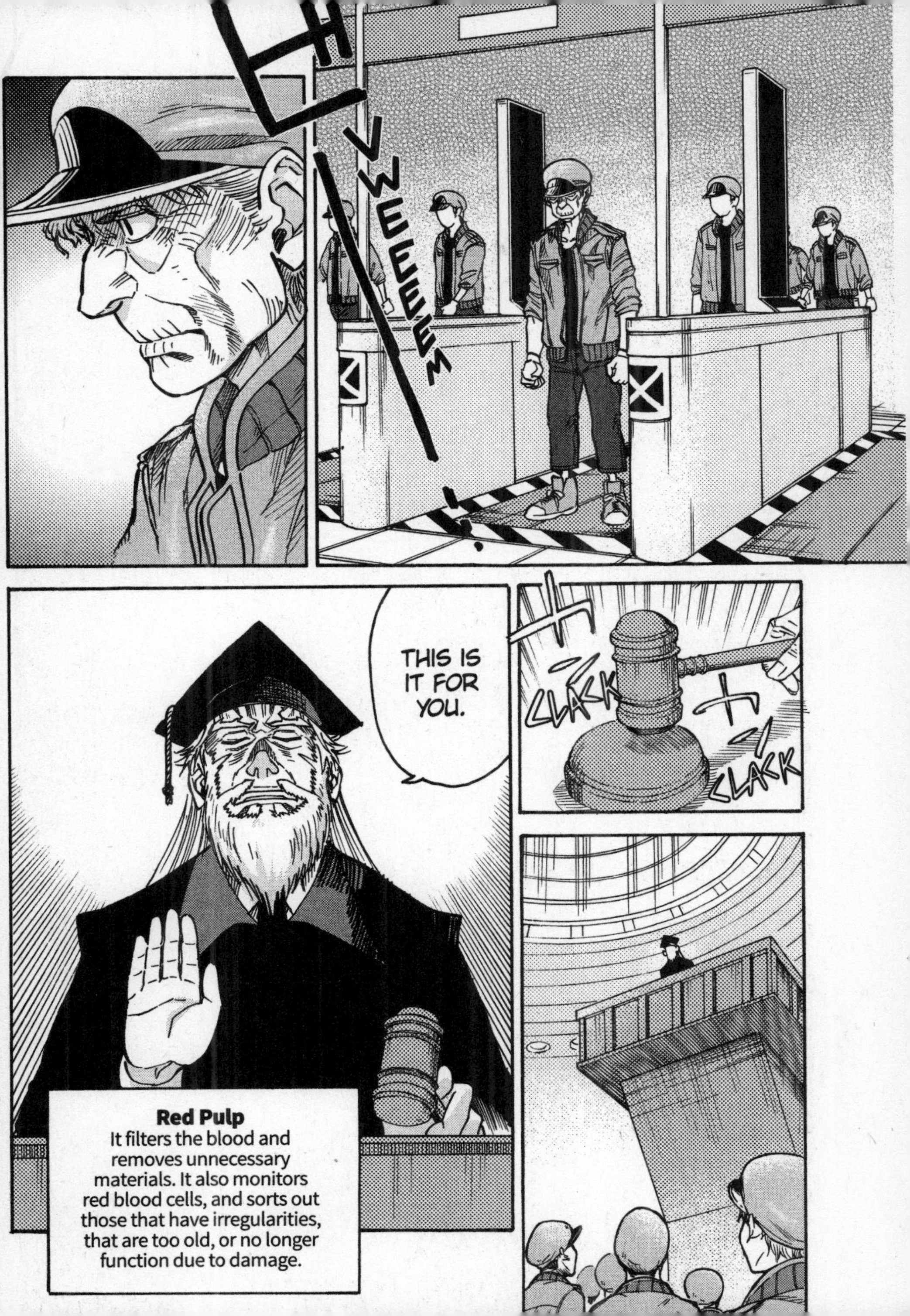
VWEEEEEM
CLACK
CLACK
THIS IS IT FOR YOU.
Red Pulp
It filters the blood and removes unnecessary materials. It also monitors red blood cells, and sorts out those that have irregularities, that are too old, or no longer function due to damage.

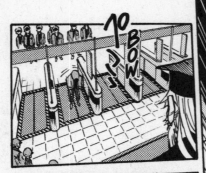

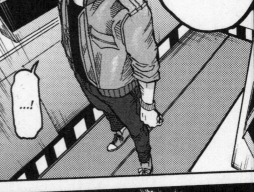

THANK YOU FOR YOUR SERVICE.

....!

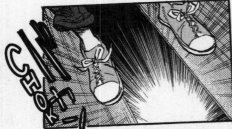

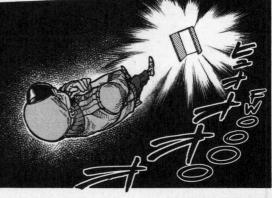

The spleen stores blood and sends it out to muscles when needed. It has several additional functions, including producing B and T lymphocytes, and destroying red blood cells sorted out by the red pulp.

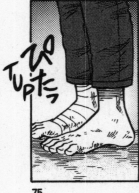

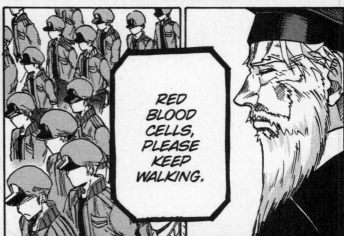

RED BLOOD CELLS, PLEASE KEEP WALKING.

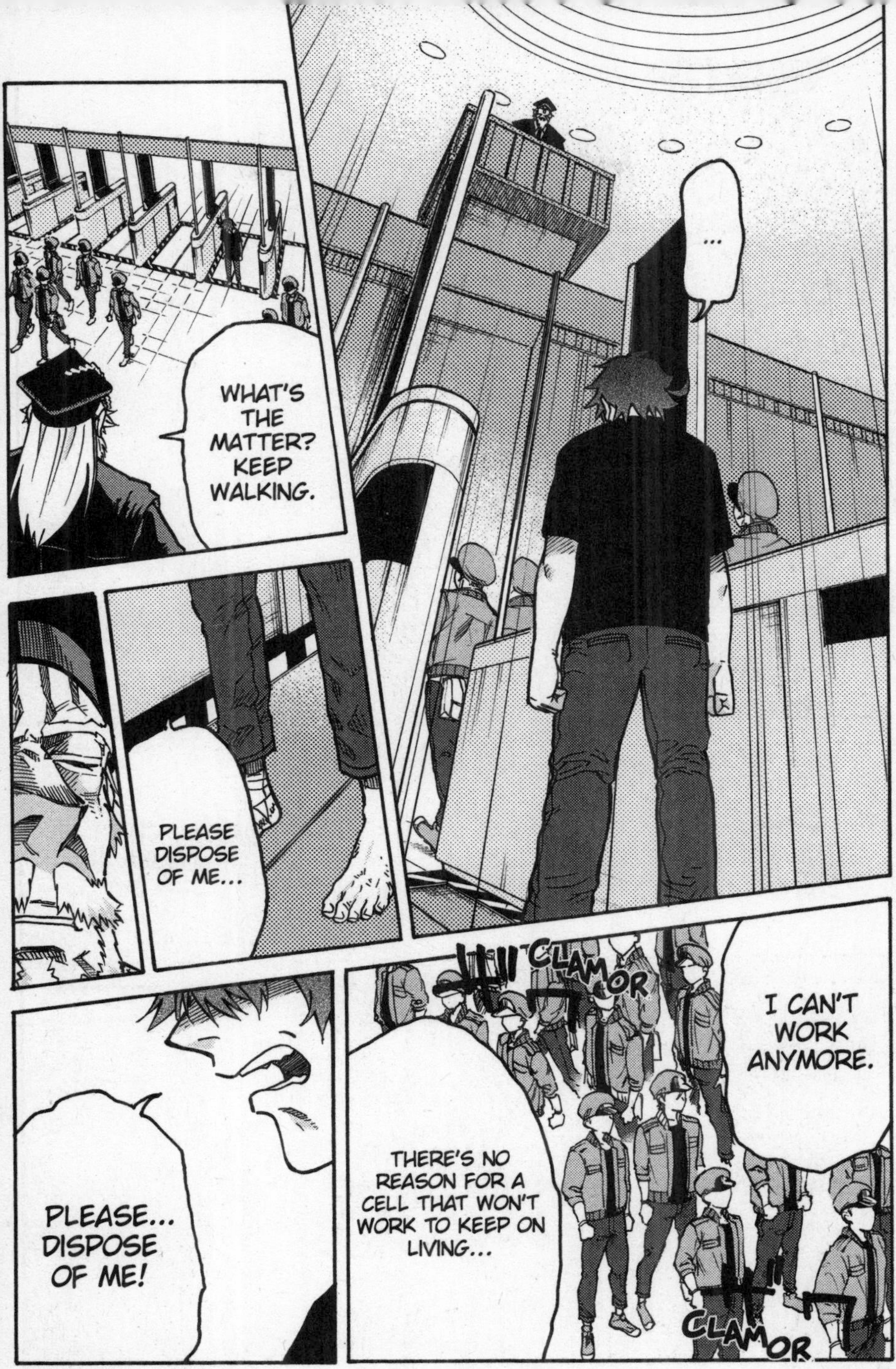
...
WHAT'S THE MATTER? KEEP WALKING.
PLEASE DISPOSE OF ME...
CLAMOR
I CAN'T WORK ANYMORE.
THERE'S NO REASON FOR A CELL THAT WON'T WORK TO KEEP ON LIVING...
CLAMOR
PLEASE... DISPOSE OF ME!

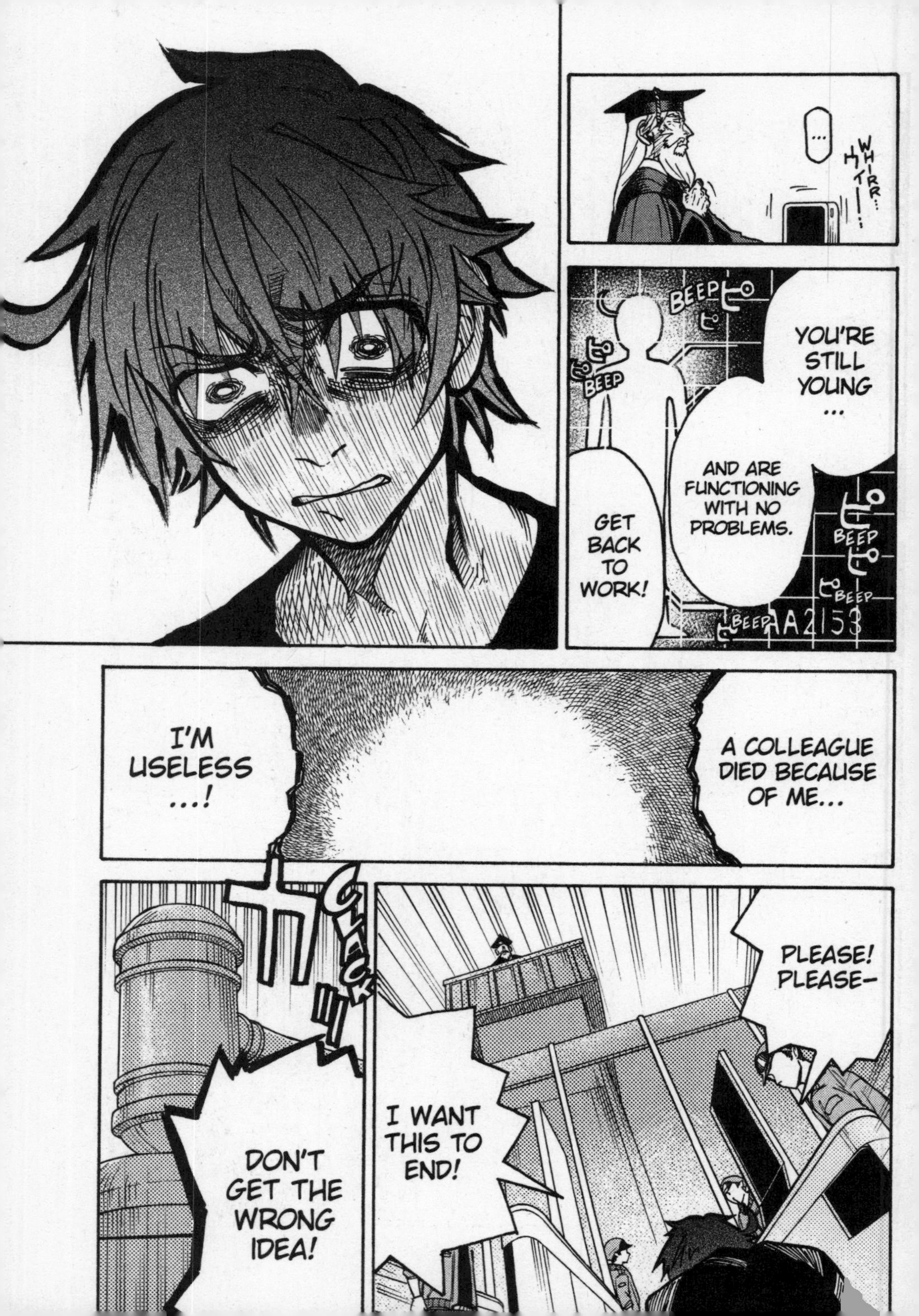
...
WHIRR...
BEEP
BEEP
YOU'RE STILL YOUNG...
AND ARE FUNCTIONING WITH NO PROBLEMS.
GET BACK TO WORK!
BEEP
BEEP
BEEP
AA2153
A COLLEAGUE DIED BECAUSE OF ME...
I'M USELESS...!
PLEASE! PLEASE-
I WANT THIS TO END!
CLACK
DON'T GET THE WRONG IDEA!

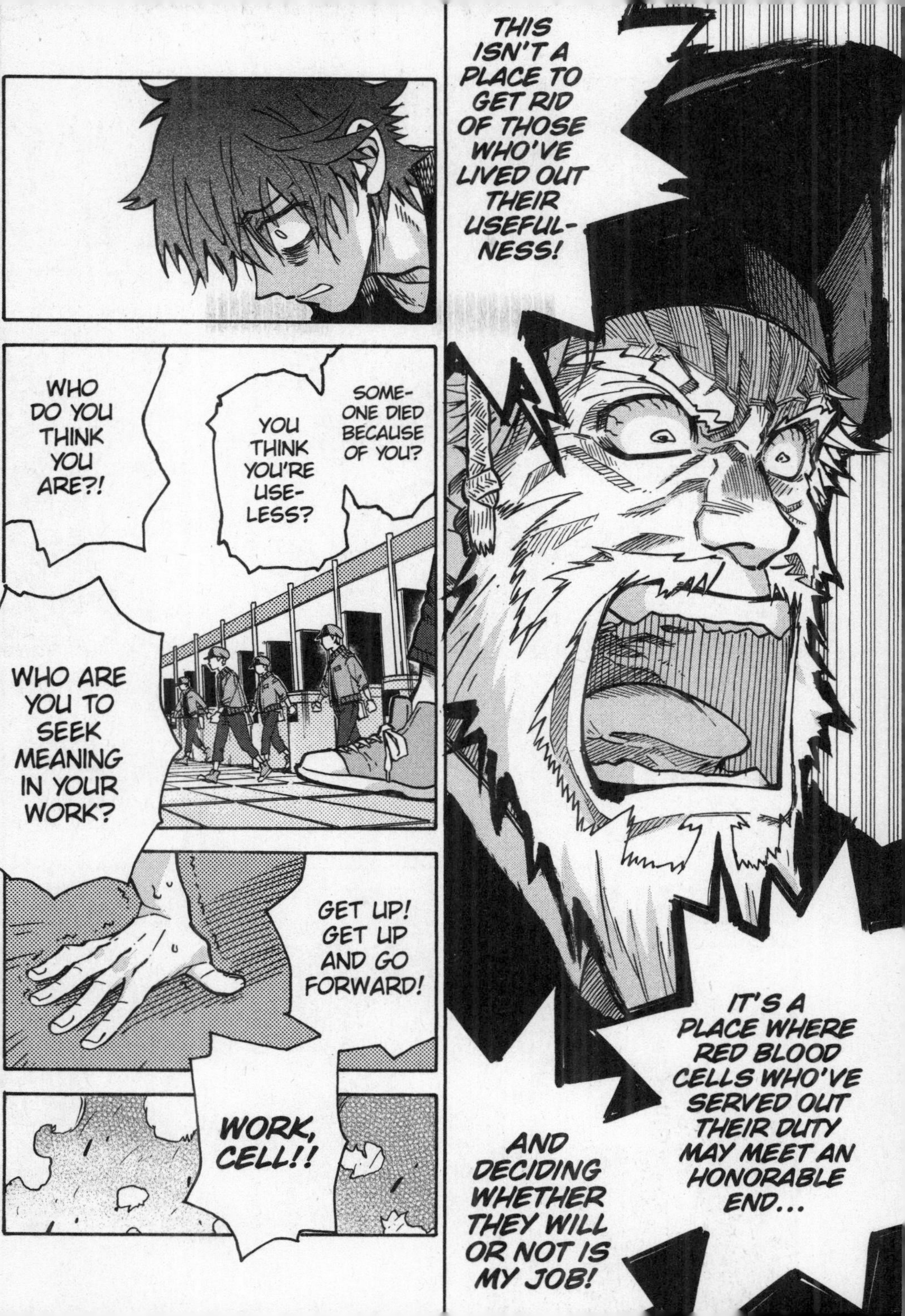
THIS ISN'T A PLACE TO GET RID OF THOSE WHO'VE LIVED OUT THEIR USEFUL-NESS!
IT'S A PLACE WHERE RED BLOOD CELLS WHO'VE SERVED OUT THEIR DUTY MAY MEET AN HONORABLE END...
AND DECIDING WHETHER THEY WILL OR NOT IS MY JOB!
SOME-ONE DIED BECAUSE OF YOU?
YOU THINK YOU'RE USE-LESS?
WHO DO YOU THINK YOU ARE?!
WHO ARE YOU TO SEEK MEANING IN YOUR WORK?
GET UP! GET UP AND GO FORWARD!
WORK, CELL!!

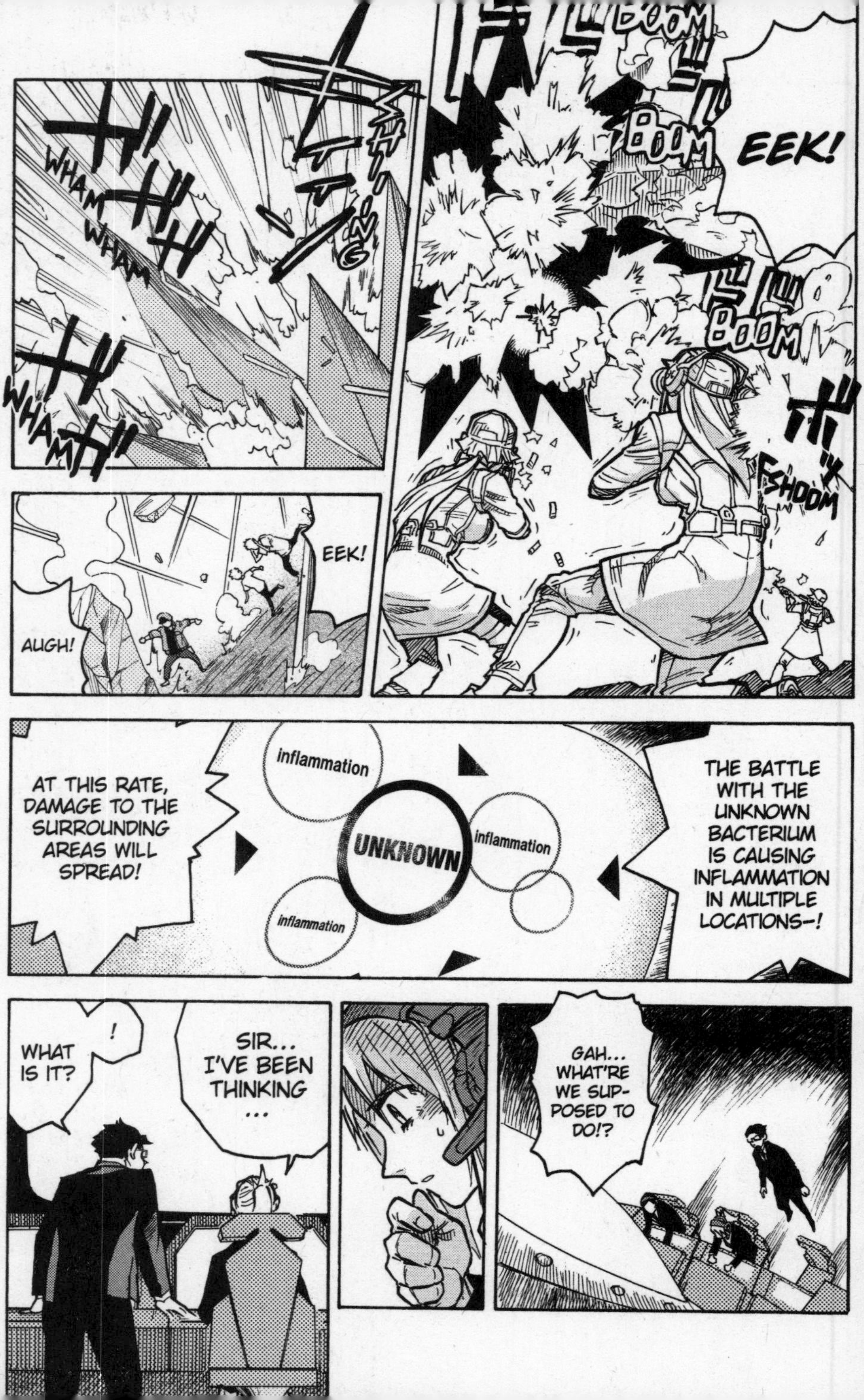
BOOM
BOOM
EEK!
BOOM
FSHOOM
WHIIING
WHAM
WHAM
WHAM
WHAM
EEK!
AUGH!
THE BATTLE WITH THE UNKNOWN BACTERIUM IS CAUSING INFLAMMATION IN MULTIPLE LOCATIONS--!
inflammation
UNKNOWN
inflammation
inflammation
AT THIS RATE, DAMAGE TO THE SURROUNDING AREAS WILL SPREAD!
GAH... WHAT'RE WE SUP-POSED TO DO!?
SIR... I'VE BEEN THINKING...
!
WHAT IS IT?

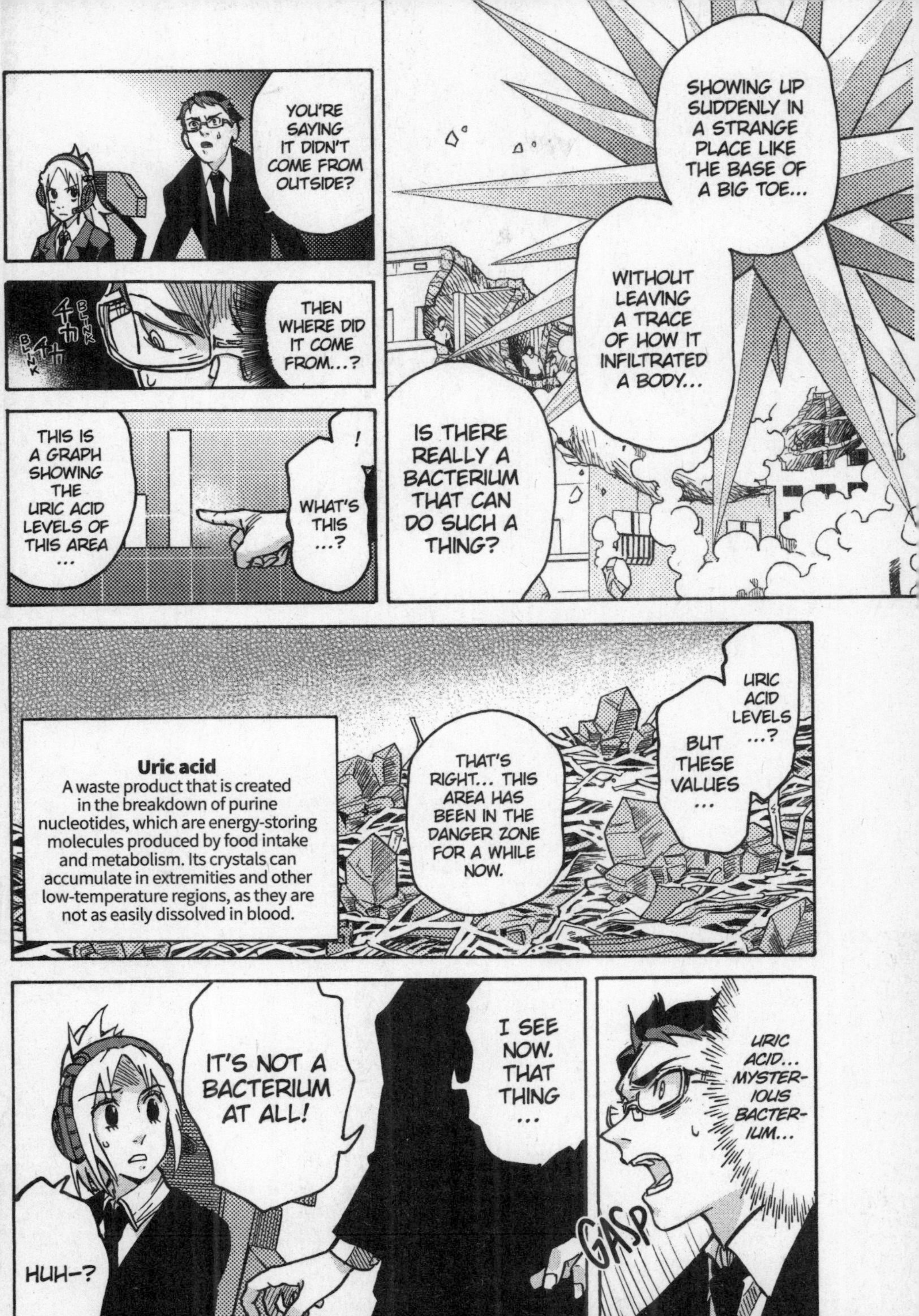
SHOWING UP SUDDENLY IN A STRANGE PLACE LIKE THE BASE OF A BIG TOE...
WITHOUT LEAVING A TRACE OF HOW IT INFILTRATED A BODY...
IS THERE REALLY A BACTERIUM THAT CAN DO SUCH A THING?
YOU'RE SAYING IT DIDN'T COME FROM OUTSIDE?
THEN WHERE DID IT COME FROM...?
BLINK BLINK
!
WHAT'S THIS ...?
THIS IS A GRAPH SHOWING THE URIC ACID LEVELS OF THIS AREA ...
URIC ACID LEVELS ...?
BUT THESE VALUES ...
THAT'S RIGHT... THIS AREA HAS BEEN IN THE DANGER ZONE FOR A WHILE NOW.
Uric acid
A waste product that is created in the breakdown of purine nucleotides, which are energy-storing molecules produced by food intake and metabolism. Its crystals can accumulate in extremities and other low-temperature regions, as they are not as easily dissolved in blood.
URIC ACID... MYSTERIOUS BACTERIUM...
GASP
I SEE NOW. THAT THING ...
IT'S NOT A BACTERIUM AT ALL!
HUH-?

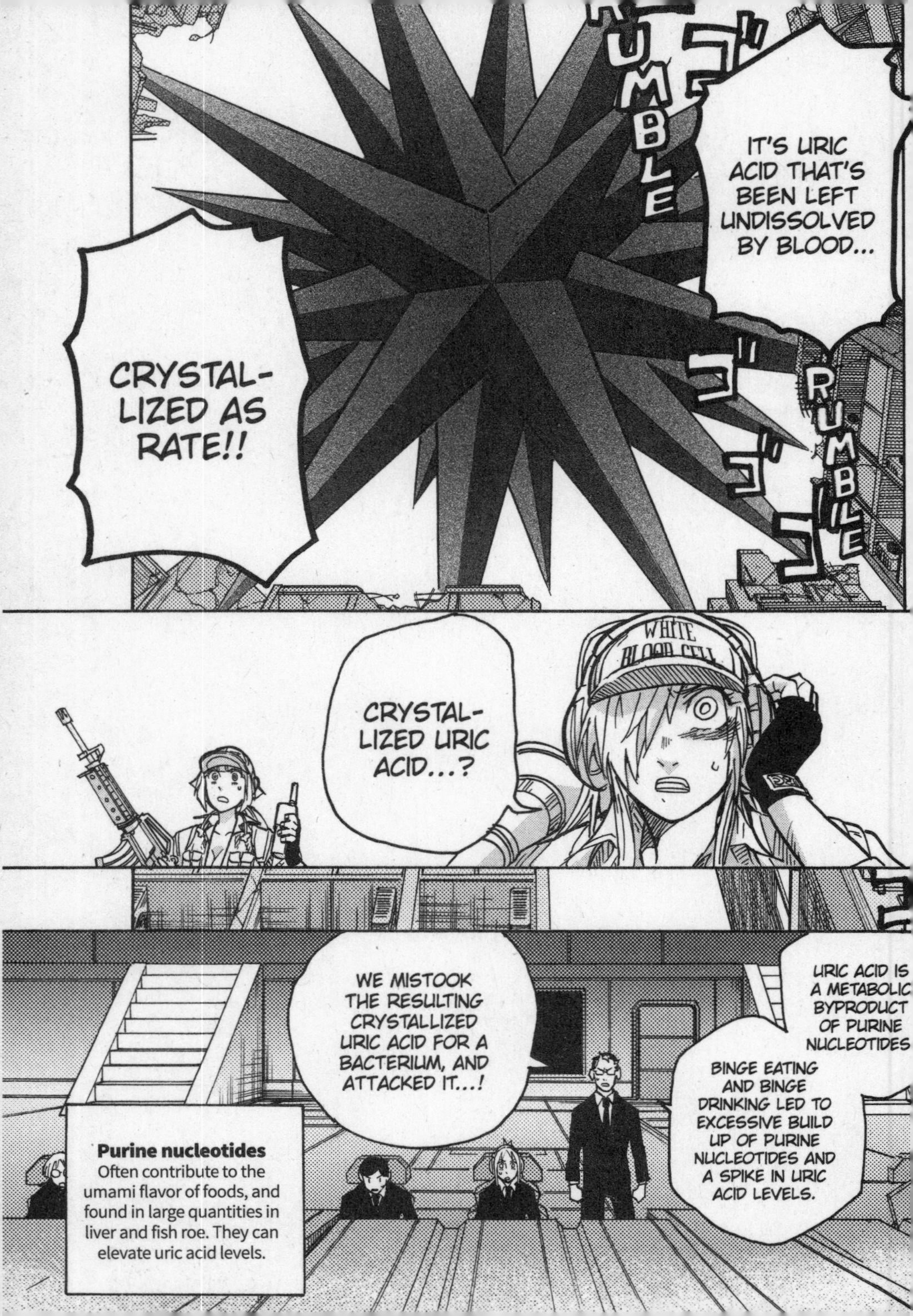
RUMBLE
IT'S URIC ACID THAT'S BEEN LEFT UNDISSOLVED BY BLOOD...
RUMBLE
CRYSTAL-LIZED AS RATE!!
WHITE BLOOD CELL
CRYSTAL-LIZED URIC ACID...?
URIC ACID IS A METABOLIC BYPRODUCT OF PURINE NUCLEOTIDES
BINGE EATING AND BINGE DRINKING LED TO EXCESSIVE BUILD UP OF PURINE NUCLEOTIDES AND A SPIKE IN URIC ACID LEVELS.
WE MISTOOK THE RESULTING CRYSTALLIZED URIC ACID FOR A BACTERIUM, AND ATTACKED IT...!
Purine nucleotides
Often contribute to the umami flavor of foods, and found in large quantities in liver and fish roe. They can elevate uric acid levels.

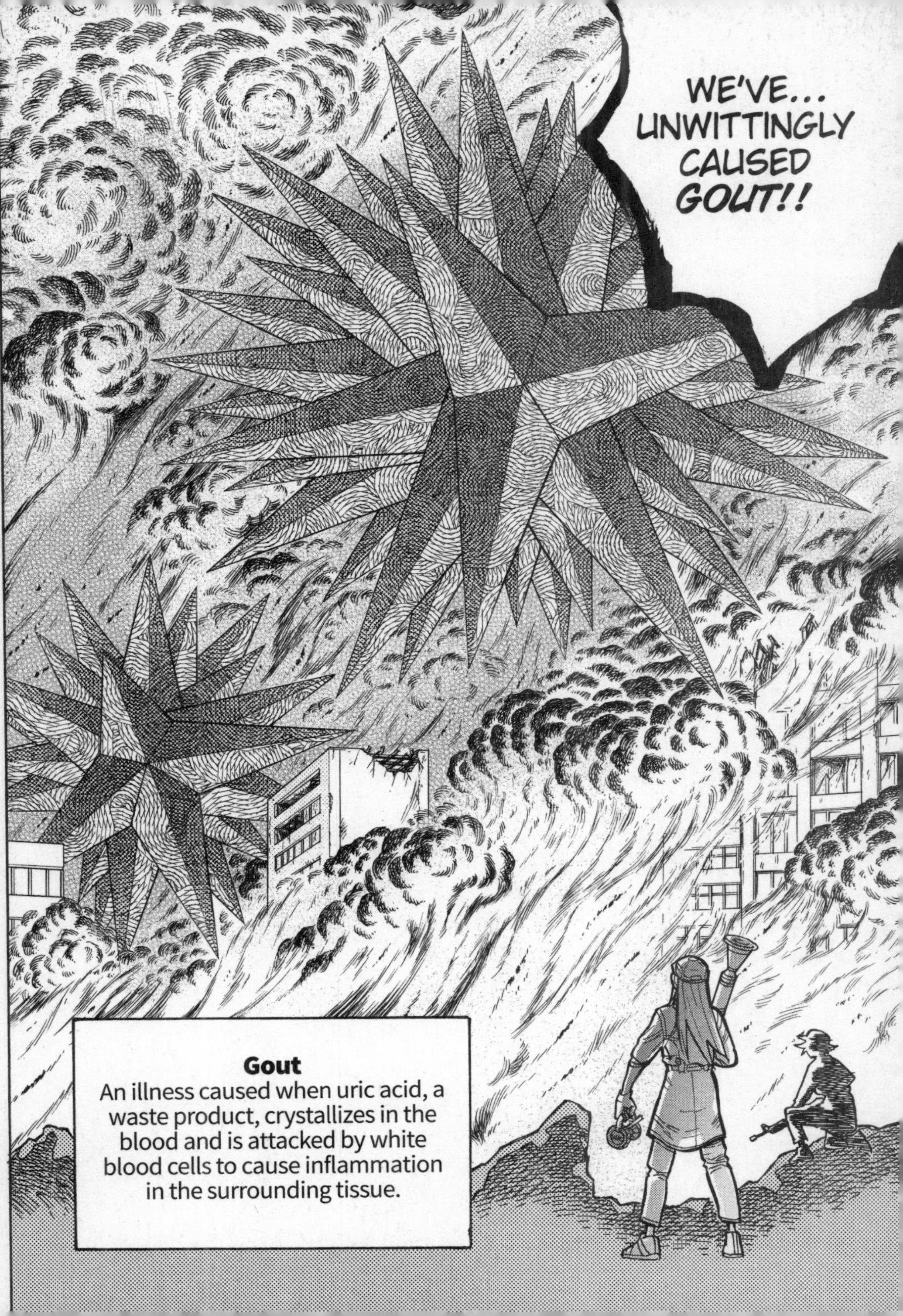
WE'VE... UNWITTINGLY CAUSED GOUT!!
Gout
An illness caused when uric acid, a waste product, crystallizes in the blood and is attacked by white blood cells to cause inflammation in the surrounding tissue.

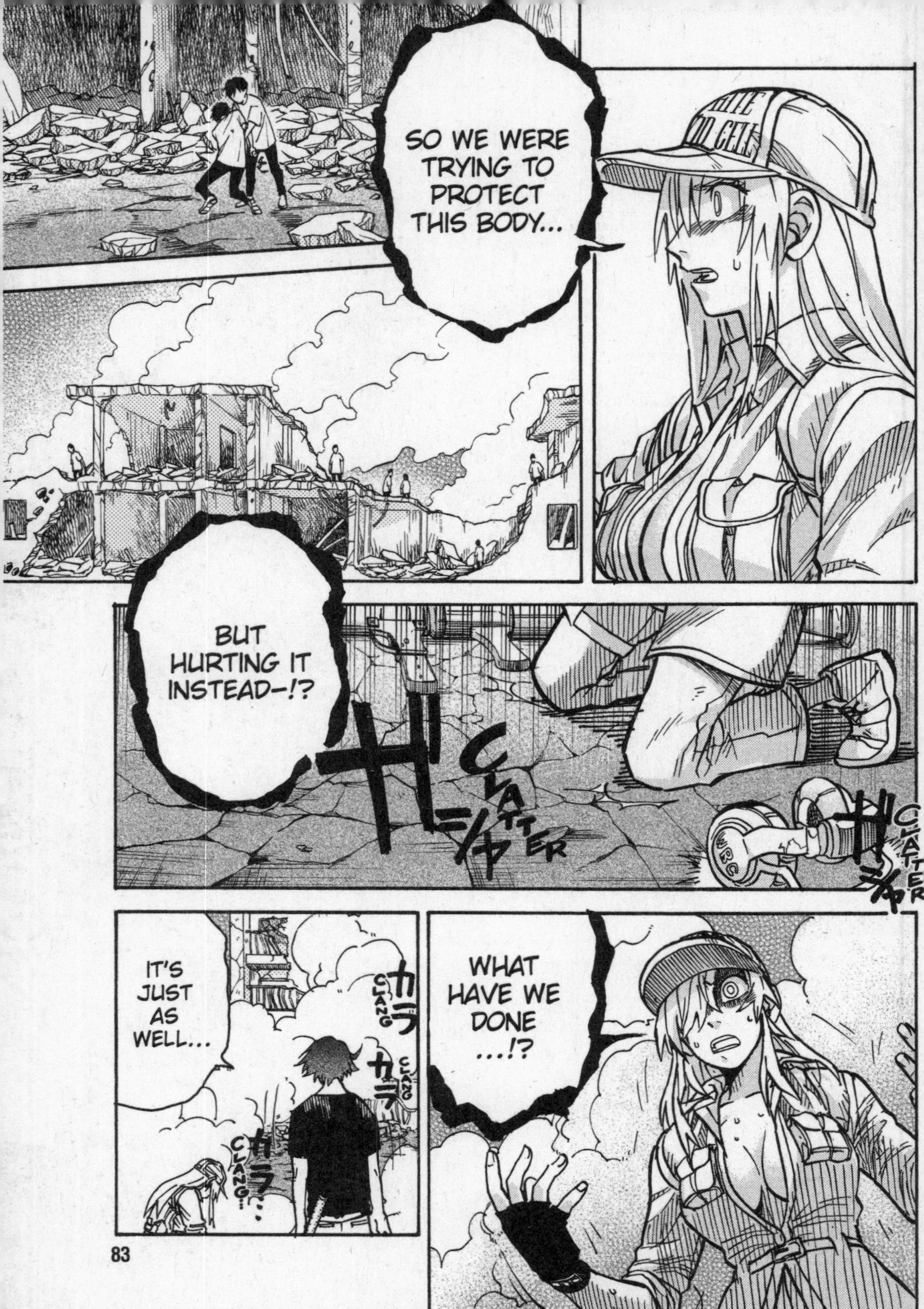
SO WE WERE TRYING TO PROTECT THIS BODY...
BUT HURTING IT INSTEAD-!?
CLATTER
CLATTER
WHAT HAVE WE DONE ...!?
IT'S JUST AS WELL...
CLANG
CLANG
CLANG...

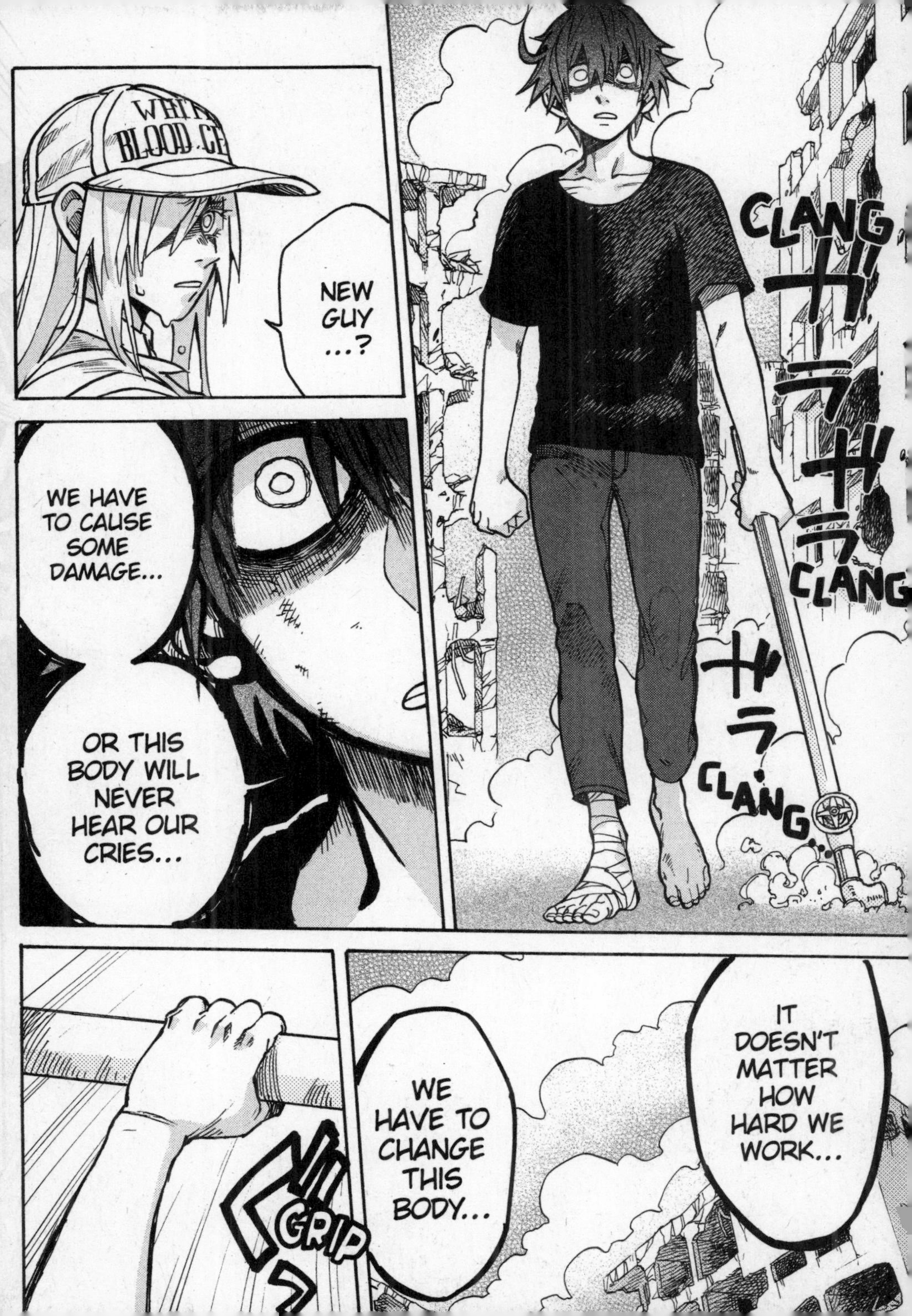
CLANG
CLANG
CLANG...
NEW GUY ...?
WE HAVE TO CAUSE SOME DAMAGE...
OR THIS BODY WILL NEVER HEAR OUR CRIES...
IT DOESN'T MATTER HOW HARD WE WORK...
WE HAVE TO CHANGE THIS BODY...
GRIP

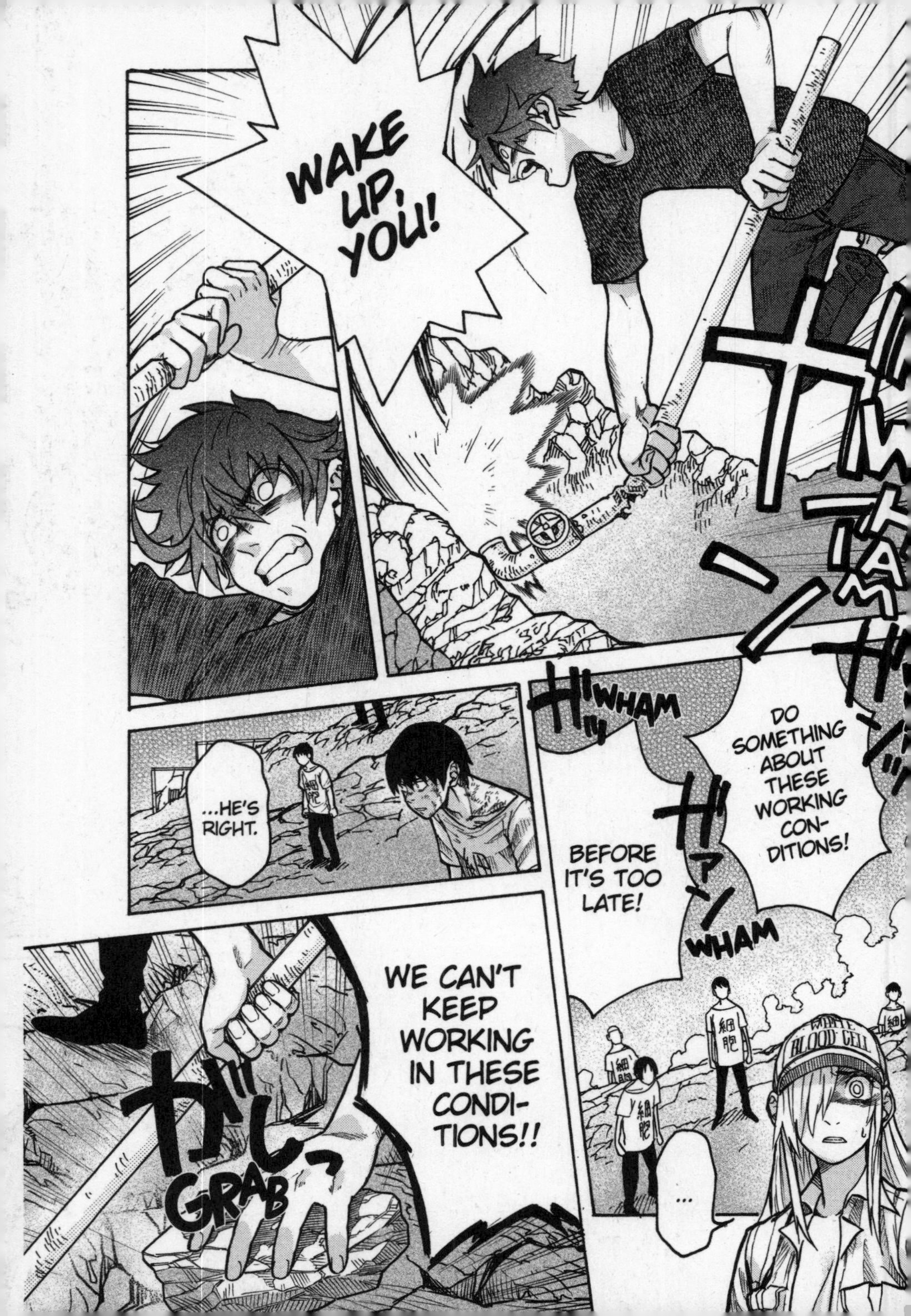
WHAM
WAKE UP, YOU!
WHAM
DO SOMETHING ABOUT THESE WORKING CON-DITIONS!
BEFORE IT'S TOO LATE!
WHAM
...HE'S RIGHT.
...
WE CAN'T KEEP WORKING IN THESE CONDI-TIONS!!
GRAB

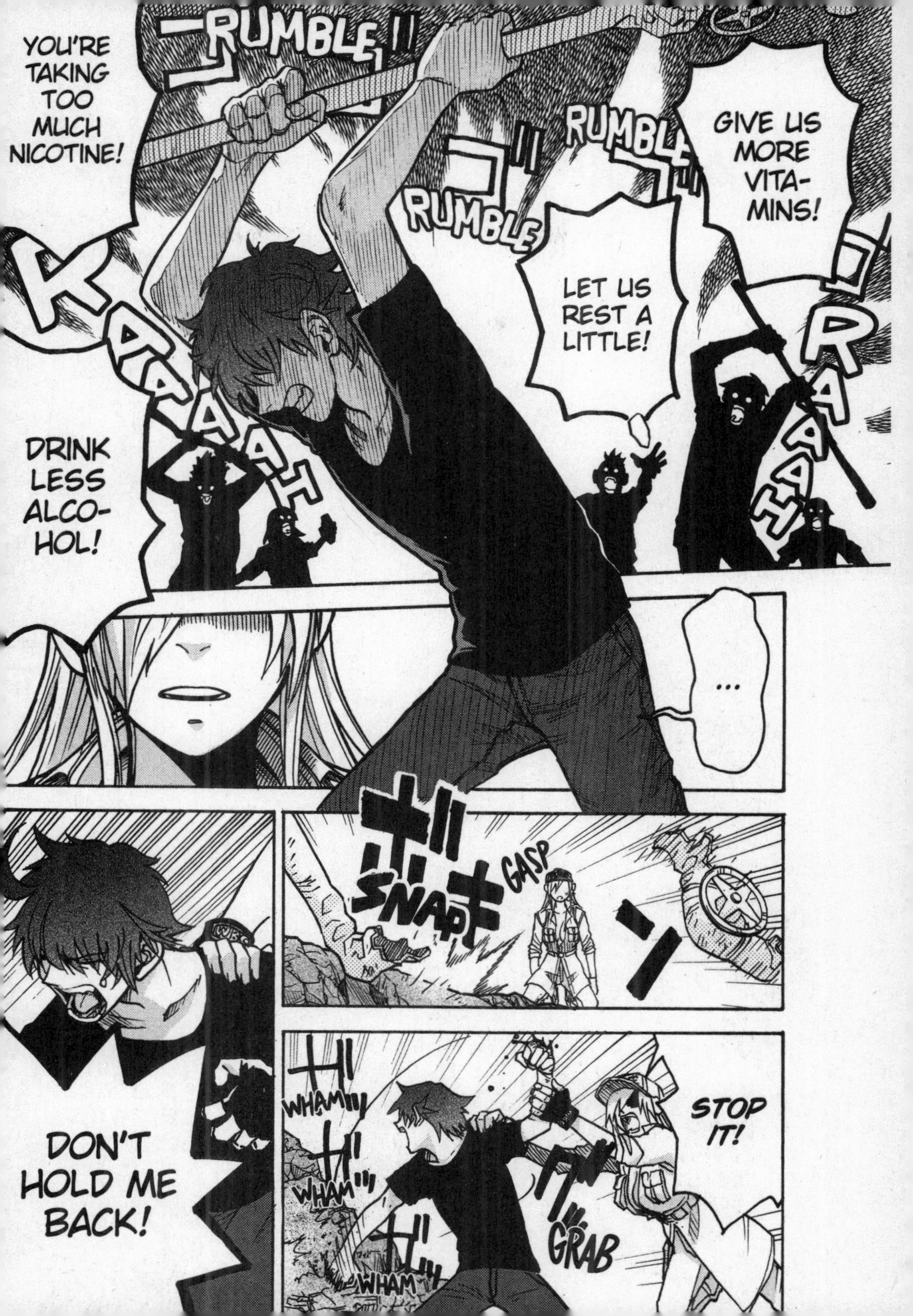
GIVE US MORE VITA-MINS!
RAAAH
LET US REST A LITTLE!
RUMBLE
RUMBLE
RUMBLE
YOU'RE TAKING TOO MUCH NICOTINE!
KAAAAH
DRINK LESS ALCO-HOL!
...
GASP
SNAP
STOP IT!
GRAB
WHAM
WHAM
WHAM
DON'T HOLD ME BACK!

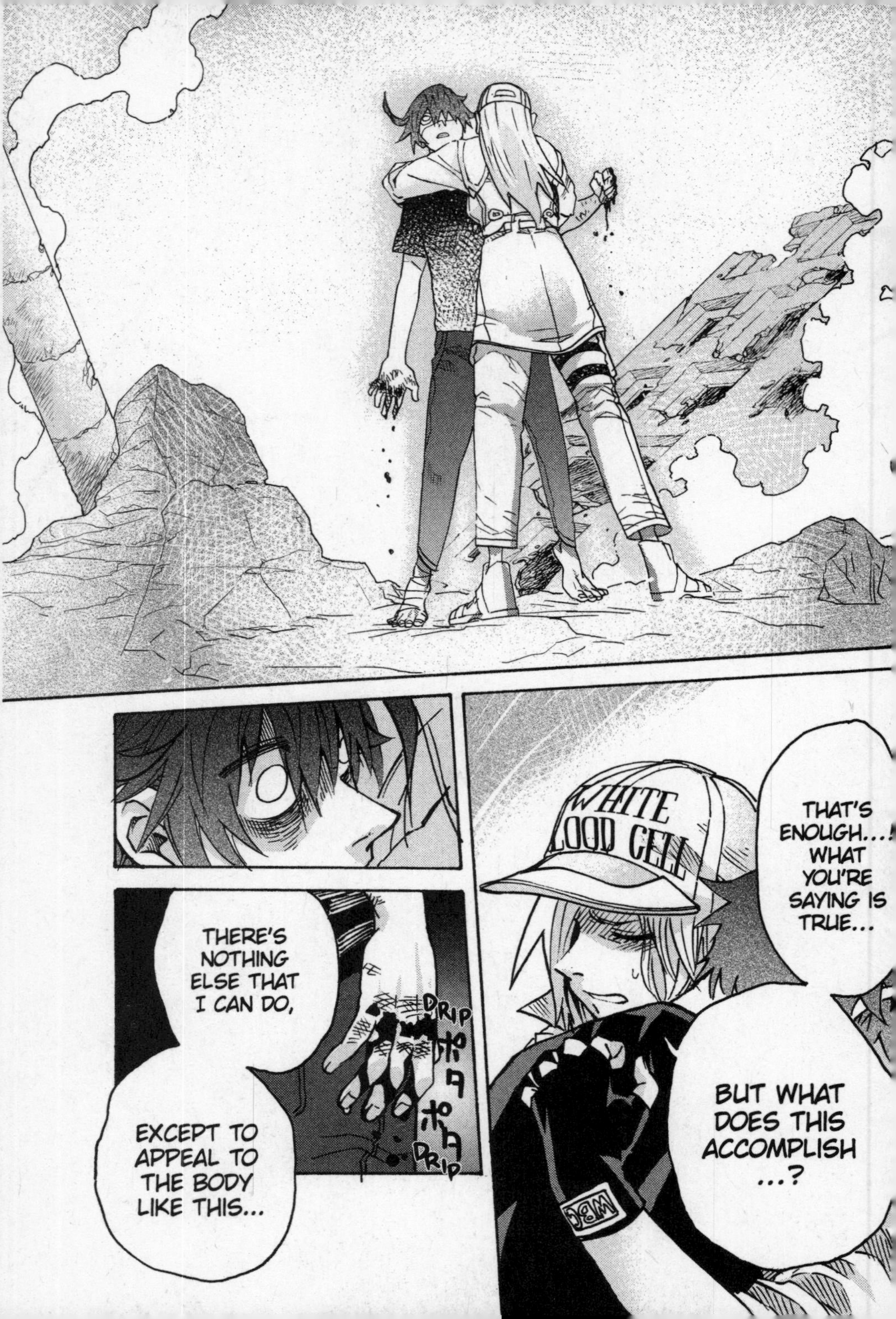
THAT'S ENOUGH.... WHAT YOU'RE SAYING IS TRUE...
BUT WHAT DOES THIS ACCOMPLISH ...?
THERE'S NOTHING ELSE THAT I CAN DO,
DRIP
ポタ
ポタ
DRIP
EXCEPT TO APPEAL TO THE BODY LIKE THIS...

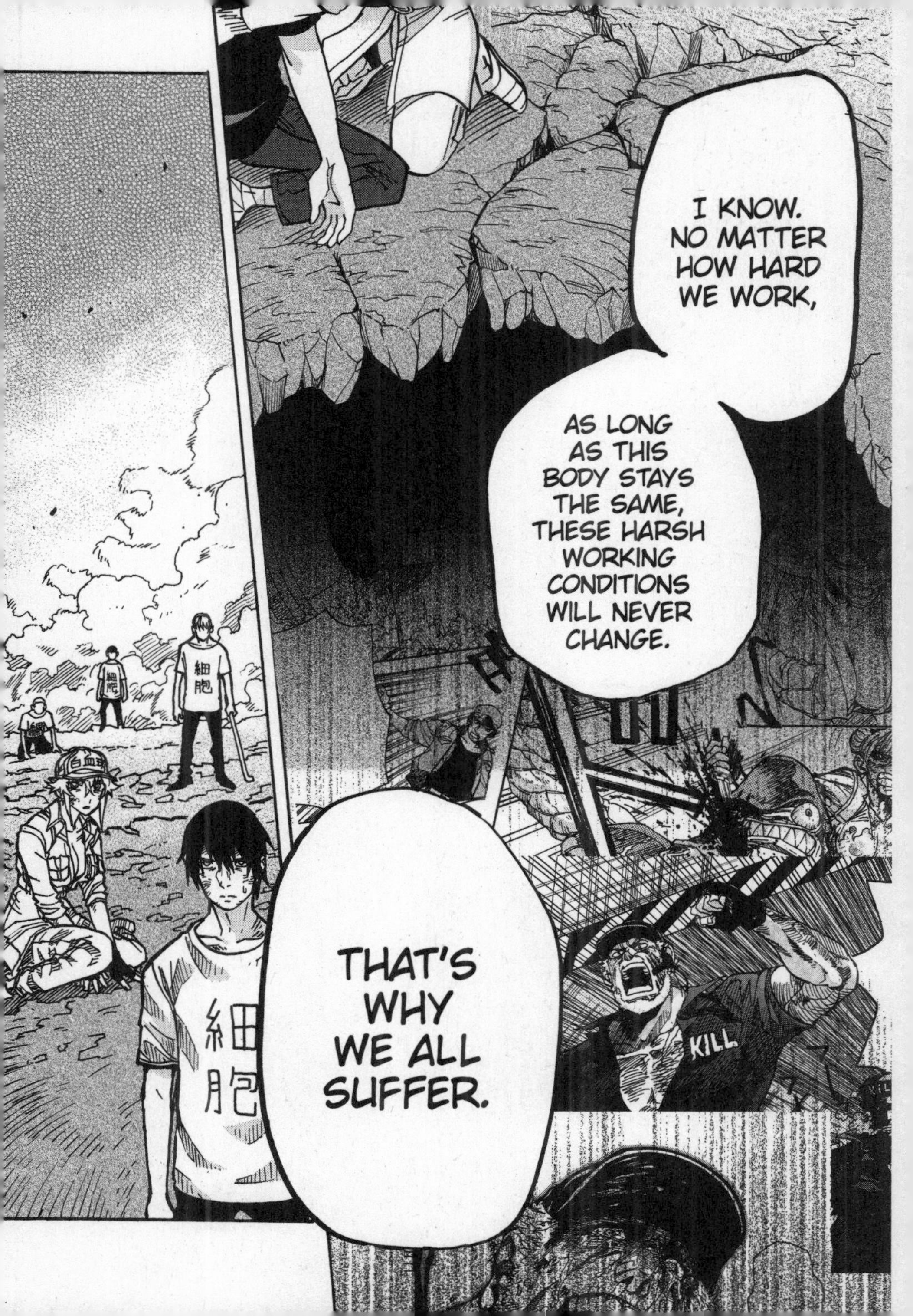
I KNOW. NO MATTER HOW HARD WE WORK,
AS LONG AS THIS BODY STAYS THE SAME, THESE HARSH WORKING CONDITIONS WILL NEVER CHANGE.
THAT'S WHY WE ALL SUFFER.
KILL
細胞

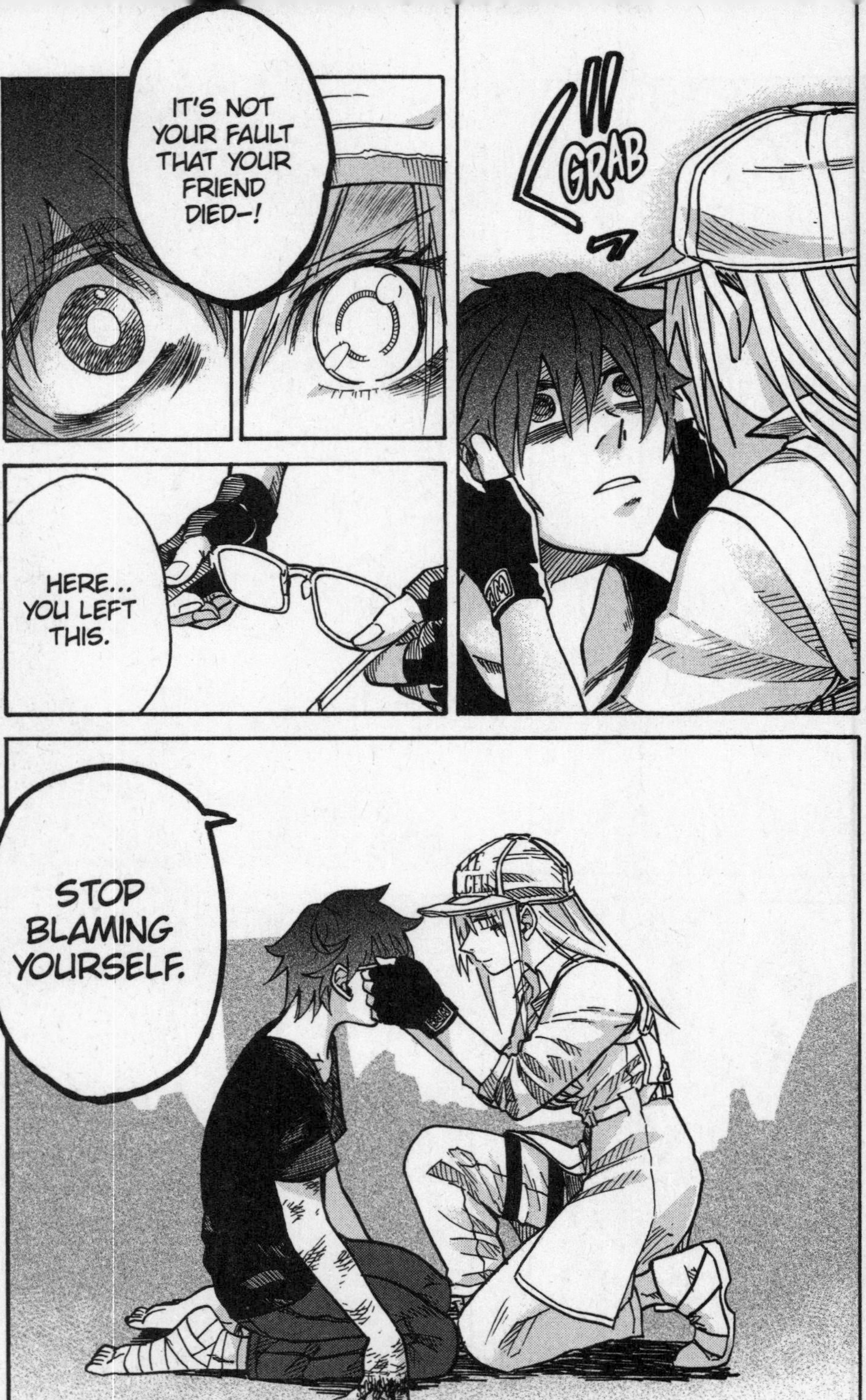
GRAB
IT'S NOT YOUR FAULT THAT YOUR FRIEND DIED-!
HERE... YOU LEFT THIS.
STOP BLAMING YOURSELF.

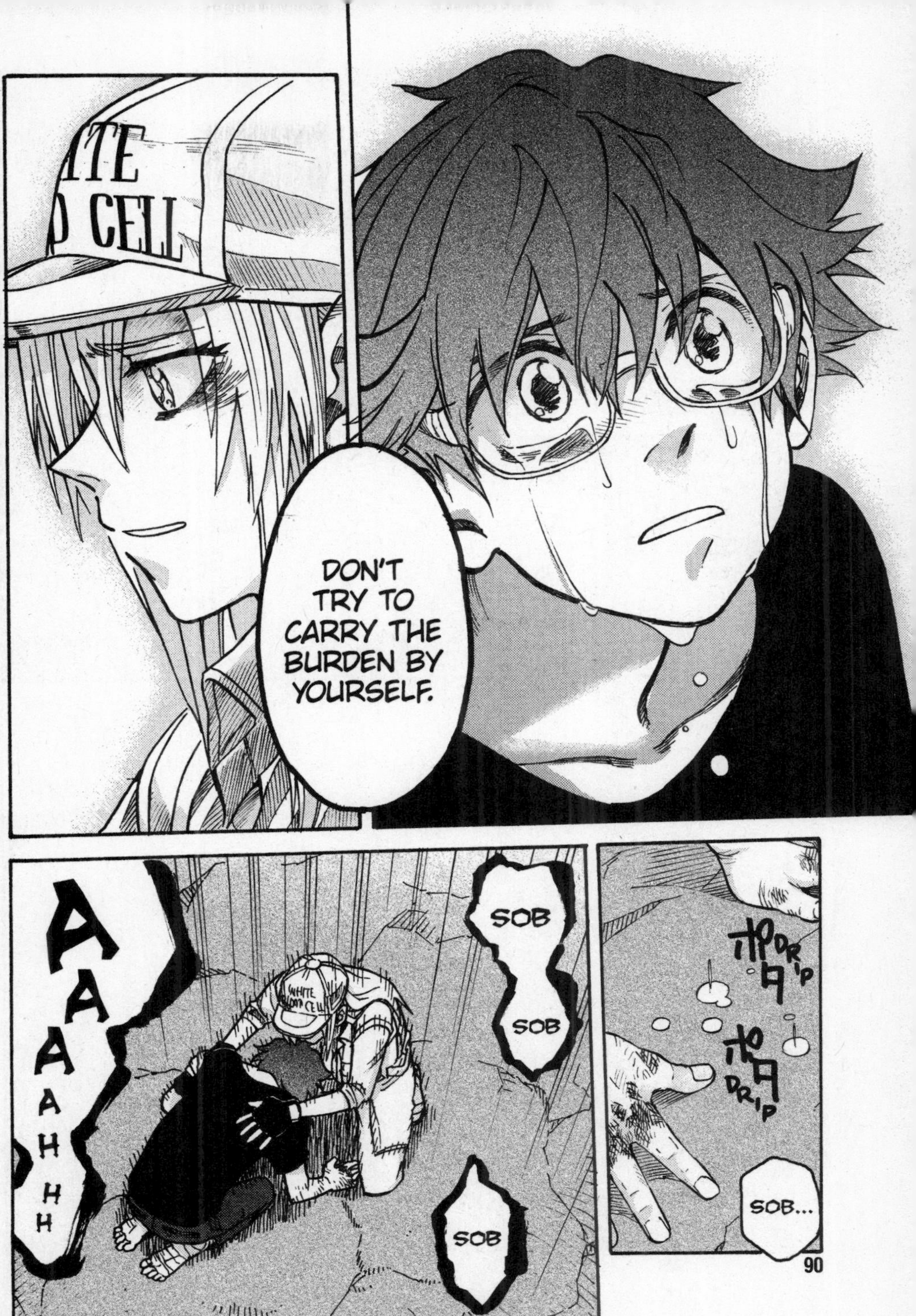
DON'T TRY TO CARRY THE BURDEN BY YOURSELF.
DRIP
DRIP
SOB...
SOB
SOB
AAAAHHH
SOB

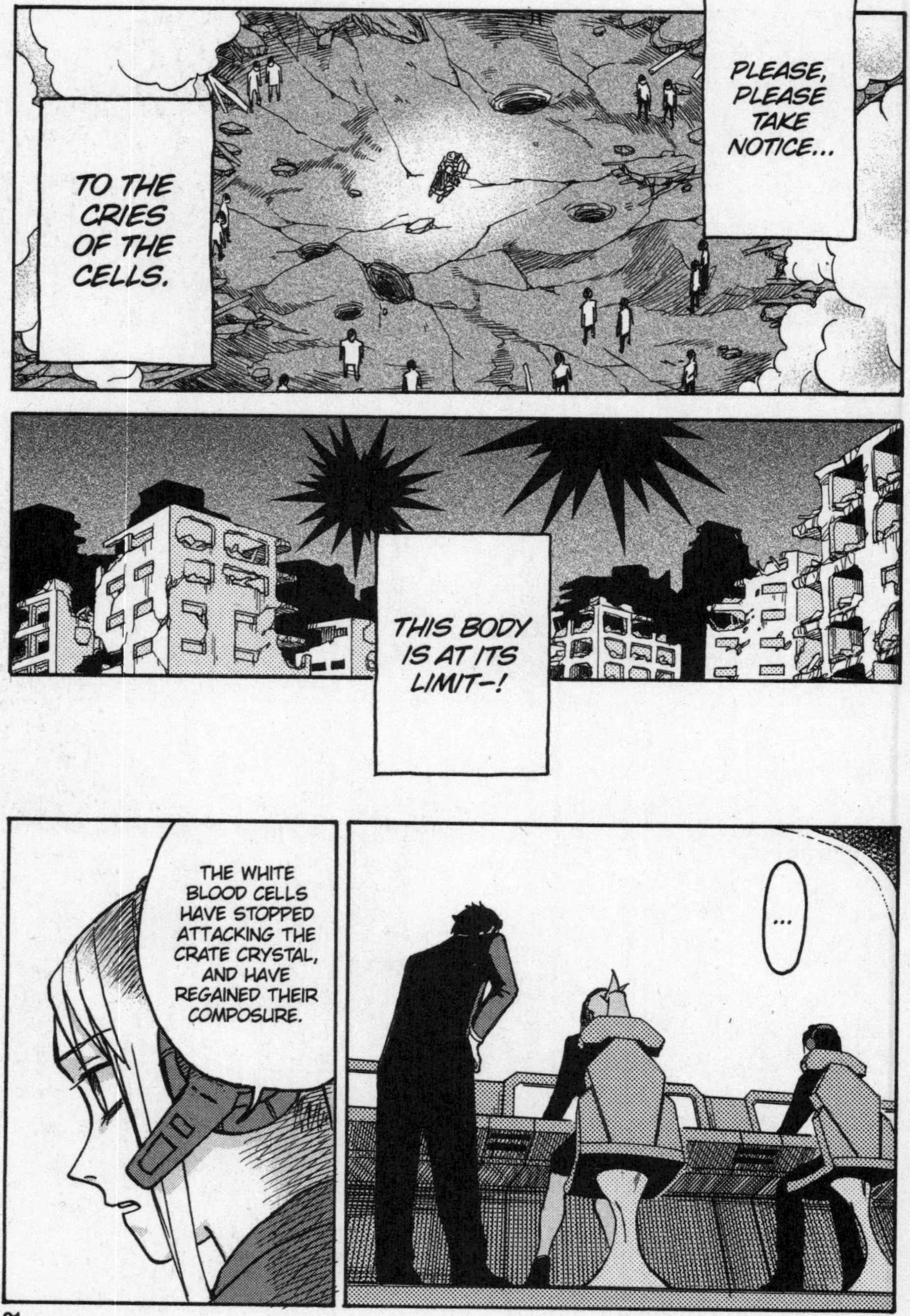
PLEASE, PLEASE TAKE NOTICE...
TO THE CRIES OF THE CELLS.
THIS BODY IS AT ITS LIMIT-!
...
THE WHITE BLOOD CELLS HAVE STOPPED ATTACKING THE CRATE CRYSTAL, AND HAVE REGAINED THEIR COMPOSURE.

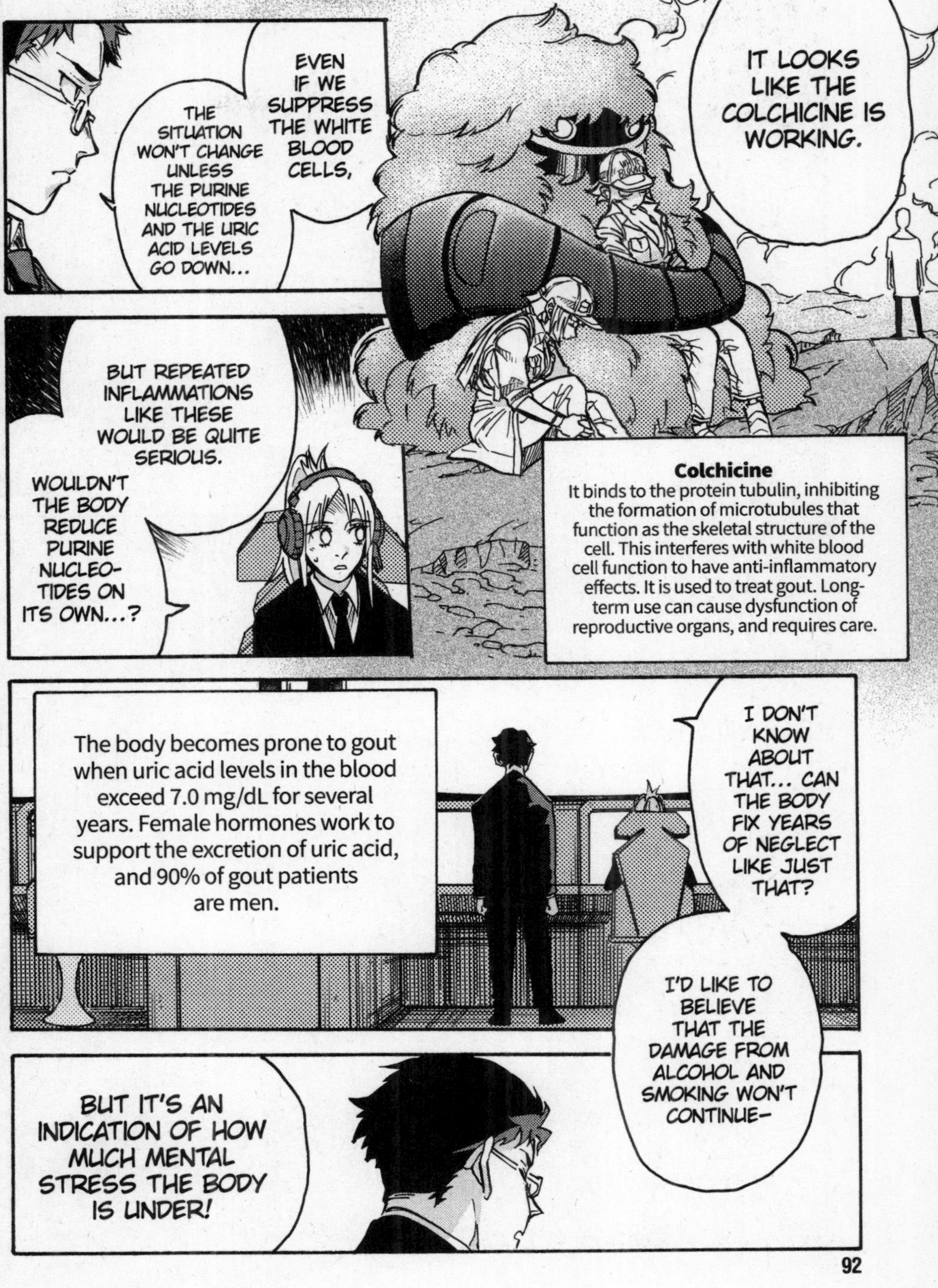
IT LOOKS LIKE THE COLCHICINE IS WORKING.
Colchicine
It binds to the protein tubulin, inhibiting the formation of microtubules that function as the skeletal structure of the cell. This interferes with white blood cell function to have anti-inflammatory effects. It is used to treat gout. Long-term use can cause dysfunction of reproductive organs, and requires care.
EVEN IF WE SUPPRESS THE WHITE BLOOD CELLS,
THE SITUATION WON'T CHANGE UNLESS THE PURINE NUCLEOTIDES AND THE URIC ACID LEVELS GO DOWN...
BUT REPEATED INFLAMMATIONS LIKE THESE WOULD BE QUITE SERIOUS.
WOULDN'T THE BODY REDUCE PURINE NUCLEO-TIDES ON ITS OWN...?
I DON'T KNOW ABOUT THAT... CAN THE BODY FIX YEARS OF NEGLECT LIKE JUST THAT?
The body becomes prone to gout when uric acid levels in the blood exceed 7.0 mg/dL for several years. Female hormones work to support the excretion of uric acid, and 90% of gout patients are men.
I'D LIKE TO BELIEVE THAT THE DAMAGE FROM ALCOHOL AND SMOKING WON'T CONTINUE—
BUT IT'S AN INDICATION OF HOW MUCH MENTAL STRESS THE BODY IS UNDER!

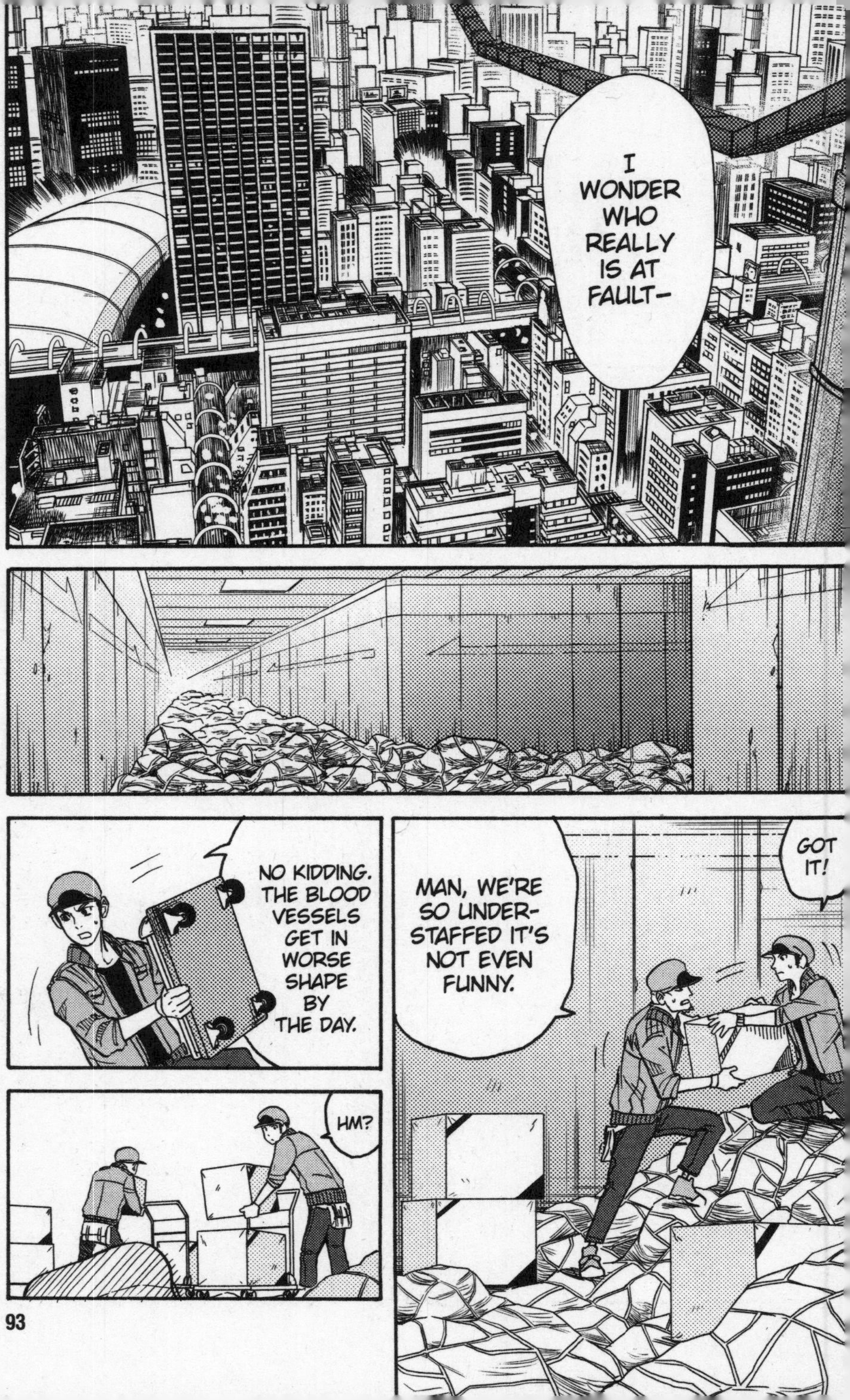
I WONDER WHO REALLY IS AT FAULT–
GOT IT!
MAN, WE'RE SO UNDER-STAFFED IT'S NOT EVEN FUNNY.
NO KIDDING. THE BLOOD VESSELS GET IN WORSE SHAPE BY THE DAY.
HM?

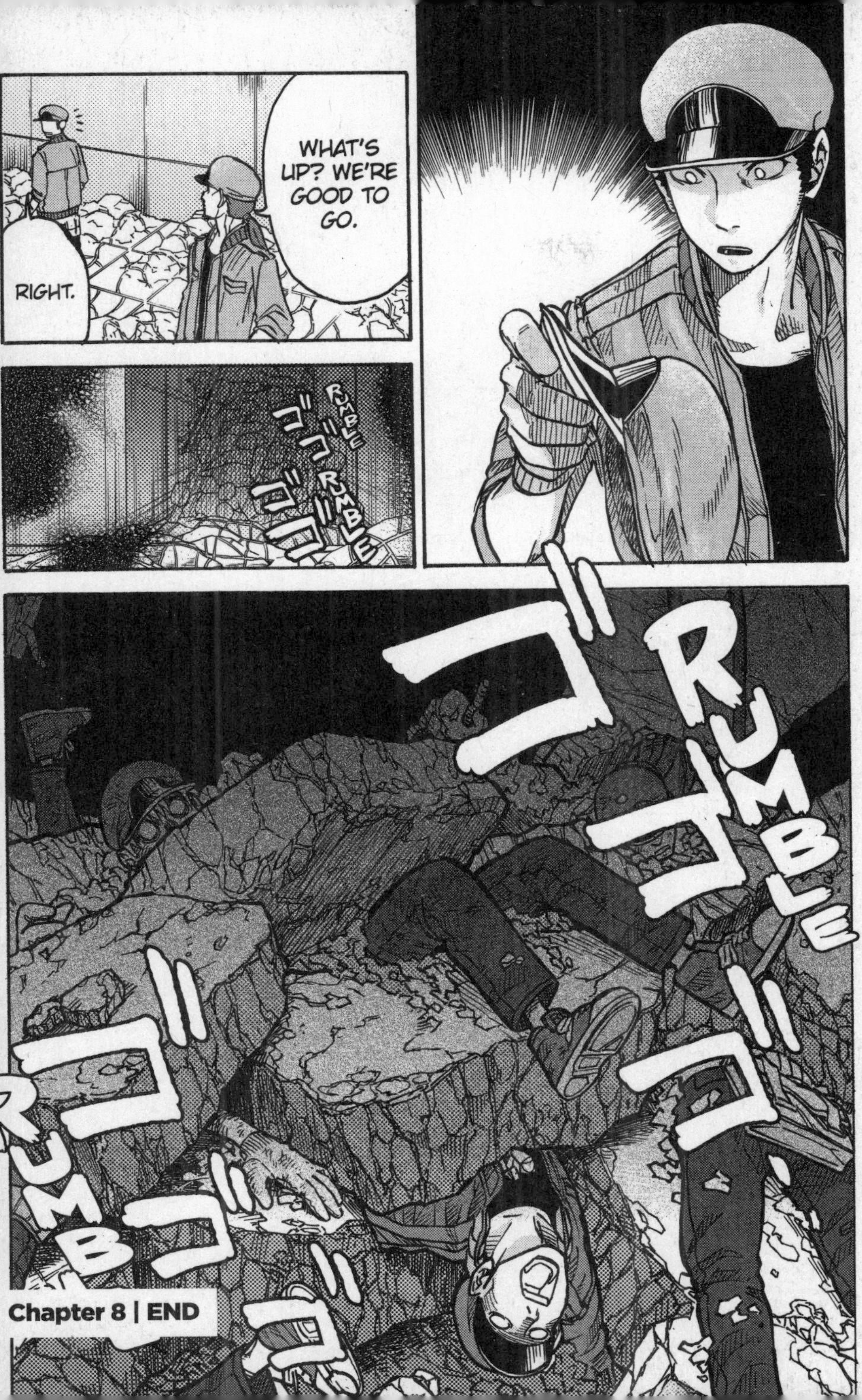
WHAT'S UP? WE'RE GOOD TO GO.
RIGHT.
RUMBLE ゴゴ RUMBLE ゴゴ
ゴゴ RUMBLE
ゴゴ RUMB

Chapter 8 | END

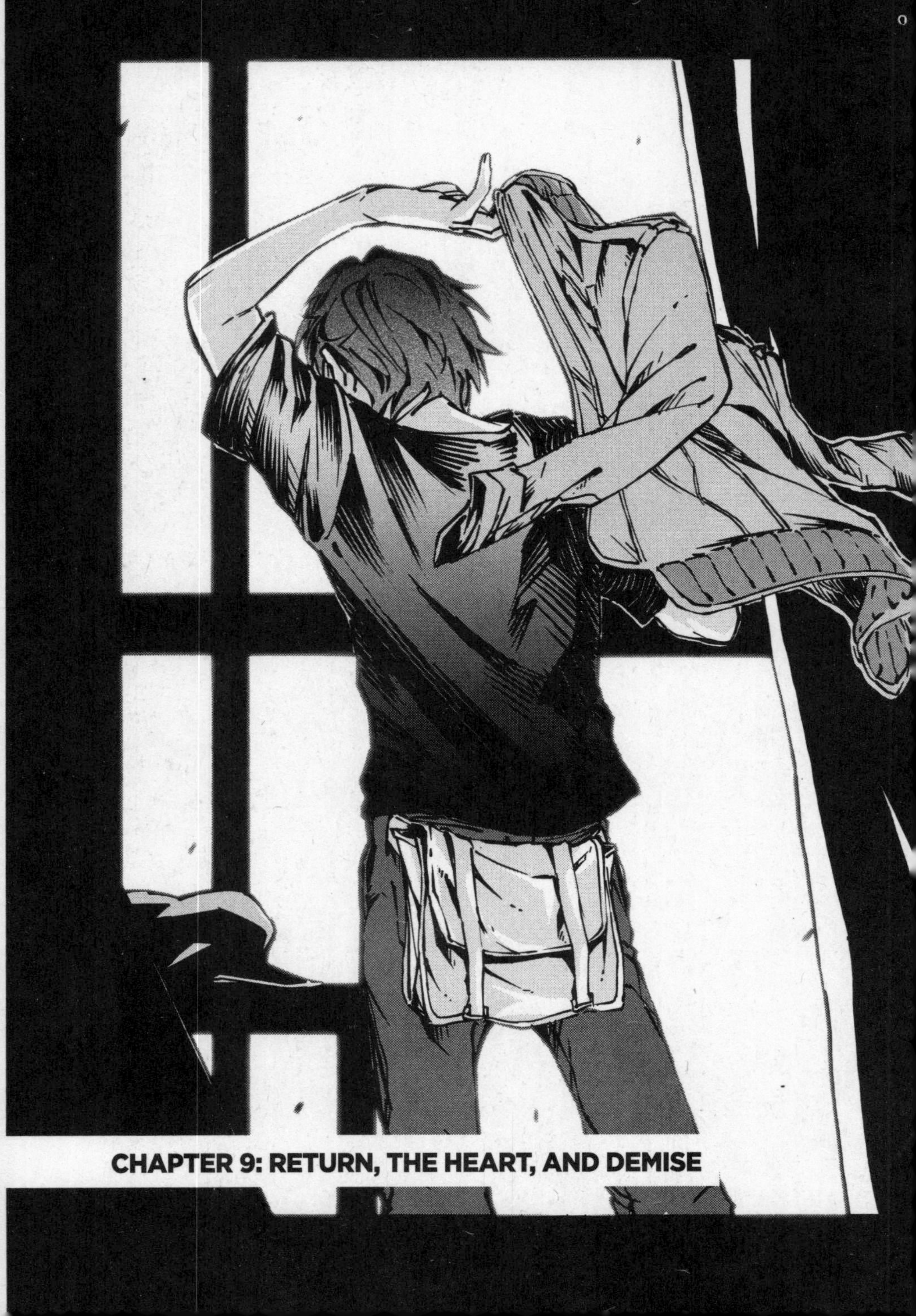
CHAPTER 9: RETURN, THE HEART, AND DEMISE

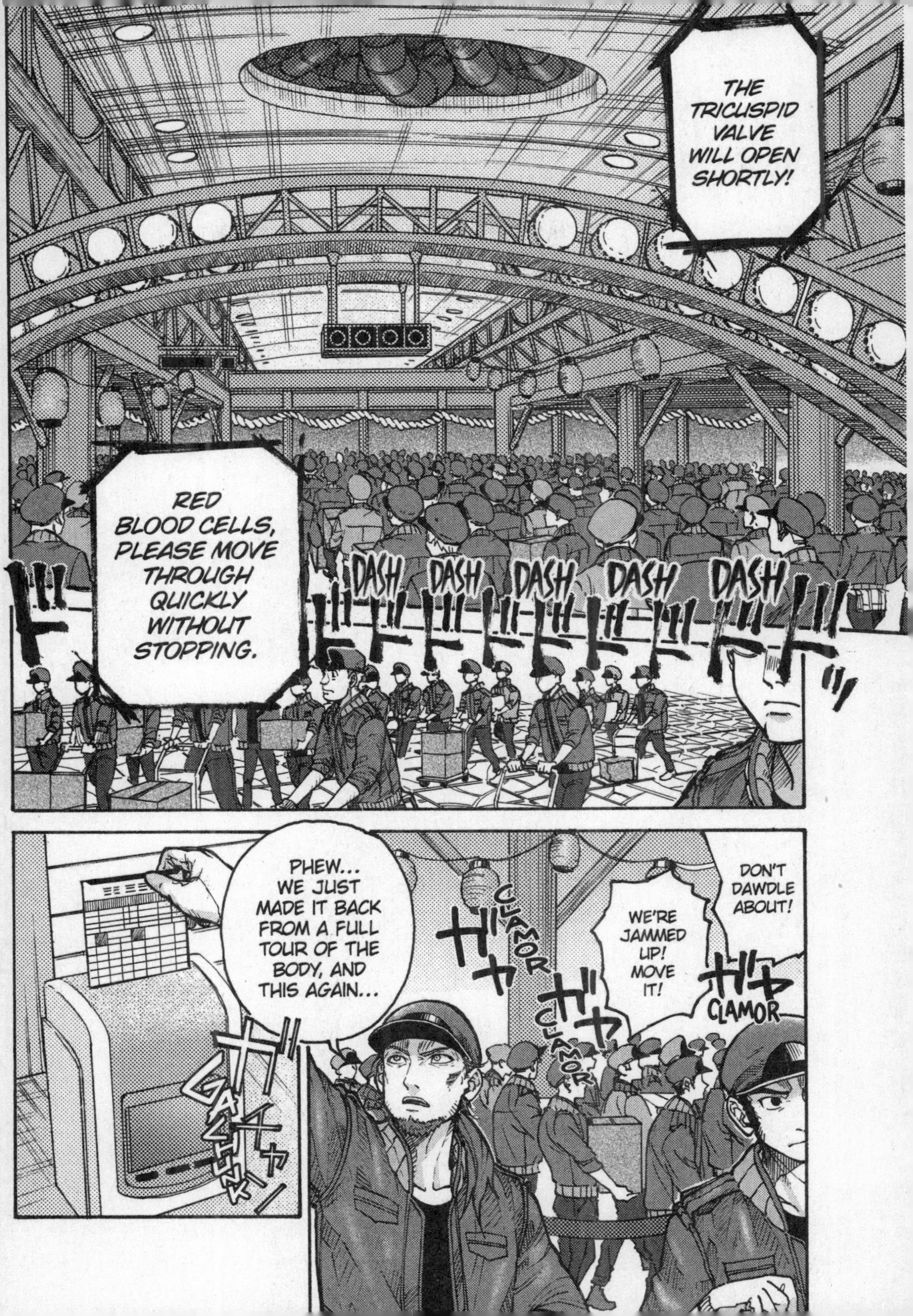
THE TRICUSPID VALVE WILL OPEN SHORTLY!
RED BLOOD CELLS, PLEASE MOVE THROUGH QUICKLY WITHOUT STOPPING.
DASH DASH DASH DASH DASH
DON'T DAWDLE ABOUT!
WE'RE JAMMED UP! MOVE IT!
CLAMOR
CLAMOR
CLAMOR
PHEW... WE JUST MADE IT BACK FROM A FULL TOUR OF THE BODY, AND THIS AGAIN...
CLAMOR
GACHUNK

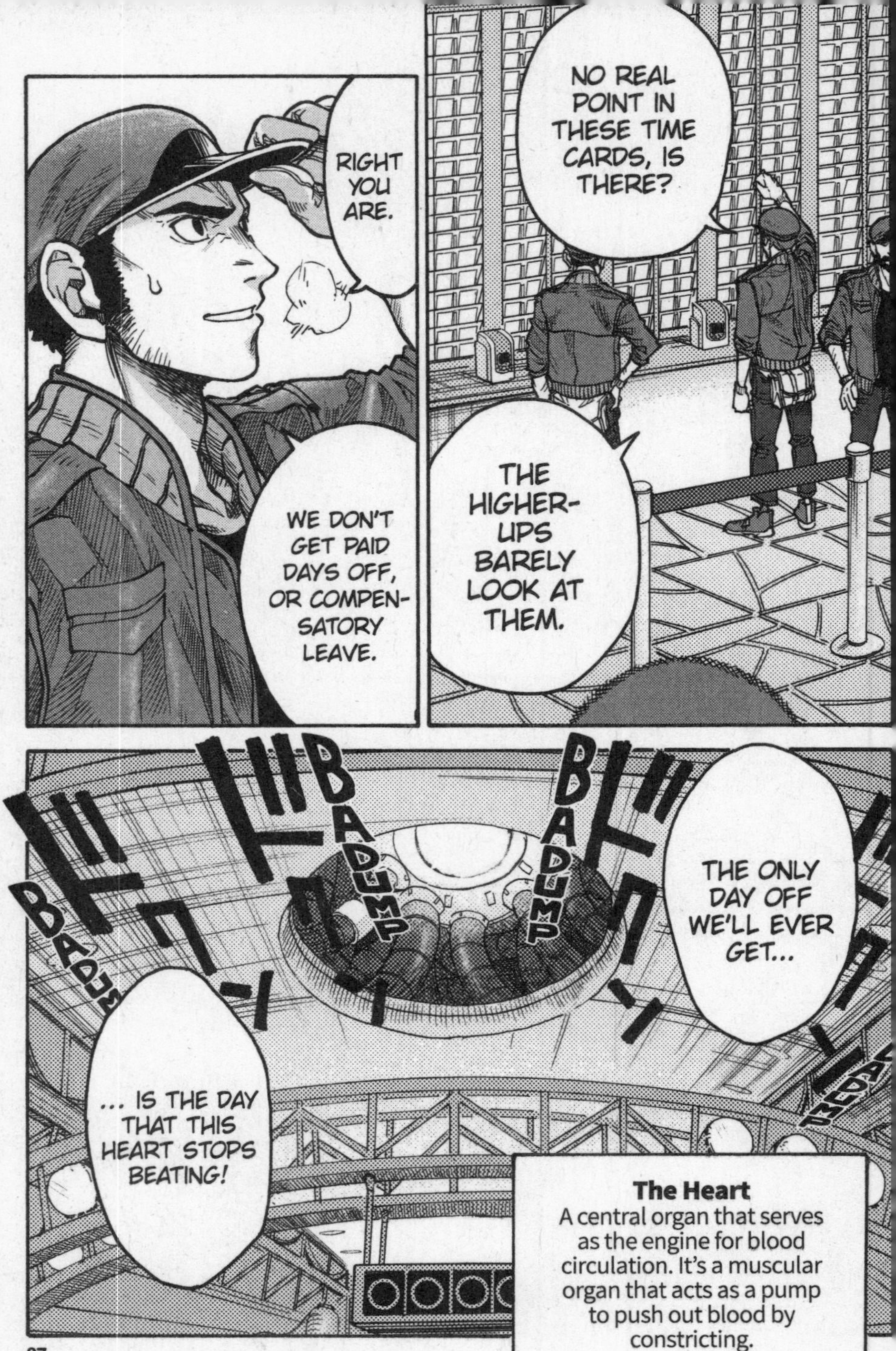
NO REAL POINT IN THESE TIME CARDS, IS THERE?
THE HIGHER-UPS BARELY LOOK AT THEM.
RIGHT YOU ARE.
WE DON'T GET PAID DAYS OFF, OR COMPEN-SATORY LEAVE.
BADUMP
BADUMP
THE ONLY DAY OFF WE'LL EVER GET...
... IS THE DAY THAT THIS HEART STOPS BEATING!
The Heart
A central organ that serves as the engine for blood circulation. It's a muscular organ that acts as a pump to push out blood by constricting.

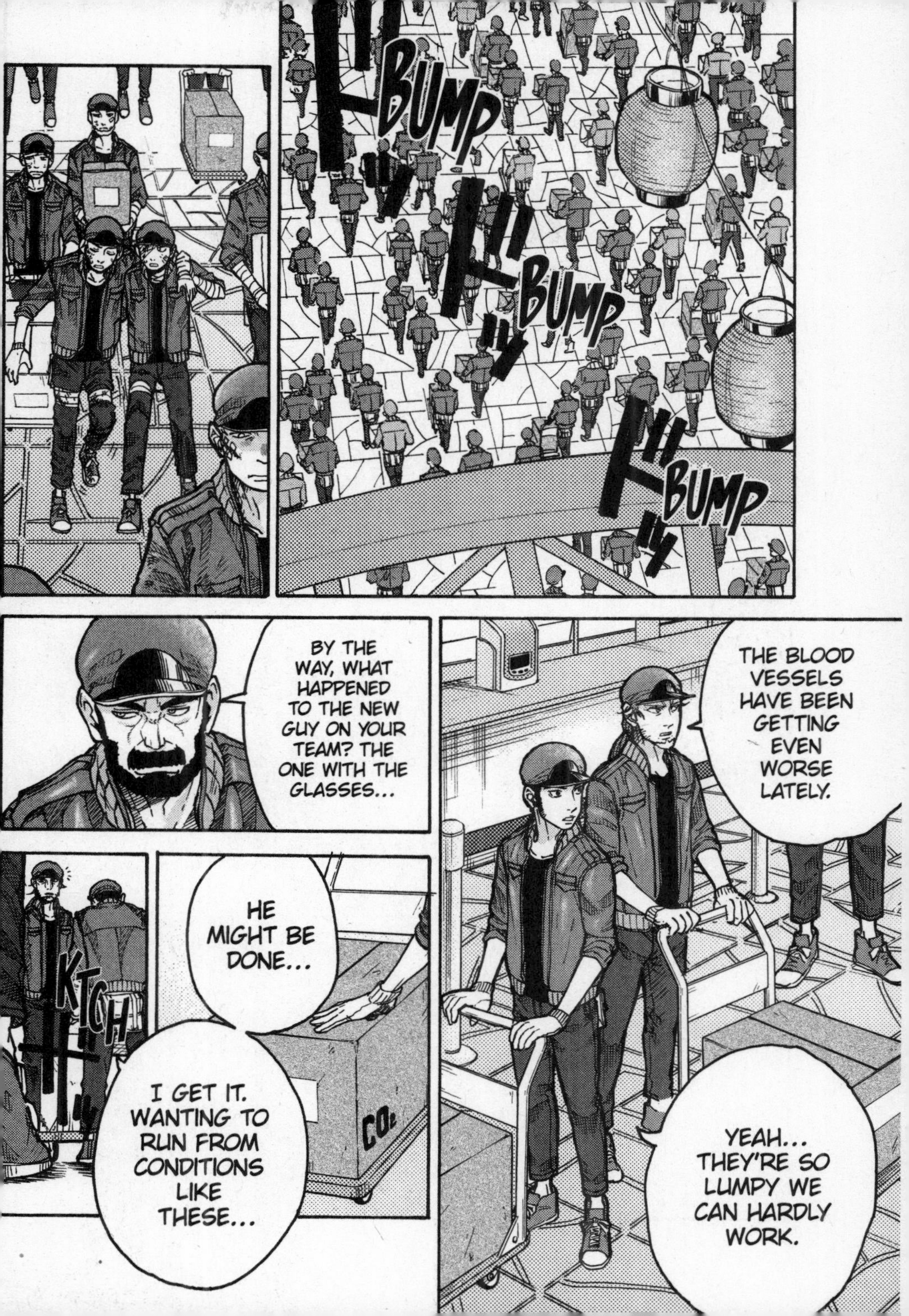
BUMP
BUMP
BUMP
THE BLOOD VESSELS HAVE BEEN GETTING EVEN WORSE LATELY.
YEAH... THEY'RE SO LUMPY WE CAN HARDLY WORK.
BY THE WAY, WHAT HAPPENED TO THE NEW GUY ON YOUR TEAM? THE ONE WITH THE GLASSES...
HE MIGHT BE DONE...
I GET IT. WANTING TO RUN FROM CONDITIONS LIKE THESE...
CO2
KTCH

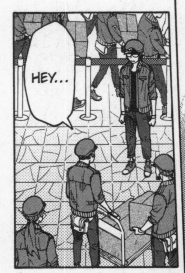

HEY...

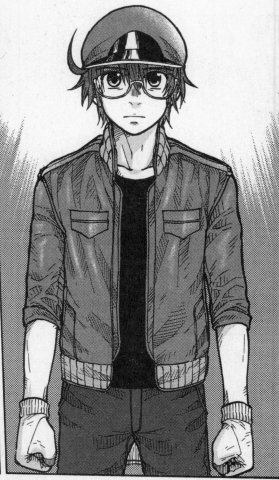

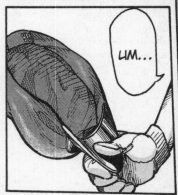

UM...

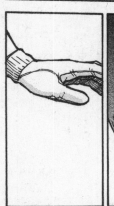

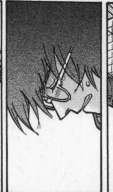

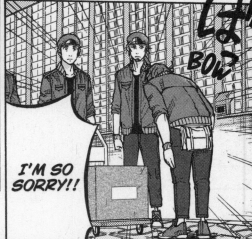

BOW

I'M SO SORRY!!

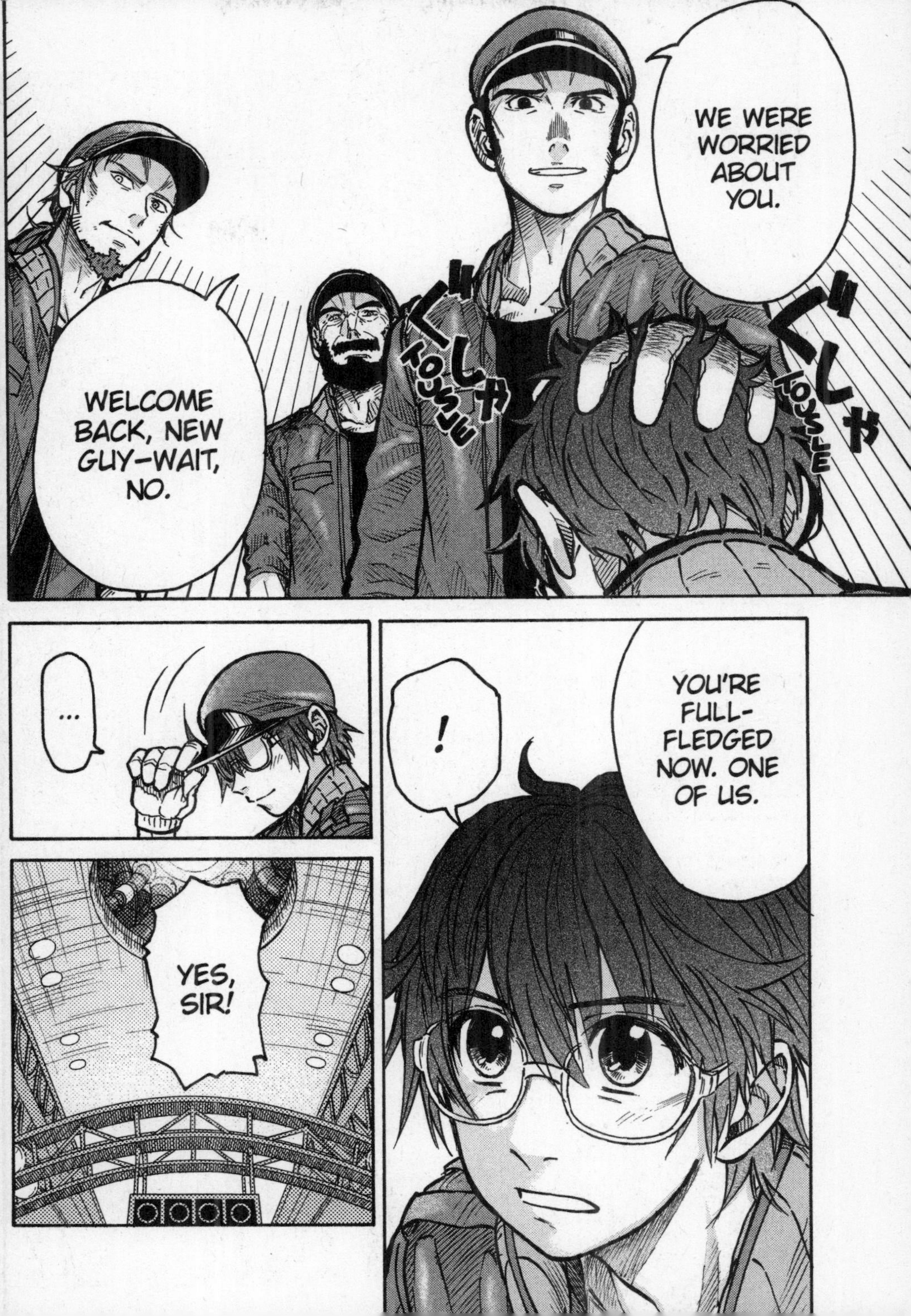
WE WERE WORRIED ABOUT YOU.
ぐしゃ
TOUSLE
ぐしゃ
TOUSLE
WELCOME BACK, NEW GUY—WAIT, NO.
YOU'RE FULL-FLEDGED NOW. ONE OF US.
!
...
YES, SIR!

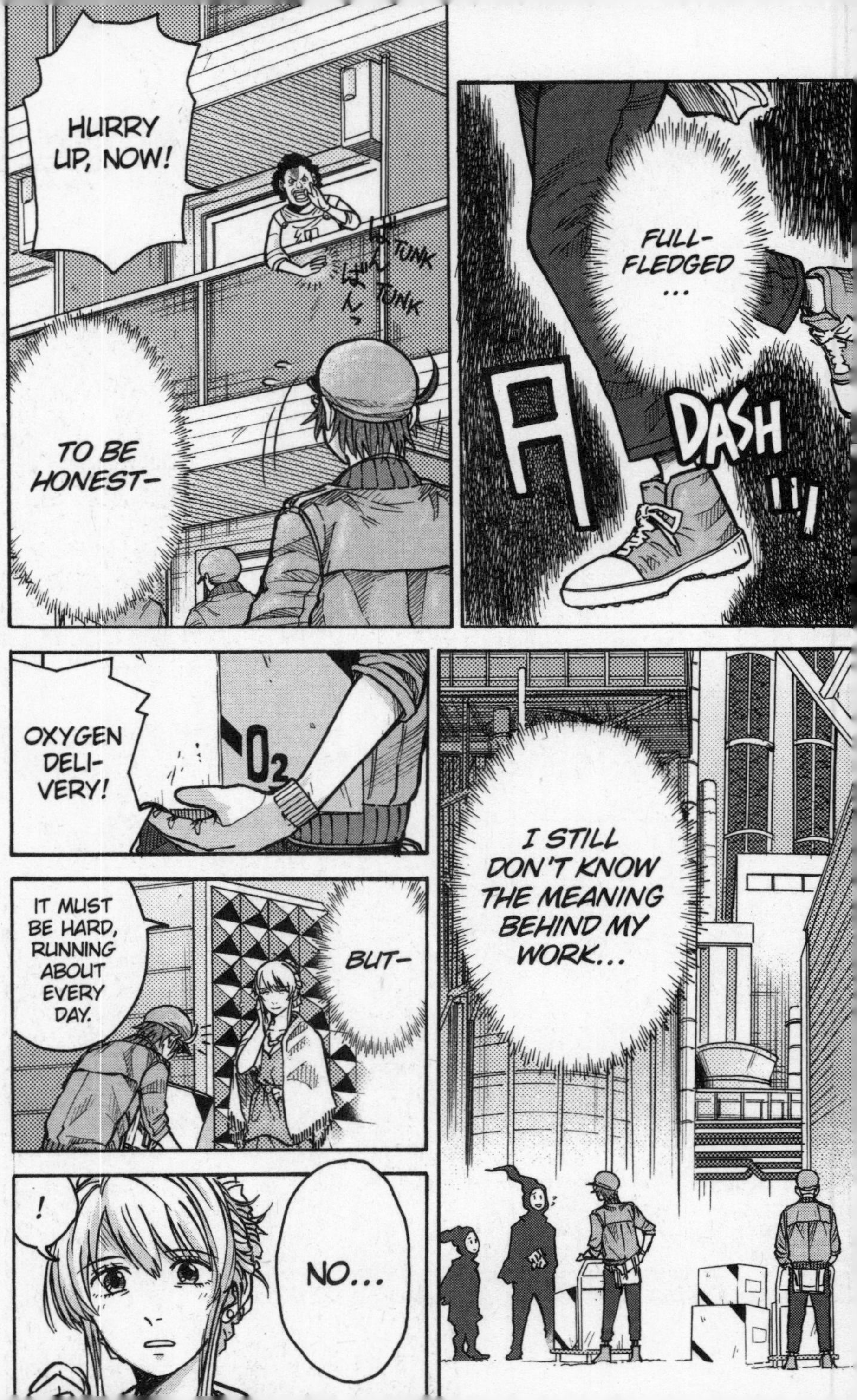
FULL-FLEDGED...
DASH
TUNK
TUNK
HURRY UP, NOW!
TO BE HONEST-
I STILL DON'T KNOW THE MEANING BEHIND MY WORK...
OXYGEN DELIVERY!
O_2
BUT-
IT MUST BE HARD, RUNNING ABOUT EVERY DAY.
NO...
!

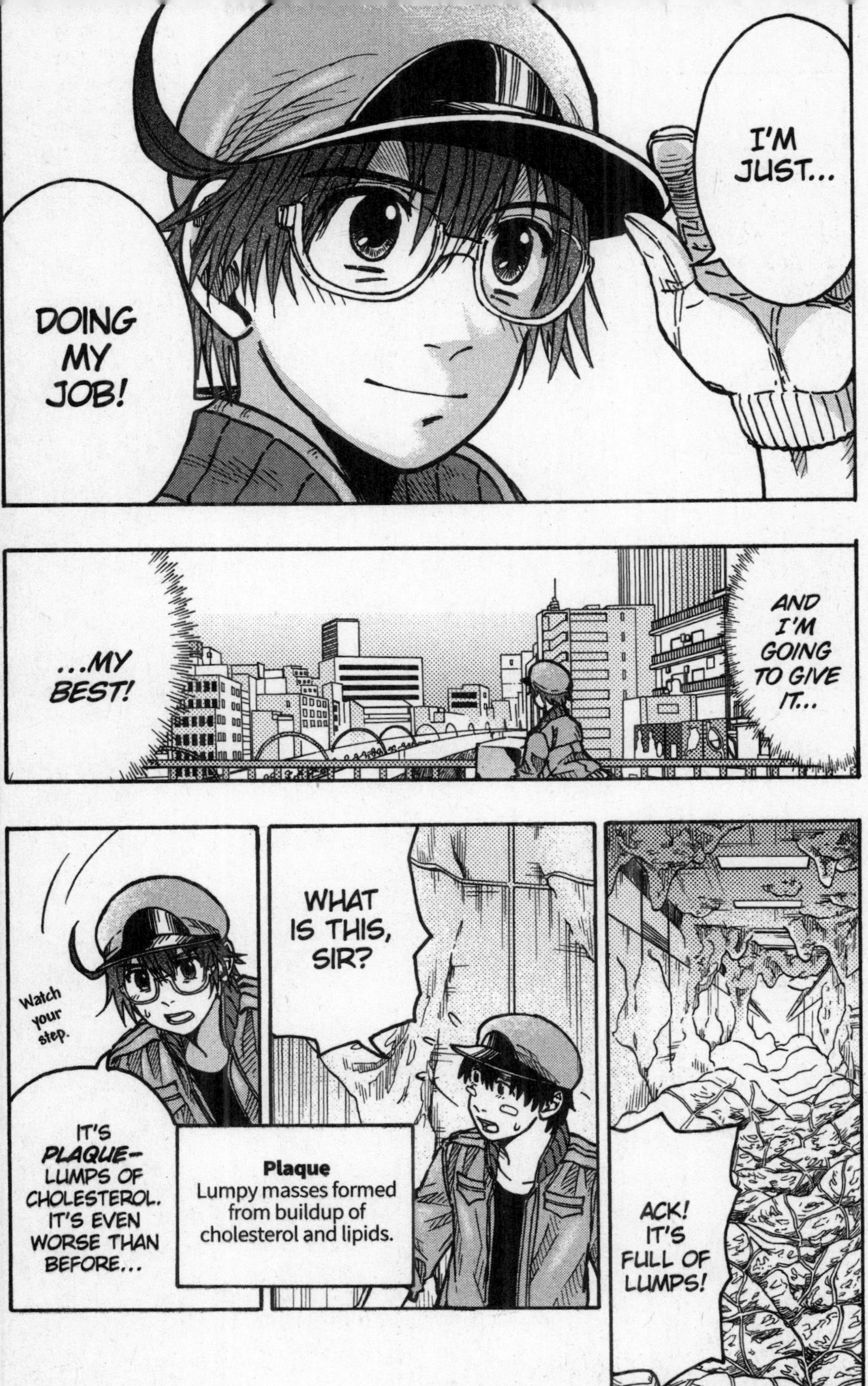
I'M JUST...
DOING MY JOB!
AND I'M GOING TO GIVE IT...
...MY BEST!
ACK! IT'S FULL OF LUMPS!
WHAT IS THIS, SIR?
Watch your step.
IT'S PLAQUE—LUMPS OF CHOLESTEROL. IT'S EVEN WORSE THAN BEFORE...
Plaque
Lumpy masses formed from buildup of cholesterol and lipids.

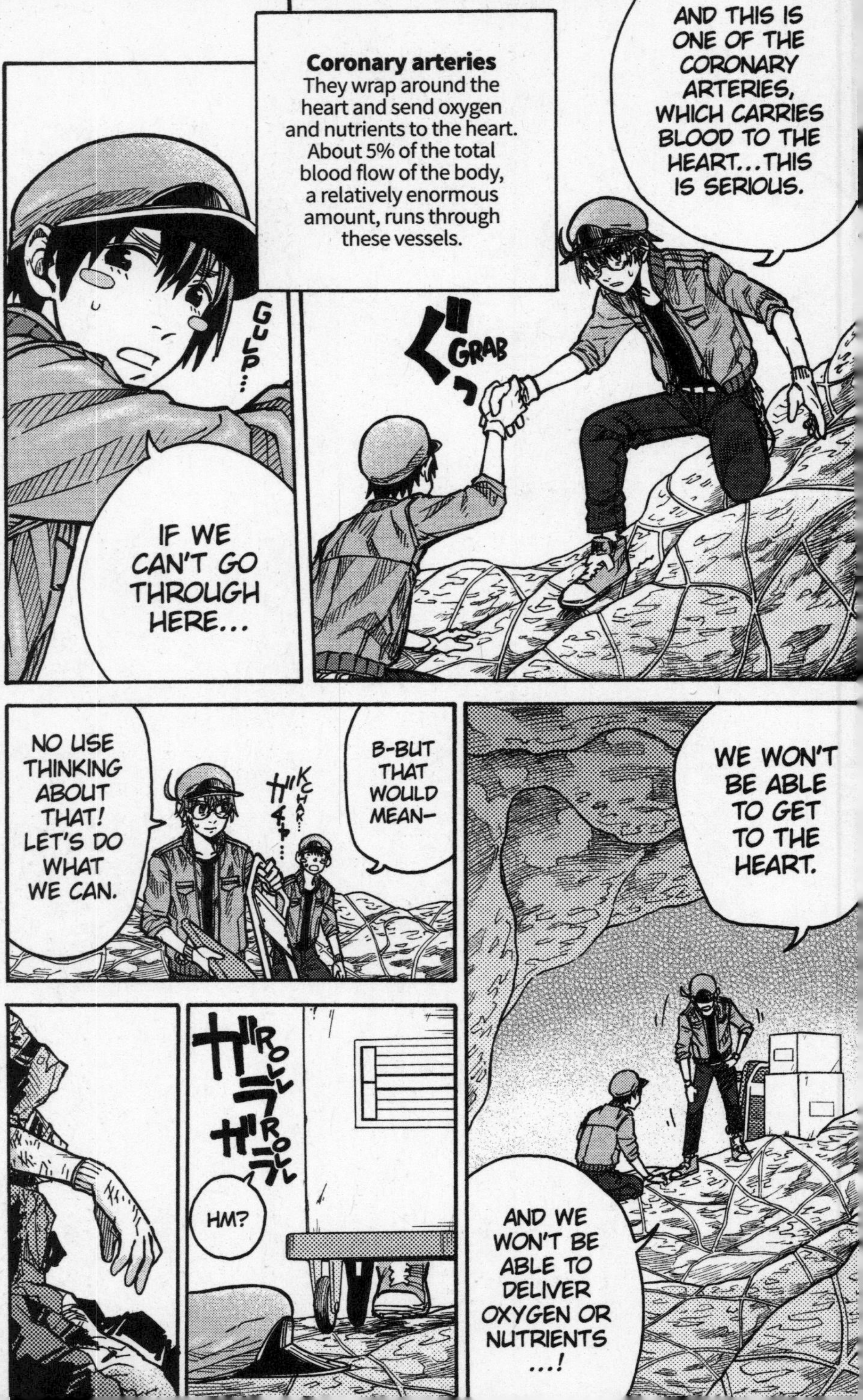
AND THIS IS ONE OF THE CORONARY ARTERIES, WHICH CARRIES BLOOD TO THE HEART...THIS IS SERIOUS.
Coronary arteries
They wrap around the heart and send oxygen and nutrients to the heart. About 5% of the total blood flow of the body, a relatively enormous amount, runs through these vessels.
GRAB
GULP...
IF WE CAN'T GO THROUGH HERE...
WE WON'T BE ABLE TO GET TO THE HEART.
AND WE WON'T BE ABLE TO DELIVER OXYGEN OR NUTRIENTS ...!
B-BUT THAT WOULD MEAN-
KCHAK...
NO USE THINKING ABOUT THAT! LET'S DO WHAT WE CAN.
ROLL
ROLL
HM?

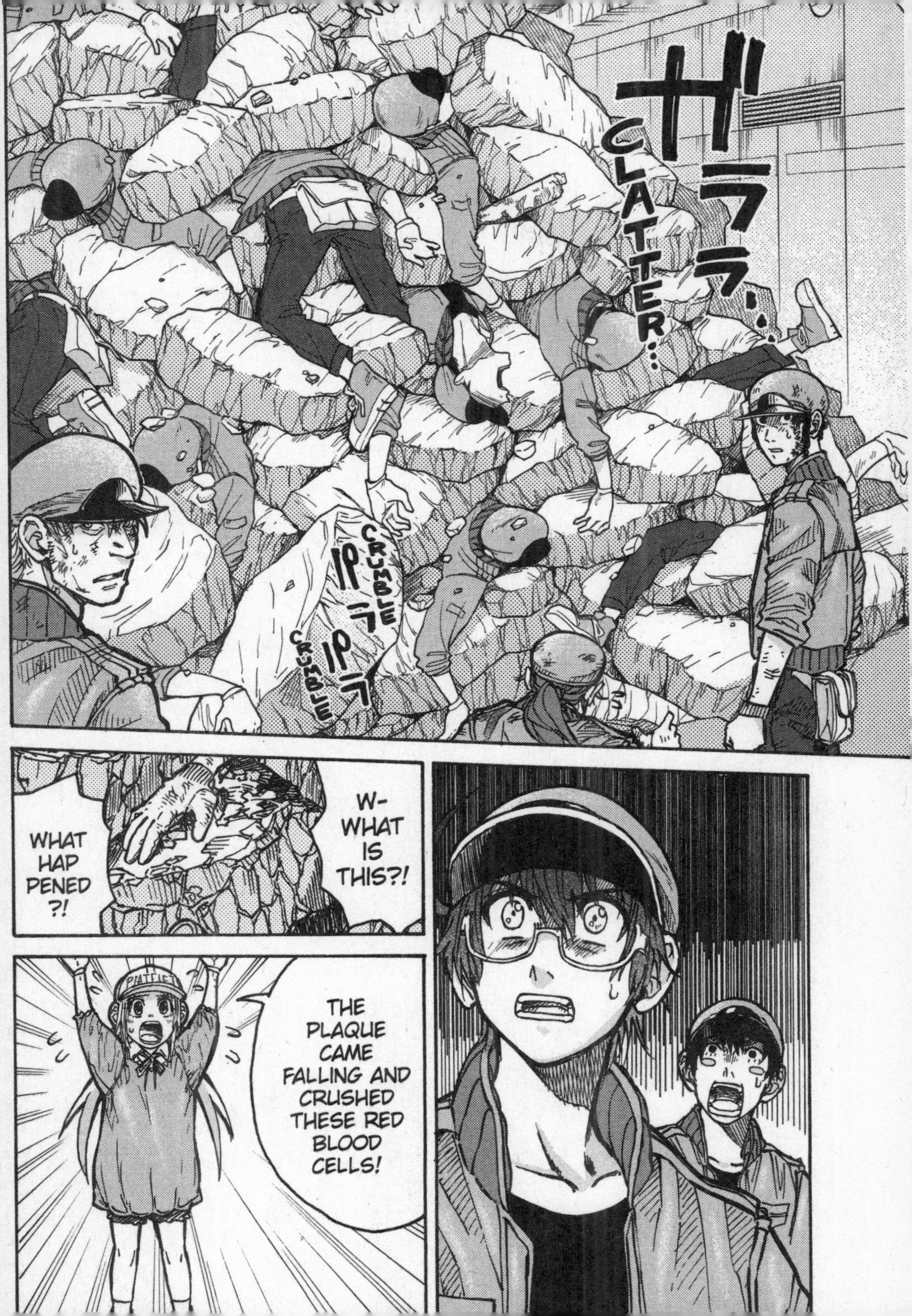
ザララ…
CLATTER...
CRUMBLE
CRUMBLE
W-WHAT IS THIS?!
WHAT HAPPENED?!
THE PLAQUE CAME FALLING AND CRUSHED THESE RED BLOOD CELLS!

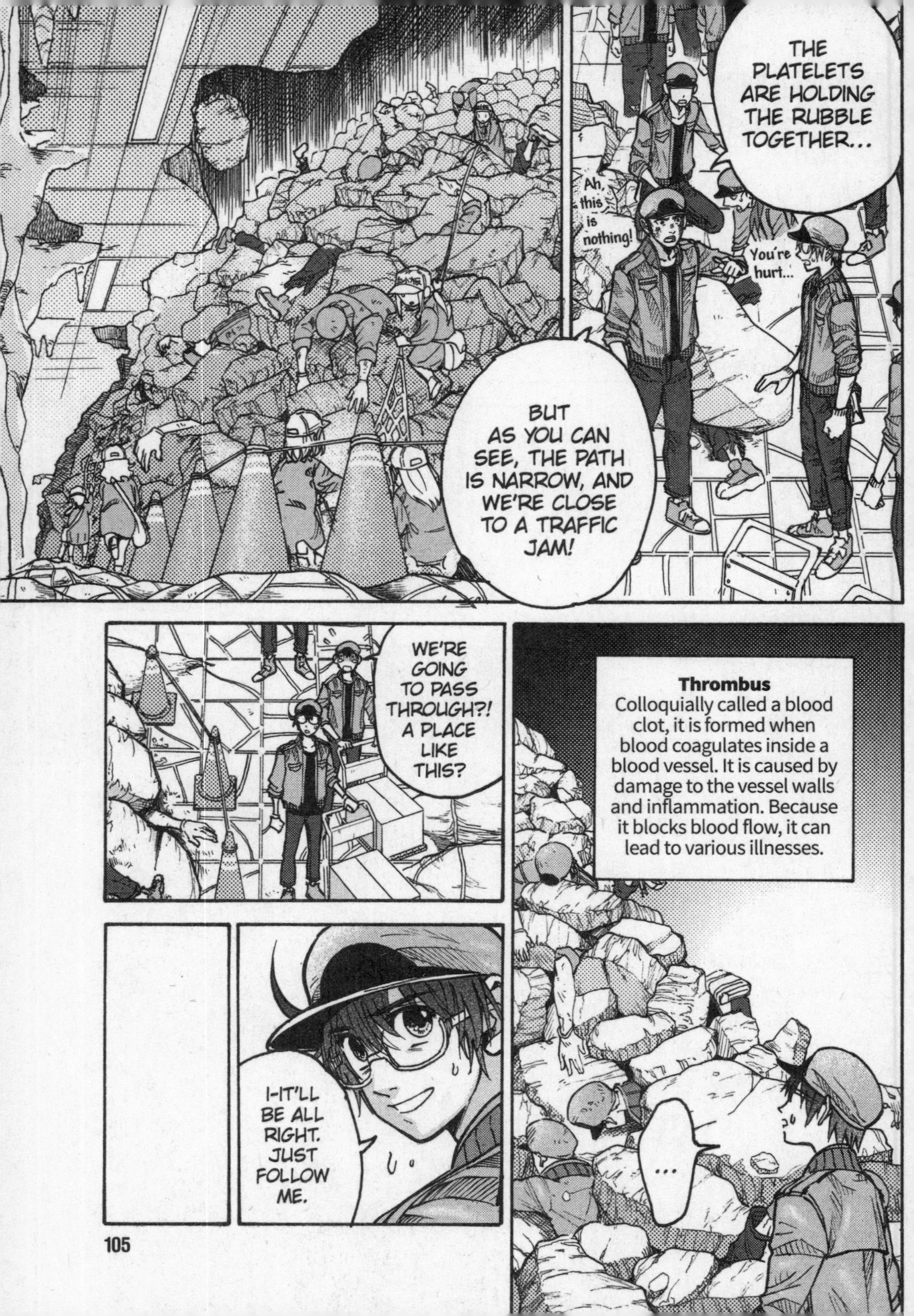
THE PLATELETS ARE HOLDING THE RUBBLE TOGETHER...
You're hurt...
Ah, this is nothing!
BUT AS YOU CAN SEE, THE PATH IS NARROW, AND WE'RE CLOSE TO A TRAFFIC JAM!
Thrombus
Colloquially called a blood clot, it is formed when blood coagulates inside a blood vessel. It is caused by damage to the vessel walls and inflammation. Because it blocks blood flow, it can lead to various illnesses.
...
WE'RE GOING TO PASS THROUGH?! A PLACE LIKE THIS?
I-IT'LL BE ALL RIGHT. JUST FOLLOW ME.

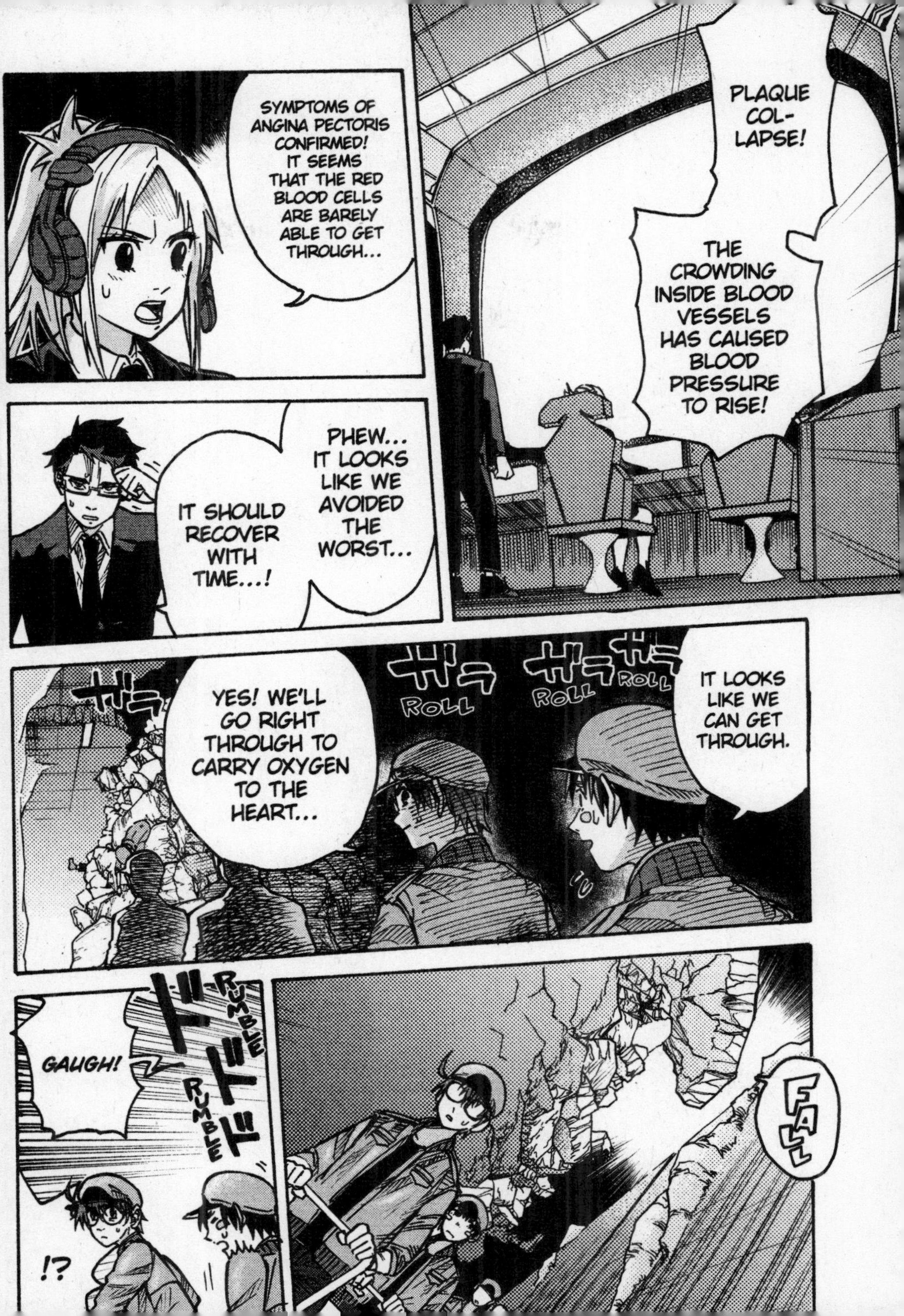
PLAQUE COL-LAPSE!
THE CROWDING INSIDE BLOOD VESSELS HAS CAUSED BLOOD PRESSURE TO RISE!
SYMPTOMS OF ANGINA PECTORIS CONFIRMED! IT SEEMS THAT THE RED BLOOD CELLS ARE BARELY ABLE TO GET THROUGH...
PHEW... IT LOOKS LIKE WE AVOIDED THE WORST...
IT SHOULD RECOVER WITH TIME...!
IT LOOKS LIKE WE CAN GET THROUGH.
ROLL
ROLL
ROLL
YES! WE'LL GO RIGHT THROUGH TO CARRY OXYGEN TO THE HEART...
FALL
RUMBLE
RUMBLE
GAUGH!
!?

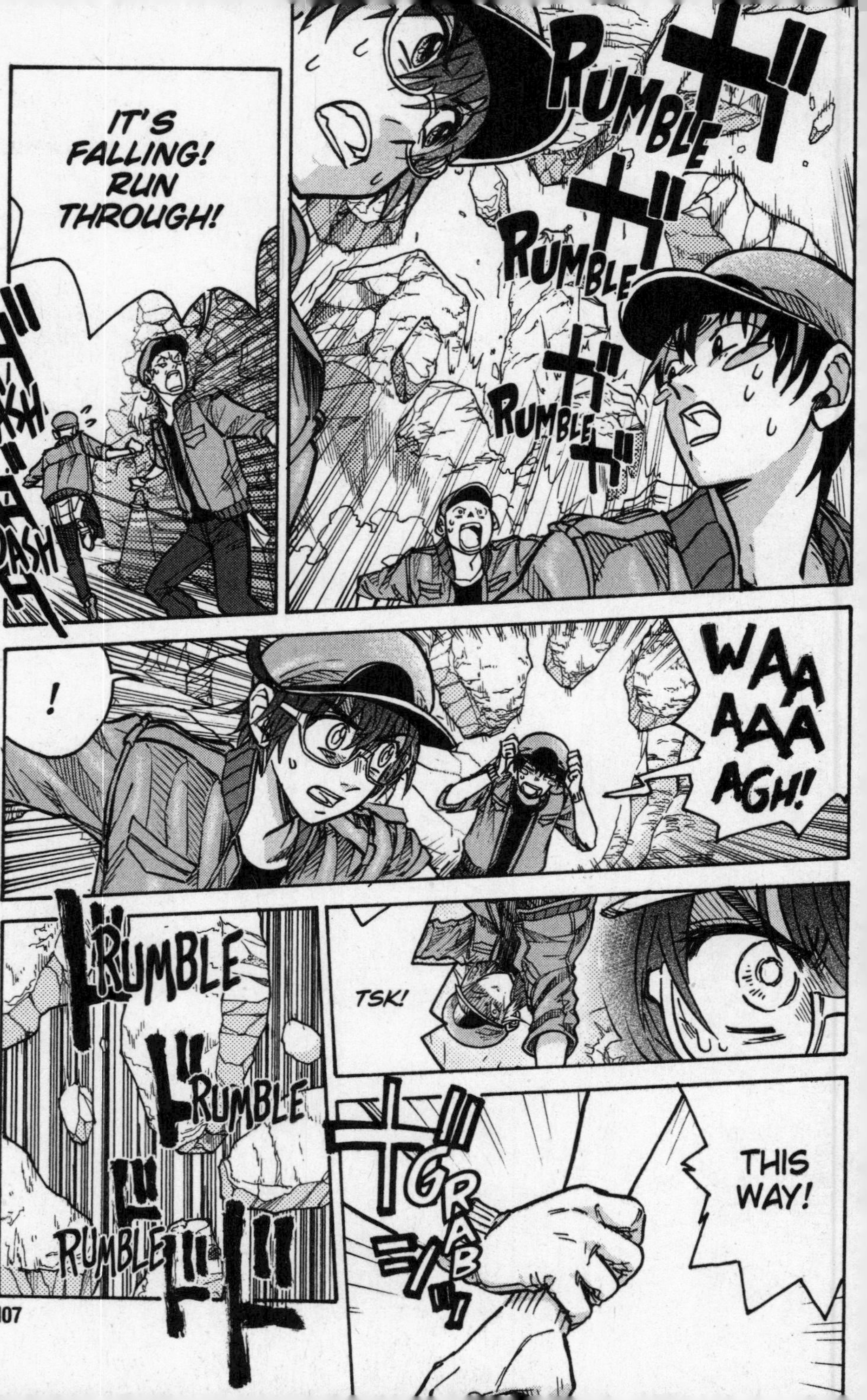
RUMBLE
RUMBLE
RUMBLE
IT'S FALLING! RUN THROUGH!
DASH
DASH
WAAAAAAGH!
!
TSK!
THIS WAY!
GRAB
RUMBLE
RUMBLE
RUMBLE

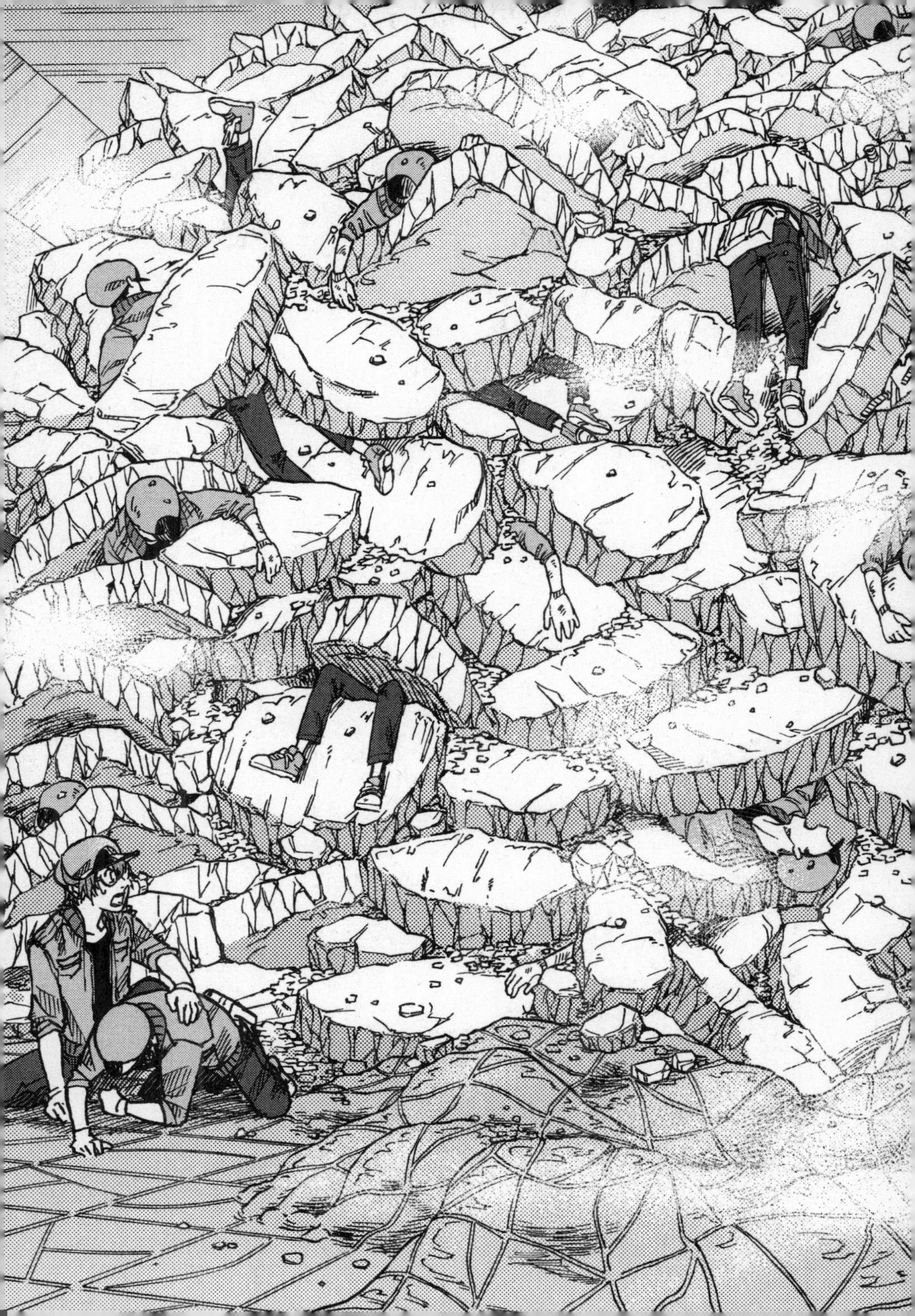

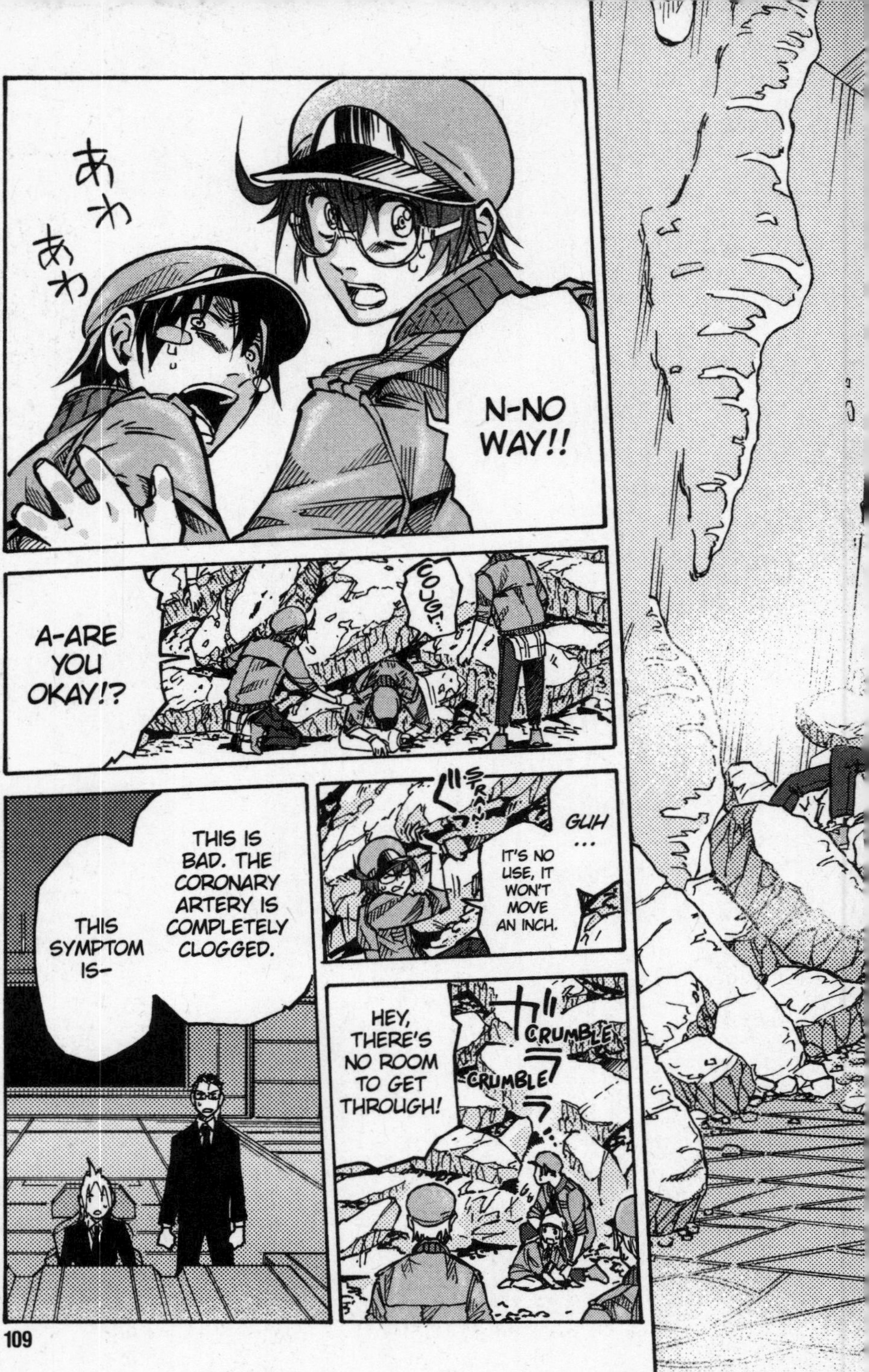
あわ あわ
N-NO WAY!!
COUGH...
A-ARE YOU OKAY!?
ぐ STRAIN
GUH...
IT'S NO USE, IT WON'T MOVE AN INCH.
HEY, THERE'S NO ROOM TO GET THROUGH!
ガ CRUMBLE
ラ CRUMBLE
THIS IS BAD. THE CORONARY ARTERY IS COMPLETELY CLOGGED.
THIS SYMPTOM IS-

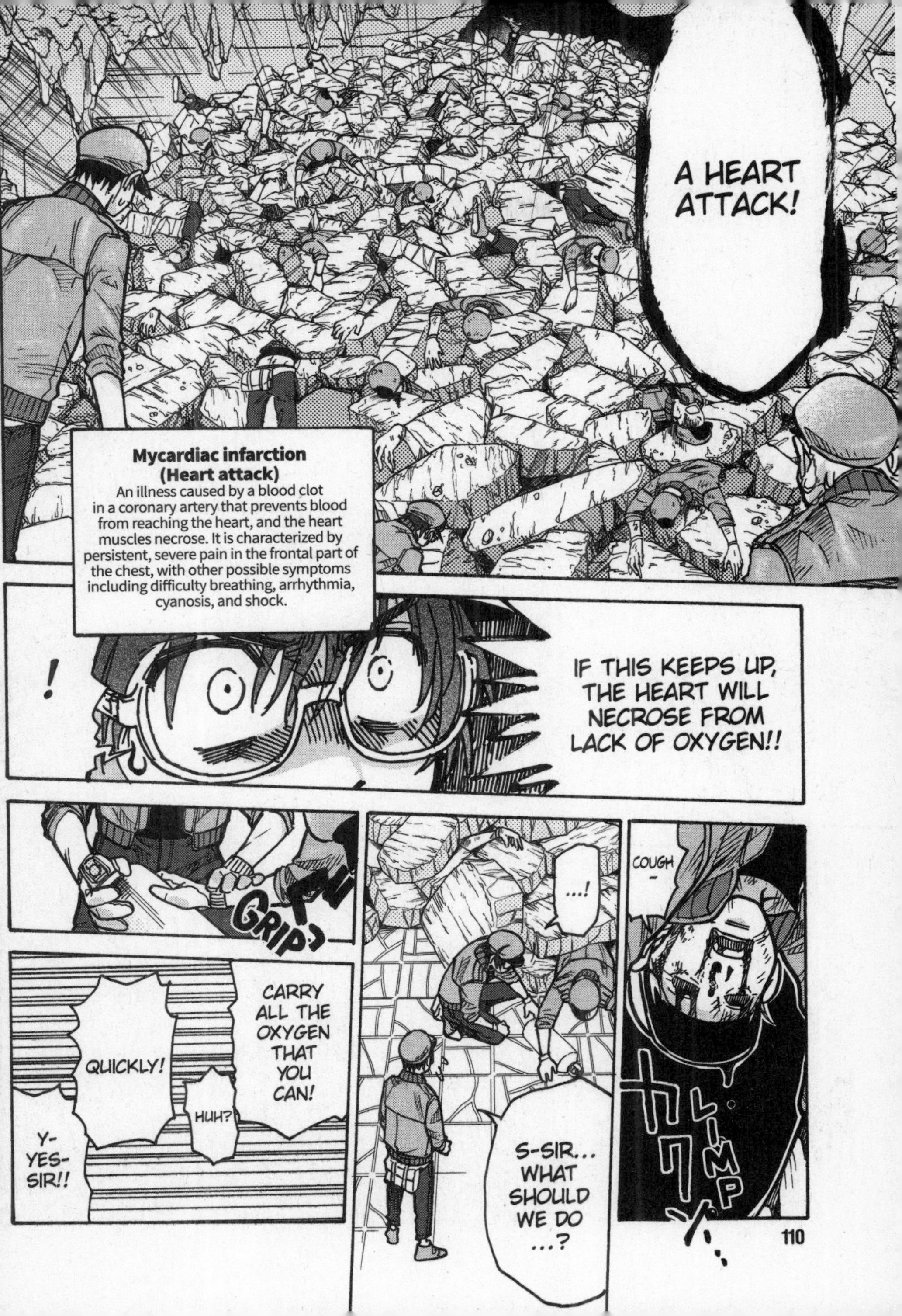
A HEART ATTACK!
Mycardiac infarction (Heart attack)
An illness caused by a blood clot in a coronary artery that prevents blood from reaching the heart, and the heart muscles necrose. It is characterized by persistent, severe pain in the frontal part of the chest, with other possible symptoms including difficulty breathing, arrhythmia, cyanosis, and shock.
IF THIS KEEPS UP, THE HEART WILL NECROSE FROM LACK OF OXYGEN!!
!
COUGH
LIMP
...!
S-SIR... WHAT SHOULD WE DO ...?
GRIP
CARRY ALL THE OXYGEN THAT YOU CAN!
QUICKLY!
HUH?
Y-YES-SIR!!

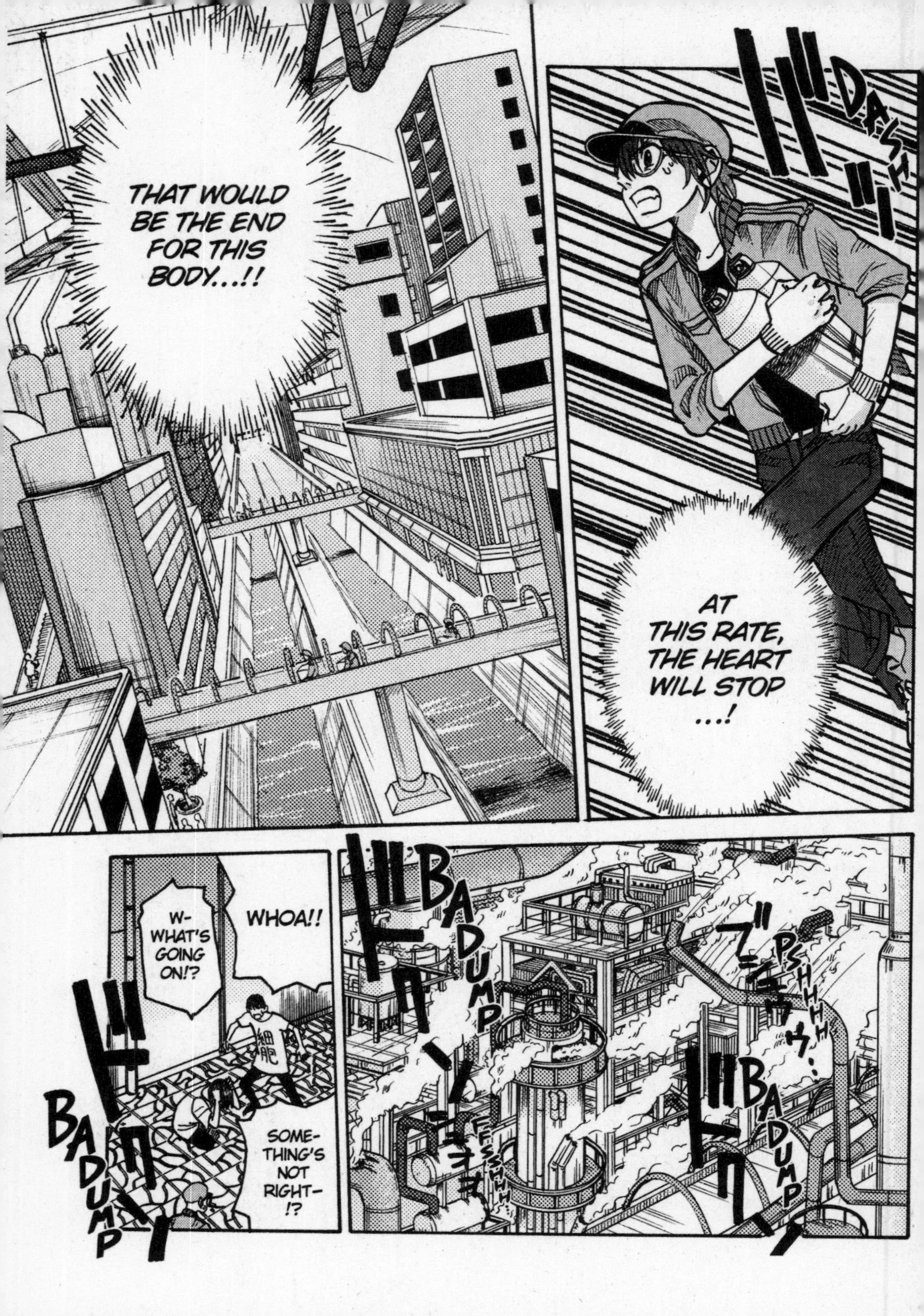
DASH
AT THIS RATE, THE HEART WILL STOP ...!
THAT WOULD BE THE END FOR THIS BODY...!!
BADUMP
PSHHHH...
FFSHHH...
BADUMP
WHOA!!
W- WHAT'S GOING ON!?
SOME- THING'S NOT RIGHT- !?
BADUMP

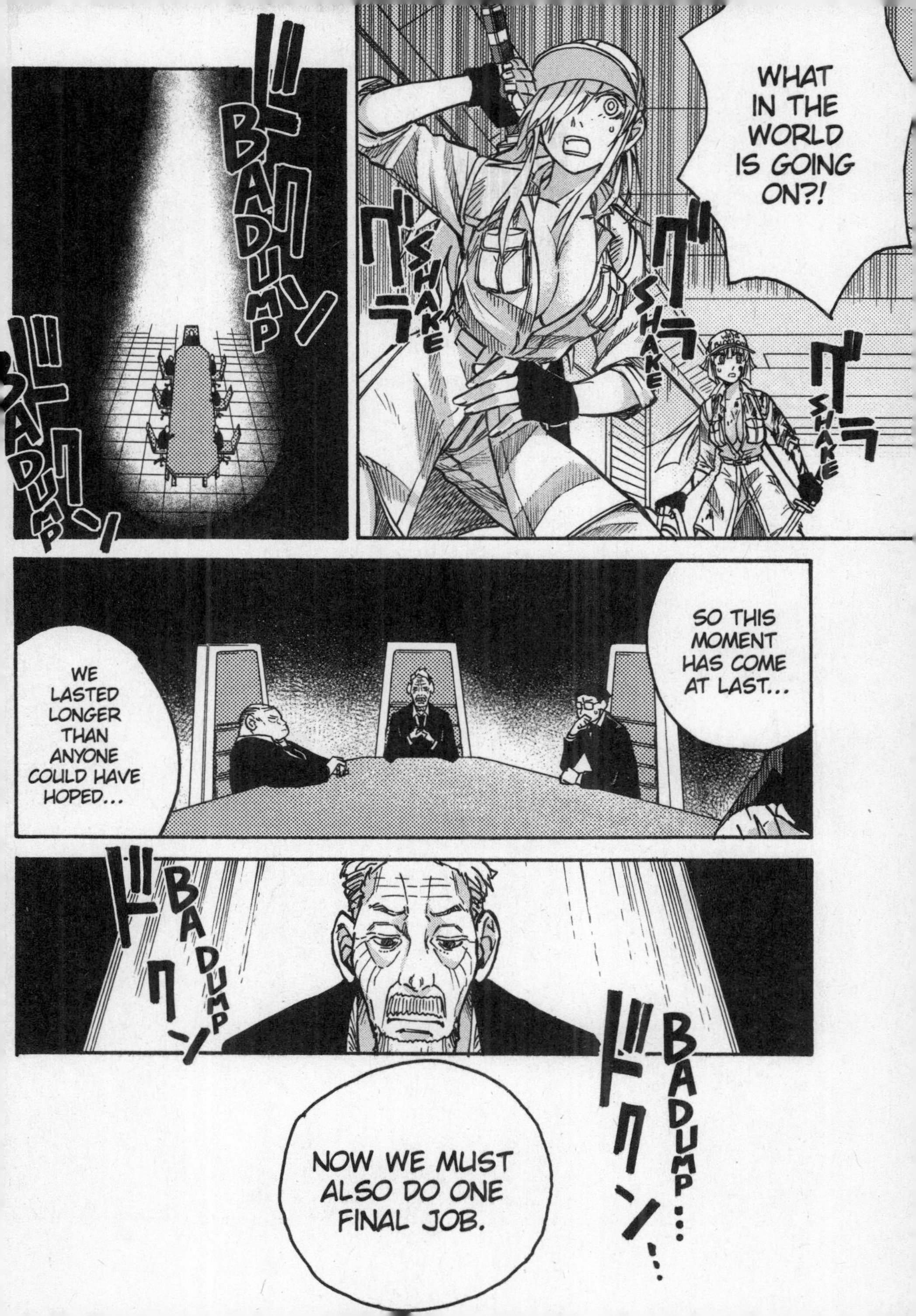

WHAT IN THE WORLD IS GOING ON?!
SHAKE
SHAKE
SHAKE
BADUMP
BADUMP
SO THIS MOMENT HAS COME AT LAST...
WE LASTED LONGER THAN ANYONE COULD HAVE HOPED...
BADUMP
BADUMP...
NOW WE MUST ALSO DO ONE FINAL JOB.

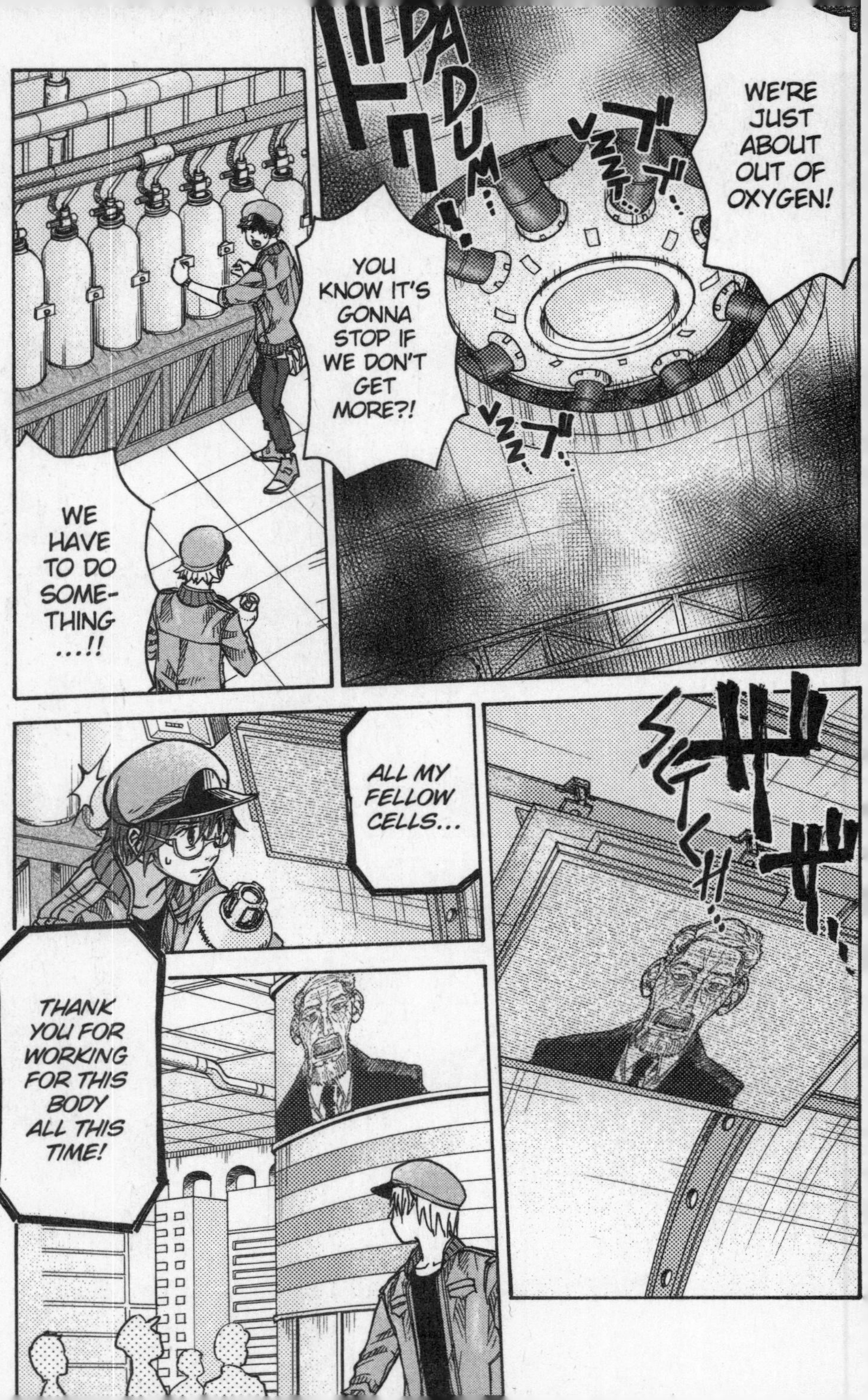
WE'RE JUST ABOUT OUT OF OXYGEN!
VZZZT...
DA DUM!!...
YOU KNOW IT'S GONNA STOP IF WE DON'T GET MORE?!
VZZZ...
WE HAVE TO DO SOME-THING...!!
ALL MY FELLOW CELLS...
THANK YOU FOR WORKING FOR THIS BODY ALL THIS TIME!

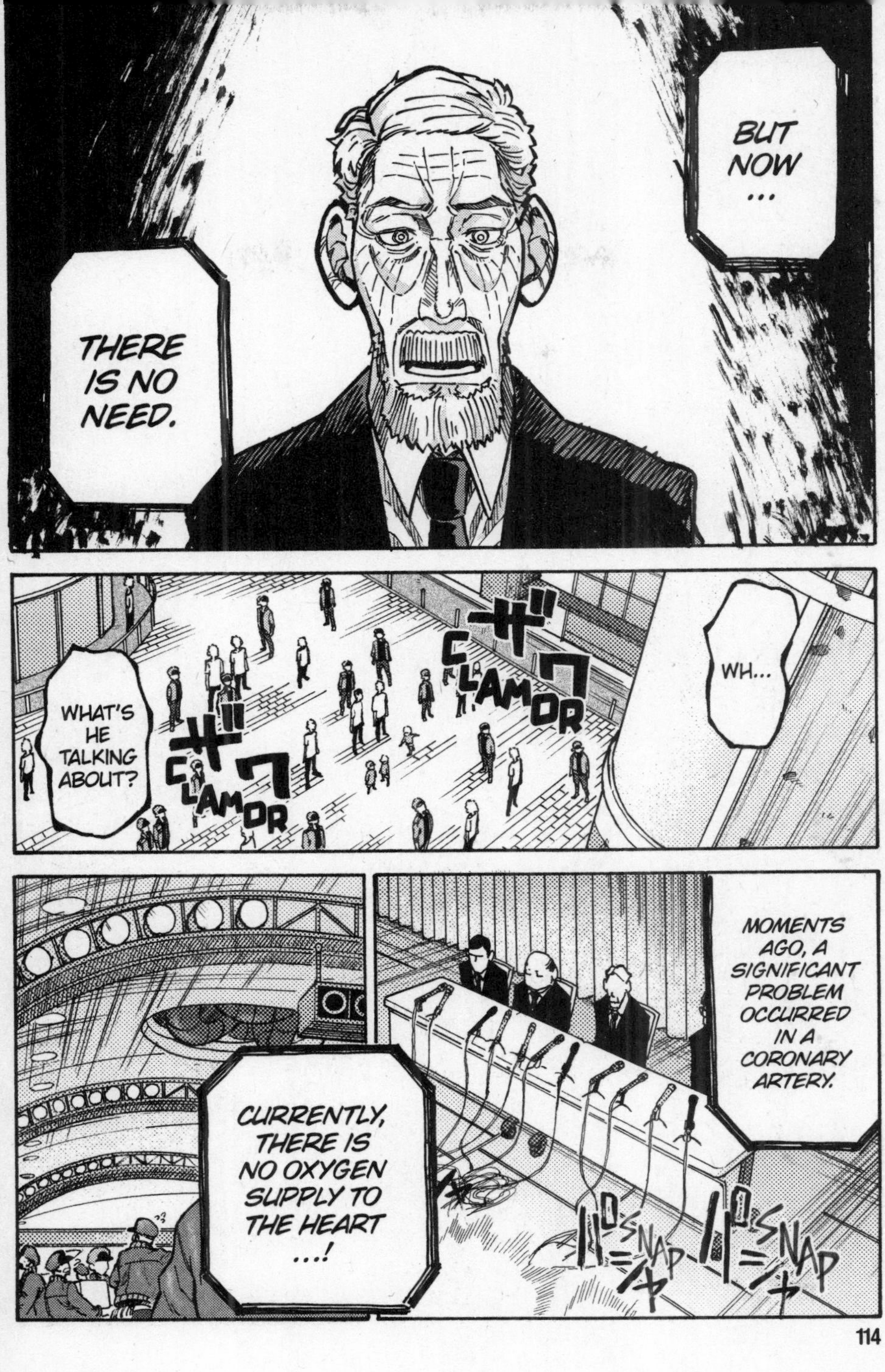
BUT NOW ...
THERE IS NO NEED.
WH...
CLAMOR
CLAMOR
WHAT'S HE TALKING ABOUT?
MOMENTS AGO, A SIGNIFICANT PROBLEM OCCURRED IN A CORONARY ARTERY.
CURRENTLY, THERE IS NO OXYGEN SUPPLY TO THE HEART ...!
SNAP
SNAP

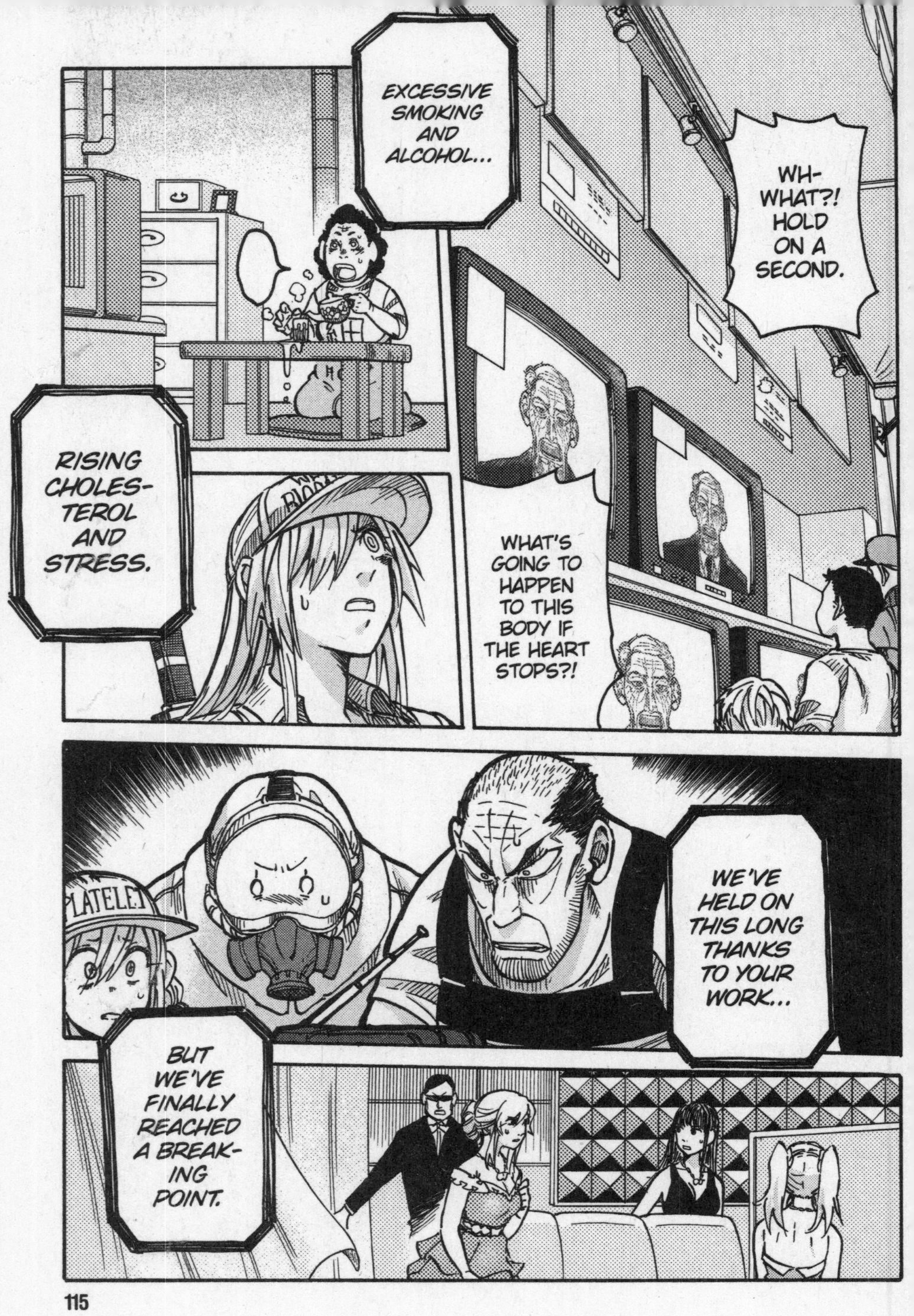
WH-WHAT?! HOLD ON A SECOND.
WHAT'S GOING TO HAPPEN TO THIS BODY IF THE HEART STOPS?!
EXCESSIVE SMOKING AND ALCOHOL...
RISING CHOLES-TEROL AND STRESS.
WE'VE HELD ON THIS LONG THANKS TO YOUR WORK...
PLATELET
BUT WE'VE FINALLY REACHED A BREAK-ING POINT.

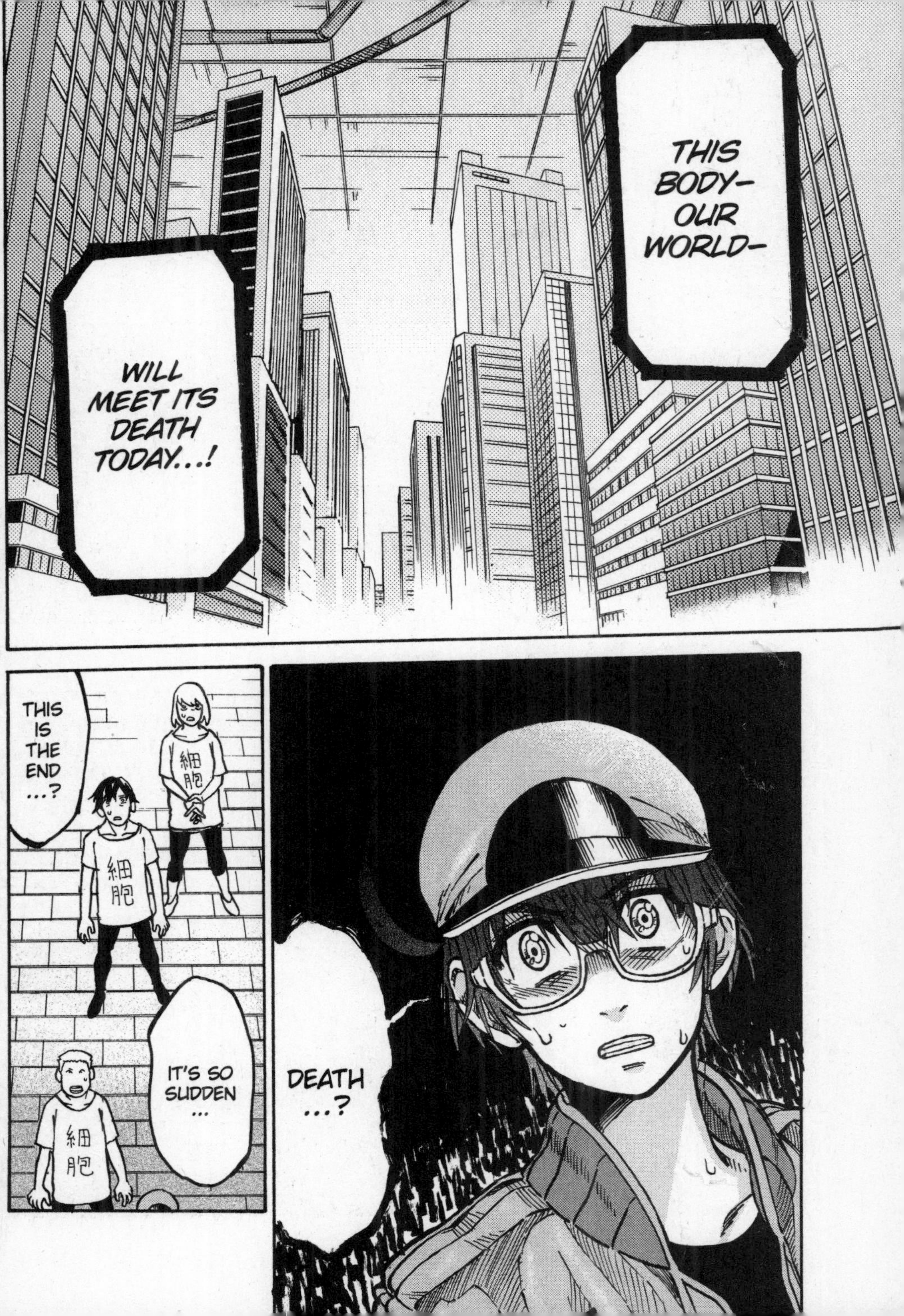
THIS BODY- OUR WORLD-
WILL MEET ITS DEATH TODAY...!
DEATH ...?
THIS IS THE END ...?
細胞
細胞
IT'S SO SUDDEN ...
細胞

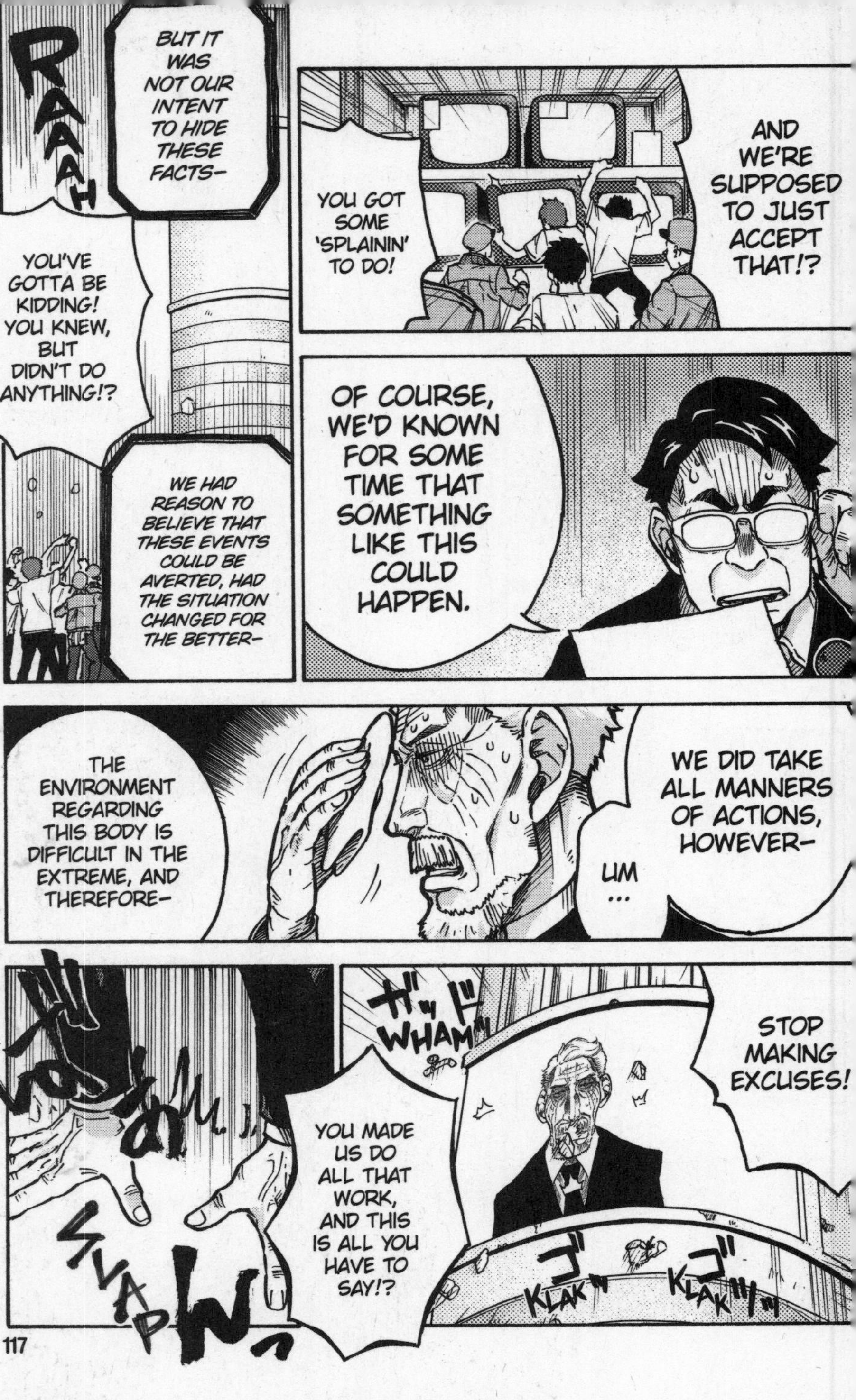
AND WE'RE SUPPOSED TO JUST ACCEPT THAT!?
YOU GOT SOME 'SPLAININ' TO DO!
OF COURSE, WE'D KNOWN FOR SOME TIME THAT SOMETHING LIKE THIS COULD HAPPEN.
BUT IT WAS NOT OUR INTENT TO HIDE THESE FACTS-
RAAAAH
YOU'VE GOTTA BE KIDDING! YOU KNEW, BUT DIDN'T DO ANYTHING!?
WE HAD REASON TO BELIEVE THAT THESE EVENTS COULD BE AVERTED, HAD THE SITUATION CHANGED FOR THE BETTER-
WE DID TAKE ALL MANNERS OF ACTIONS, HOWEVER-
UM ...
THE ENVIRONMENT REGARDING THIS BODY IS DIFFICULT IN THE EXTREME, AND THEREFORE-
STOP MAKING EXCUSES!
WHAM
KLAK KLAK
YOU MADE US DO ALL THAT WORK, AND THIS IS ALL YOU HAVE TO SAY!?
SLAP

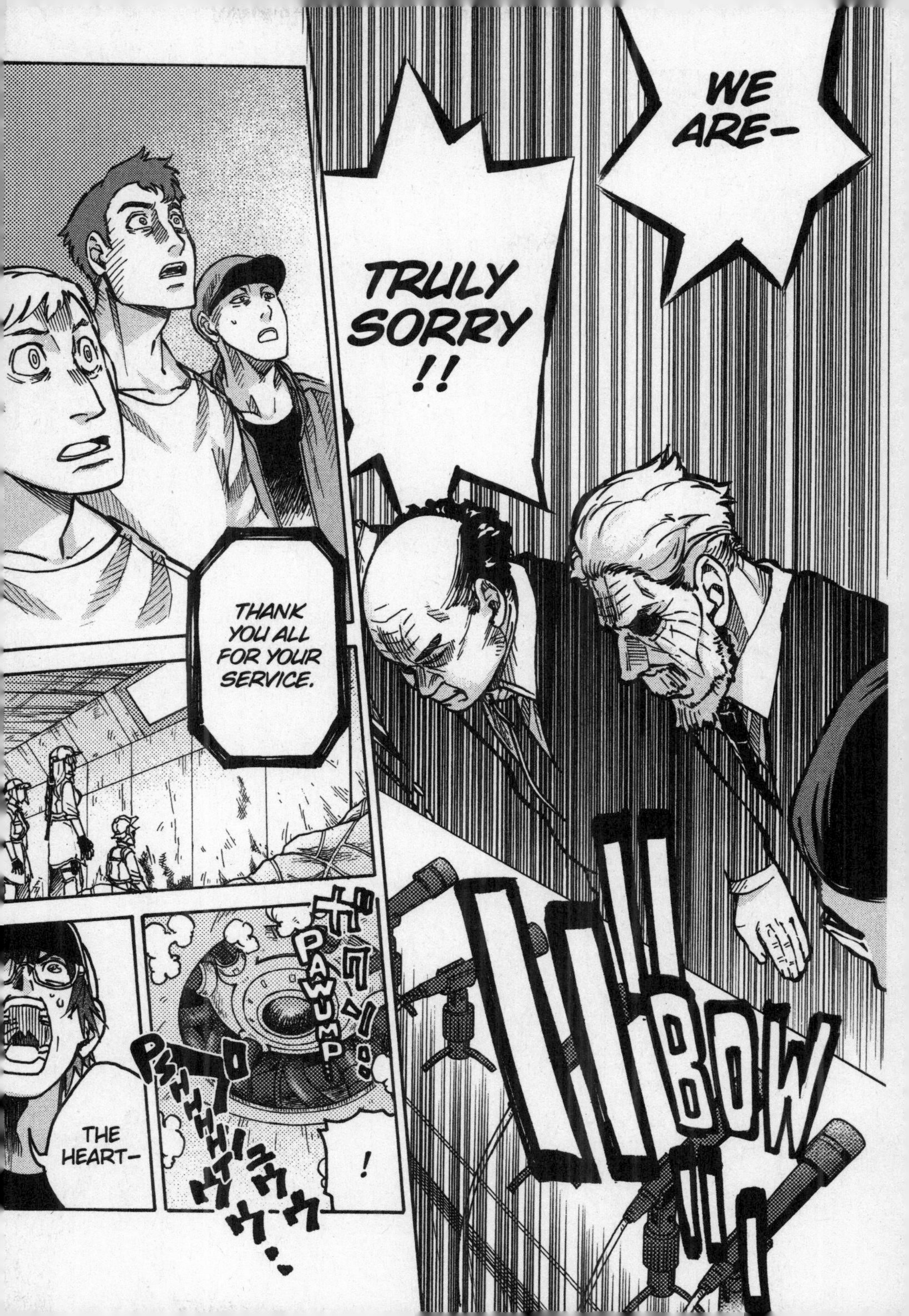
WE ARE-
TRULY SORRY!!
BOW
THANK YOU ALL FOR YOUR SERVICE.
PAWUMP...
PSHHHHH
!
THE HEART-

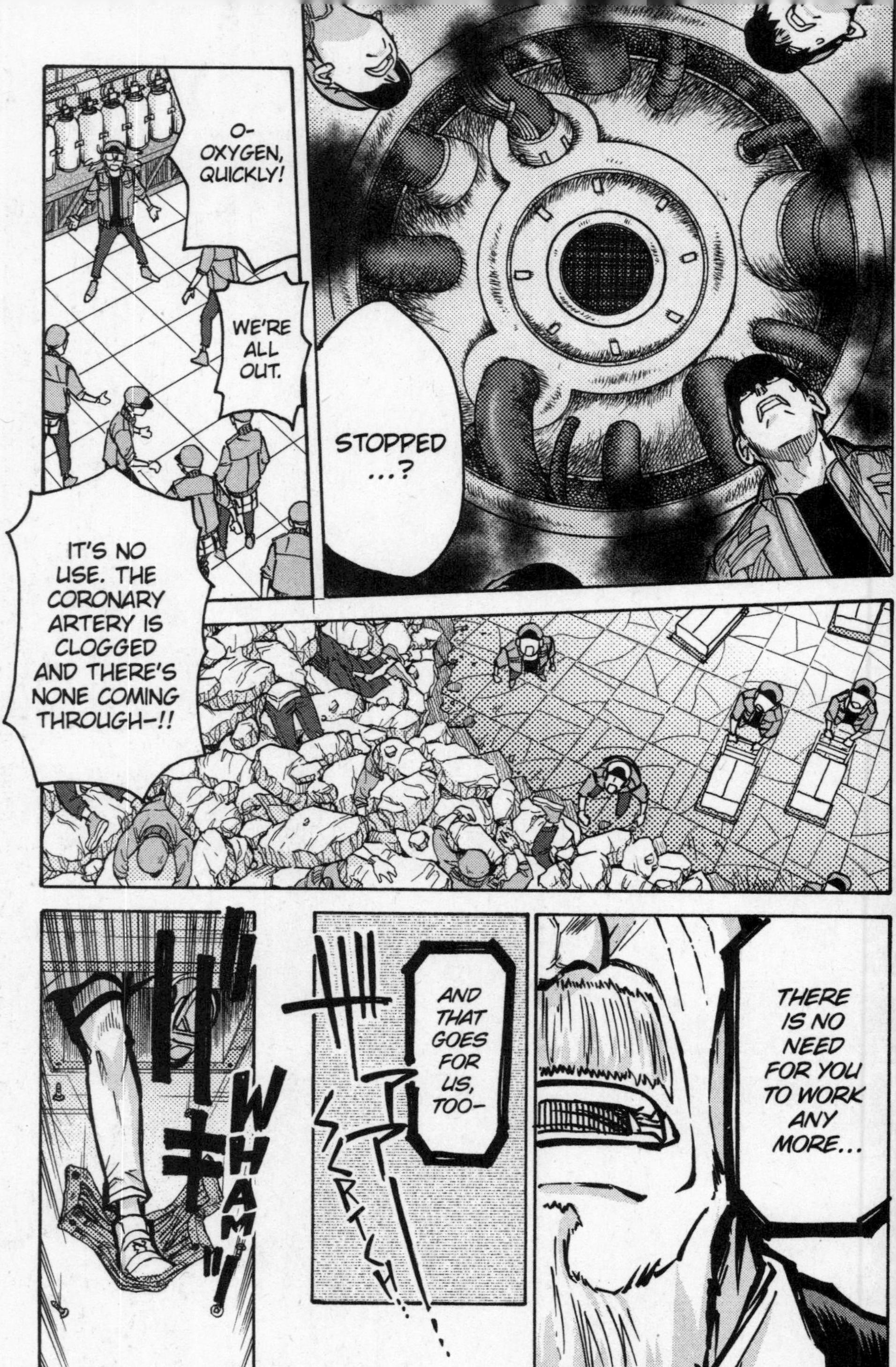
STOPPED ...?
O-OXYGEN, QUICKLY!
WE'RE ALL OUT.
IT'S NO USE. THE CORONARY ARTERY IS CLOGGED AND THERE'S NONE COMING THROUGH-!!
THERE IS NO NEED FOR YOU TO WORK ANY MORE...
AND THAT GOES FOR US, TOO-
SLRTLH...!
WHAM!!

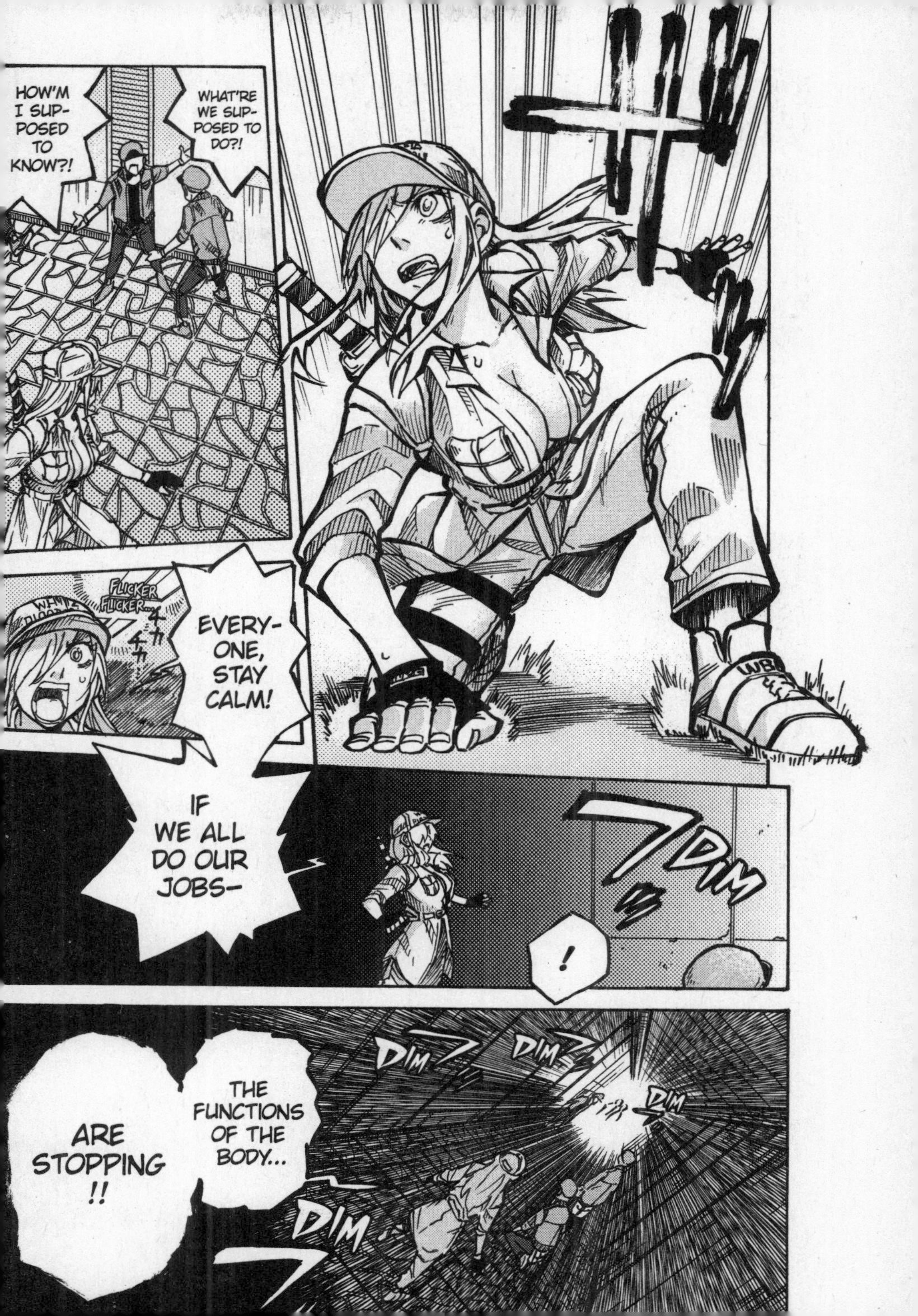
WHAT'RE WE SUP-POSED TO DO?!
HOW'M I SUP-POSED TO KNOW?!
FLICKER FLICKER...
EVERY-ONE, STAY CALM!
DIM
!
IF WE ALL DO OUR JOBS-
DIM
DIM
DIM
THE FUNCTIONS OF THE BODY...
ARE STOPPING !!
DIM

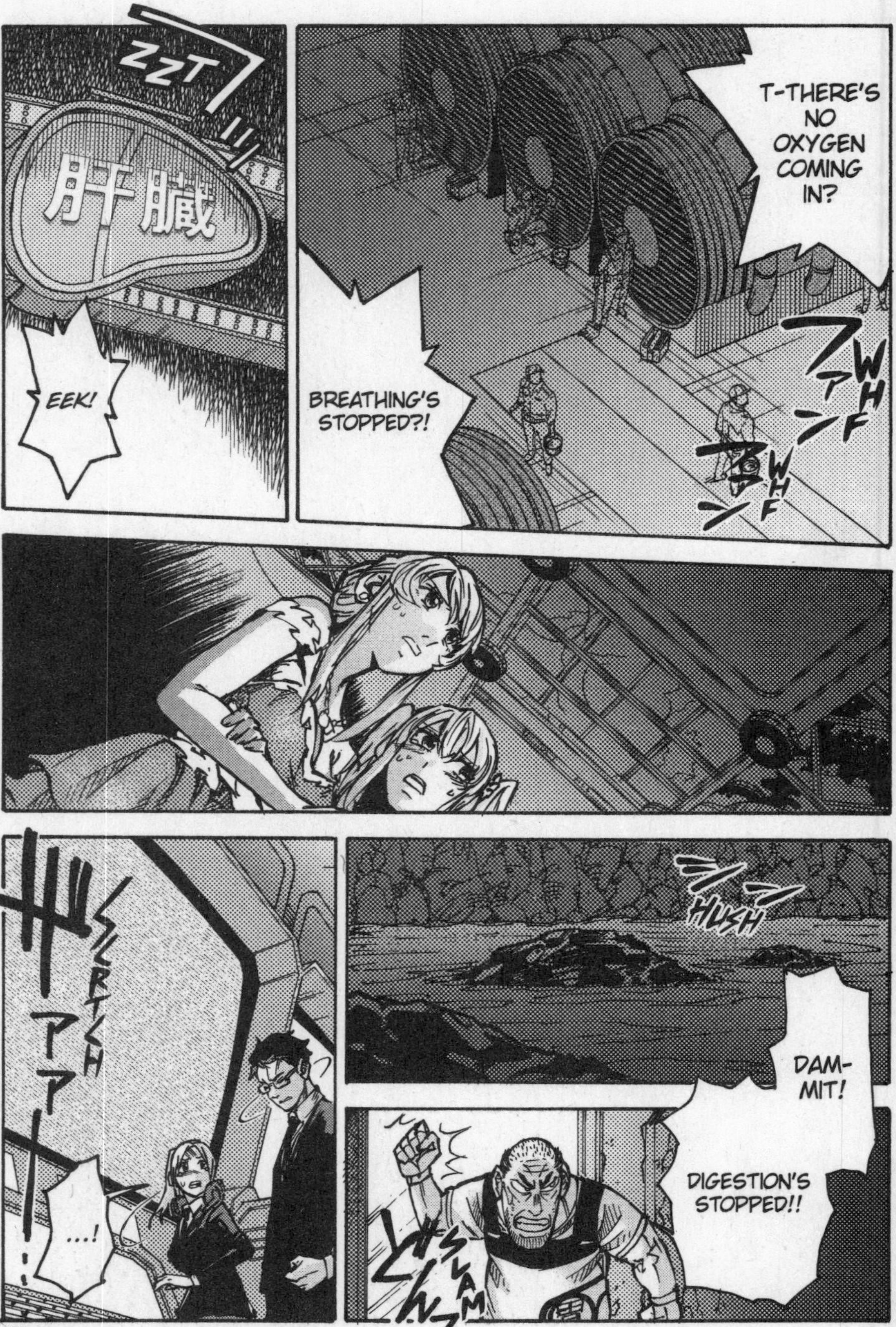
T-THERE'S NO OXYGEN COMING IN?
BREATHING'S STOPPED?!
WHF
WHF
ZZT
肝臓
EEK!
HUSH
DAM-MIT!
DIGESTION'S STOPPED!!
SLAM
SCRTCH
...!

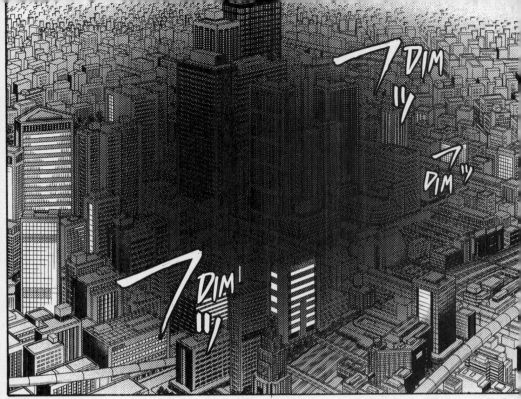

DIM ''

DIM ''

DIM ''

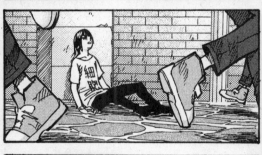

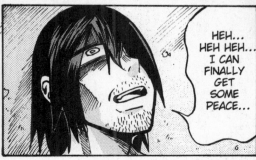

HEH... HEH HEH... I CAN FINALLY GET SOME PEACE...

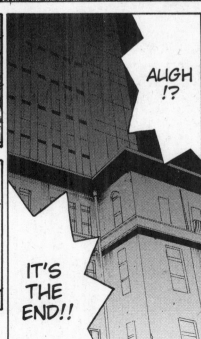

AUGH !?

IT'S THE END!!

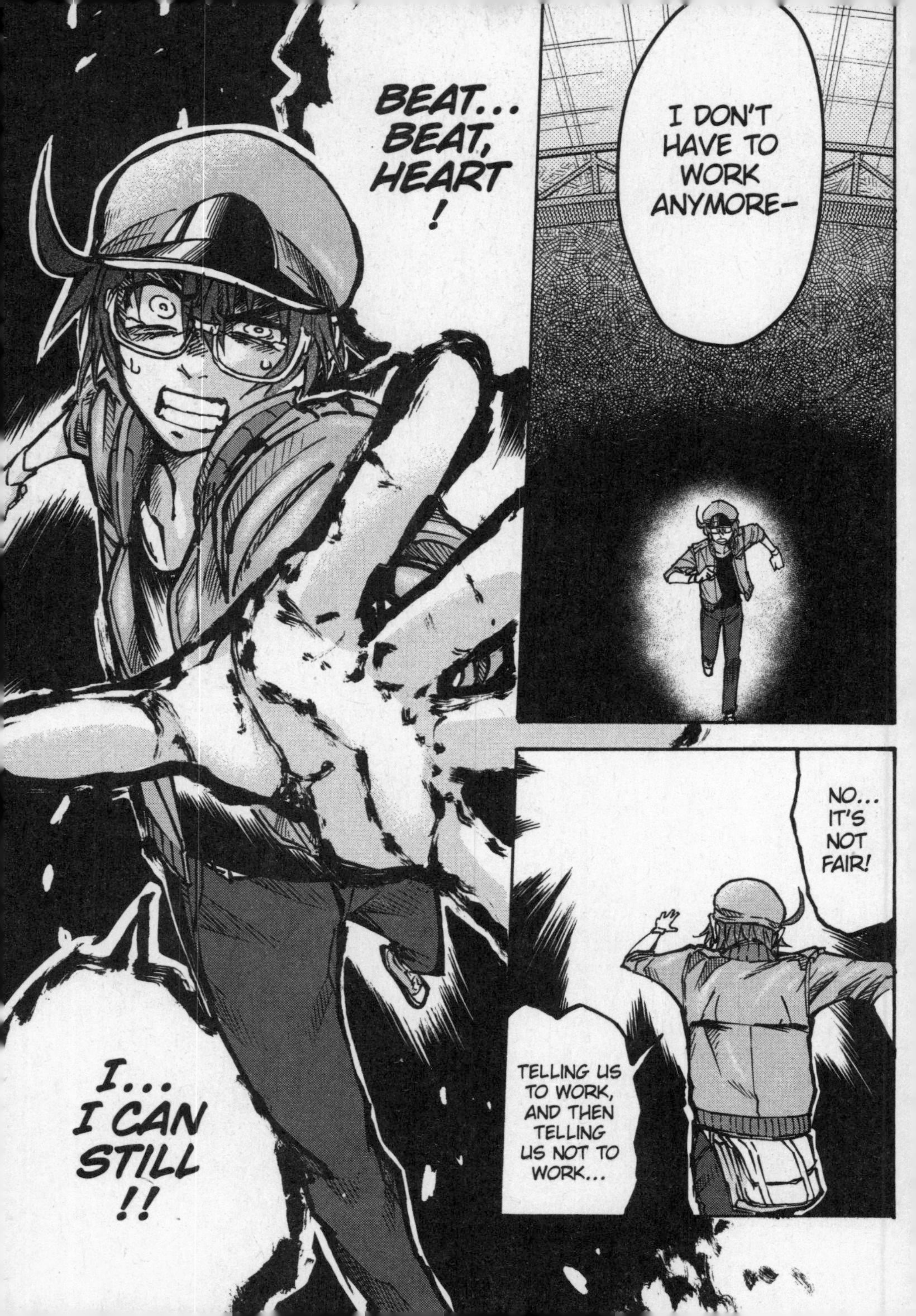
I DON'T HAVE TO WORK ANYMORE-
NO... IT'S NOT FAIR!
TELLING US TO WORK, AND THEN TELLING US NOT TO WORK...
BEAT... BEAT, HEART!
I... I CAN STILL!!

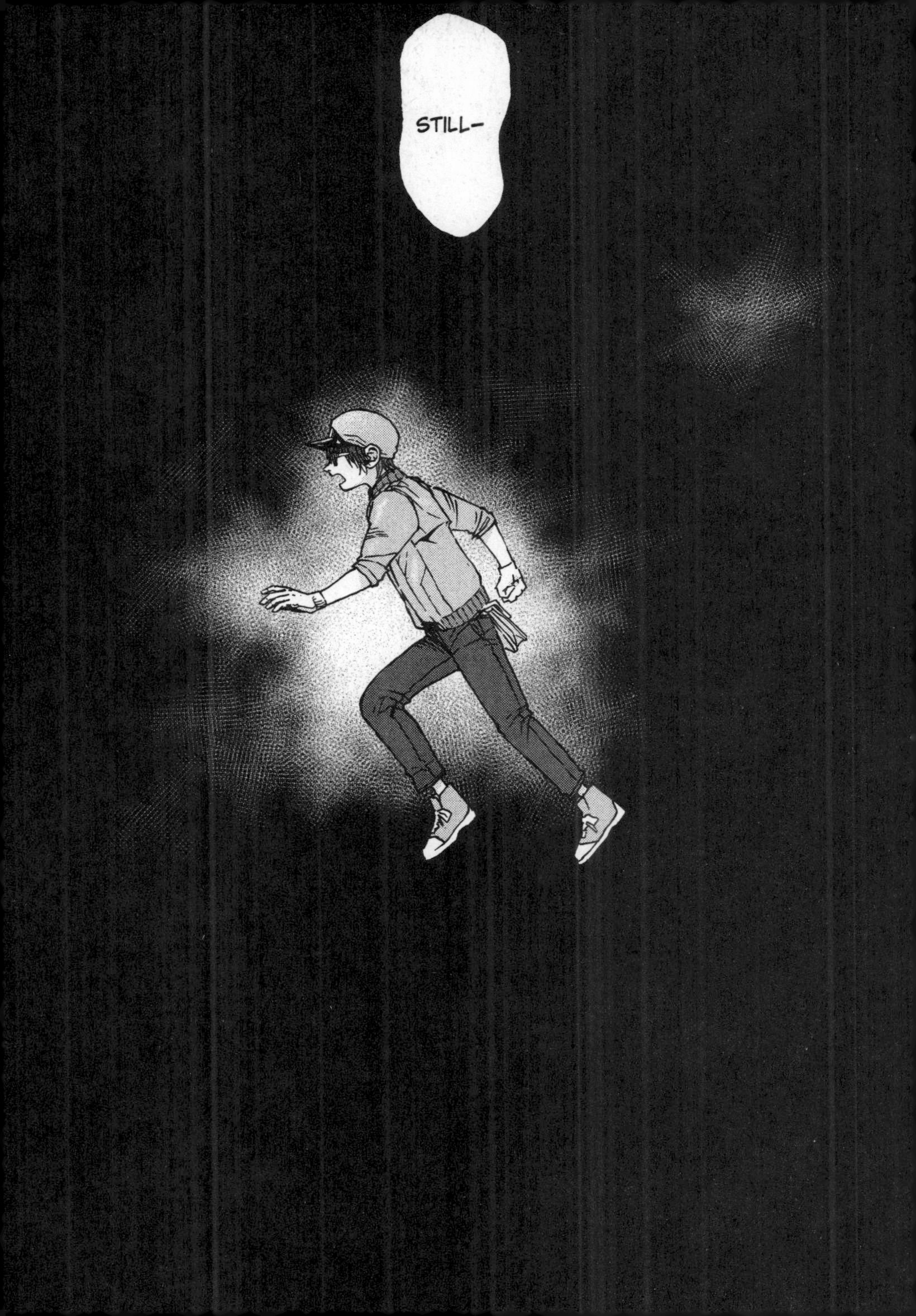
STILL-

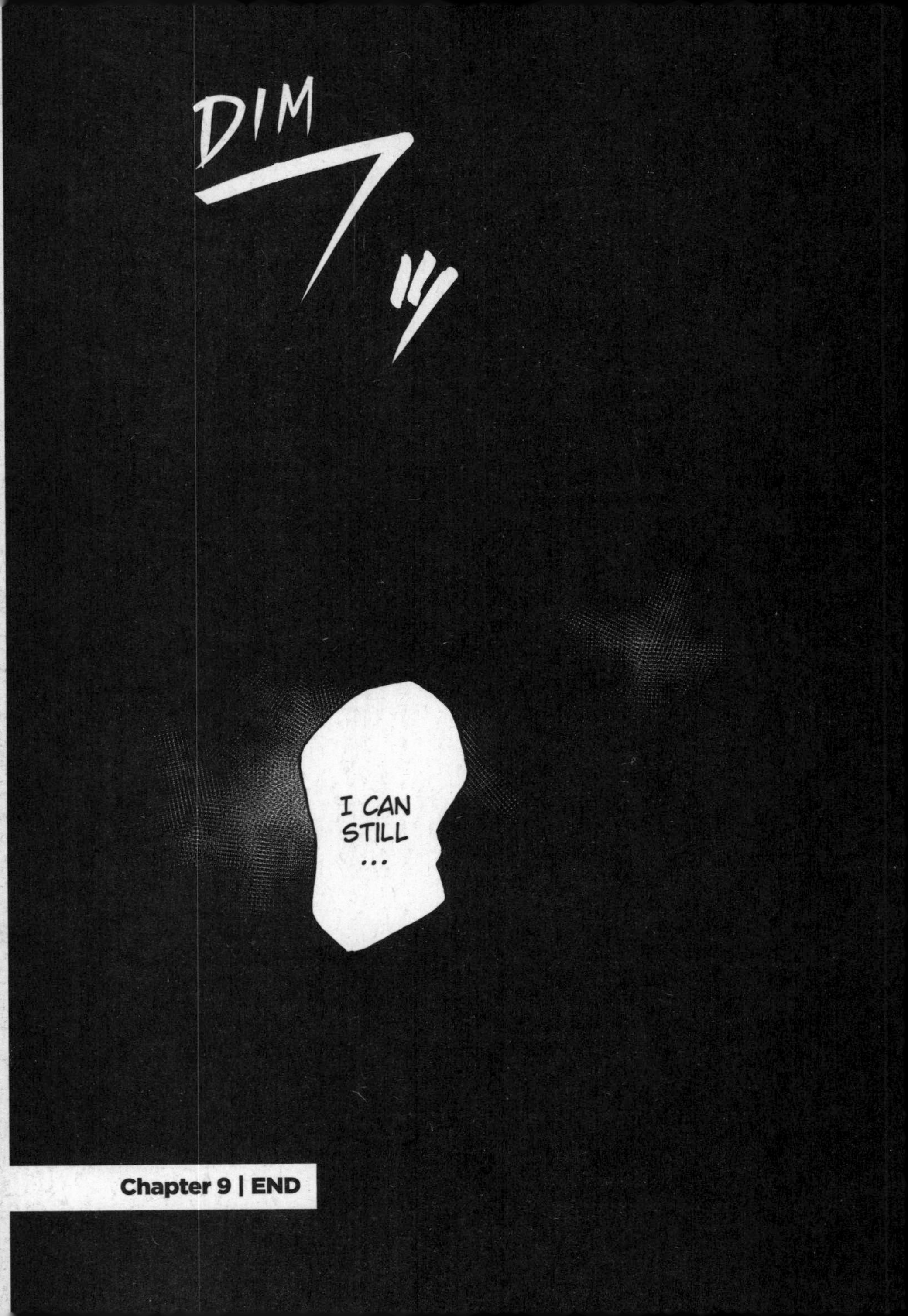
DIM
I CAN STILL
...

Chapter 9 | END

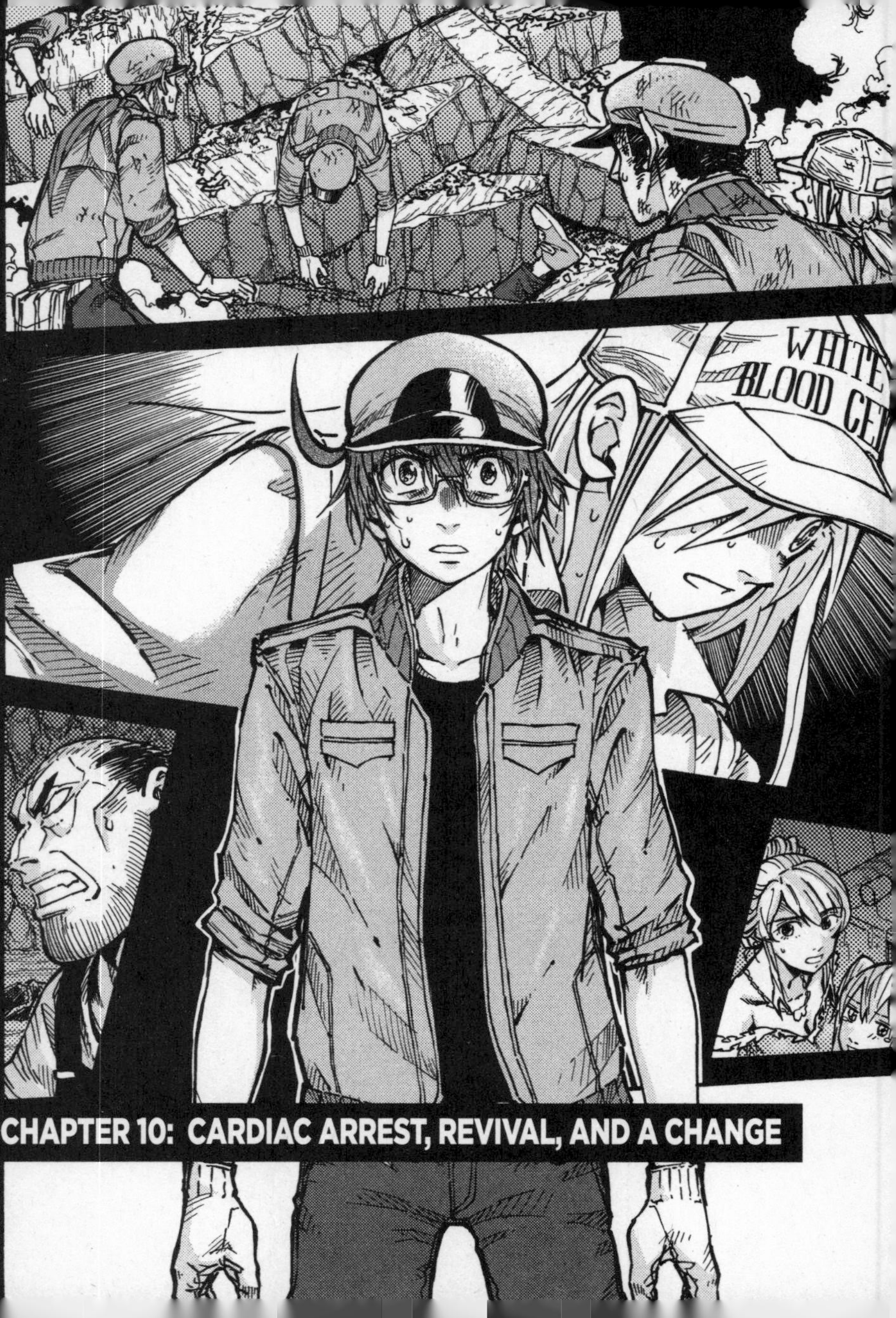
WHITE
BLOOD CE

CHAPTER 10: CARDIAC ARREST, REVIVAL, AND A CHANGE

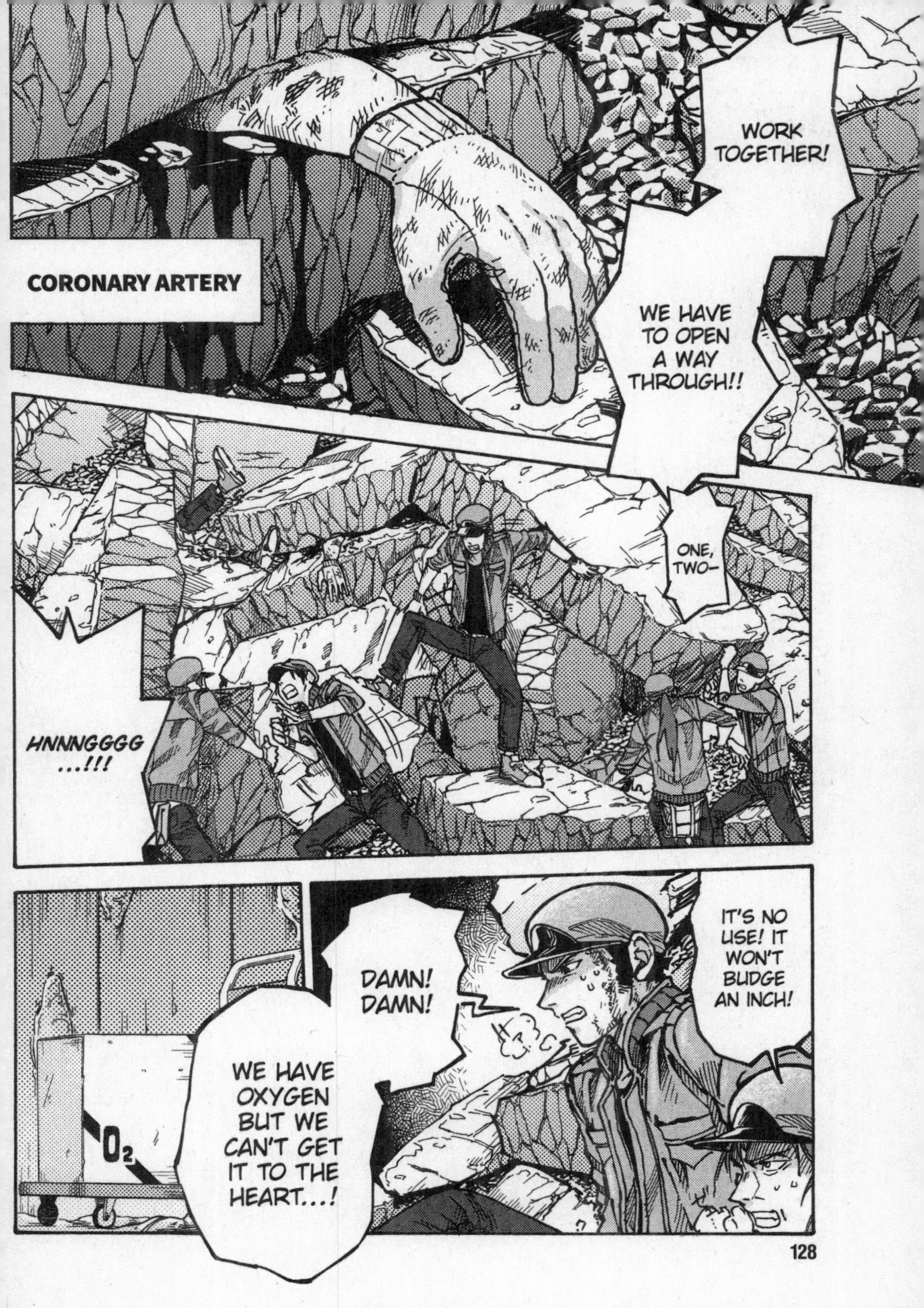
CORONARY ARTERY
WORK TOGETHER!
WE HAVE TO OPEN A WAY THROUGH!!
ONE, TWO—
HNNNGGGG ...!!!
IT'S NO USE! IT WON'T BUDGE AN INCH!
DAMN! DAMN!
WE HAVE OXYGEN BUT WE CAN'T GET IT TO THE HEART...!
O2

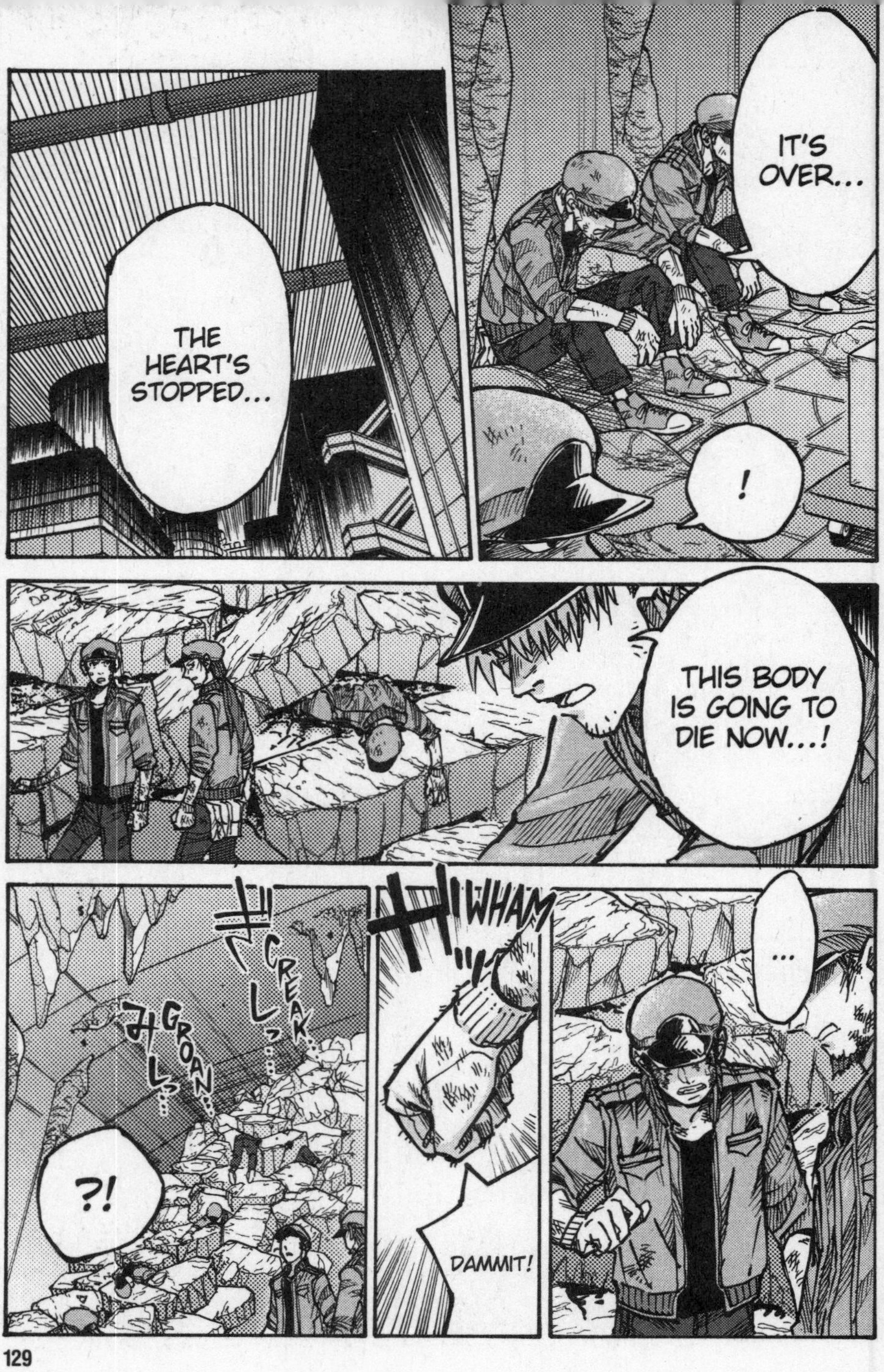
IT'S OVER...
!
THE HEART'S STOPPED...
THIS BODY IS GOING TO DIE NOW...!
...
WHAM
DAMMIT!
CREAK...
GROAN...
?!

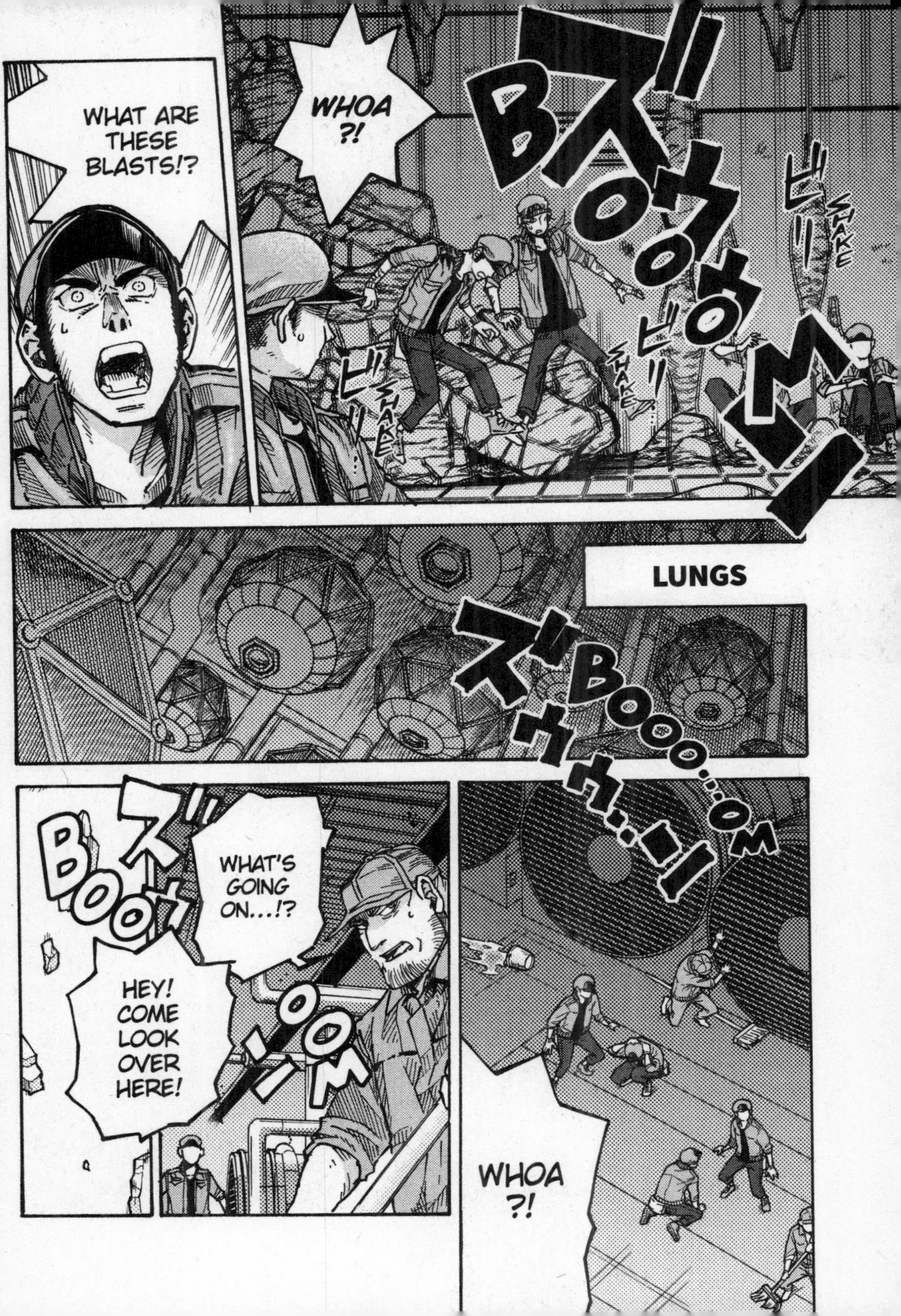

WHOA ?!
BOOM
SHAKE
SHAKE
SHAKE
WHAT ARE THESE BLASTS!?
LUNGS
BOOO...OM
WHOA ?!
BOOO
WHAT'S GOING ON...!?
HEY! COME LOOK OVER HERE!
...OOM

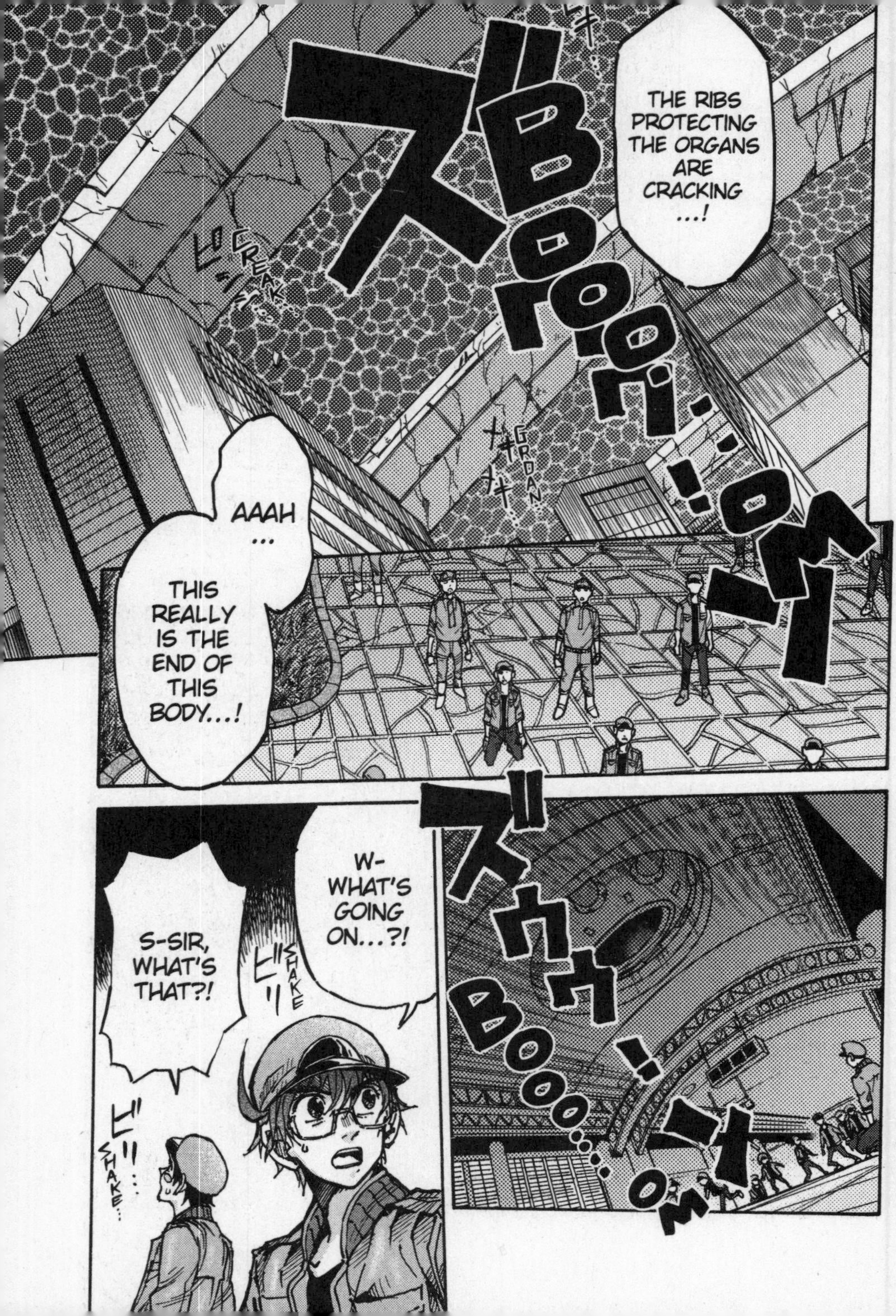
THE RIBS PROTECTING THE ORGANS ARE CRACKING ...!
BOOOOOM!!
CREAK...
GRDAN...
AAAH ... THIS REALLY IS THE END OF THIS BODY...!
BOOOO...OM
W- WHAT'S GOING ON...?!
SHAKE
S-SIR, WHAT'S THAT?!
SHAKE...

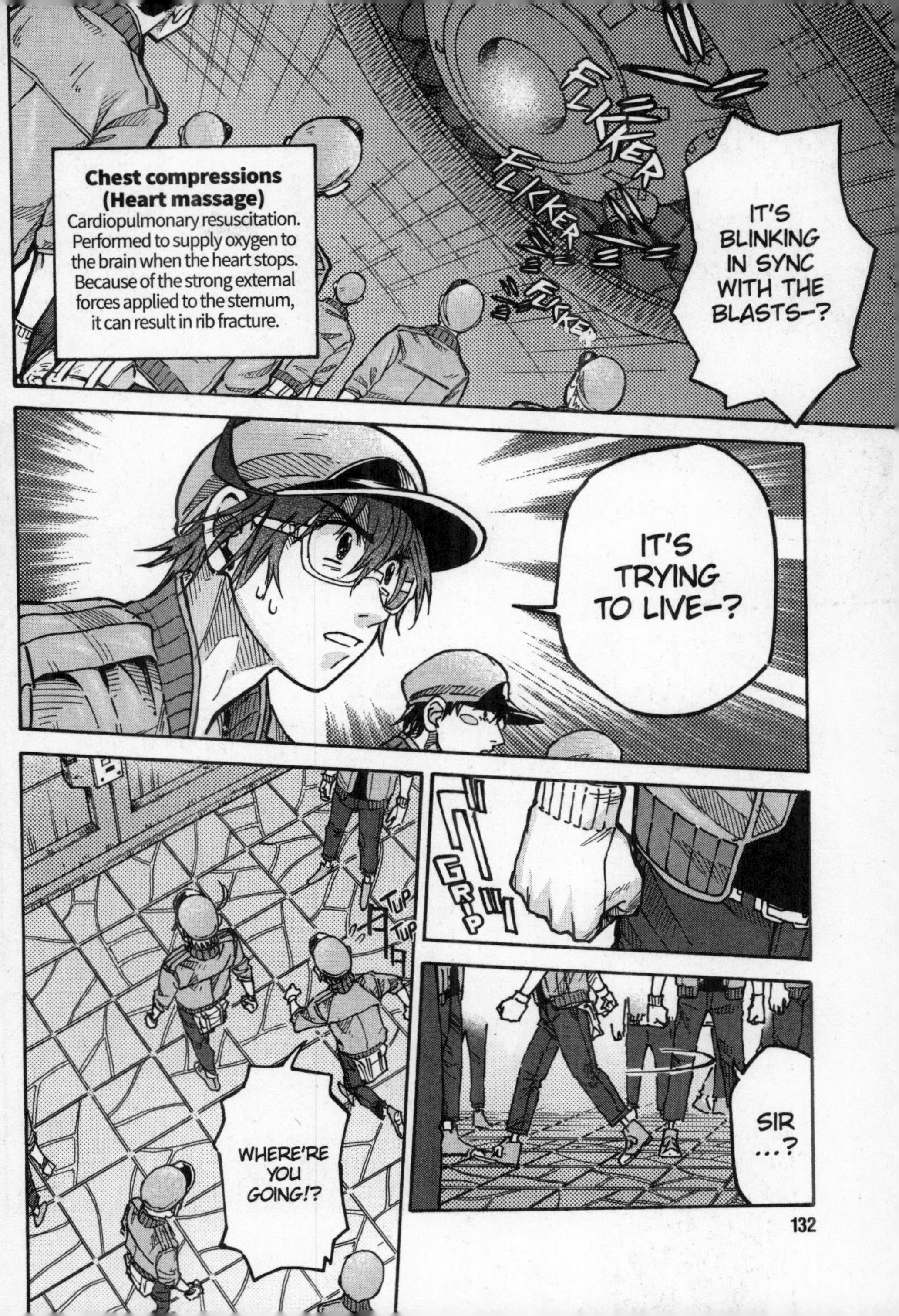
FLICKER
FLICKER
FLICKER
FLICKER
IT'S BLINKING IN SYNC WITH THE BLASTS-?
Chest compressions (Heart massage)
Cardiopulmonary resuscitation. Performed to supply oxygen to the brain when the heart stops. Because of the strong external forces applied to the sternum, it can result in rib fracture.
IT'S TRYING TO LIVE-?
GRIP
SIR ...?
TUP TUP
WHERE'RE YOU GOING!?

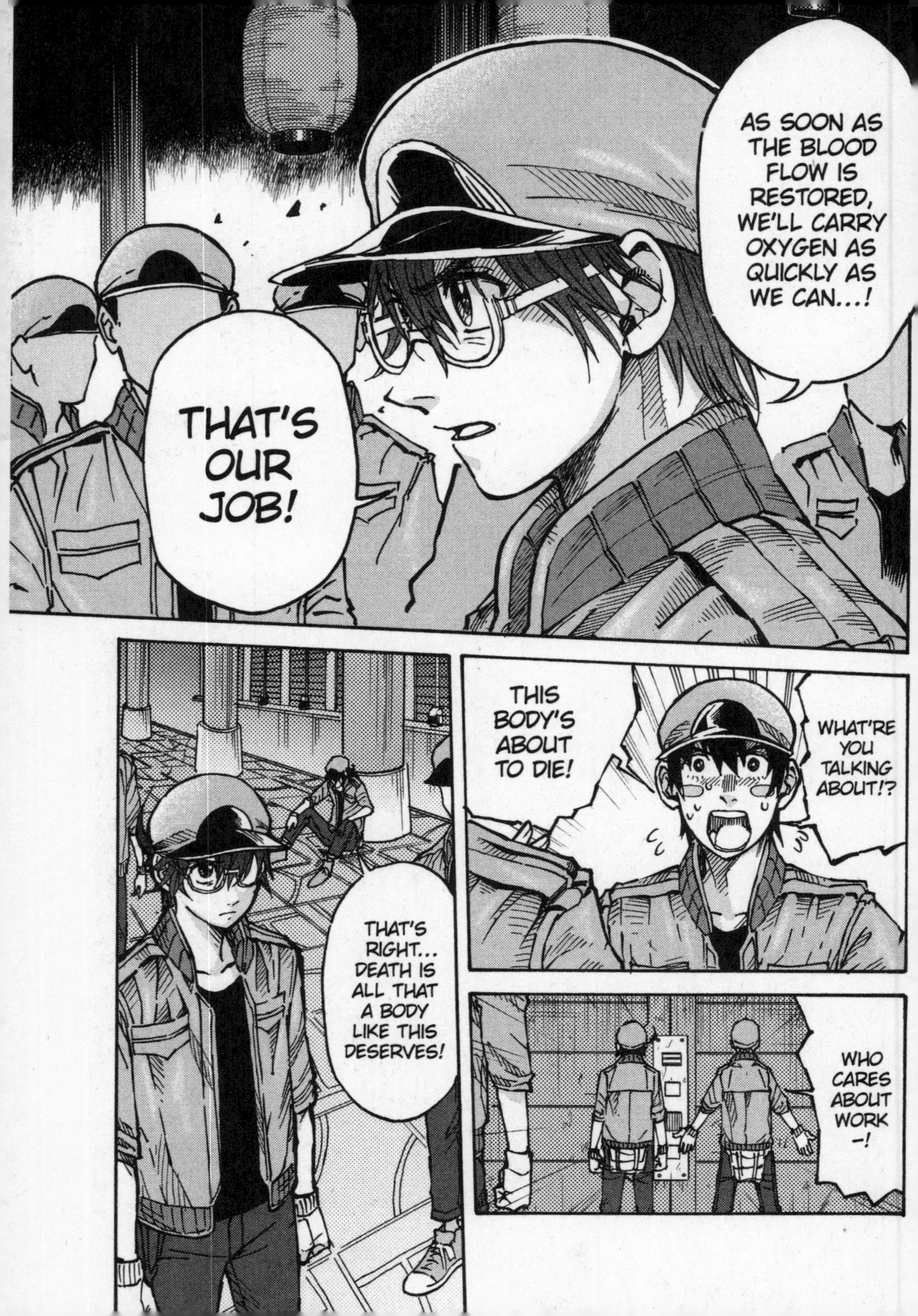
AS SOON AS THE BLOOD FLOW IS RESTORED, WE'LL CARRY OXYGEN AS QUICKLY AS WE CAN...!
THAT'S OUR JOB!
WHAT'RE YOU TALKING ABOUT!?
THIS BODY'S ABOUT TO DIE!
WHO CARES ABOUT WORK —!
THAT'S RIGHT... DEATH IS ALL THAT A BODY LIKE THIS DESERVES!

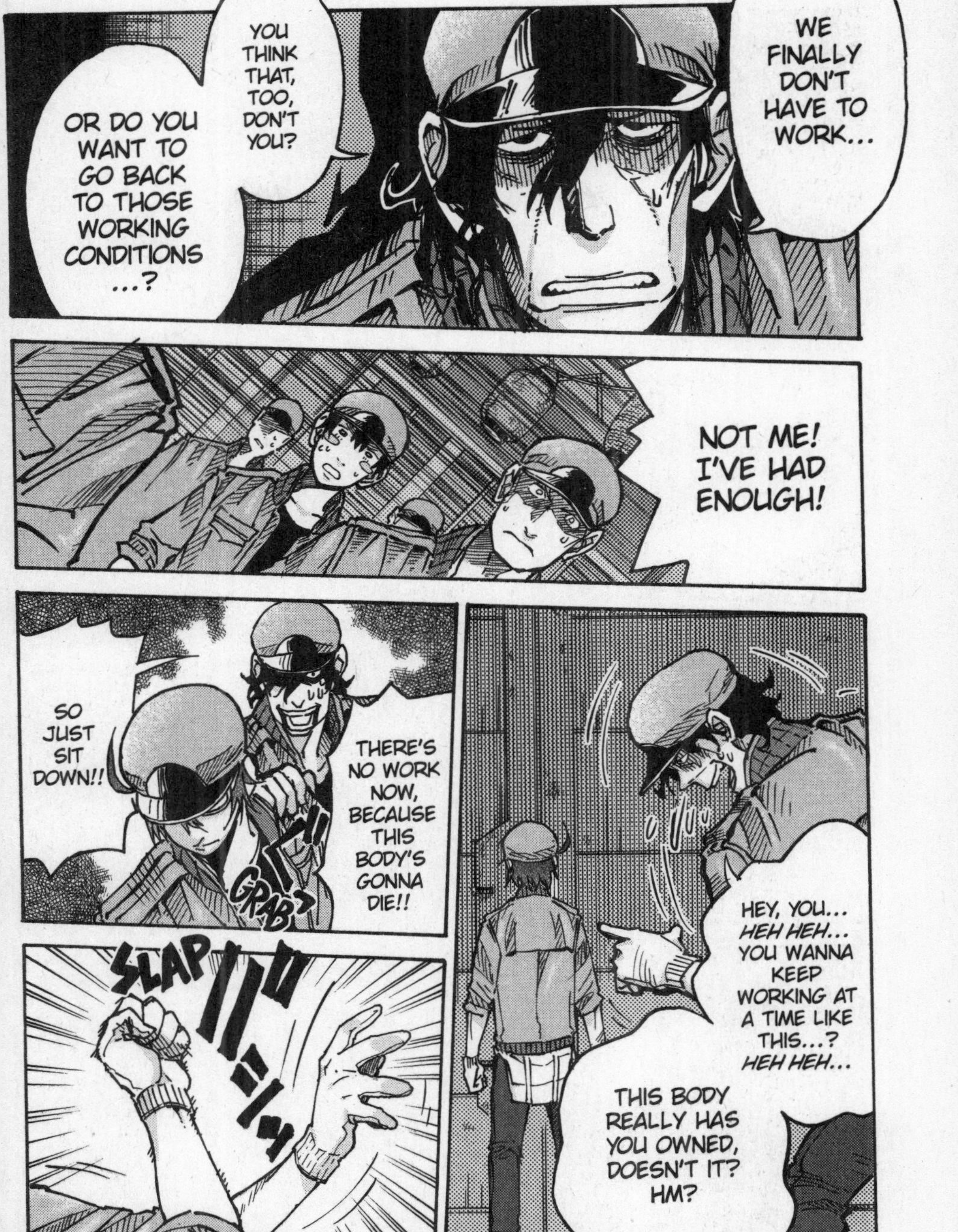
WE FINALLY DON'T HAVE TO WORK...
YOU THINK THAT, TOO, DON'T YOU?
OR DO YOU WANT TO GO BACK TO THOSE WORKING CONDITIONS ...?
NOT ME! I'VE HAD ENOUGH!
HEY, YOU... *HEH HEH...* YOU WANNA KEEP WORKING AT A TIME LIKE THIS...? *HEH HEH...*
THIS BODY REALLY HAS YOU OWNED, DOESN'T IT? HM?
THERE'S NO WORK NOW, BECAUSE THIS BODY'S GONNA DIE!!
SO JUST SIT DOWN!!
GRAB
SLAP

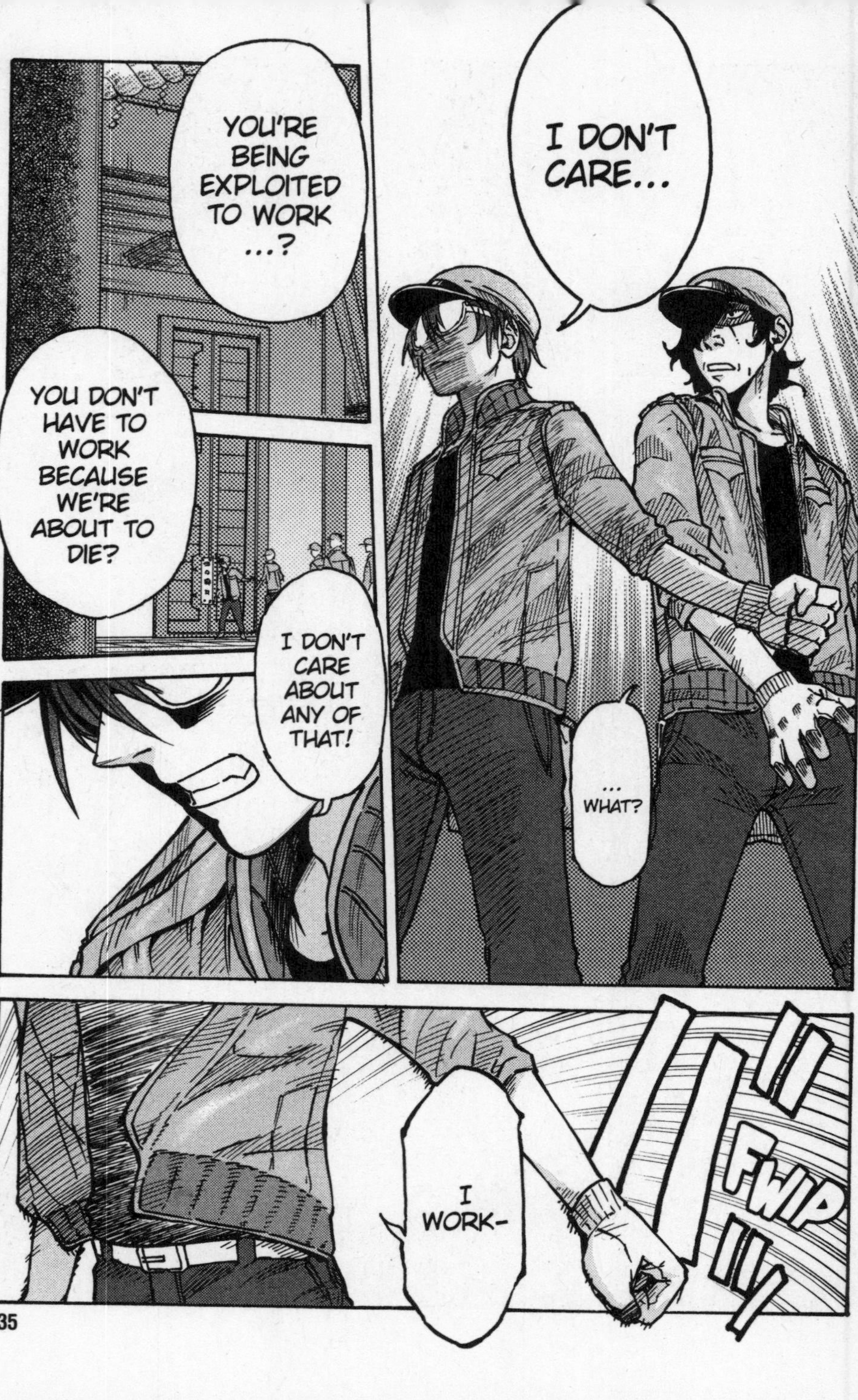
I DON'T CARE...
...WHAT?
YOU'RE BEING EXPLOITED TO WORK ...?
YOU DON'T HAVE TO WORK BECAUSE WE'RE ABOUT TO DIE?
I DON'T CARE ABOUT ANY OF THAT!
FWIP
I WORK-

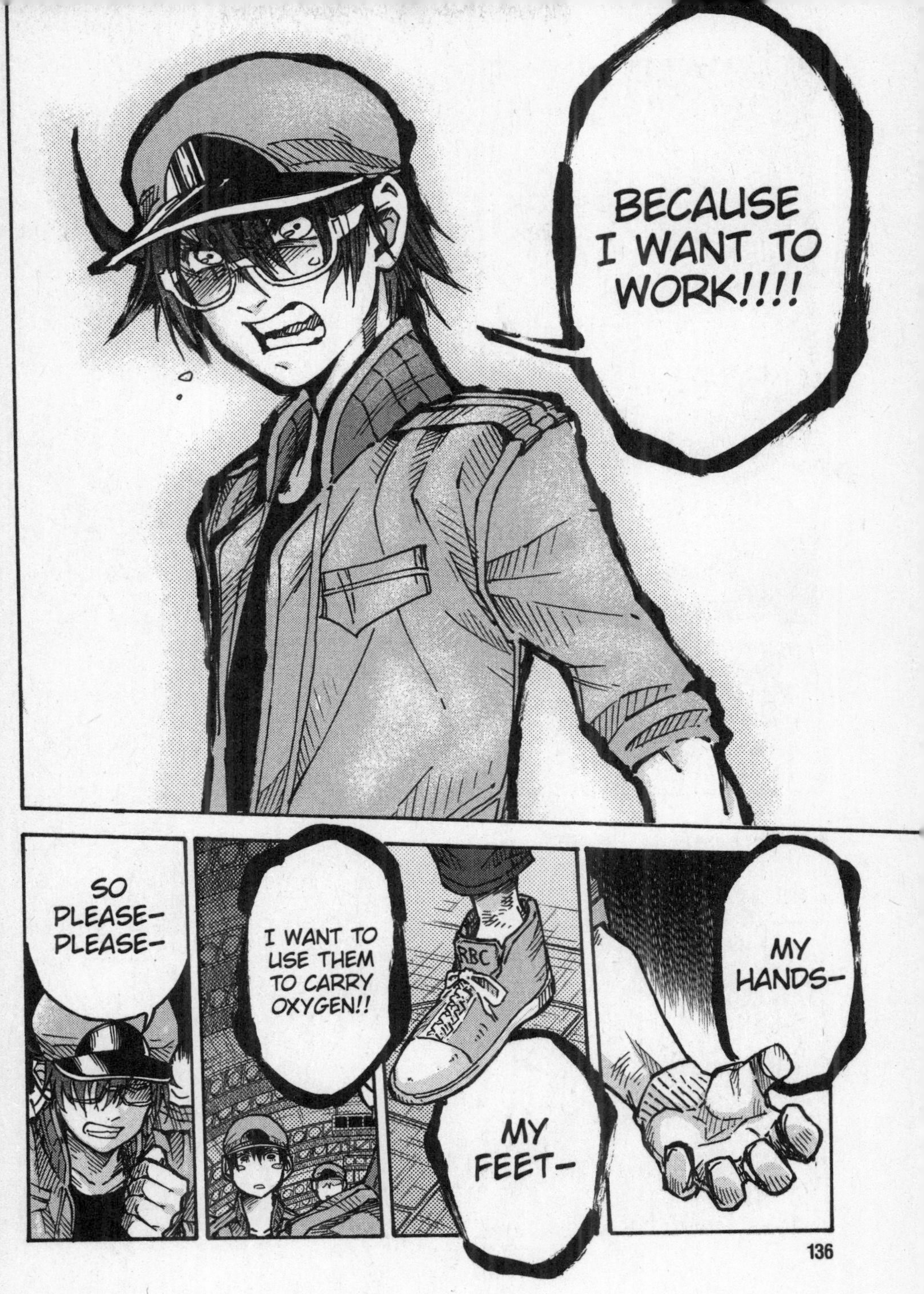
BECAUSE I WANT TO WORK!!!!
MY HANDS-
MY FEET-
RBC
I WANT TO USE THEM TO CARRY OXYGEN!!
SO PLEASE-PLEASE-

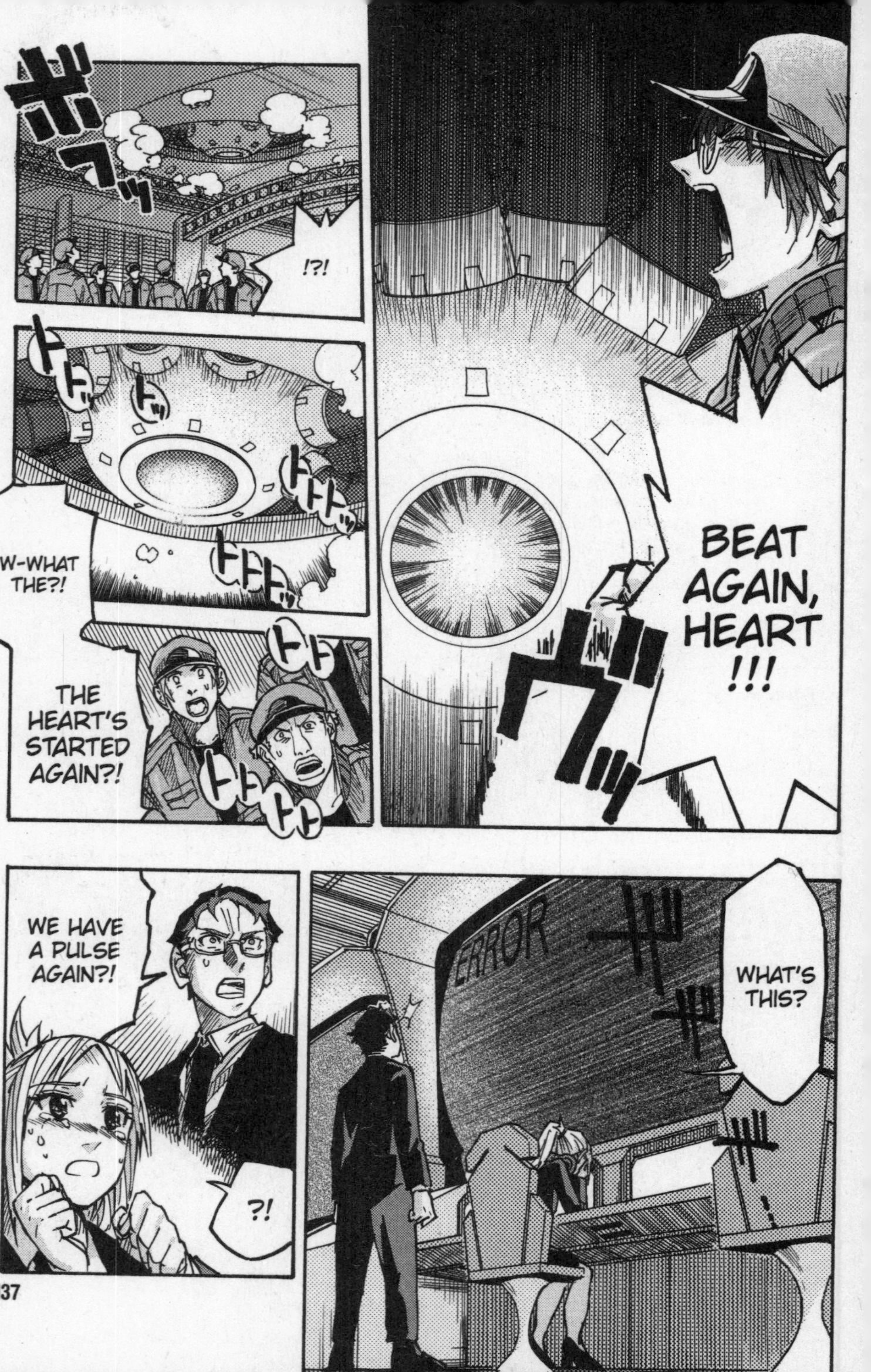
BEAT AGAIN, HEART!!!
!?!
W-WHAT THE?!
THE HEART'S STARTED AGAIN?!
ERROR
WHAT'S THIS?
WE HAVE A PULSE AGAIN?!
?!

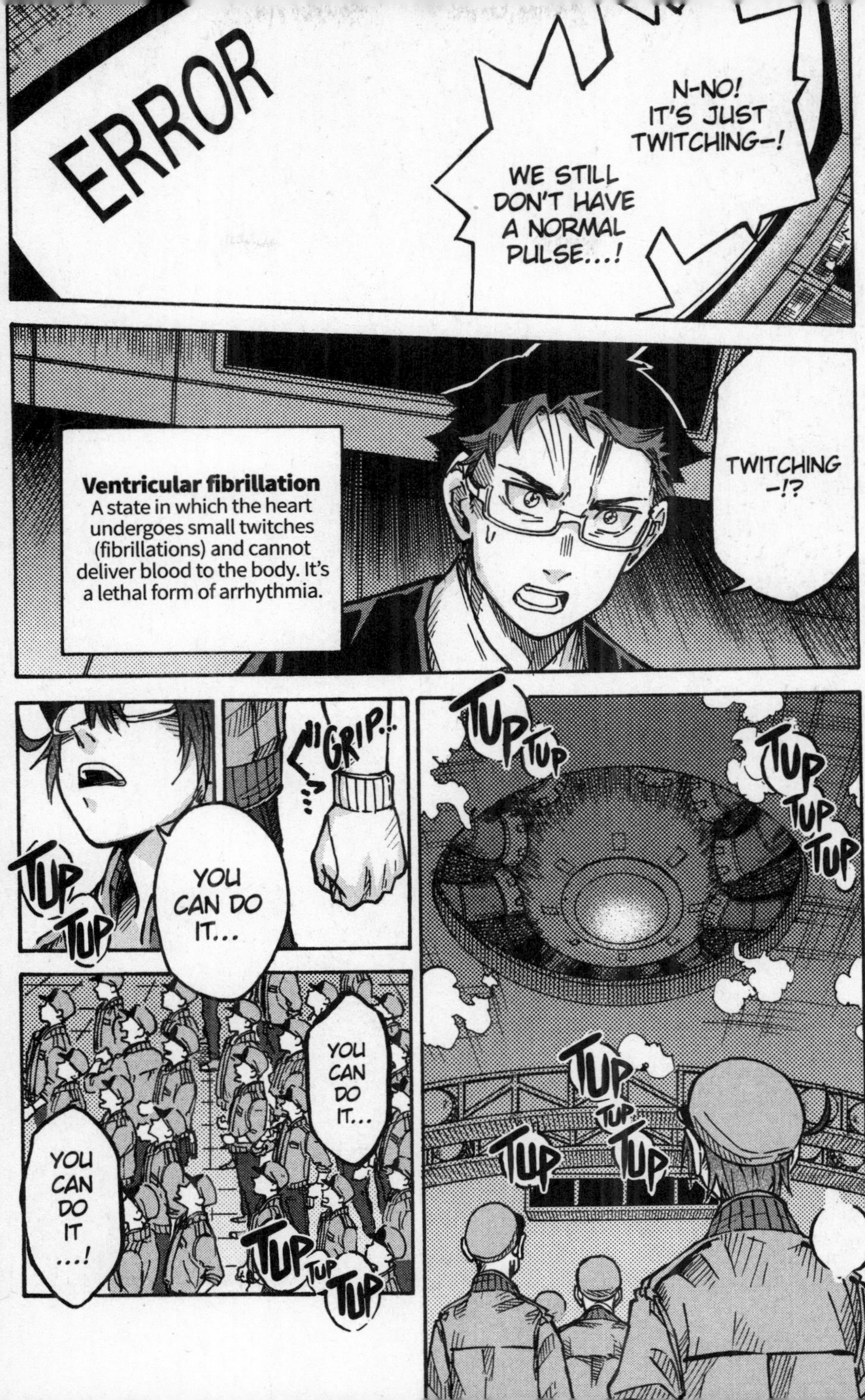
ERROR
N-NO! IT'S JUST TWITCHING-!
WE STILL DON'T HAVE A NORMAL PULSE...!
TWITCHING -!?
Ventricular fibrillation
A state in which the heart undergoes small twitches (fibrillations) and cannot deliver blood to the body. It's a lethal form of arrhythmia.
TUP TUP
TUP TUP TUP
TUP TUP TUP TUP
GRIP...
TUP TUP
YOU CAN DO IT...
YOU CAN DO IT...
YOU CAN DO IT ...!
TUP TUP TUP

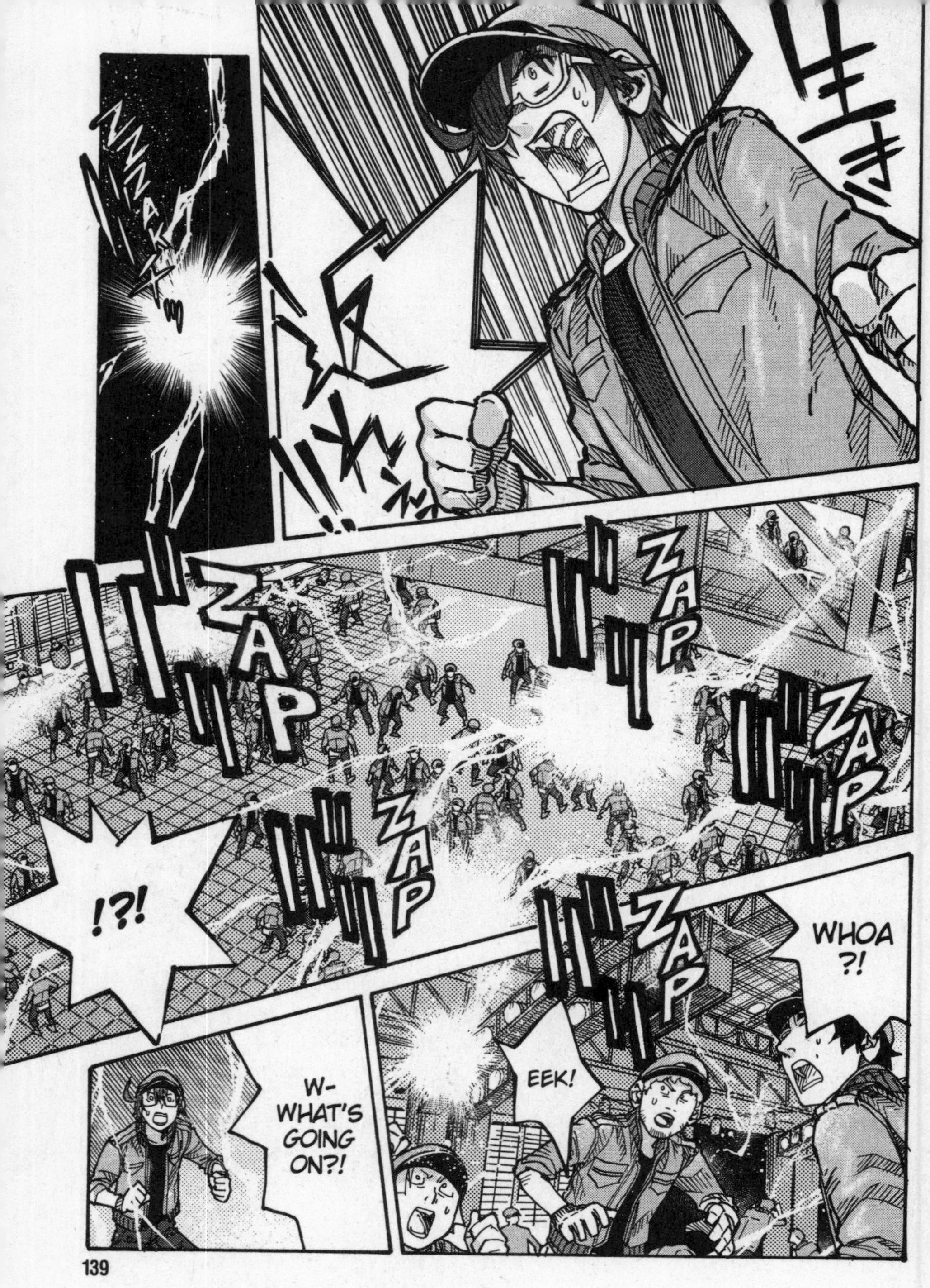
ZZZZAK
ZAP
ZAP
ZAP
ZAP
ZAP
!?!
WHOA ?!
EEK!
W- WHAT'S GOING ON?!

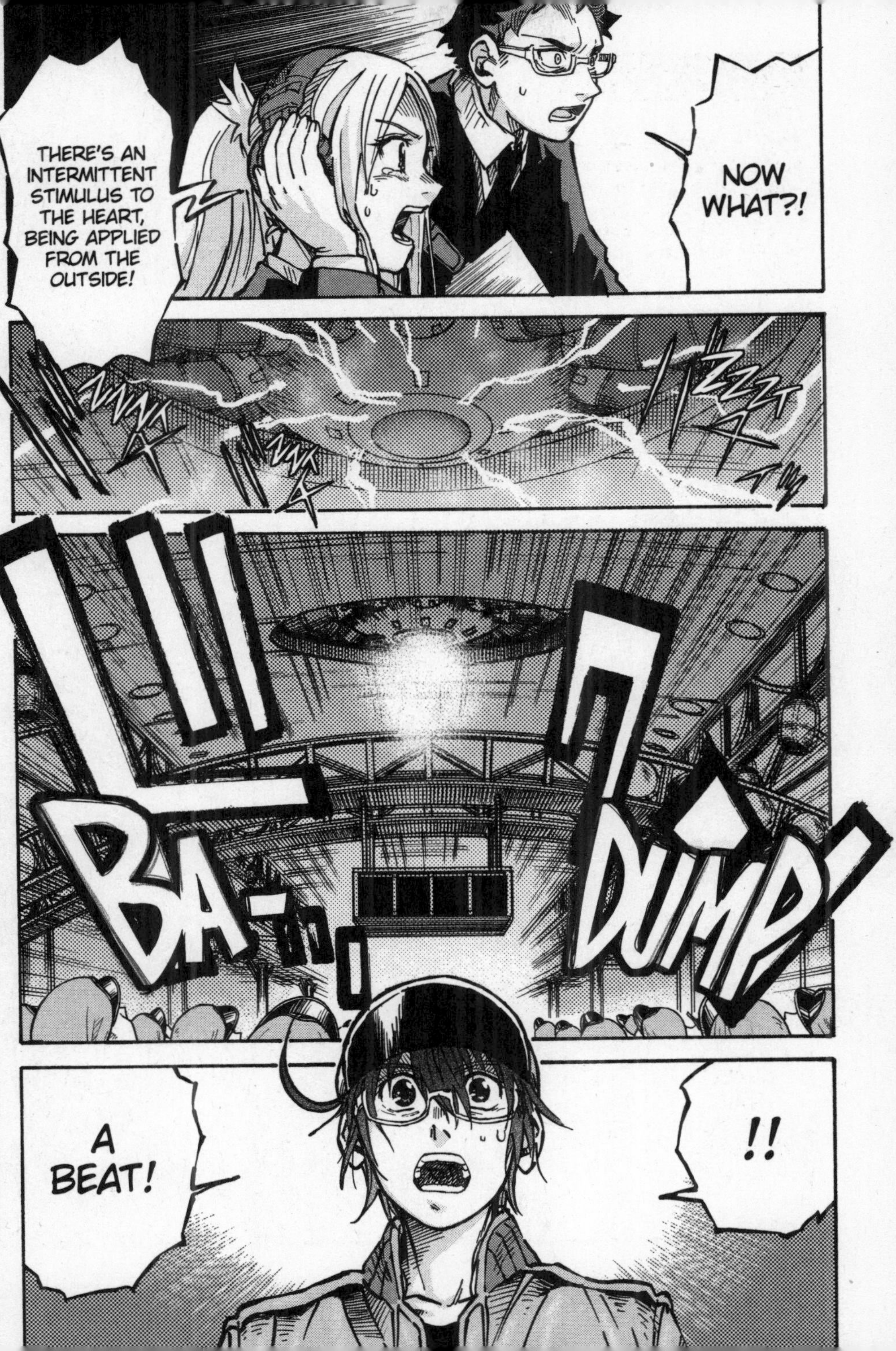
NOW WHAT?!
THERE'S AN INTERMITTENT STIMULUS TO THE HEART, BEING APPLIED FROM THE OUTSIDE!
BA-DUMP!
!!
A BEAT!

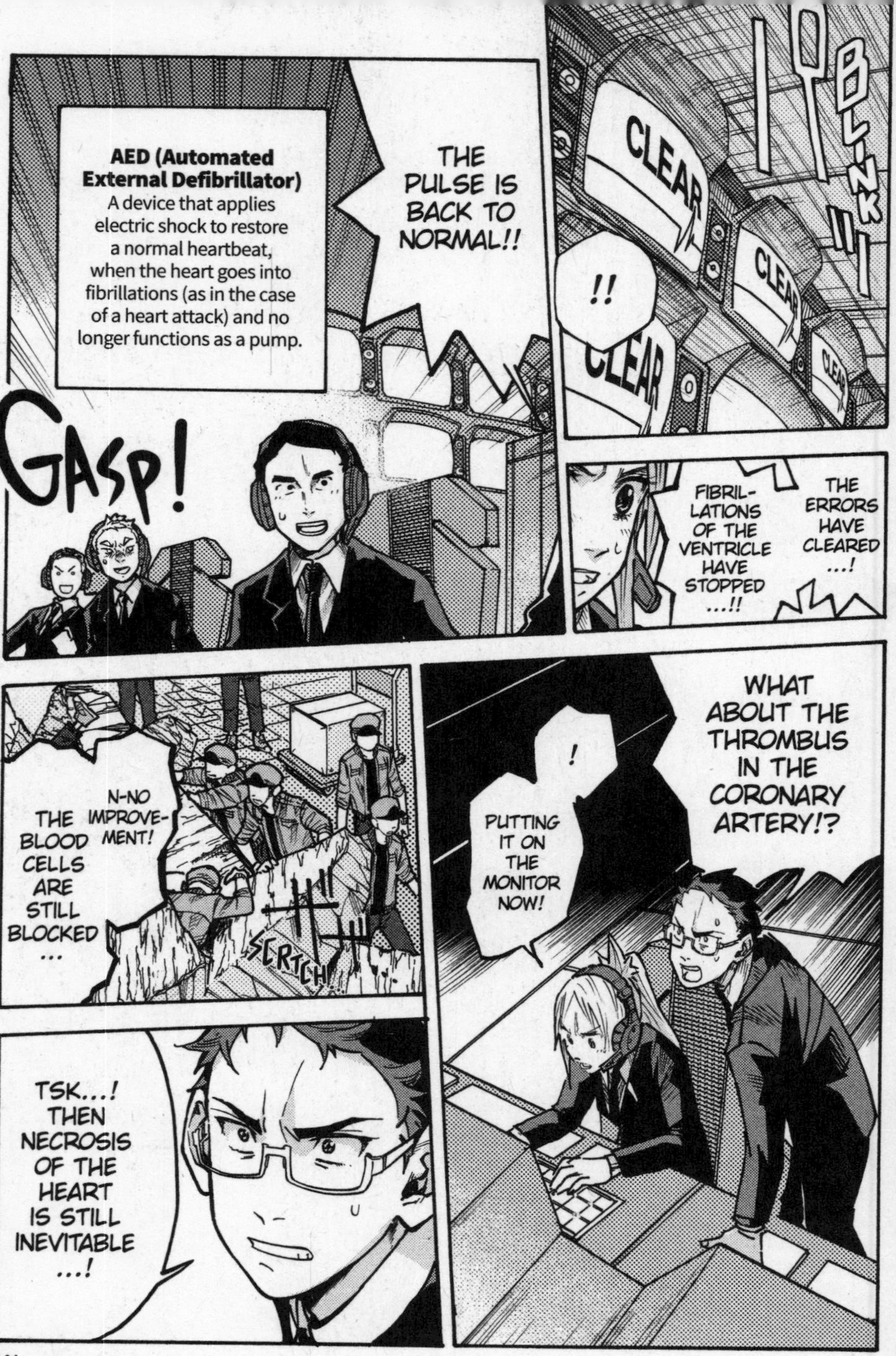
CLEAR
CLEAR
CLEAR
CLEAR
BLINK
!!
THE ERRORS HAVE CLEARED ...!
FIBRIL-LATIONS OF THE VENTRICLE HAVE STOPPED ...!!
AED (Automated External Defibrillator)
A device that applies electric shock to restore a normal heartbeat, when the heart goes into fibrillations (as in the case of a heart attack) and no longer functions as a pump.
THE PULSE IS BACK TO NORMAL!!
GASP!
WHAT ABOUT THE THROMBUS IN THE CORONARY ARTERY!?
!
PUTTING IT ON THE MONITOR NOW!
N-NO IMPROVE-MENT!
THE BLOOD CELLS ARE STILL BLOCKED ...
SCRTCH
TSK...! THEN NECROSIS OF THE HEART IS STILL INEVITABLE ...!

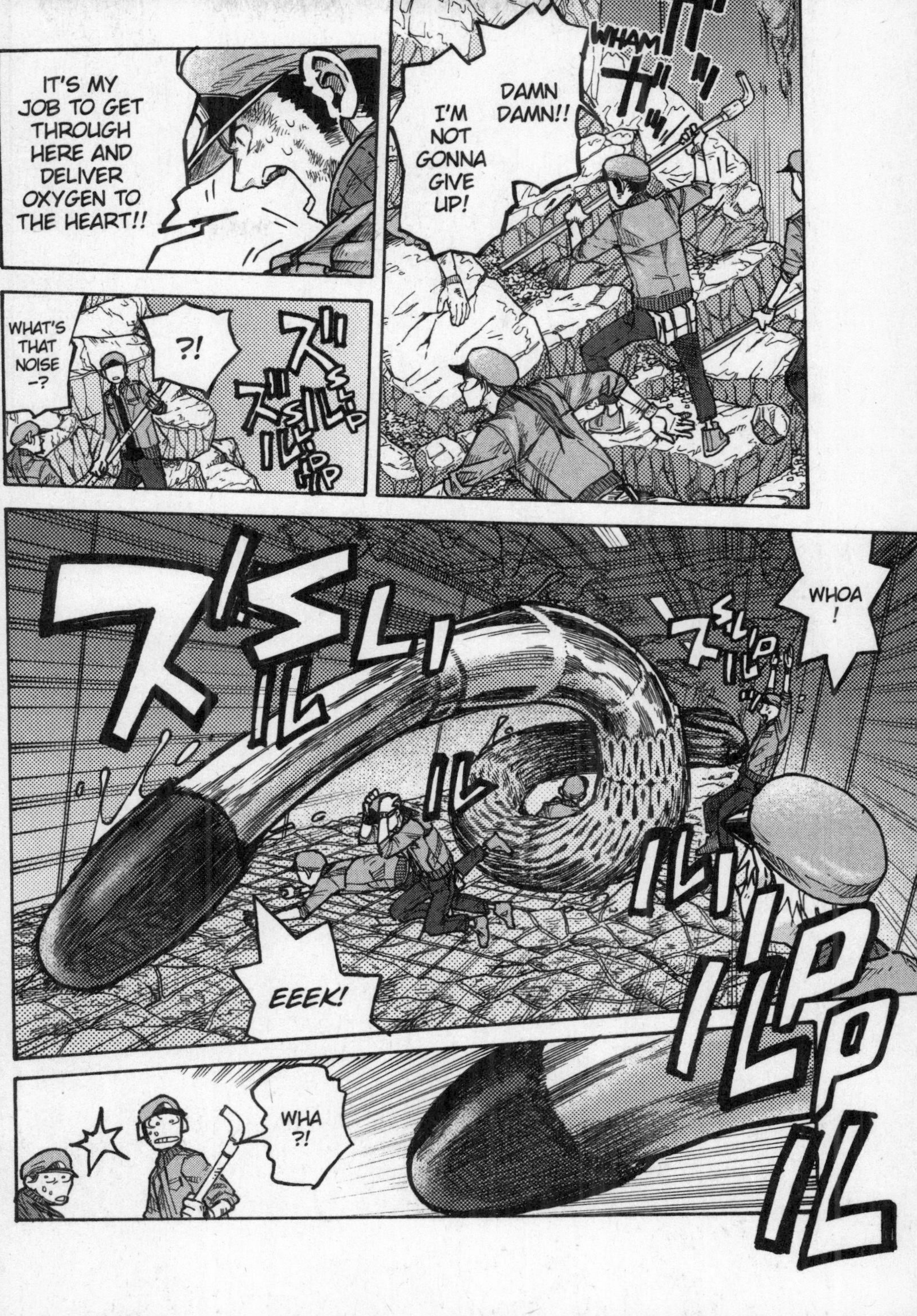
WHAM
DAMN DAMN!!
I'M NOT GONNA GIVE UP!
IT'S MY JOB TO GET THROUGH HERE AND DELIVER OXYGEN TO THE HEART!!
SLIP
?!
WHAT'S THAT NOISE-?
WHOA!
SLIP
EEEK!
WHA?!

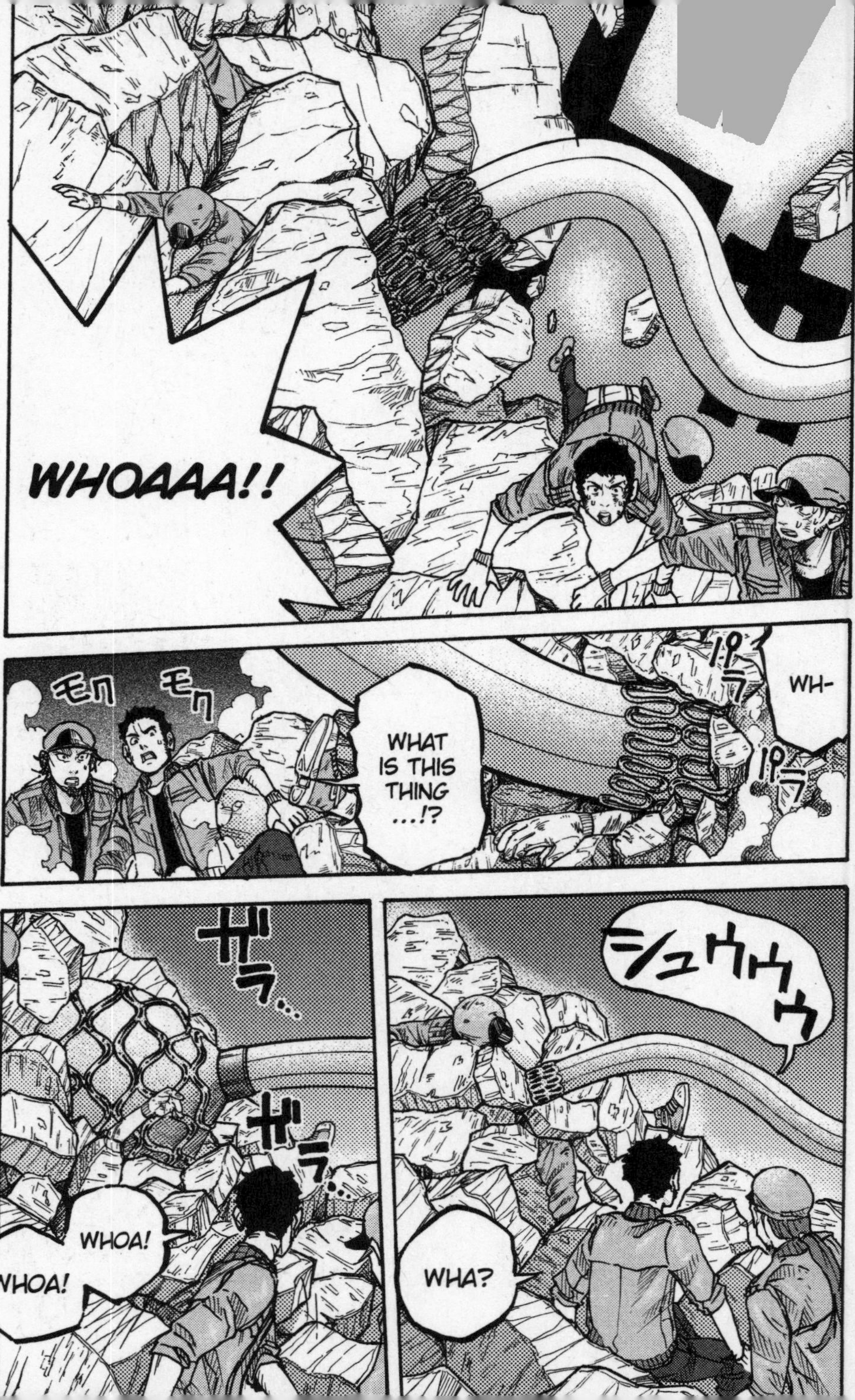
WHOAAA!!
WH-
パラ
パラ
WHAT IS THIS THING ...!?
モク
モク
シュウウウウ
WHA?
ザラ...
ザラ...
WHOA!
WHOA!

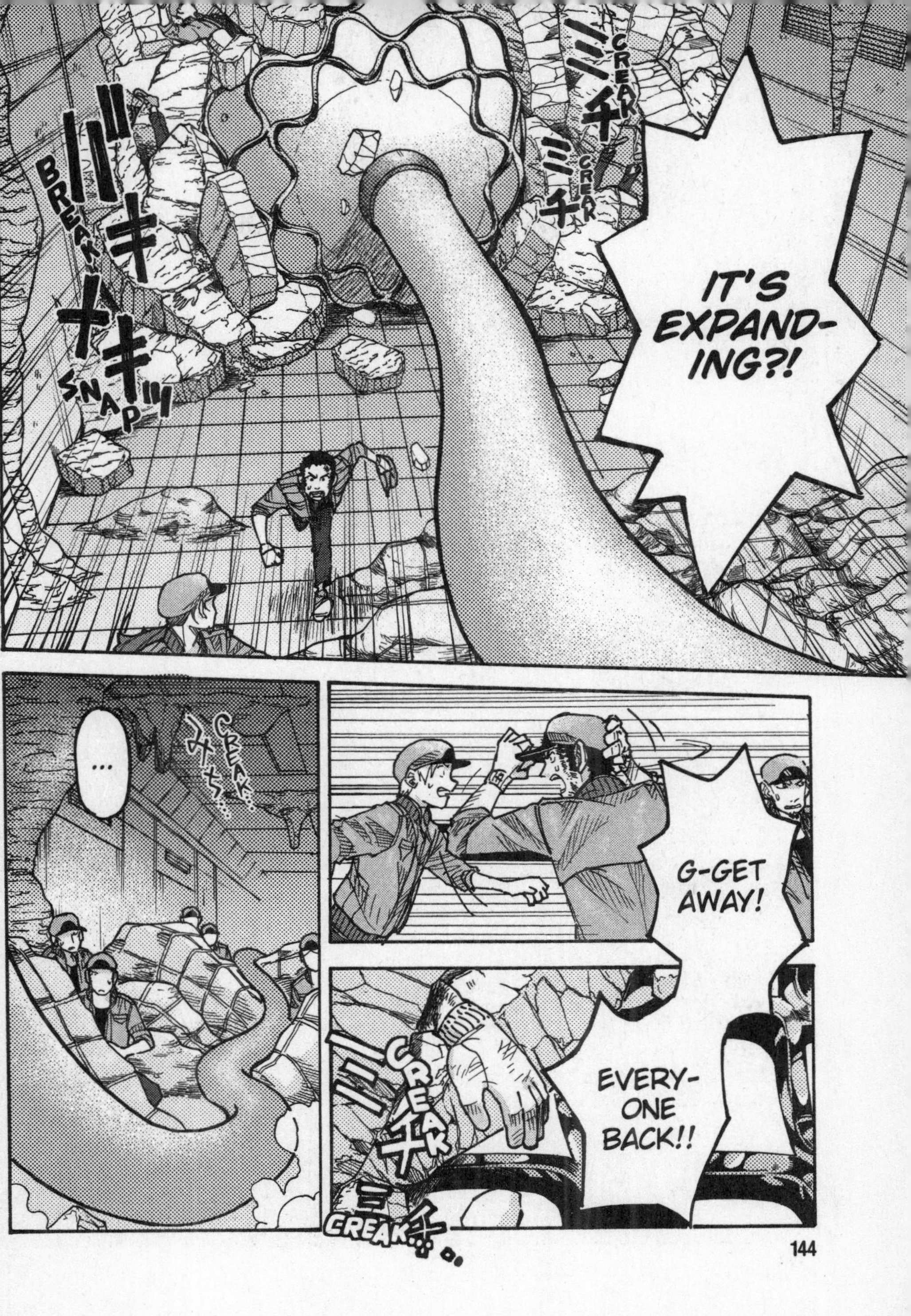

CREAK
CREAK
IT'S EXPANDING?!
BREAK
SNAP
G-GET AWAY!
EVERY-ONE BACK!!
CREAK
CREAK...
...
CREAK...

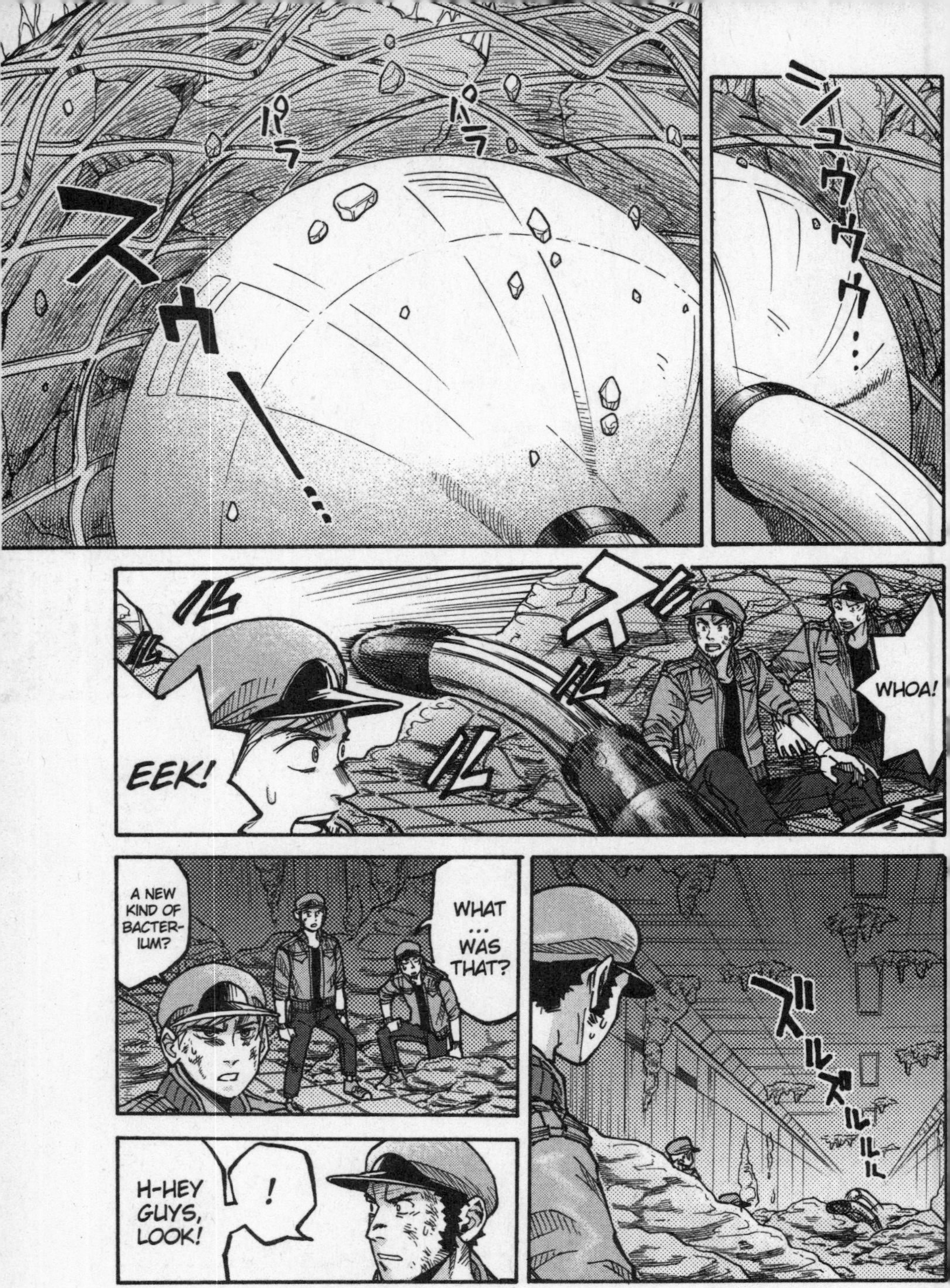

シュウウウ…
パラパラ
スウー…
WHOA!
ズルル
ルル
EEK!
ズルズルルル
WHAT ... WAS THAT?
A NEW KIND OF BACTER-IUM?
!
H-HEY GUYS, LOOK!

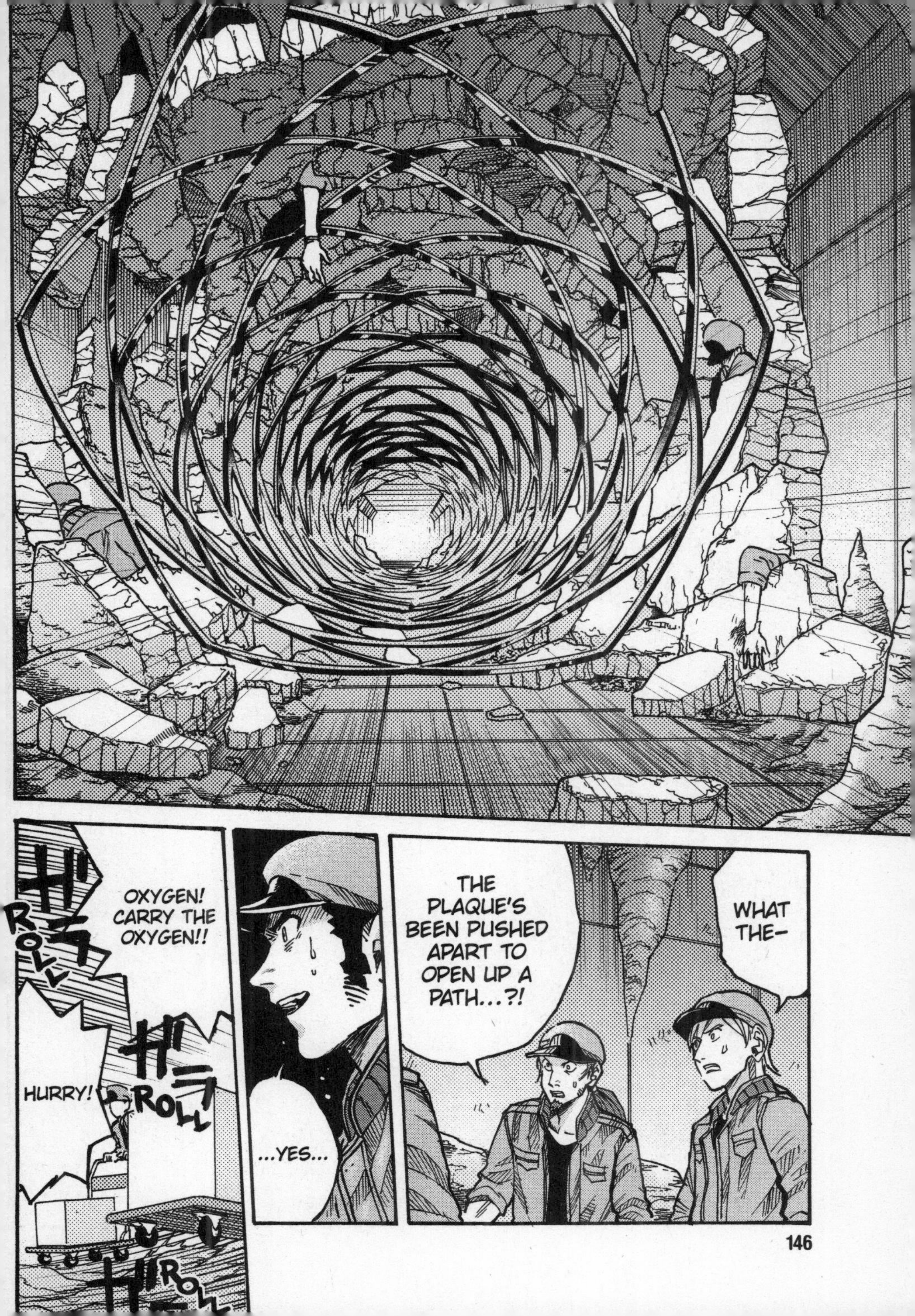
WHAT THE-
THE PLAQUE'S BEEN PUSHED APART TO OPEN UP A PATH...?!
...YES...
OXYGEN! CARRY THE OXYGEN!!
ROLL
HURRY!
ROLL
ROLL

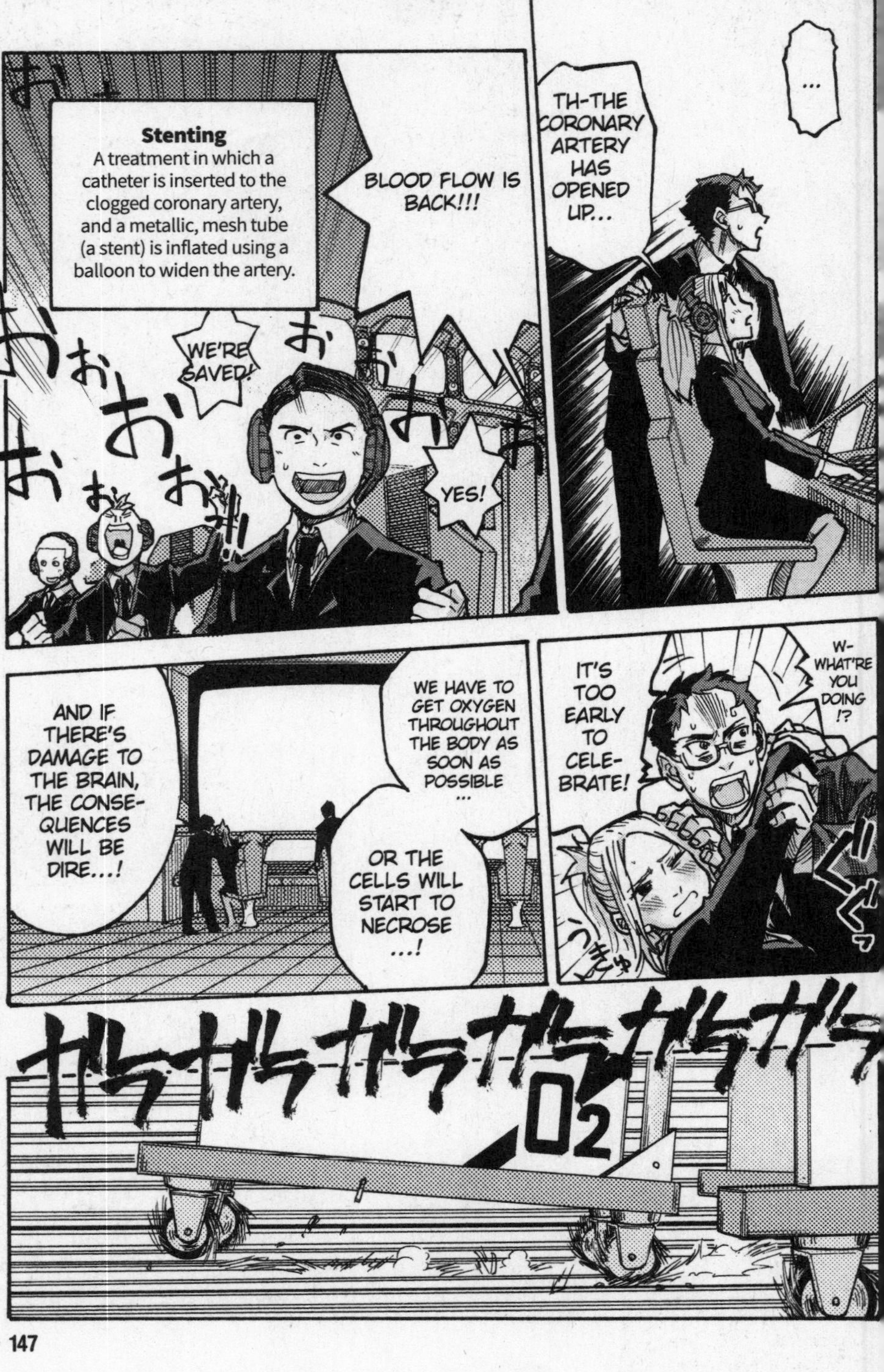
...
TH-THE CORONARY ARTERY HAS OPENED UP...
BLOOD FLOW IS BACK!!!
Stenting
A treatment in which a catheter is inserted to the clogged coronary artery, and a metallic, mesh tube (a stent) is inflated using a balloon to widen the artery.
WE'RE SAVED!
YES!
W-WHAT'RE YOU DOING!?
IT'S TOO EARLY TO CELEBRATE!
WE HAVE TO GET OXYGEN THROUGHOUT THE BODY AS SOON AS POSSIBLE...
OR THE CELLS WILL START TO NECROSE...!
AND IF THERE'S DAMAGE TO THE BRAIN, THE CONSEQUENCES WILL BE DIRE...!
O2

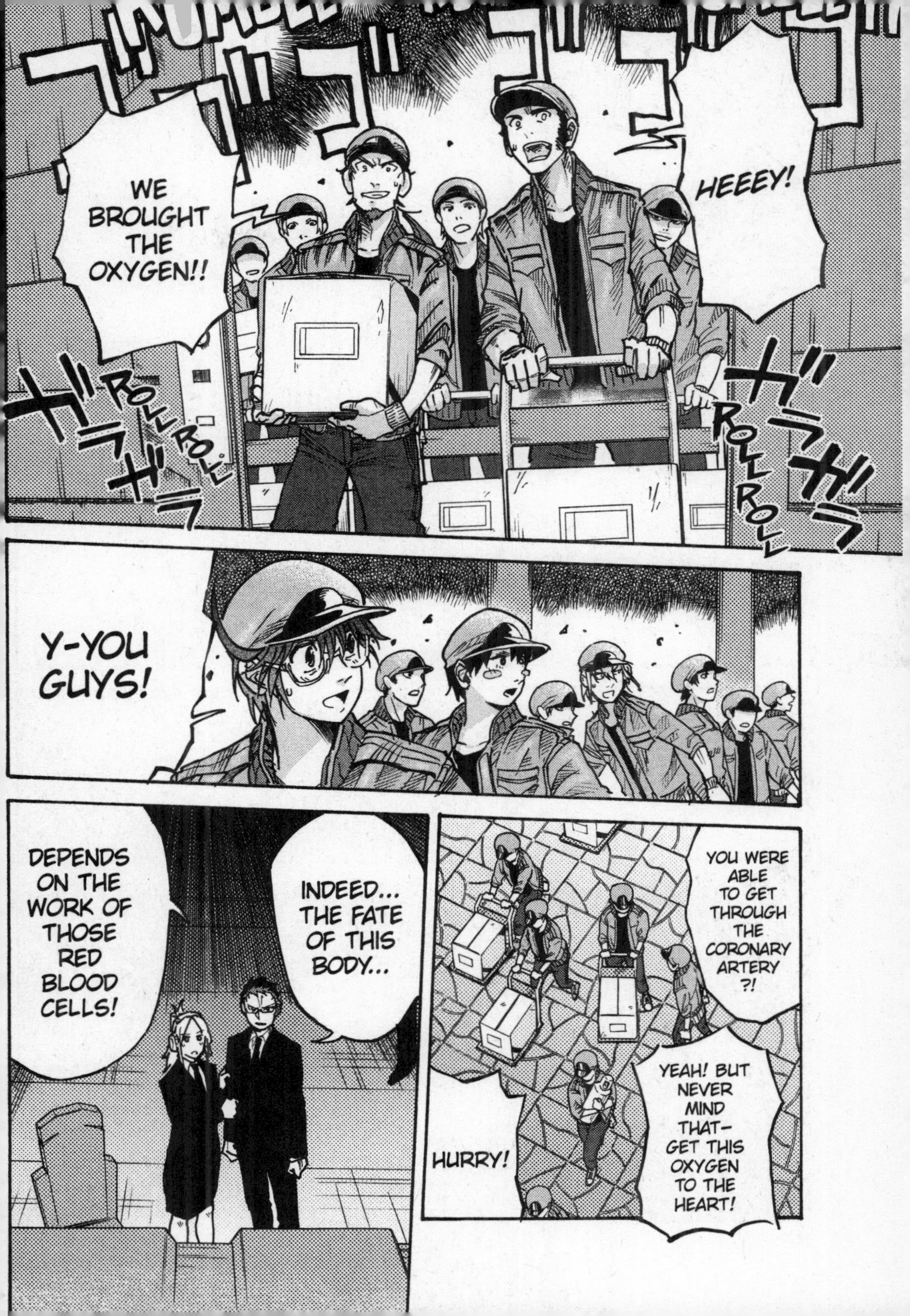
HEEEY!
WE BROUGHT THE OXYGEN!!
ROLL ROLL
ROLL ROLL
Y-YOU GUYS!
YOU WERE ABLE TO GET THROUGH THE CORONARY ARTERY ?!
YEAH! BUT NEVER MIND THAT— GET THIS OXYGEN TO THE HEART!
HURRY!
INDEED... THE FATE OF THIS BODY...
DEPENDS ON THE WORK OF THOSE RED BLOOD CELLS!

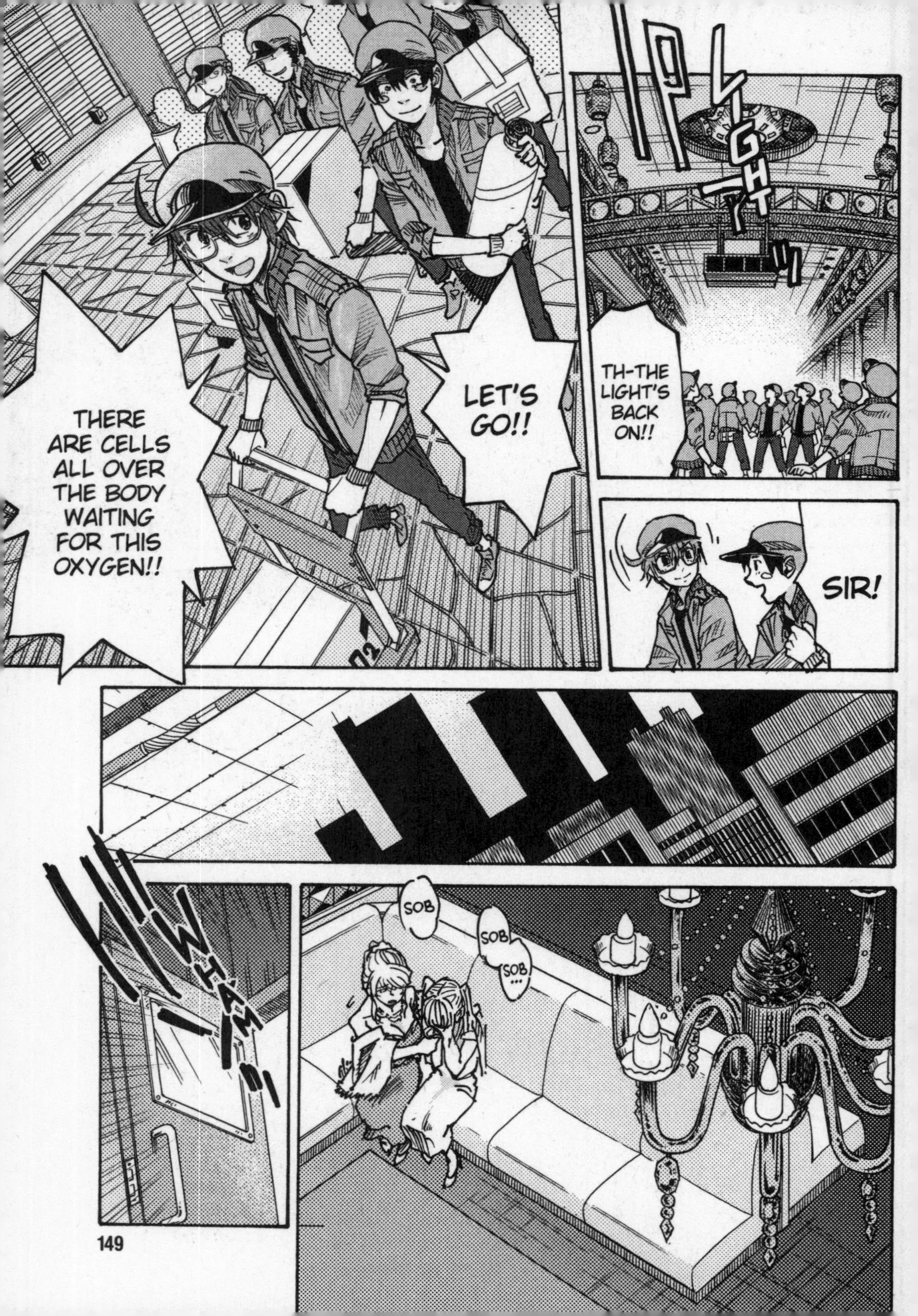
LIGHT
TH-THE LIGHT'S BACK ON!!
SIR!
THERE ARE CELLS ALL OVER THE BODY WAITING FOR THIS OXYGEN!!
LET'S GO!!
SOB
SOB
SOB...
WHAM

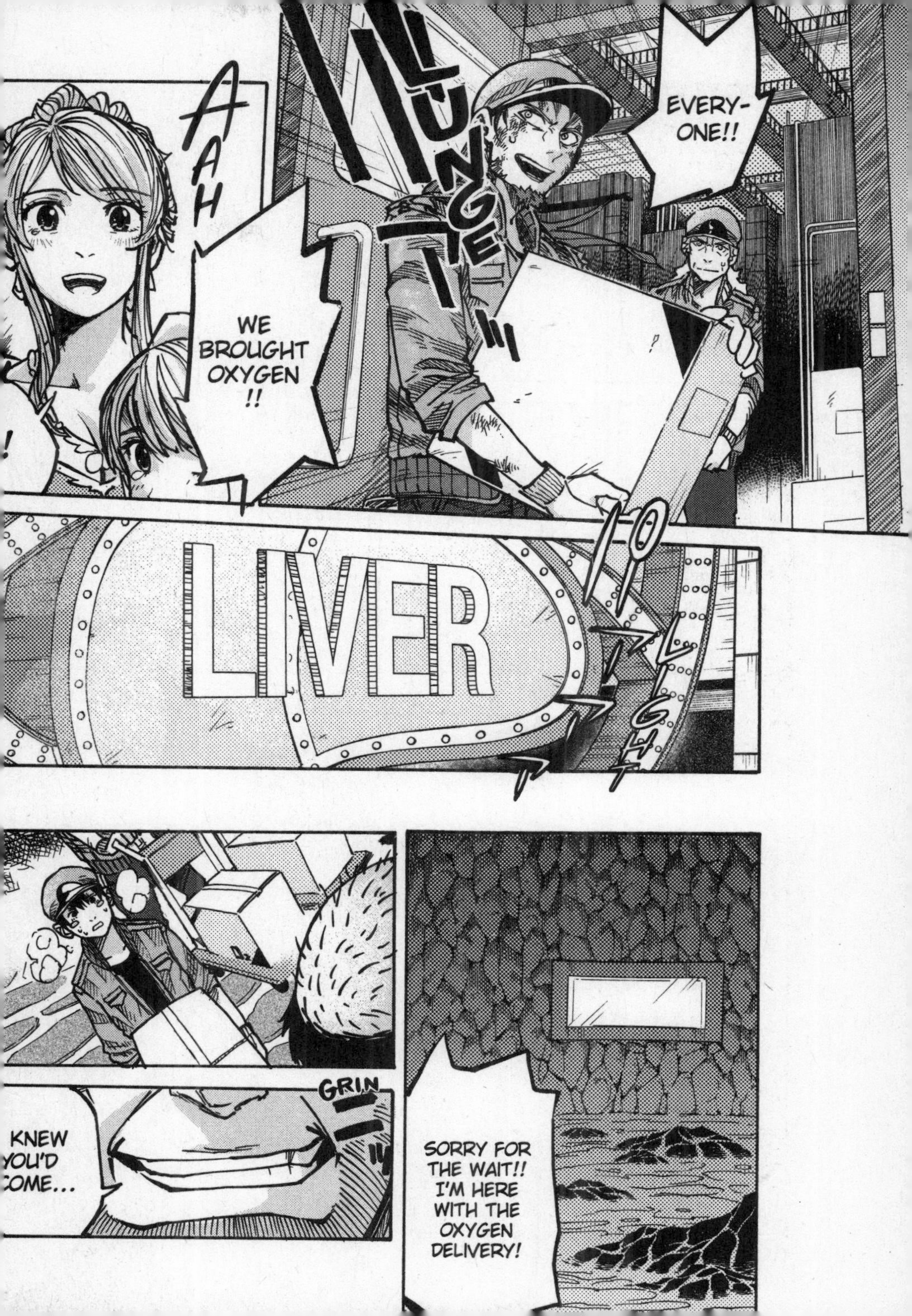
EVERY-ONE!!
LUNGE
AAH
WE BROUGHT OXYGEN !!
LIVER
SLIGHT
SORRY FOR THE WAIT!! I'M HERE WITH THE OXYGEN DELIVERY!
GRIN
KNEW YOU'D COME...

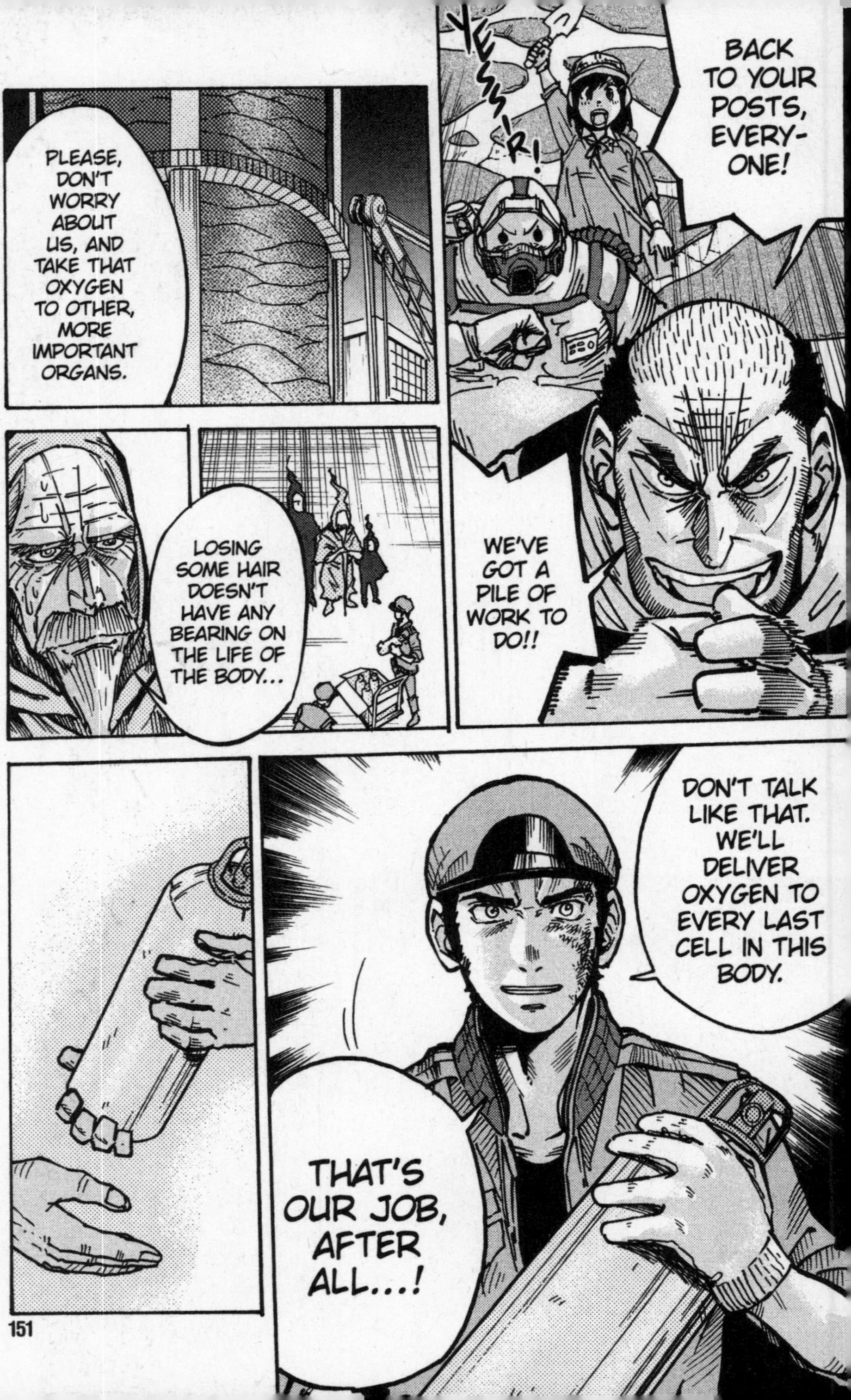
BACK TO YOUR POSTS, EVERYONE!
YESSIR!
WE'VE GOT A PILE OF WORK TO DO!!
PLEASE, DON'T WORRY ABOUT US, AND TAKE THAT OXYGEN TO OTHER, MORE IMPORTANT ORGANS.
LOSING SOME HAIR DOESN'T HAVE ANY BEARING ON THE LIFE OF THE BODY...
DON'T TALK LIKE THAT. WE'LL DELIVER OXYGEN TO EVERY LAST CELL IN THIS BODY.
THAT'S OUR JOB, AFTER ALL...!

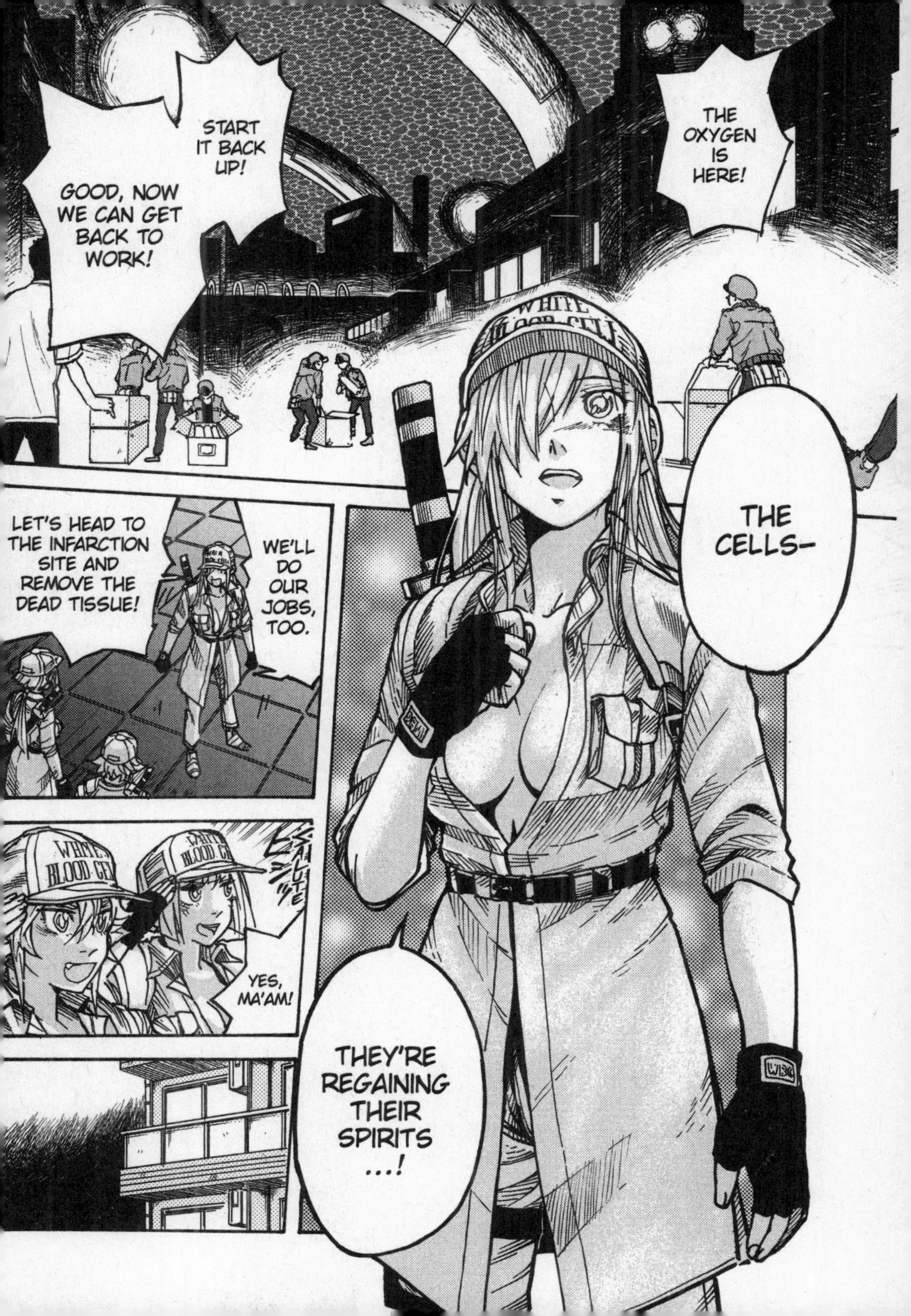
THE OXYGEN IS HERE!
START IT BACK UP!
GOOD, NOW WE CAN GET BACK TO WORK!
THE CELLS-
THEY'RE REGAINING THEIR SPIRITS ...!
WE'LL DO OUR JOBS, TOO.
LET'S HEAD TO THE INFARCTION SITE AND REMOVE THE DEAD TISSUE!
SALUTE
YES, MA'AM!

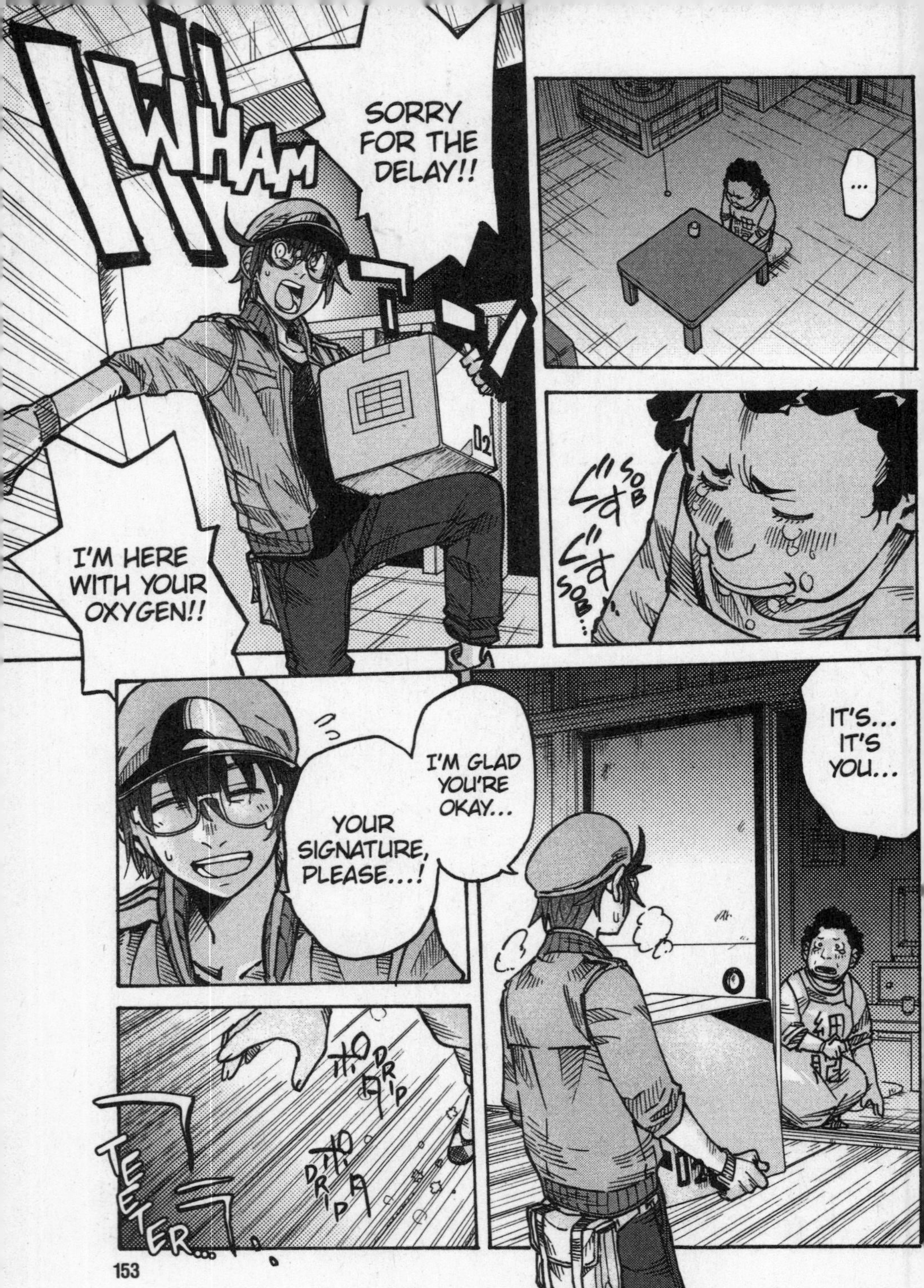
...
ぐす SOB
ぐす SOB...
WHAM
SORRY FOR THE DELAY!!
I'M HERE WITH YOUR OXYGEN!!
IT'S... IT'S YOU...
I'M GLAD YOU'RE OKAY...
YOUR SIGNATURE, PLEASE...!
DRIP
DRIP
TEETER...

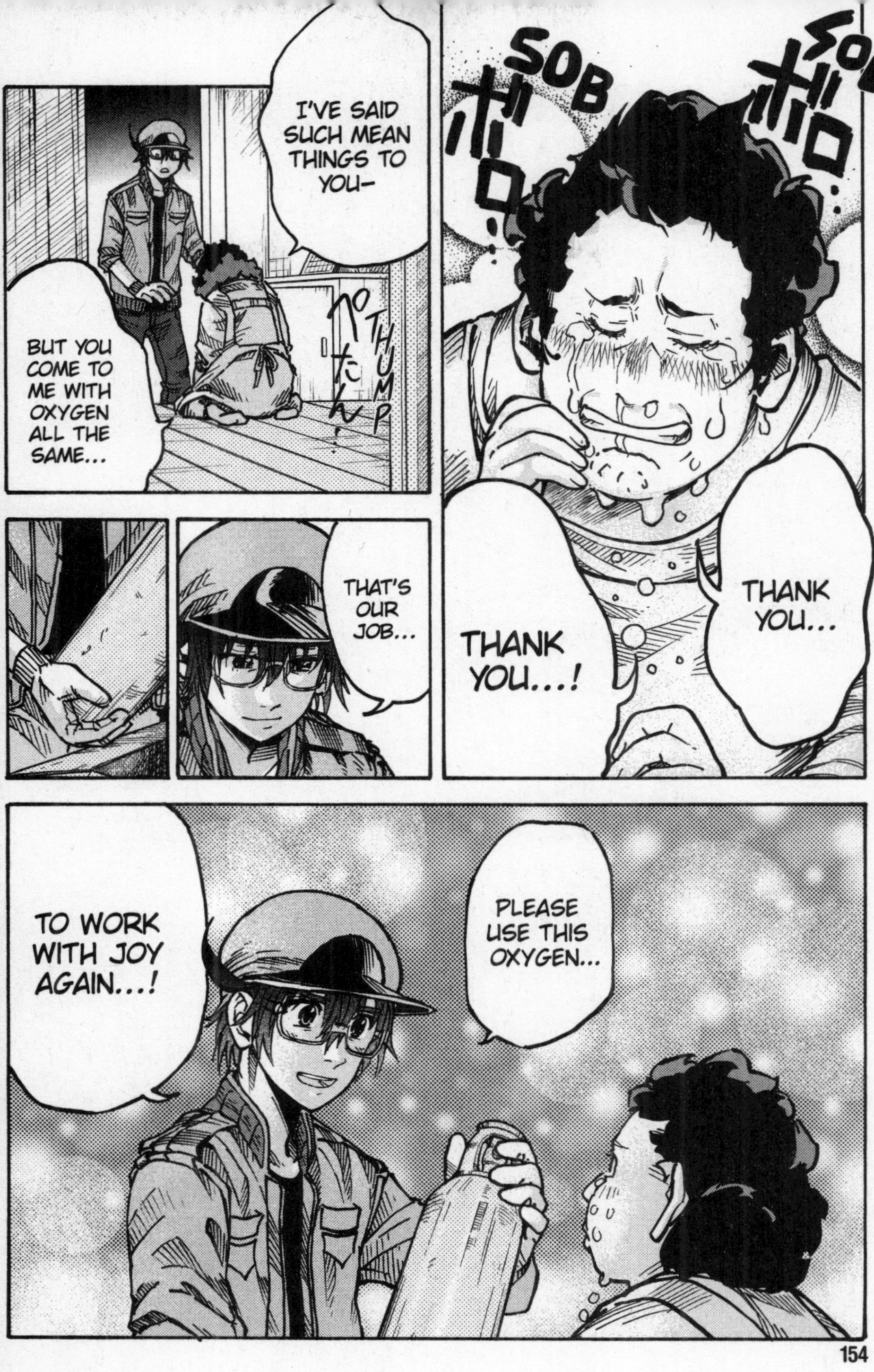
ボロ
SOB...
ボロ
SOB
THANK YOU...
THANK YOU...!
I'VE SAID SUCH MEAN THINGS TO YOU-
ぺたん
THUMP
BUT YOU COME TO ME WITH OXYGEN ALL THE SAME...
THAT'S OUR JOB...
PLEASE USE THIS OXYGEN...
TO WORK WITH JOY AGAIN...!

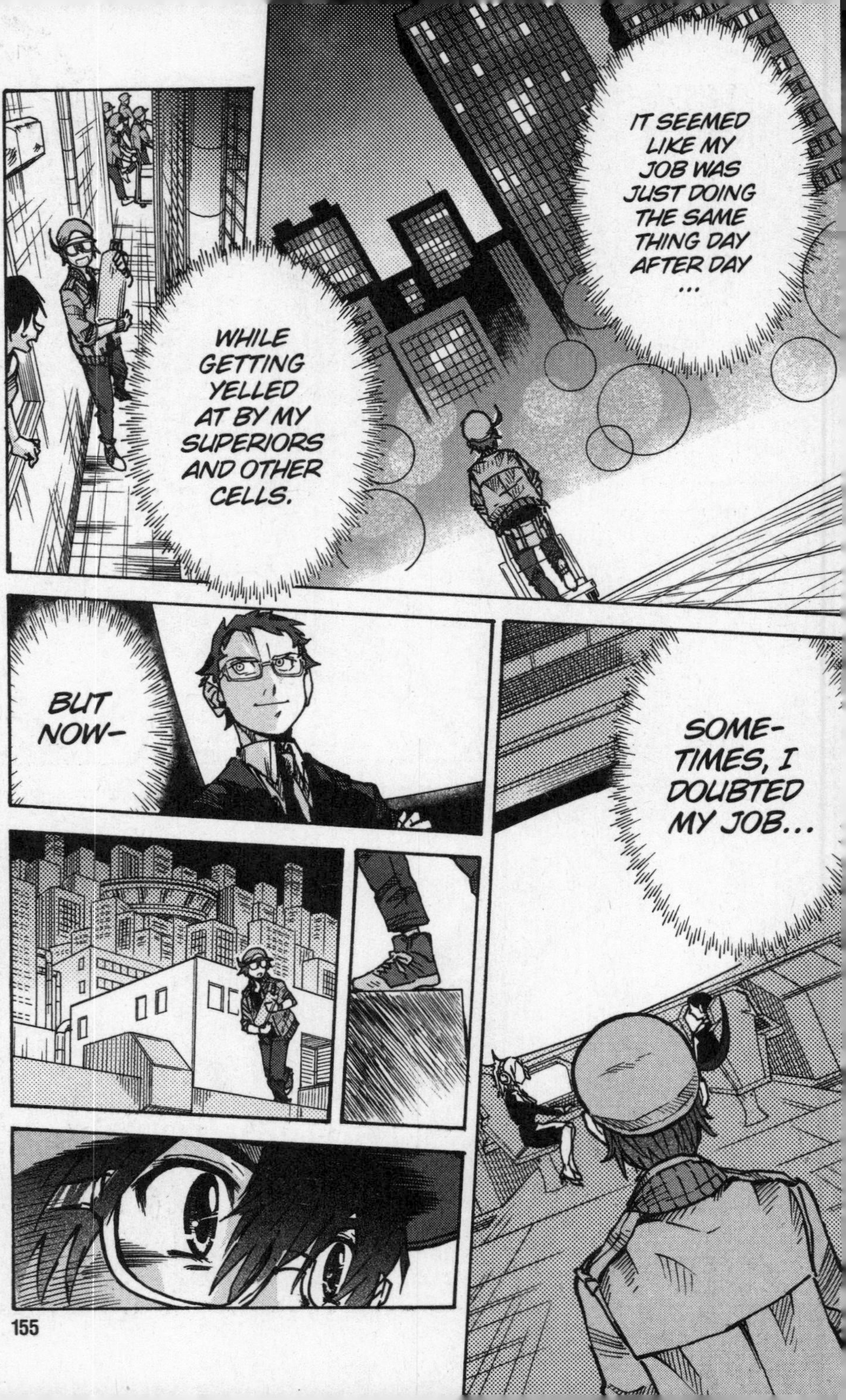
IT SEEMED LIKE MY JOB WAS JUST DOING THE SAME THING DAY AFTER DAY ...
WHILE GETTING YELLED AT BY MY SUPERIORS AND OTHER CELLS.
SOME-TIMES, I DOUBTED MY JOB...
BUT NOW-

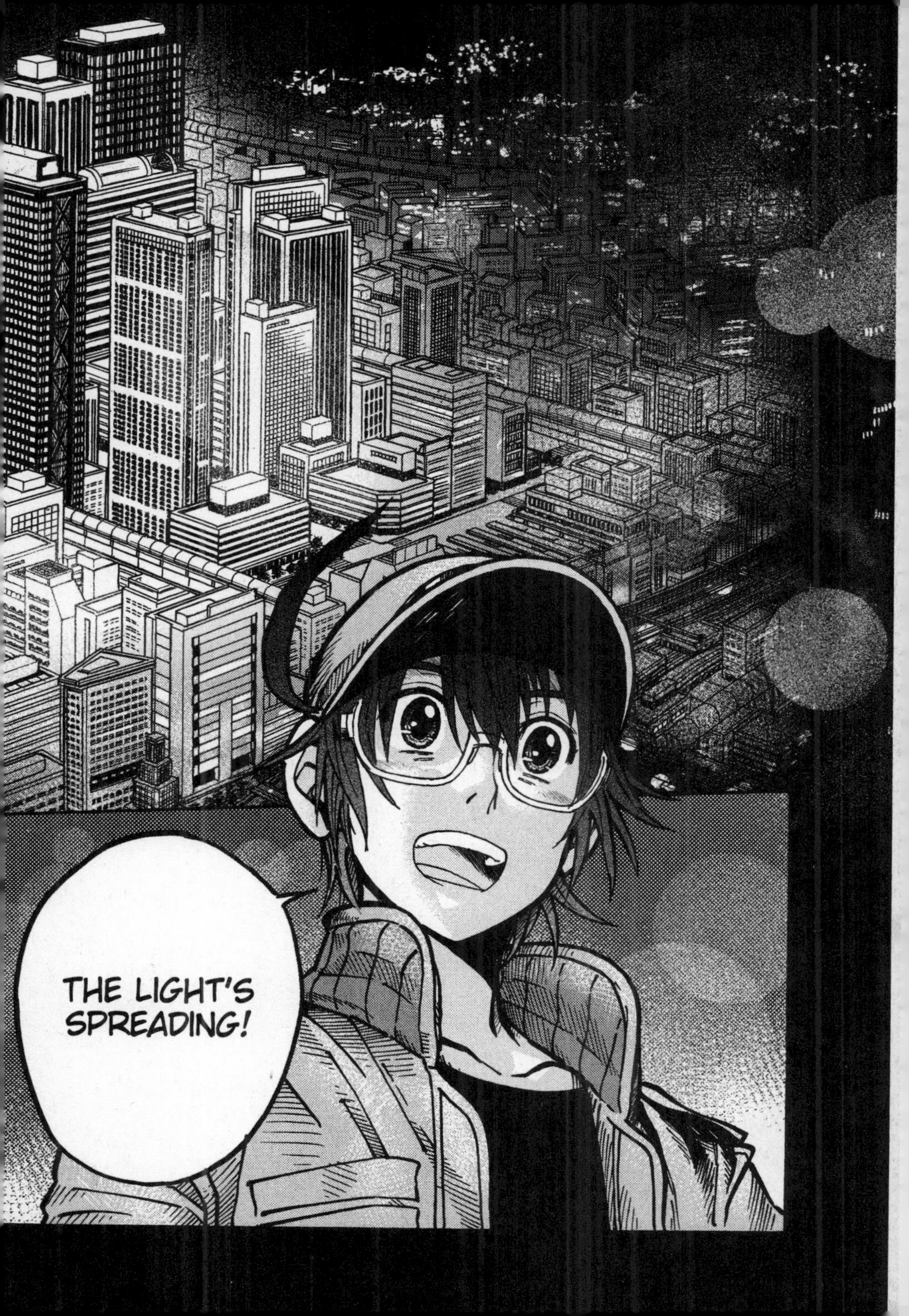
THE LIGHT'S SPREADING!

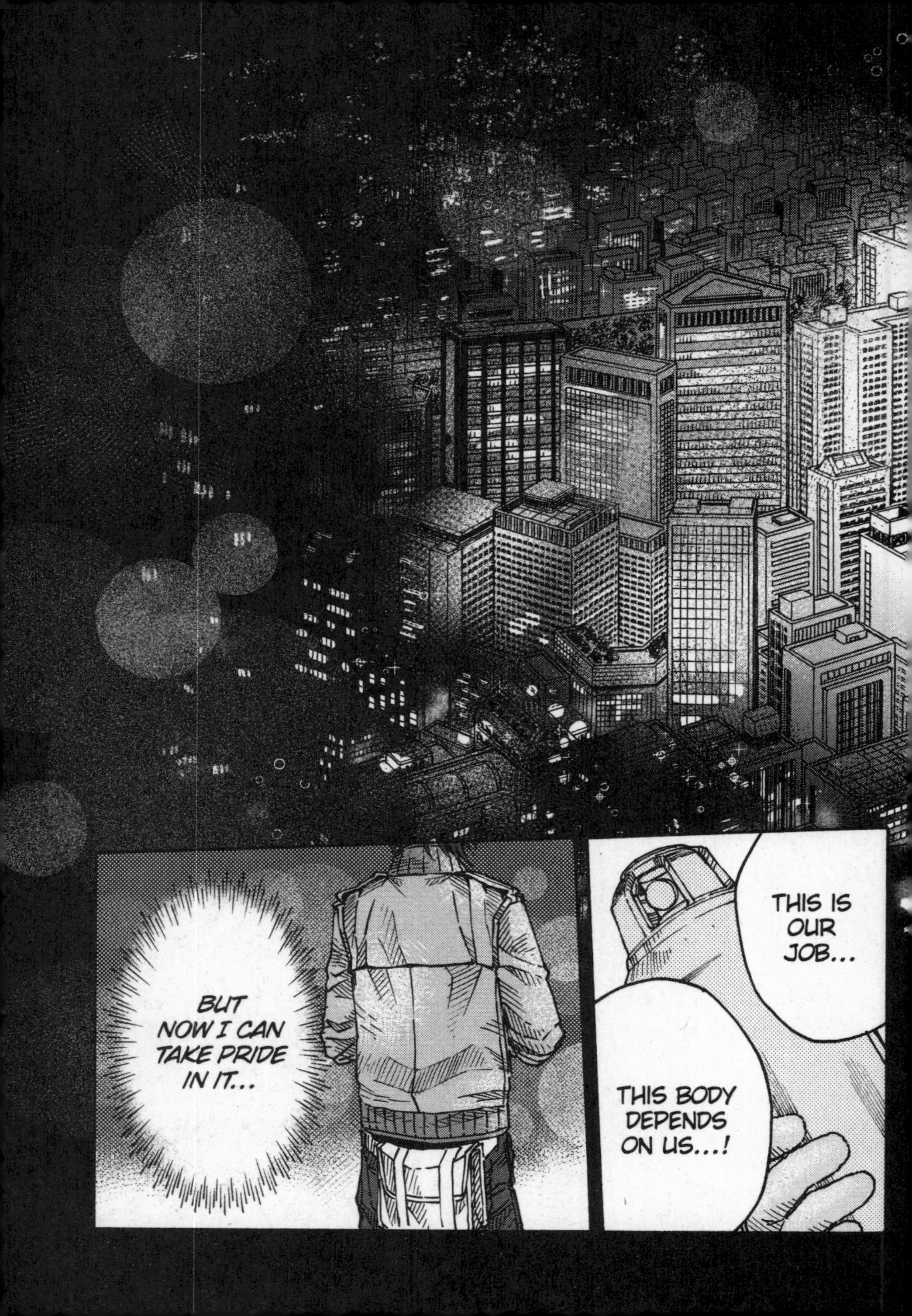
THIS IS OUR JOB...
THIS BODY DEPENDS ON US...!
BUT NOW I CAN TAKE PRIDE IN IT...

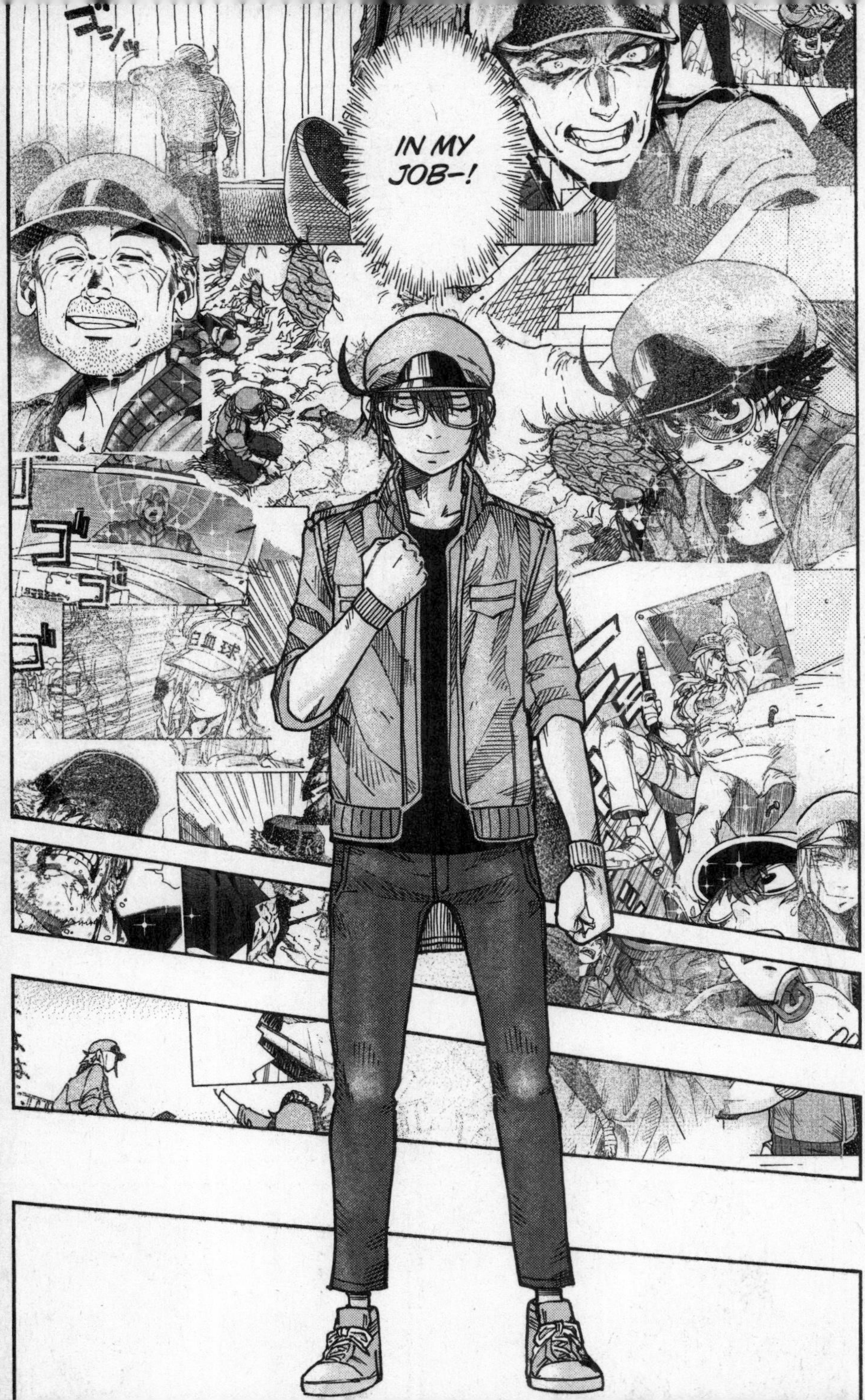
IN MY JOB–!

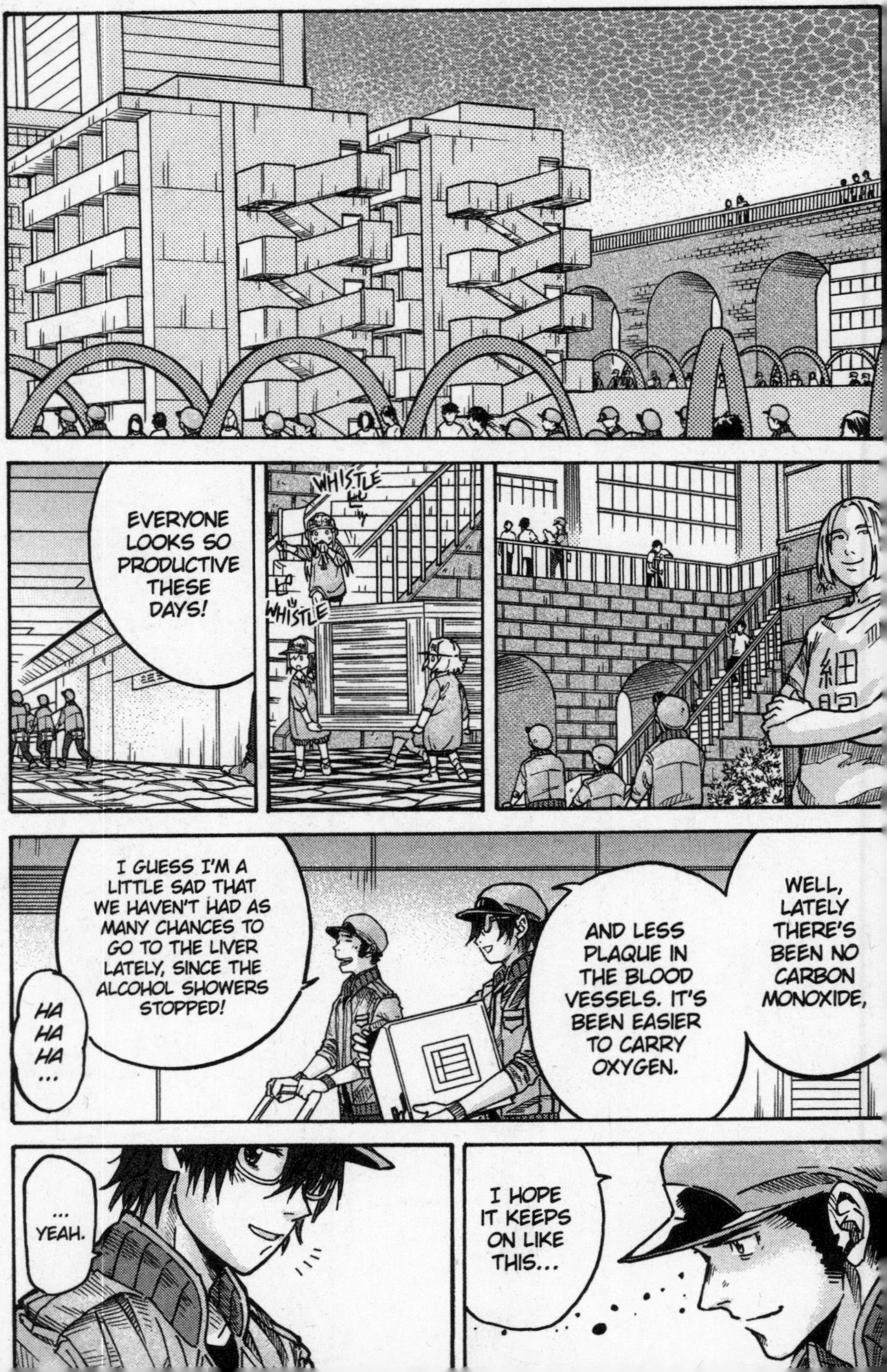
WHISTLE
WHISTLE
EVERYONE LOOKS SO PRODUCTIVE THESE DAYS!
WELL, LATELY THERE'S BEEN NO CARBON MONOXIDE,
AND LESS PLAQUE IN THE BLOOD VESSELS. IT'S BEEN EASIER TO CARRY OXYGEN.
I GUESS I'M A LITTLE SAD THAT WE HAVEN'T HAD AS MANY CHANCES TO GO TO THE LIVER LATELY, SINCE THE ALCOHOL SHOWERS STOPPED!
HA HA HA ...
I HOPE IT KEEPS ON LIKE THIS...
... YEAH.

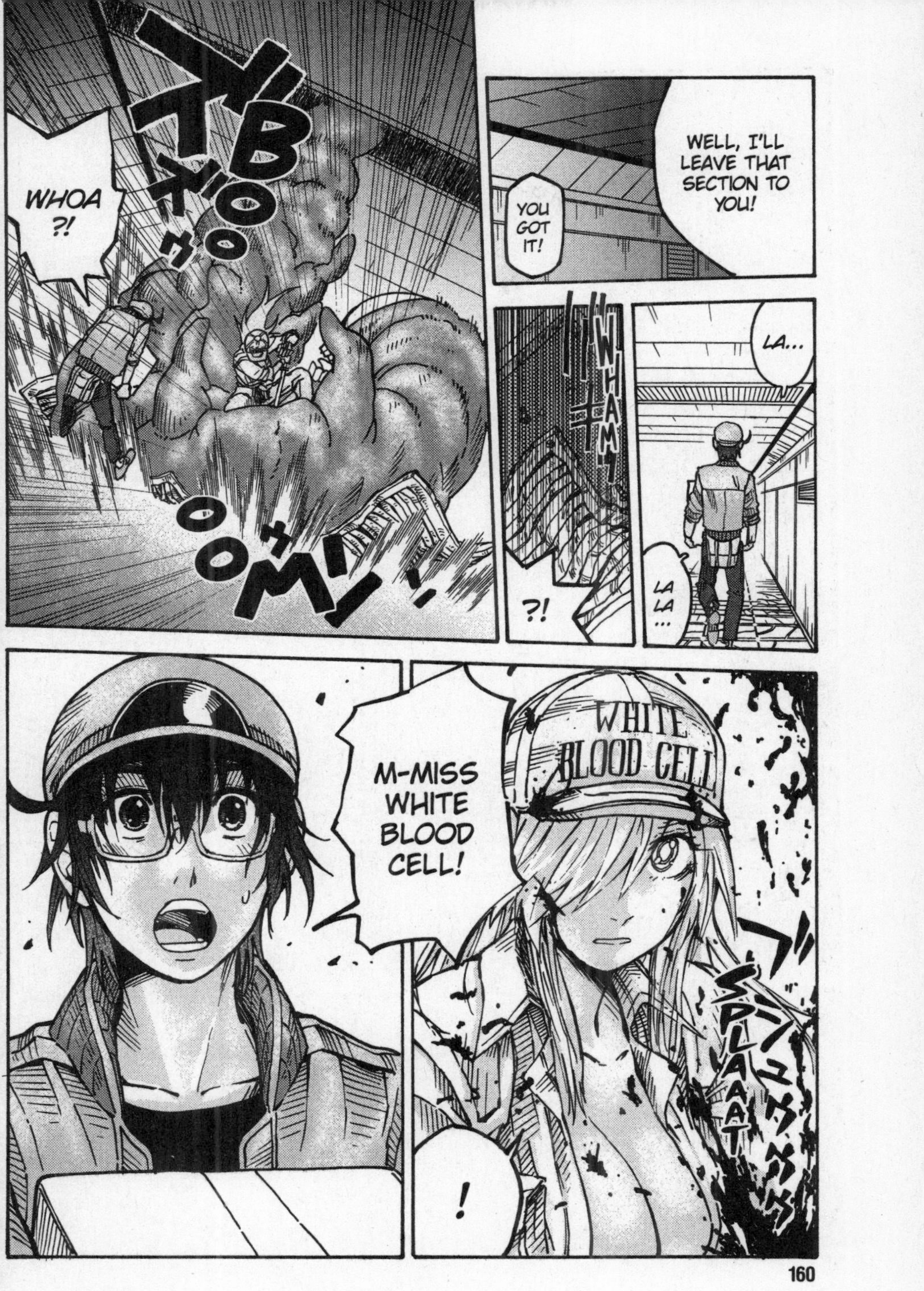
WELL, I'LL LEAVE THAT SECTION TO YOU!
YOU GOT IT!
LA...
LA LA...
WHAM!
?!
BOOOOM!
WHOA ?!
WHITE BLOOD CELL
SPLAAAT
!
M-MISS WHITE BLOOD CELL!

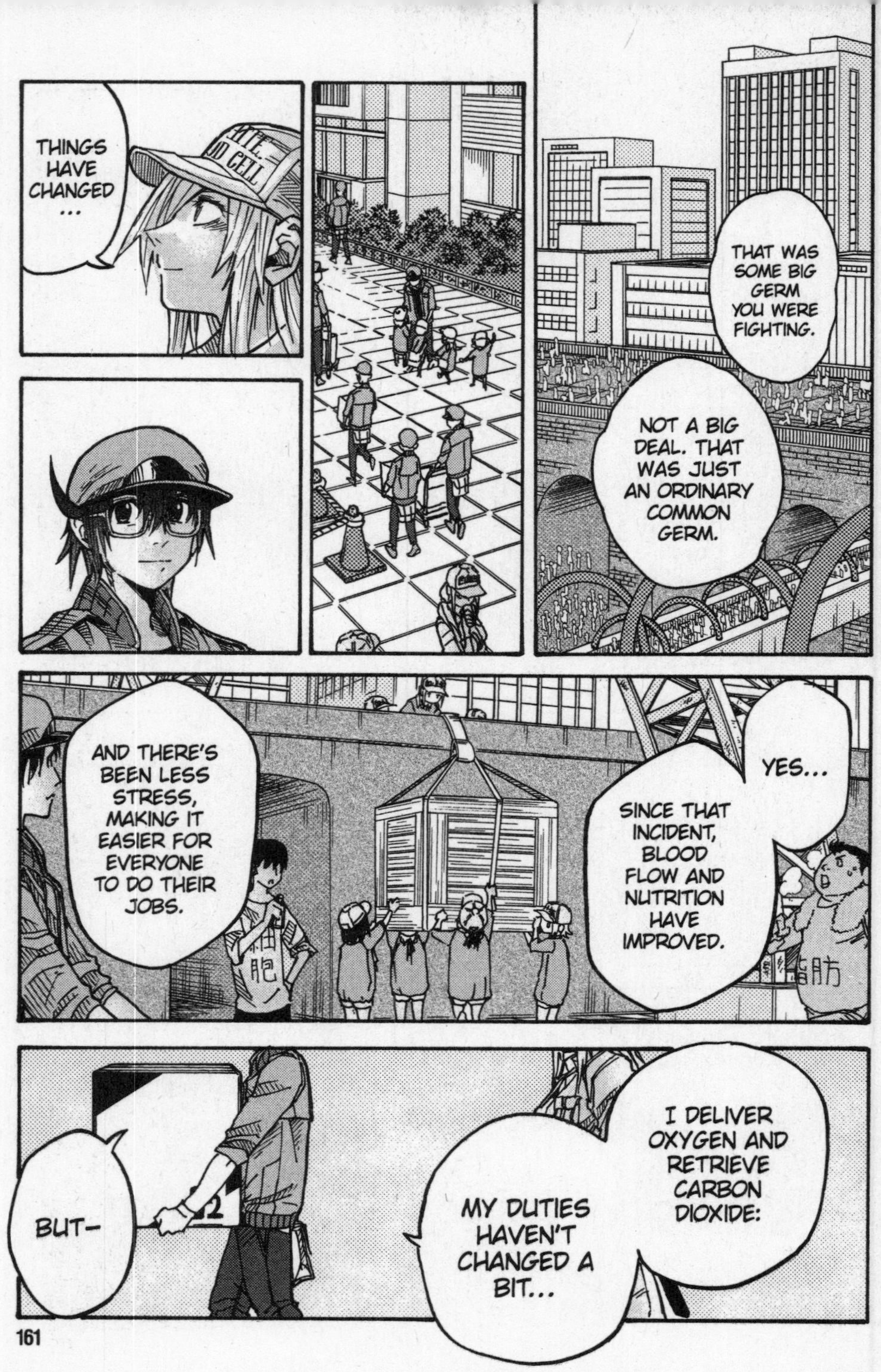
THAT WAS SOME BIG GERM YOU WERE FIGHTING.
NOT A BIG DEAL. THAT WAS JUST AN ORDINARY COMMON GERM.
THINGS HAVE CHANGED ...
YES...
SINCE THAT INCIDENT, BLOOD FLOW AND NUTRITION HAVE IMPROVED.
脂肪
AND THERE'S BEEN LESS STRESS, MAKING IT EASIER FOR EVERYONE TO DO THEIR JOBS.
細胞
I DELIVER OXYGEN AND RETRIEVE CARBON DIOXIDE:
MY DUTIES HAVEN'T CHANGED A BIT...
BUT-

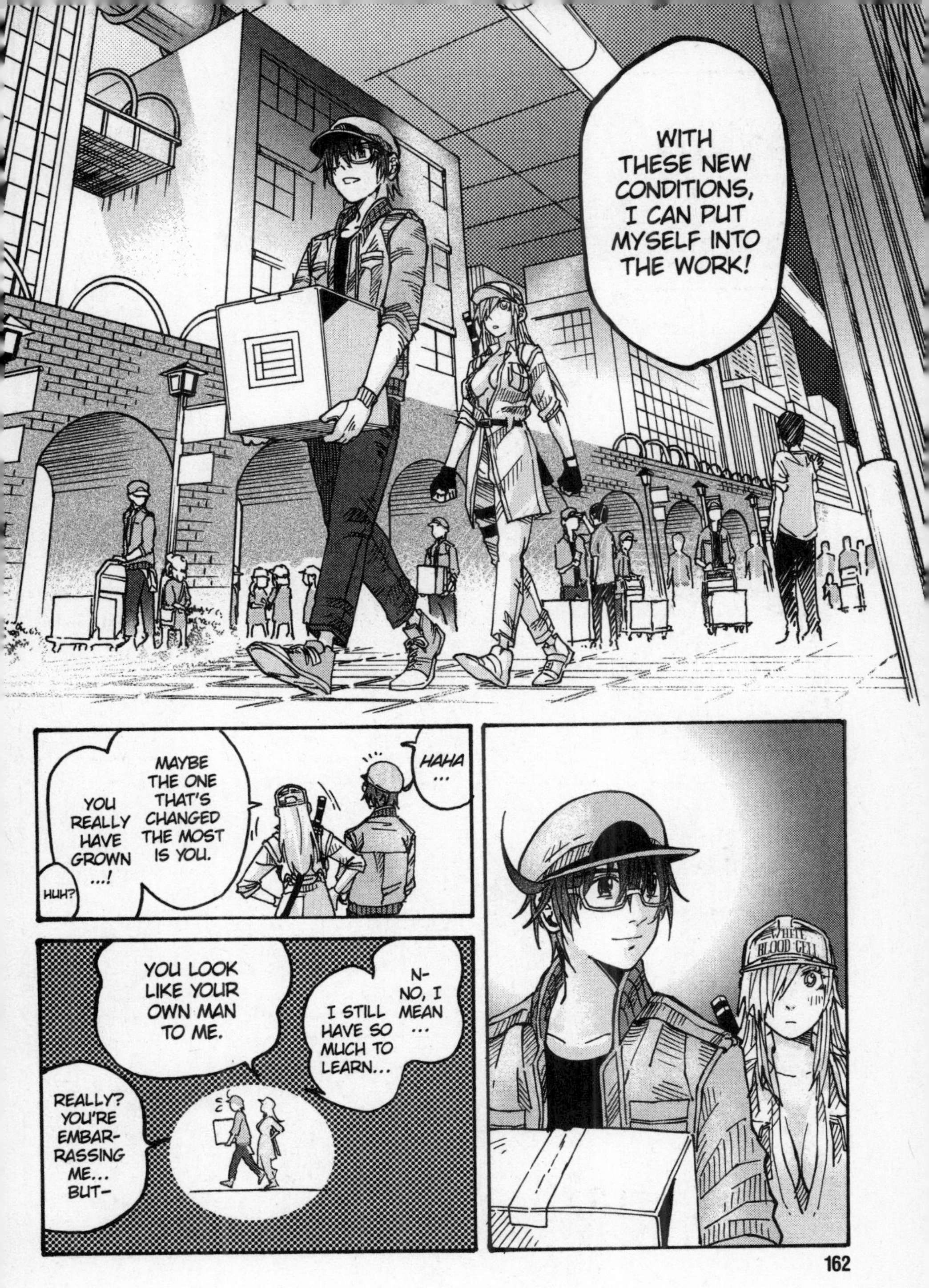
WITH THESE NEW CONDITIONS, I CAN PUT MYSELF INTO THE WORK!
WHITE BLOOD CELL
HAHA...
MAYBE THE ONE THAT'S CHANGED THE MOST IS YOU.
YOU REALLY HAVE GROWN...!
HUH?
N-NO, I MEAN...
I STILL HAVE SO MUCH TO LEARN...
YOU LOOK LIKE YOUR OWN MAN TO ME.
REALLY? YOU'RE EMBARRASSING ME... BUT-

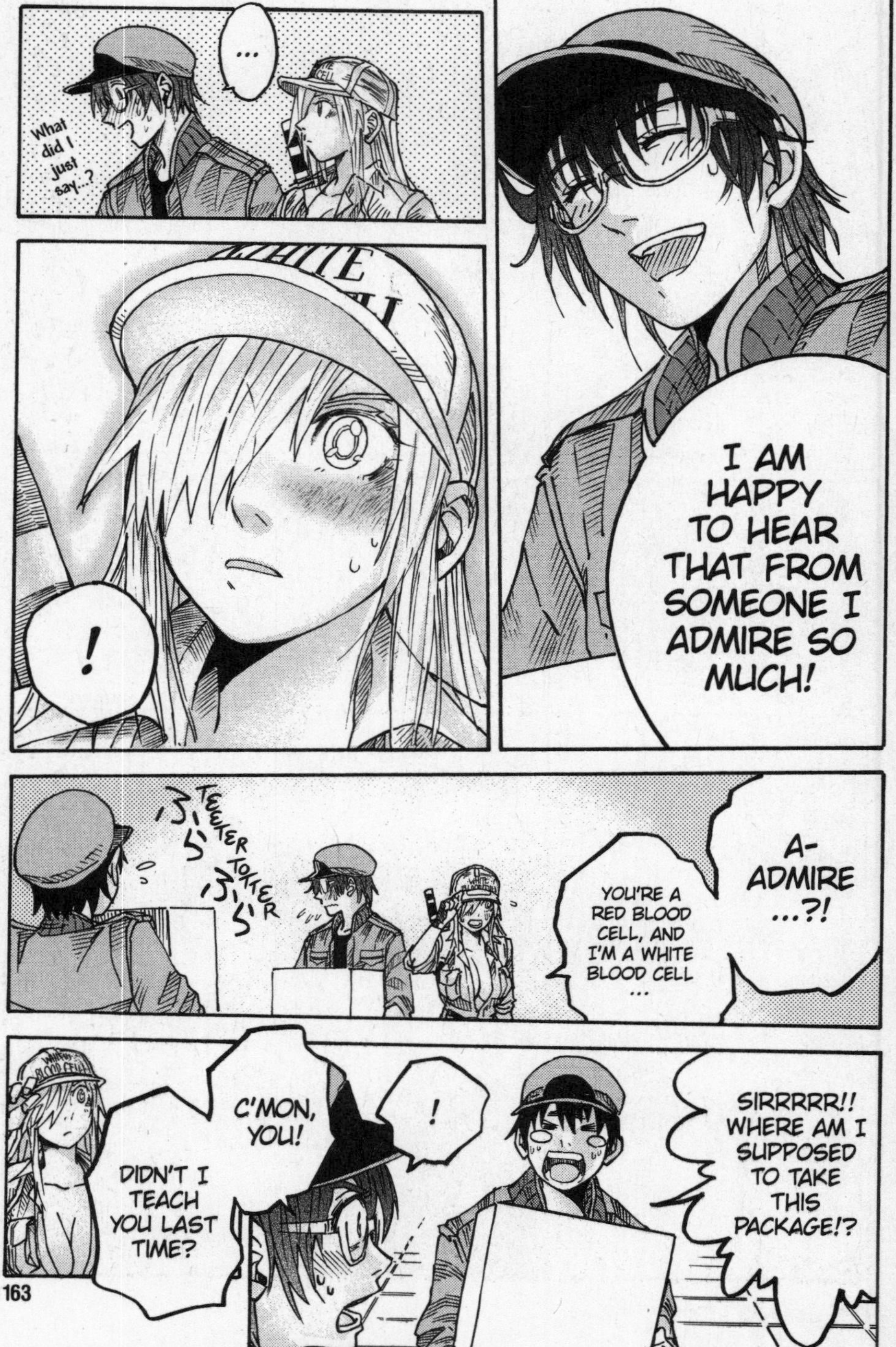
I AM HAPPY TO HEAR THAT FROM SOMEONE I ADMIRE SO MUCH!
...
What did I just say...?
!
A- ADMIRE ...?!
YOU'RE A RED BLOOD CELL, AND I'M A WHITE BLOOD CELL ...
TEETER TOTTER
SIRRRRR!! WHERE AM I SUPPOSED TO TAKE THIS PACKAGE!?
!
C'MON, YOU!
DIDN'T I TEACH YOU LAST TIME?

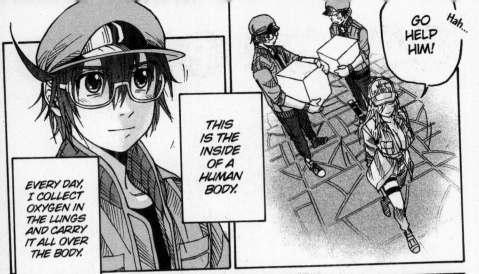

Hah...
GO HELP HIM!
THIS IS THE INSIDE OF A HUMAN BODY.
EVERY DAY, I COLLECT OXYGEN IN THE LUNGS AND CARRY IT ALL OVER THE BODY.
IT MAY SEEM SIMPLE.
BUT... THAT'S THE JOB OF US RED BLOOD CELLS!

Chapter 10 | END

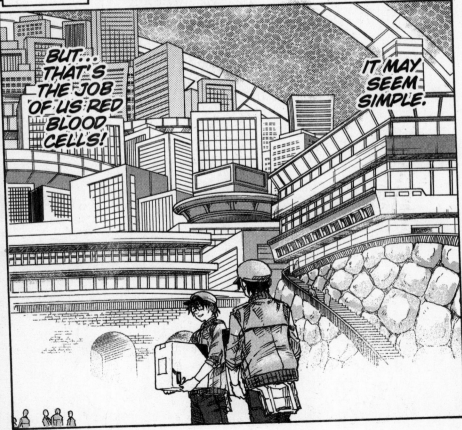

BONUS PAGES

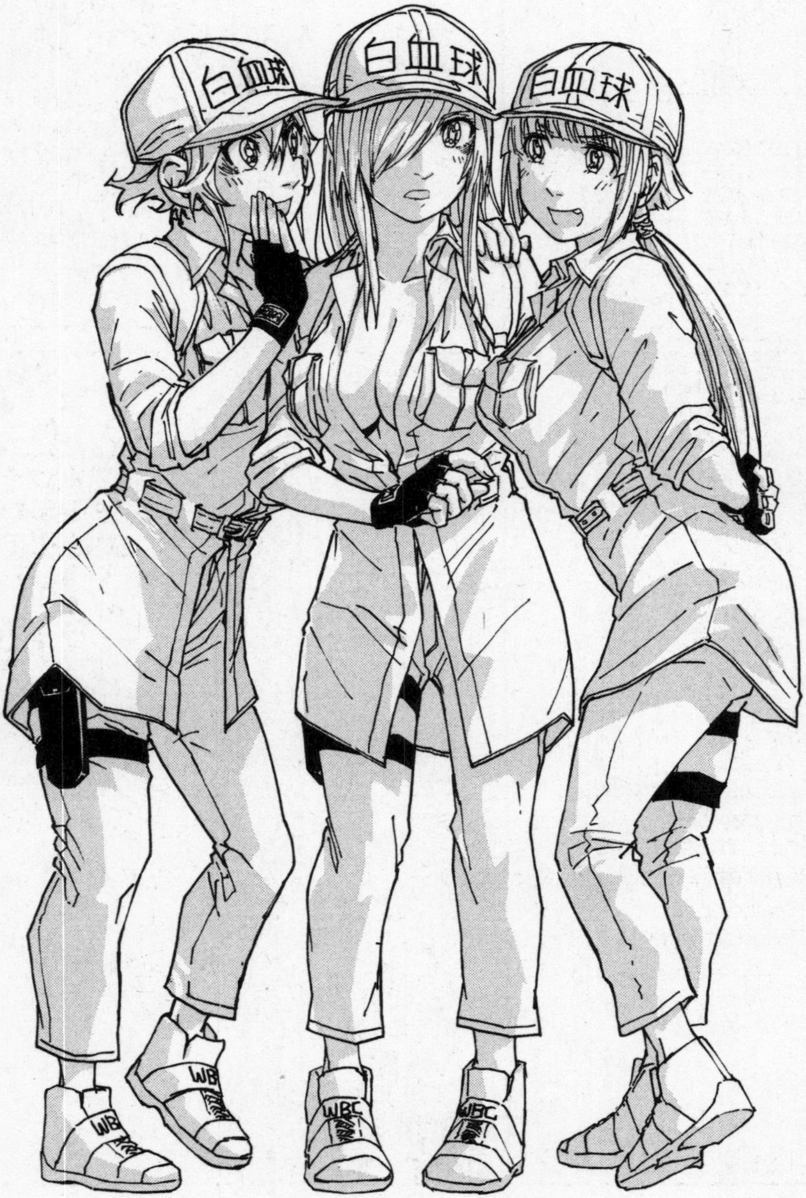
白血球
白血球
白血球
WBC
WBC
WBC
WBC

Bonus Part 1

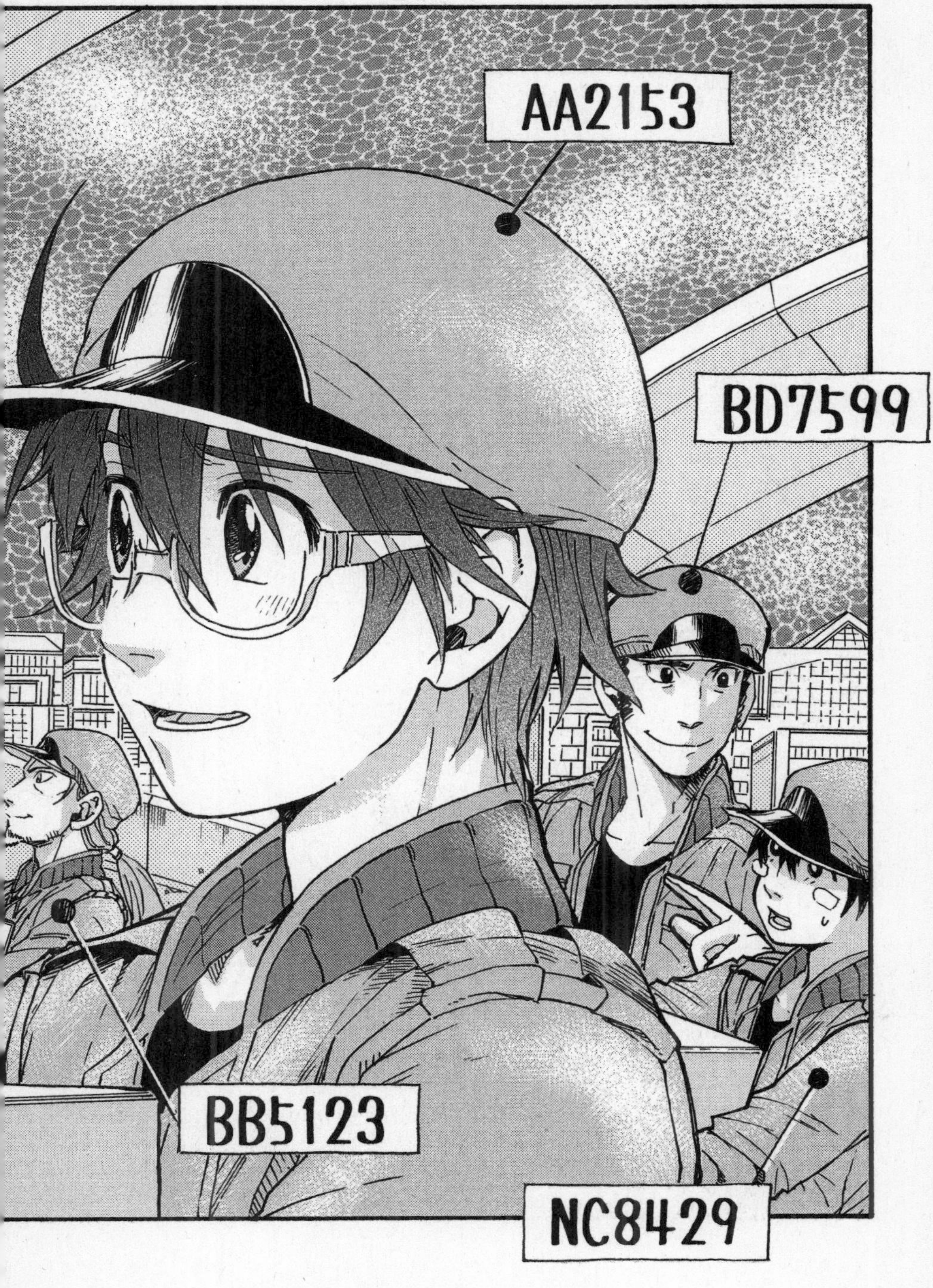
AA2153
BD7599
BB5123
NC8429

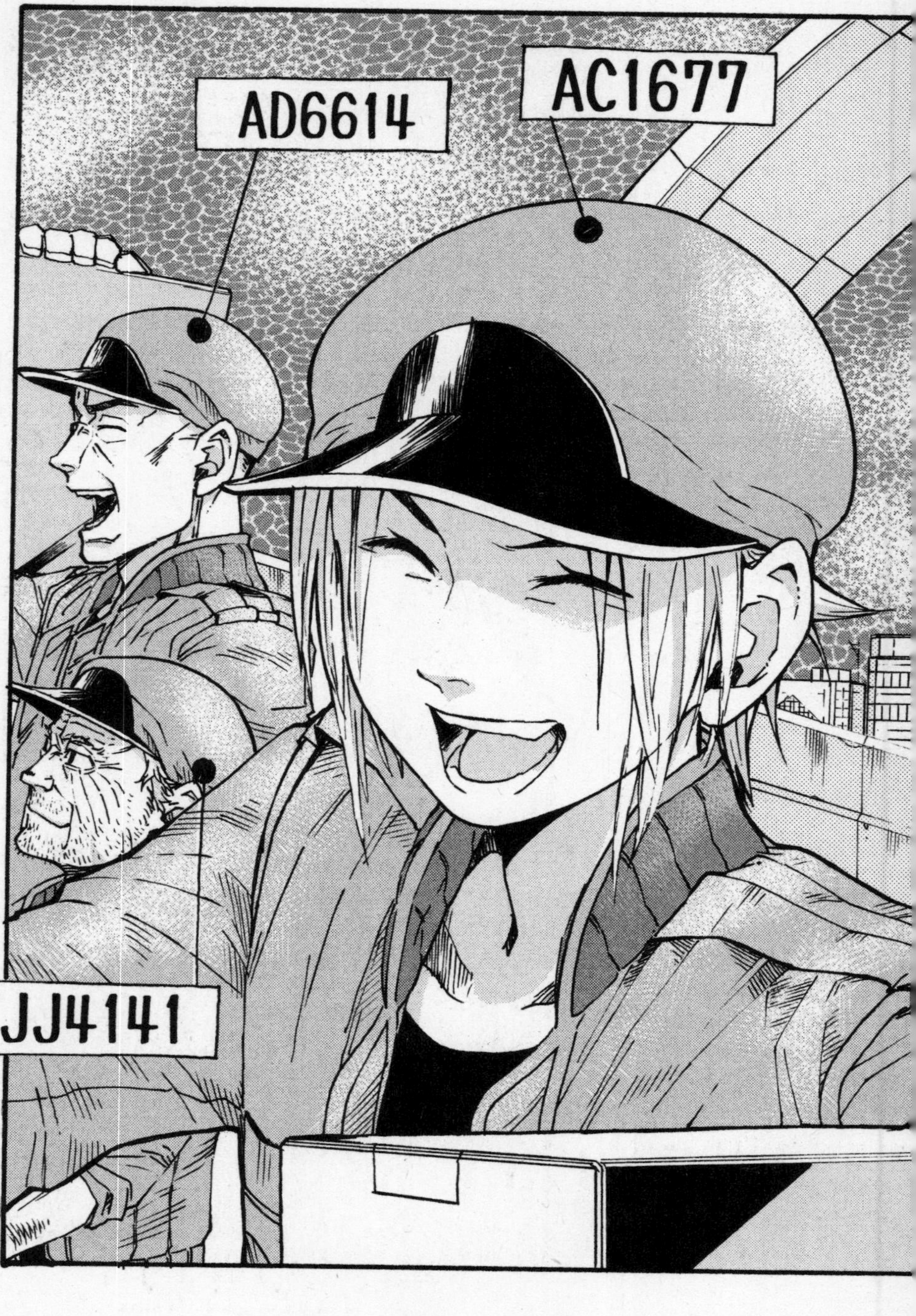
AC1677
AD6614
JJ4141

Bonus Part 2

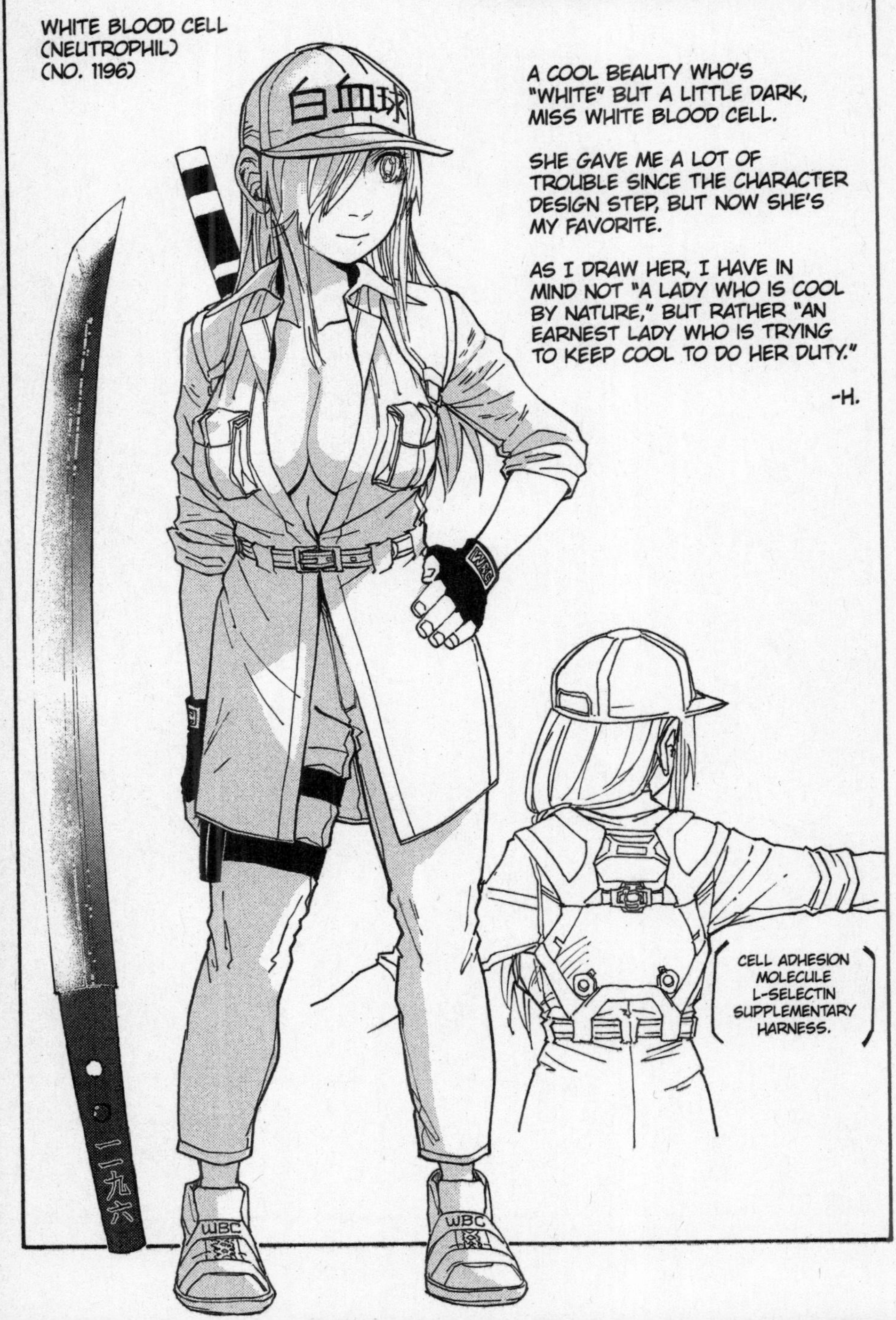
WHITE BLOOD CELL
(NEUTROPHIL)
(NO. 1196)
白血球
A COOL BEAUTY WHO'S "WHITE" BUT A LITTLE DARK, MISS WHITE BLOOD CELL.
SHE GAVE ME A LOT OF TROUBLE SINCE THE CHARACTER DESIGN STEP, BUT NOW SHE'S MY FAVORITE.
AS I DRAW HER, I HAVE IN MIND NOT "A LADY WHO IS COOL BY NATURE," BUT RATHER "AN EARNEST LADY WHO IS TRYING TO KEEP COOL TO DO HER DUTY."
-H.
WBC
CELL ADHESION MOLECULE L-SELECTIN SUPPLEMENTARY HARNESS.
一一九六
WBC
WBC

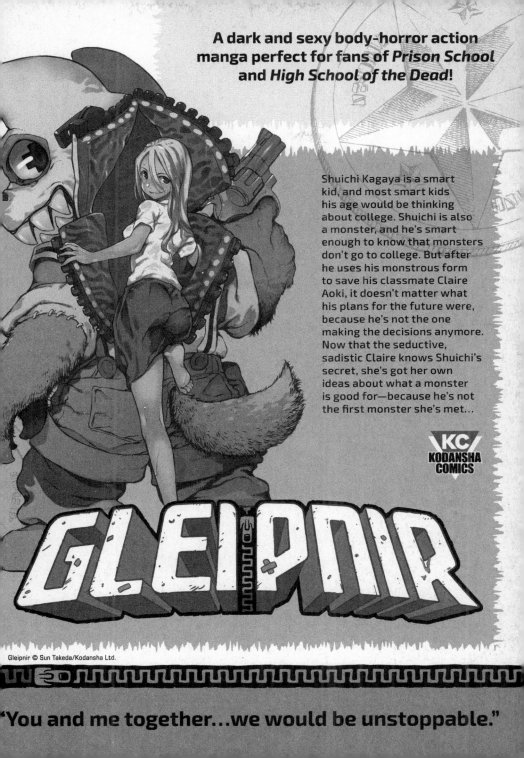

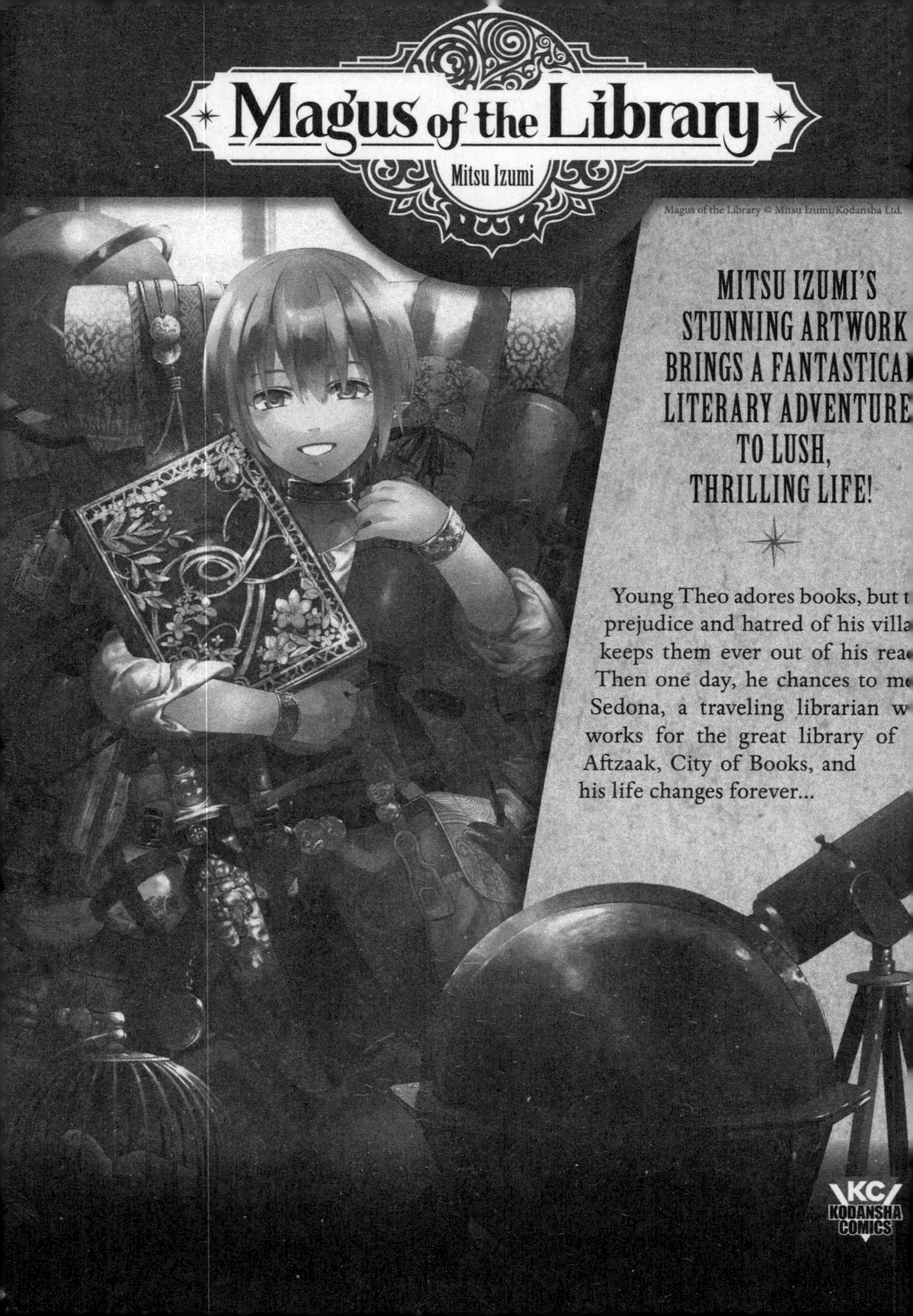
Magus of the Library
Mitsu Izumi
Magus of the Library © Mitsu Izumi/Kodansha Ltd.
MITSU IZUMI'S STUNNING ARTWORK BRINGS A FANTASTICA
LITERARY ADVENTURE TO LUSH, THRILLING LIFE!
Young Theo adores books, but t
prejudice and hatred of his villa
keeps them ever out of his rea
Then one day, he chances to m
Sedona, a traveling librarian w
works for the great library of
Aftzaak, City of Books, and
his life changes forever...
KC KODANSHA COMICS

Acclaimed screenwriter and director Mari Okada (*Maquia, anohana*) teams up with manga artist Nao Emoto (*Forget Me Not*) in this moving, funny, so-true-it's-embarrassing coming-of-age series!

When Kazusa enters high school, she joins the Literature Club, and leaps from reading innocent fiction to diving into the literary classics. But these novels are a bit more...*adult* than she was prepared for. Between euphemisms like fresh dewy grass and pork stew, crushing on the boy next door, and knowing you want to do that *one thing* before you die—discovering your budding sexuality is no easy feat! As if puberty wasn't awkward enough, the club consists of a brooding writer, the prettiest girl in school, an agreeable comrade, and an outspoken prude. Fumbling over their own discomforts, these five teens get thrown into chaos over three little letters: *S...E...X...!*

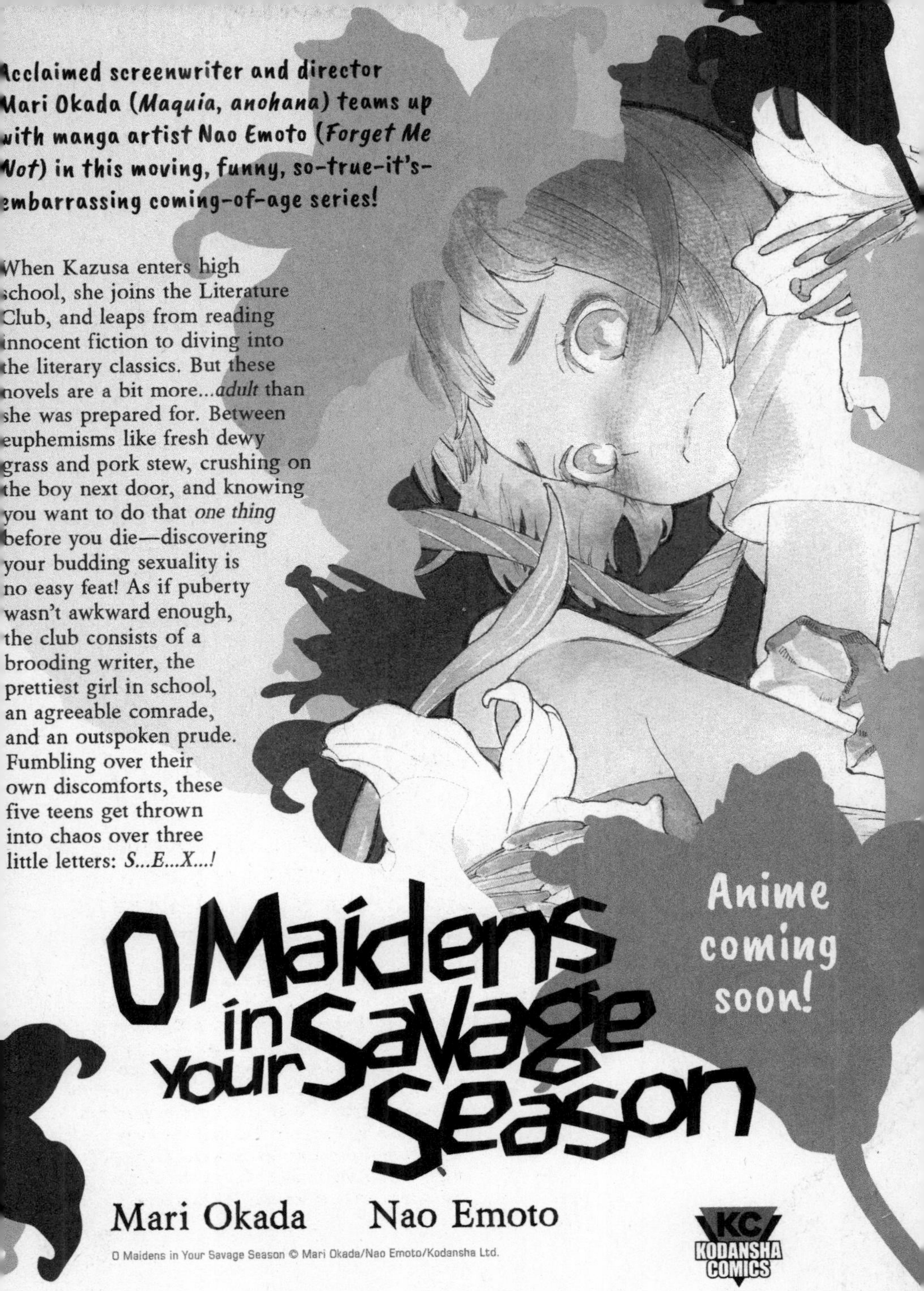

Anime coming soon!

O Maidens in Your Savage Season

Mari Okada Nao Emoto

KC KODANSHA COMICS

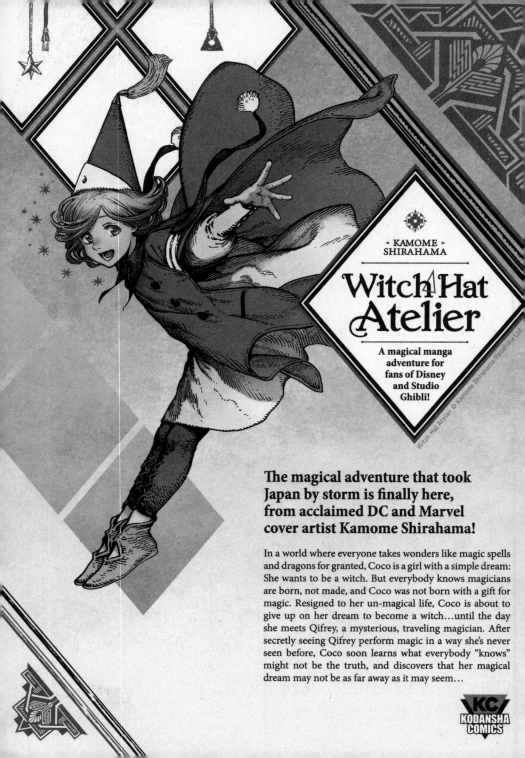

‹ KAMOME ›
SHIRAHAMA

Witch Hat Atelier

A magical manga
adventure for
fans of Disney
and Studio
Ghibli!

The magical adventure that took Japan by storm is finally here, from acclaimed DC and Marvel cover artist Kamome Shirahama!

In a world where everyone takes wonders like magic spells
and dragons for granted, Coco is a girl with a simple dream:
She wants to be a witch. But everybody knows magicians
are born, not made, and Coco was not born with a gift for
magic. Resigned to her un-magical life, Coco is about to
give up on her dream to become a witch...until the day
she meets Qifrey, a mysterious, traveling magician. After
secretly seeing Qifrey perform magic in a way she's never
seen before, Coco soon learns what everybody "knows"
might not be the truth, and discovers that her magical
dream may not be as far away as it may seem...

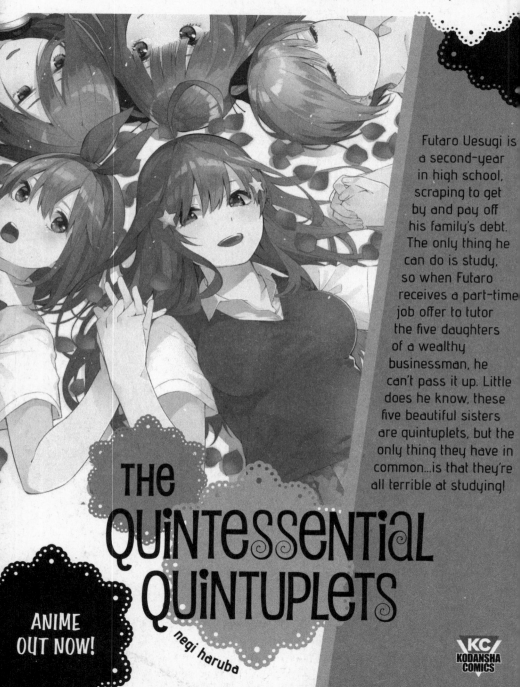

A Kodansha Comics Trade Paperback Original
Cells at Work! CODE BLACK 2 copyright © 2018 Shigemitsu Harada/Issei Hatsuyoshiya/ Akane Shimizu
nglish translation copyright © 2019 Shigemitsu Harada/Issei Hatsuyoshiya/Akane Shimizu

Published in the United States by Kodansha Comics, an imprint of Kodansha USA Publishing, LLC, New York.

Publication rights for this English edition arranged through Kodansha Ltd., Tokyo.

First published in Japan in 2018 by Kodansha Ltd., Tokyo as *Hataraku Saibou BLACK*, volume 2.

ISBN 978-1-63236-895-9

Printed in the United States of America.

www.kodanshacomics.com

9 8 7 6 5 4 3 2 1
Translation: Yamato Tanaka
Lettering: E. K. Weaver
Editing: Paul Starr
Kodansha Comics edition cover design by Phil Balsman

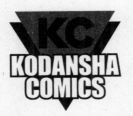

Publisher: Kiichiro Sugawara
Managing editor: Maya Rosewood
Vice president of marketing & publicity: Naho Yamada

Director of publishing services: Ben Applegate
Associate director of operations: Stephen Pakula
Publishing services managing editor: Noelle Webster
Assistant production manager: Emi Lotto

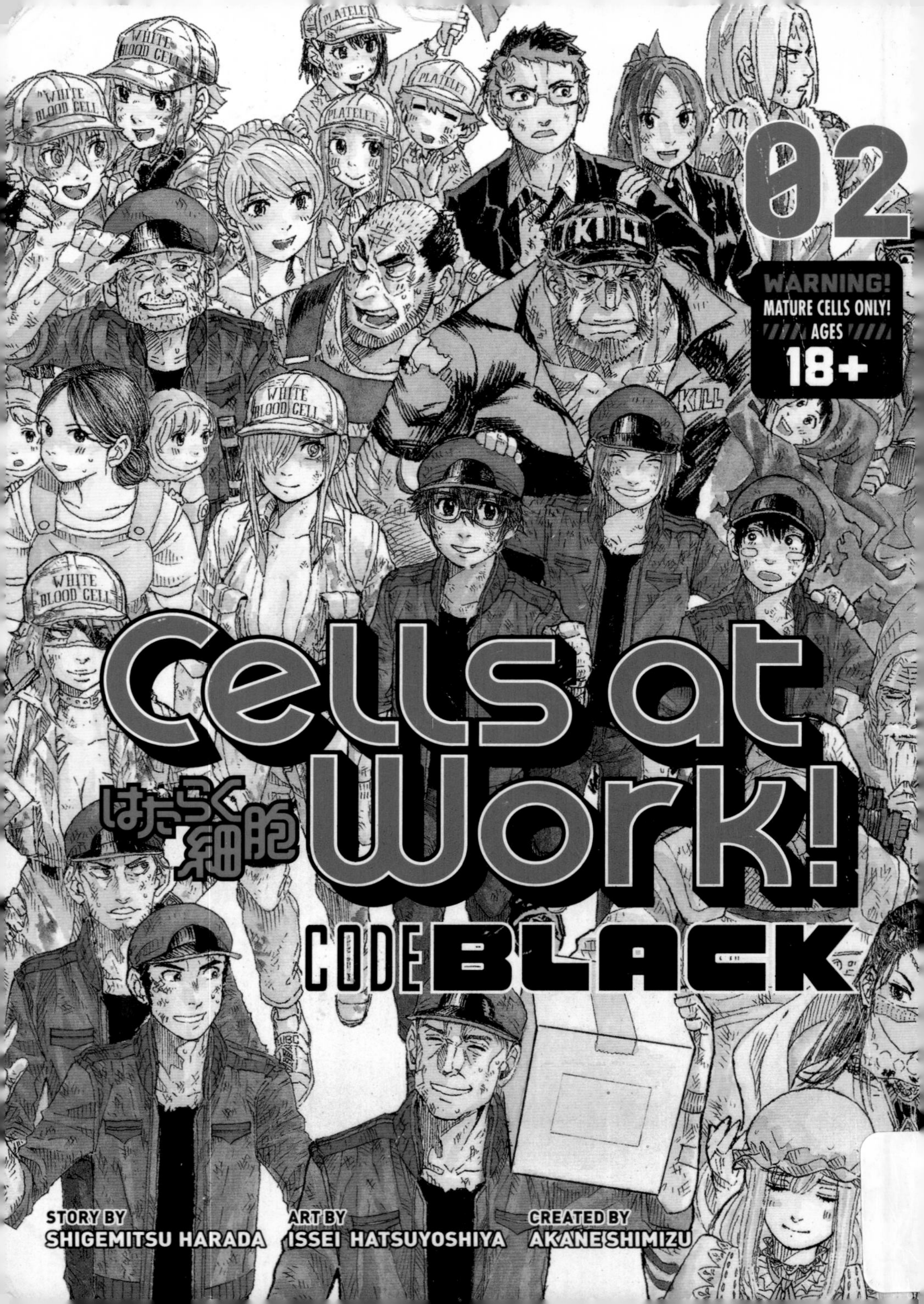
02
WARNING!
MATURE CELLS ONLY!
AGES
18+
Cells at Work!
はたらく細胞
CODE BLACK
STORY BY
SHIGEMITSU HARADA
ART BY
ISSEI HATSUYOSHIYA
CREATED BY
AKANE SHIMIZU
WHITE BLOOD CELL
PLATELET
KILL